THE DOT MEDICAL EXAMINATION

AN UNOFFICIAL GUIDE TO COMMERCIAL DRIVERS' MEDICAL CERTIFICATION

SIXTH EDITION

NATALIE P. HARTENBAUM
MD, MPH, FACOEM, EDITOR

OEM Press
8 West Street
Beverly Farms, MA 01915
978-921-7300
www.oempress.com

Cover design: Ellen Weinberger
Interior design & composition: Mayerchak + Company, LLC

Special thanks and appreciation to Alexis Rautio, Editorial Director at OEM Press, for her help in making this edition possible.

ISBN 978-1-883595-75-3

The information contained in this book is based on documents provided by the Federal Motor Carrier Safety Administration (FMCSA), its expert panels, and the medical literature. The information in this book should be used as guidance unless specifically indicated as regulation. Sound medical knowledge and an understanding of the underlying disease process, its treatment, and prognosis must guide the final medical certification determination.

Library of Congress Cataloging-in-Publication Data

Names: Hartenbaum, Natalie P., editor. | United States. Department of
   Transportation.
Title: The DOT medical examination : an unofficial guide to commercial
   drivers' medical certification / Natalie P. Hartenbaum, editor.
Description: Sixth edition. | Beverly Farms, MA : OEM Press, [2017] |
   Includes bibliographical references and index.
Identifiers: LCCN 2017021220 (print) | LCCN 2017022174 (ebook) | ISBN
   9781883595777 (e-book) | ISBN 9781883595753 (pbk.) | ISBN 9781883595791
   (pbk. & ebook bundle) | ISBN 9781883595777 (ebook)
Subjects: | MESH: Automobile Driving--standards | Licensure--standards |
   Commerce--standards | Physical Examination | United States
Classification: LCC TL152.35 (ebook) | LCC TL152.35 (print) | NLM WA 275 |
   DDC 629.28/330973--dc23
LC record available at https://lccn.loc.gov/2017021220

OEM Press® is a registered trademark of OEM Health Information, Inc.

Questions or comments regarding this book should be directed to:

OEM Health Information, Inc.
8 West Street
Beverly Farms, MA 01915-2226
978-921-7300
978-921-0304 (fax)
www.oempress.com
5 4 3 2

CONTENTS

CONTRIBUTING AUTHORS

Natalie P. Hartenbaum, MD, MPH, FACOEM
President and Chief Medical Officer
OccuMedix, Inc.
Maple Glen, Pennsylvania

Eric Wood, MD, MPH, FACOEM
Occupational Medicine Residency Program Director
Rocky Mountain Center for Occupational and Environmental Health
University of Utah
Salt Lake City, Utah

FOREWORD

"Develop a comprehensive medical oversight program for interstate commercial drivers...." Thus begins a Safety Recommendation issued to the Federal Motor Carrier Safety Administration (FMCSA) by the National Transportation Safety Board (NTSB) in 2001 in response to "serious flaws" in the medical certification process for commercial drivers. The FMCSA has made halting progress toward this goal, but Dr. Natalie Hartenbaum continues to edit the single most important source of guidance for those commercial driver medical examiners who would make transportation safety their highest priority.

As the FMCSA works to transition toward a more systematic process for commercial driver medical evaluation, it is even more important that those performing the exams have a ready reference for the often-complex questions they will need to address. The FMCSA's process clearly lays responsibility for the consistent performance of commercial driver certification examinations at the foot of the certified examiner. This book fills the gaps between what such examiners are obligated to do by their position and what will best provide for highway safety. The book has always served as a concise collection of the critical regulatory and guidance information on the process of the examination, specific data-driven recommendations on how to perform and evaluate various portions of the exam itself, and straightforward acknowledgment of where the science or directives (or both) may fall short.

The first edition of this book was published at about the same time that I was beginning my tenure as the Medical Officer at the NTSB, and I have come to know Natalie as a passionate and tireless advocate for transportation safety. She has taught for over two decades on the commercial driver examination process, edited the American College of Occupational and Environmental Medicine (ACOEM) Commercial Driver Medical Examiner Review for over 15 years, served as the ACOEM Transportation Section Chair for more than 10 years, and is a past president of ACOEM. She brings to this edition of *The DOT*

Medical Examination both her extensive expertise in the realm of transportation medicine and her firsthand knowledge of the uncertainties that examiners have about the exams they are regularly performing.

Mitchell A. Garber, MD, MPH, MSME
Senior Managing Consultant
Engineering Systems, Inc.

PREFACE

It is hard to believe that it's been over 20 years since the first edition of this guide was published. Our hope for the first edition was that it would serve not only as a resource to occupational health professionals but also as a convenient reference for others involved in the commercial driver medical certification process. The extent to which this manual has been utilized has been beyond our imagination.

Although much of the original guidance information had been available for years, it was not easily accessible, nor were many examiners aware of its existence or location. While the first edition attempted to collate the information primarily from the Federal Highway Administration (FHWA) conference reports, the next few editions focused on the "official" guidance from FHWA and later the Federal Motor Carrier Safety Administration (FMCSA) but included relevant information from the medical literature. The fifth edition took things even further from our original goal, presenting not only the "official" guidance, but inclusion of the "less official" information from the FMCSA's Medical Review Board (MRB) and Medical Expert Panels (MEP).

The long gap prior to this sixth edition saw major changes in the commercial driver medical certification process—we kept waiting for the dust to settle. The FMCSA Medical Examiner Handbook was taken down for update and, several years later, we are still waiting for its return. Since 2007, FMCSA has heard recommendations from numerous MEPs and the MRB, but none of those have been incorporated into "official" guidance. The greatest change was the implementation of the National Registry of Certified Medical Examiners (NRCME) along with a new form (several changes even to that) and a lot of bumps in the road. The NRCME limited the performance of the commercial driver medical examinations (CDME) to those who meet specific criteria, including training and certification. This is a far cry from when many of us started performing these examinations, having little to no guidance and no available training.

In addition to attempting to collate the most recent "official" guidance from FMCSA, recommendations from FMCSA advisory groups (that have not been formally adopted), and the medical literature, this edition will attempt to clarify many of the confusing issues that have arisen from the NRCME. But, as many of you know, I am very careful in separating what is regulation, FMCSA guidance, other information, and my opinion, and will continue to do so. It has always been true that FMCSA expects examiners to consider the guidance as a starting point, and that they will utilize current best medical practice in reaching their final certification determination.

The sixth edition beings us into the electronic age; the electronic version will have updates at least twice a year. I suspect that some would prefer only the traditional hard copy and some only the electronic but from the beginning, I envisioned this as a bundled product—both paper and electronic. I could not see any value in preparing a book that would be out of date possibly before it was published.

I continue to be grateful to those who have contributed to earlier editions of this book: Dr. Sam Caughron, Dr. Tuenis Zondag, Dr. Kurt Hegmann, and, of course, to Dr. Eric Wood, who joined with the prior edition and continues to put up with me. The support and encouragement by Curtis Vouwie of OEM Press continues to be invaluable.

And, of course, I want to thank my family for their support: Dave, who accepts my quirks, and "the girls." Many of you have heard me refer to the Alissa and Sara test, the ultimate criteria to evaluate whether an individual is safe to drive a bus or other commercial motor vehicle. When I started in occupational medicine and with the training programs for commercial driver medical examiners, Alissa was an infant and Sara only a dream. As the CDME process has progressed since the first edition, so have they; both are now confident young women.

We hope this sixth edition meets your expectations and needs.

And please remember:

The information contained in this book is based on documents provided by FMCSA, its expert panels, and the medical literature. The information in this book should be used as guidance unless specifically indicated as regulation. Sound medical knowledge and an understanding of the underlying disease process, its treatment, and prognosis must guide the final medical certification determination.

—*Natalie P. Hartenbaum, MD, MPH, FACOEM*

PART I

The Examination Process

CHAPTER 1

Commercial Driver Medical Qualification: Past, Present, and Future

NATALIE P. HARTENBAUM, MD, MPH, FACOEM

Since the prior edition of this book, the Commercial Driver Medical Examiner (CDME) processes have undergone significant changes, mostly related to the National Registry of Certified Medical Examiners (NRCME). In 2014, the Federal Motor Carrier Safety Administration Medical Examiner Handbook (ME Handbook) was taken off the Federal Motor Carrier Safety Administration (FMCSA) website for update and revision. As this edition is being prepared, examiners still should consider guidance from the prior handbook, as that is what is being taught in the training programs, but should base their final decision on current best medical practice remembering that our ultimate responsibility is to ensure the safety of the motoring public to the extent reasonably possible. Chapters will include information from the most recent ME Handbook, Medical Expert Panel (MEP) reports, and Medical Review Board (MRB) recommendations as well as other relevant reports and literature.

As significant changes occur, they will be noted at the end of each chapter in the online version of this book at least twice a year.

For the first five editions of this book, we saw incremental changes in the commercial driver medical certification process. Since the fifth edition, the announcement and implementation of the National Registry of Certified Medical Examiners (NRCME)[1,2] represents the greatest change in the process in many years.

The original medical criteria of June 7, 1939, only required drivers to meet the minimum qualifications of "good physical and mental health; good eyesight; adequate hearing; no addiction to narcotic drugs; and no excessive use of alcoholic beverages or liquors."[3] While the Motor Carrier Safety Act of 1935 granted the Interstate Commerce

Commission (ICC) the authority to require medical certification for operators of commercial motor vehicles (CMVs), a physical examination and Certificate of Physical Evaluation were not required until January 1, 1954.

The U.S. Department of Transportation (DOT) was created by an act of Congress in 1970; responsibility for commercial driver qualification was then transferred to the DOT. Tighter medical qualification standards were announced 30 years after issuance of the initial criteria, on June 7, 1969.[4]

In the original notice, insulin use in the 12 months preceding the examination was disqualifying, as was a blood pressure above 160/90 mm Hg. The audiometric criterion in the Notice of Proposed Rulemaking (NPRM) was an average loss not greater than 25 to 30 dB in the better ear. Examinations were proposed to be required annually. However, in the Final Rule, issued on April 22, 1970,[5] the frequency of the examination was changed to biennial. The blood pressure criterion also was changed to its current form, disqualifying only those whose elevated blood pressure was "likely to interfere with the driver's ability to safely operate a commercial motor vehicle." The Final Rule also stated that only current use of insulin would be considered cause for disqualification. The use of hearing aids to meet the audiometric standard became permissible in 1971. At that time, the maximal permissible hearing loss was increased to an average loss not greater than 40 dB in the better ear. Since 1971, although the medical advisory criteria and other guidance have been updated, the physical qualification standards themselves have remained essentially unchanged. The only change was in clarifying the agency's position on medical marijuana by modifying 49 CFR 391.41(b)(12) by specifically prohibiting any Schedule 1 substance even if under the direction of a health care professional.[6]

Motor carrier safety had been under the authority of the Federal Highway Administration (FHWA) until October 1999, when responsibility was transferred to the Federal Motor Carrier Safety Administration (FMCSA), which reports directly to the secretary of the DOT.[7]

Over the years, there have been several changes to the medical examination process. When controlled substance testing was initially implemented, testing was part of the periodic medical fitness examination. Once a company was conducting random tests at a 50 percent annual rate, periodic controlled substance testing could be discontinued. In July 1997, reference to subpart H, drug testing, was formally eliminated, and any reference to drug testing as part of the physical examination was removed.[8] Currently, the only situation in which the drug test conducted under federal testing requirements and the examination might be done during the same office visit is in a pre-employment situation (drug testing can be performed pre-employment, but examinations cannot be conducted until at least a contingent offer of employment is made). Even in this circumstance, the medical evaluation and the drug test should be considered as two separate and unrelated processes.

A 1992 amendment to the Federal Motor Carrier Safety Regulations (FMCSRs) allowed licensed health care professionals other than physicians — including physician assistants, advanced practice nurses under physician supervision, and some chiropractors — to perform the commercial driver medical examinations.[9] These providers can perform commercial driver medical examinations, however, only if the state in which they are licensed permits them to perform such examinations. The hope was that, by expanding the examiner pool, there would be greater flexibility in arranging the required examination and possibly lower cost. Training and certification of examiners was not required until implementation of the NRCME.[2]

Drivers who have been unable to meet the first or second medical standard because of a loss or impairment of an extremity are eligible for what had formerly been known as a limb waiver. In May 2000,[10] terminology for this variance from the standards was changed to Skill Performance Evaluation (SPE) certificate rather than a waiver. A road test is also required prior to issuance of the SPE.

As a result of the Americans with Disabilities Act (ADA), Congress directed the FHWA to perform a thorough review of the physical qualifications. Announcements that studies were proposed to consider the feasibility of relaxing the vision[11] and diabetes[12] standards were published in the *Federal Register* in 1992 and 1993, respectively. The diabetes waiver program permitted some drivers with at least a 3-year record of safe commercial vehicle driving to drive a CMV in interstate commerce. Several other conditions were set, including blood sugar monitoring and the reporting of any accident, whether or not it normally would have been reportable. Some commercial drivers with at least a 3-year safe driving record and at least 20/40 vision corrected or uncorrected in the better eye were eligible for the vision waiver program.

A suit filed by the Advocates for Highway and Auto Safety requested a review of the issuance of waivers to individuals who otherwise did not meet the federal standard. In 1994, the U.S. Court of Appeals for the D.C. Circuit found that the "agency's determination that the waiver program(s) will not adversely affect the safe operation of CMVs is devoid of empirical support".[13] The waiver programs were discontinued at that time, but those drivers holding waivers were grandfathered in to continue to operate in interstate commerce provided that they continue to meet requirements.[14,15]

In 1996, an Eighth Circuit Court decision, *Rauenhorst v. United States Department of Transportation*, required the agency to consider granting a waiver to a driver who met the criteria for a waiver prior to the programs being closed.[16] Interim procedures for waivers, exemptions, and pilot programs were announced in 1998,[17] which were adopted as a Final Rule in 2004.[18] Waivers and exemptions are temporary relief from one or more of the Federal Motor Carrier Safety Regulations (FMCSRs). Waivers are valid for up to 3 months, whereas exemptions may be valid for up to 2 years and are renewable. For both, the applicant must indicate how the same or a greater level of safety could be achieved if the relief were granted. An exemption decision requires an opportunity for public comment through publication in the *Federal Register*, whereas waivers do not.

A 2000 report to Congress[19] on the feasibility of qualifying individuals with insulin-treated diabetes reviewed the issue and offered suggestions on how to permit some drivers on insulin to operate commercial vehicles in interstate commerce. A July 31, 2001 *Federal Register*[20] notice requested comments on whether some insulin-treated diabetics should be granted exemptions. An exemption program was announced in September 2003;[21] the first four exemptions were granted in September 2005.[22] There were very specific criteria for eligibility, including at least 3 years of safe operation of a CMV while on insulin.

The Safe, Accountable, Flexible, Efficient Transportation Equity Act: A Legacy for Users (SAFETEA-LU)[23] required FMCSA to eliminate the 3-year commercial driving requirement for insulin-treated diabetics; these changes were announced in November 2005.[24] In March 2006,[25] comments were sought on whether the prohibition on insulin-treated diabetics should be further modified, possibly eliminating the need for an exemption and allowing the medical examiner and/ or the treating provider to determine whether the driver should be medically qualified.

In May 2015, FMCSA published an NPRM[26] in the *Federal Register* that would allow drivers with stable, well-controlled insulin-treated diabetes mellitus (ITDM) to be qualified to operate CMVs in interstate commerce. After review of comments by the MRB, FMCSA published those recommendations in the *Federal Register* and sought comments.[27]

Potential changes to the vision exemption program that were proposed in 2013 would reduce or eliminate the 3-year safe driving requirement.[28] To date, there has been no action on that notice.

Until 2013, only vision and diabetes exemptions had been granted, although the FMCSA Frequently Asked Questions[29] indicates: "A CMV driver may apply for an exemption from any of the standards. Exemptions are granted only in those instances where the driver can show that safety would not be diminished by granting the exemption." A hearing waiver program to review the hearing standard was proposed in 1993,[30] but not until after a 2012 petition from the National Association for the Deaf[31] were hearing exemptions granted in 2013.[32]

Notice of applications from five drivers in 2006 and 15 in 2008 for exemption from the prohibition of drivers with epilepsy or other condition likely to cause the loss of consciousness[33-35] had been published in the *Federal Register*. Until early 2012, however, there was no action on those requests. On January 5, 2012,[36] FMCSA announced receipt of 15 new applications for exemption from the seizure criteria and in the January 15, 2013 *Federal Register*,[37] the agency announced the granting of 22 exemptions from applications as far back as 2006.

Application for exemptions have also been accepted from drivers with narcolepsy or with implantable cardioverter defibrillators; to date, exemptions have not been granted for those conditions.[38-39]

SAFETEA-LU[23] contained many other requirements for the CMV operator medical program in addition to changes in the insulin exemption eligibility. A Chief Medical Officer was also required by SAFETEA-LU, as was the establishment of a Medical Review Board (MRB). The role of the MRB is to provide scientific advice to FMCSA on ongoing medical issues, including identification of appropriate physical qualifications of CMV drivers, medical standards, and guidelines. They were to be involved in the development of the educational curriculum for training medical examiners that certify that drivers meet the physical qualification standards and functional tests for drivers with certain disabilities,[40] but they were not involved in that activity. The MRB hears reports from the various Medical Expert Panels (MEPs) that are convened to review the existing regulations and guidance. So far, while the MRB — whose members have totally turned over since the original appointments — has heard reports from the several MEPs and has made recommendations of their own based on the opinions of the MEP and the evidence reports, none of those recommendations have been adopted by FMCSA. Hegmann et al. prepared a summary of the first five years of work of the MRB.[41] It may not be simple for examiners or others interested in reports, presentations, or meeting summaries of the meetings to locate a report. Table 1-1 lists meetings and topics by date. Material may be listed under either proceeding or meetings on the Medical Review Board website, https://www.fmcsa.dot.gov/mrb.

The definition of a CMV under §390.5 — which is used for determining which vehicles are subject to the FMCSRs, including the medical standards (but not drug testing) or a commercial driver's license (CDL) — was updated with the Transportation Equity Act for the Twenty-First Century (TEA-21).[42] The definition now included vehicles designed for or used to carry more than eight passengers (including the driver) for direct compensation greater than 75 air miles. In the same announcement, FMCSA delayed requiring operators of smaller vehicles to meet the medical criteria. In 2003 however, it published a Final Rule requiring these operators of smaller vehicles to also meet medical criteria.[43] A more recent announcement[44] eliminated the 75-air-mile criteria, and now all operators of vehicles designed to transport between 8 and 15 passengers for direct compensation are required to meet FMCSA medical criteria. These drivers are not required to undergo controlled substance or alcohol testing.

A 2001 Advanced Notice of Proposed Rulemaking[45] requested comments on requiring school bus drivers involved in interstate transport of students (excluding home to school and return) to comply with the FMCSRs, including a medical examination. In 2004, this rulemaking was withdrawn.[46]

TABLE 1-1 FMCSA Medical Review Board Meetings and Topics

October 24–25, 2016 Joint Meeting with MCSAC	Obstructive Sleep Apnea, Driver Health and Wellness, Medications
August 22–23, 2016	Obstructive Sleep Apnea
August 10, 2016 Joint Meeting with MCSAC	Driver Health and Wellness Working Group
September 21–22, 2015 Joint Meeting with MCSAC	Driver Health and Wellness
July 21–22, 2015	Diabetes Mellitus and Vision Standard
October 27, 2014 Joint Meeting with MCSAC	Schedule II Controlled Substances
July 29–30, 2014	Schedule II Controlled Substances
September 11, 2013	Schedule II Medications
September 9–10, 2013 Joint Meeting with MCSAC	Motorcoach Hours of Service; Schedule II Medications .
February 2013	Bus Driver Fatigue
October 19, 2012	Field of Vision
February 6, 2012 Joint Meeting with MCSAC	Obstructive Sleep Apnea
January 4–5, 2012	Obstructive Sleep Apnea
December 2 and 5, 2011	Obstructive Sleep Apnea
June 30, 2011	Diabetes, Cochlear Implants, Obstructive Sleep Apnea
January 6, 2010	Parkinson's Disease, Multiple Sclerosis; Narcolepsy, Traumatic Brain Injury; Diabetes and Crash Risk
July 1, 2000	Psychiatric Disorders; Circadian Rhythm Disorders; Implantable Cardioverter Defibrillators and Cardiac Resynchronization; Musculoskeletal Disorders
January 12, 2009	Stroke
October 6, 2008	Hearing, Vestibular Function; Psychiatric Disorders
July 18, 2008	Chronic Kidney Disease
April 7, 2008	Chronic Kidney Disease; Vision Deficiency
January 28, 2008	Obstructive Sleep Apnea; Seizures
July 26, 2007	Seizures
April 25, 2007	Cardiovascular
January 10, 2007	Schedule II Medication
November 1, 2006	Diabetes

MCSAC, Motor Carrier Safety Advisory Committee; MRB, Medical Review Board.

For many years, there has been criticism of the medical certification program. The National Transportation Safety Board (NTSB), in its report on the 1999 New Orleans bus accident,[47] identified the failure of the medical certification program to detect the driver's medical problems and remove him from service as one of the probable causes of the accident. Board members indicated that the new form, which had been introduced since the crash, was a substantial improvement in serving as a resource for the medical examiner. As part of a congressional review, the Government Accountability Office (GAO) prepared the report, Commercial Drivers — Certification Process for Drivers with Serious Medical Conditions.[48] By comparing commercial license data from the Department of Transportation with medical disability data from the Social Security Administration, Office of Personnel Management, and Departments of Veterans Affairs and Labor, the GAO found that about 563,000 individuals with CDLs, over 4% of all CDLs in the DOT database, were also found by the federal government to be eligible for full disability benefits. An analysis of 12 states found that about 85% of these individuals had active licenses, with the majority issued after the driver was approved for full disability benefits.

A second part of the congressional review involved the staff of the Committee on Transportation and Infrastructure. In their report for the committee, *Challenges in Verifying the Authenticity of Commercial Drivers' Medical Certificates*,[49] they detailed the process and findings in verifying accuracy of medical certificates. They collected 614 medical certificates during roadside inspections. For 23 of these, they were unable to validate the existence of the medical examiner through searches of state licensing databases and the Internet. Copies of the remaining medical certificates were sent to the medical examiners who performed the examinations and the examiners were requested to confirm the certificate. Of these, 441 examiners responded, 404 indicating that the certificates were valid while 7 reported that the certificates were invalid — either forged or altered — and 4 examiners were unable to determine if certificates were valid. Their conclusion was that opportunities existed for commercial drivers to "fabricate or adulterate" a medical certificate.

Over the years, the medical examination form has also undergone many changes; some may remember the two-sided, one-sheet examination form that had been in use for many years (Figure 1.1).

An updated form was proposed in 1998,[50] with the Final Rule published on October 5, 2000.[51] On the new form, some questions or items were deleted, such as a question on venereal disease or a place for recording serology. Examiners were instructed to review medication, and a question on sleep disorders was added with the revised form. The testing and physical examination pages include many of the standards adjacent to where the examiner would enter findings, such as for vision or blood pressure. Pulse after exercise had been required in the past; this component of the examination has been eliminated. Unlike on the earlier one-sheet form, the drivers were required to complete the history segment and then sign a statement indicating that the history they provided is accurate, and that the option for certification for less than 24 months if a medical condition is present that does not disqualify, but would require more frequent monitoring, is clearly stated. In 2003, a minor update to the form was announced that included the new hypertension guidelines and other changes in the advisory criteria[52] (Figure 1.2). Details on the current form will be discussed in Chapter 2.

FIGURE 1-1 Examination Form (pre-2000)

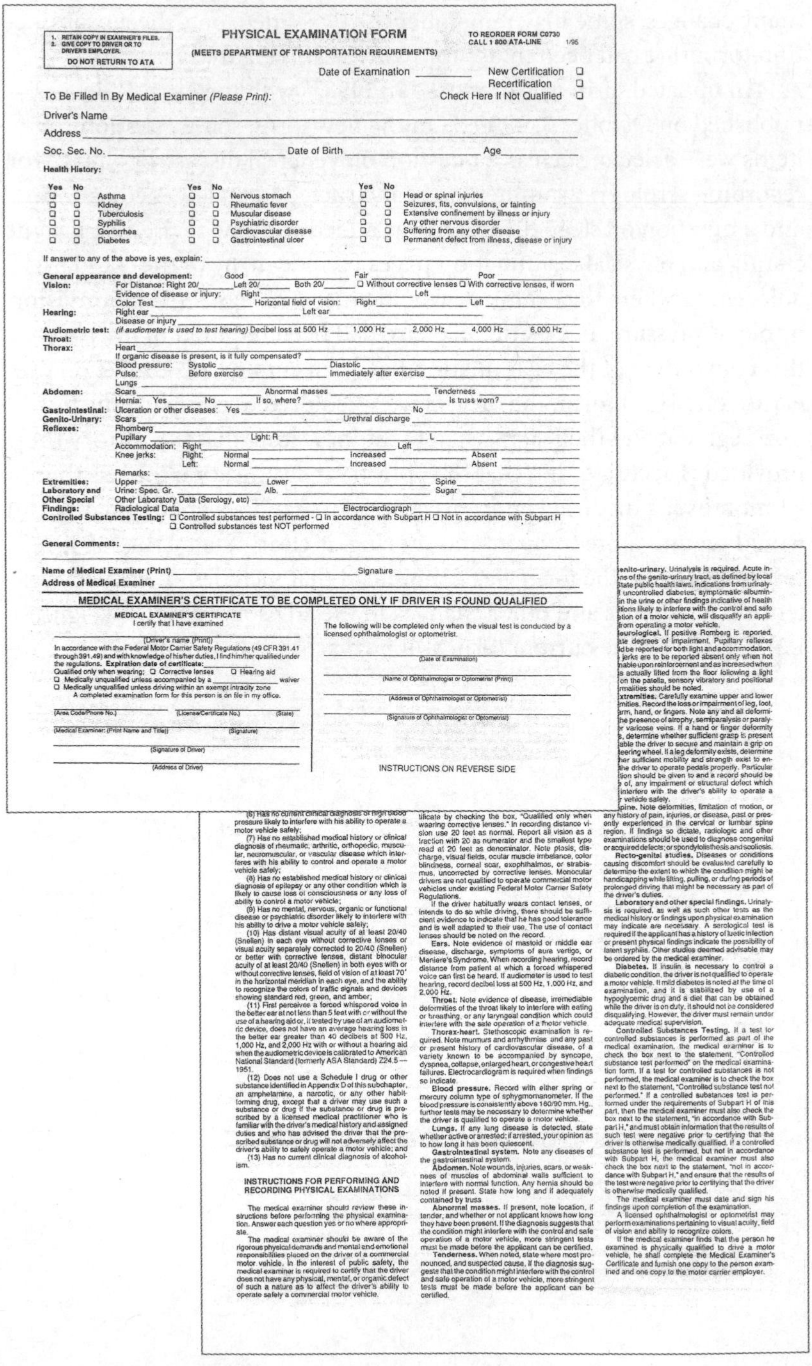

1. RETAIN COPY IN EXAMINER'S FILES.
2. GIVE COPY TO DRIVER OR TO DRIVER'S EMPLOYER.

DO NOT RETURN TO ATA

PHYSICAL EXAMINATION FORM

(MEETS DEPARTMENT OF TRANSPORTATION REQUIREMENTS)

TO REORDER FORM C0730
CALL 1 800 ATA-LINE 1/95

Date of Examination ______ New Certification ☐
Recertification ☐
To Be Filled In By Medical Examiner *(Please Print)*: Check Here If Not Qualified ☐

Driver's Name ______
Address ______
Soc. Sec. No. ______ Date of Birth ______ Age ______

Health History:

Yes	No		Yes	No		Yes	No	
☐	☐	Asthma	☐	☐	Nervous stomach	☐	☐	Head or spinal injuries
☐	☐	Kidney	☐	☐	Rheumatic fever	☐	☐	Seizures, fits, convulsions, or fainting
☐	☐	Tuberculosis	☐	☐	Muscular disease	☐	☐	Extensive confinement by illness or injury
☐	☐	Syphilis	☐	☐	Psychiatric disorder	☐	☐	Any other nervous disorder
☐	☐	Gonorrhea	☐	☐	Cardiovascular disease	☐	☐	Suffering from any other disease
☐	☐	Diabetes	☐	☐	Gastrointestinal ulcer	☐	☐	Permanent defect from illness, disease or injury

If answer to any of the above is yes, explain: ______

General appearance and development: Good ______ Fair ______ Poor ______
Vision: For Distance: Right 20/____ Left 20/____ Both 20/____ ☐ Without corrective lenses ☐ With corrective lenses, if worn
Evidence of disease or injury: Right ______ Left ______
Color Test ______ Horizontal field of vision: Right ______ Left ______
Hearing: Right ear ______ Left ear ______
Disease or injury ______
Audiometric test: *(if audiometer is used to test hearing)* Decibel loss at 500 Hz ____ 1,000 Hz ____ 2,000 Hz ____ 4,000 Hz ____ 6,000 Hz ____
Throat: ______
Thorax: Heart ______
If organic disease is present, is it fully compensated? ______
Blood pressure: Systolic ______ Diastolic ______
Pulse: Before exercise ______ Immediately after exercise ______
Lungs ______
Abdomen: Scars ______ Abnormal masses ______ Tenderness ______
Hernia: Yes ____ No ____ If so, where? ______ Is truss worn? ______
Gastrointestinal: Ulceration or other diseases: Yes ______ No ______
Genito-Urinary: Scars ______ Urethral discharge ______
Reflexes: Rhomberg ______
Pupillary ______ Light: R ______ L ______
Accommodation: Right ______ Left ______
Knee jerks: Right: Normal ______ Increased ______ Absent ______
Left: Normal ______ Increased ______ Absent ______
Remarks: ______
Extremities: Upper ______ Lower ______ Spine ______
Laboratory and Other Special Findings: Urine: Spec. Gr. ______ Alb. ______ Sugar ______
Other Laboratory Data (Serology, etc) ______
Radiological Data ______ Electrocardiograph ______
Controlled Substances Testing: ☐ Controlled substances test performed - ☐ In accordance with Subpart H ☐ Not in accordance with Subpart H
☐ Controlled substances test NOT performed

General Comments: ______

Name of Medical Examiner (Print) ______ Signature ______
Address of Medical Examiner ______

MEDICAL EXAMINER'S CERTIFICATE TO BE COMPLETED ONLY IF DRIVER IS FOUND QUALIFIED

MEDICAL EXAMINER'S CERTIFICATE
I certify that I have examined

______
(Driver's name (Print))

In accordance with the Federal Motor Carrier Safety Regulations (49 CFR 391.41 through 391.49) and with knowledge of his/her duties, I find him/her qualified under the regulations. **Expiration date of certificate:** ______
Qualified only when wearing: ☐ Corrective lenses ☐ Hearing aid
☐ Medically unqualified unless accompanied by a ______ waiver
☐ Medically unqualified unless driving within an exempt intracity zone
A completed examination form for this person is on file in my office.

(Area Code/Phone No.) (License/Certificate No.) (State)

(Medical Examiner: (Print Name and Title)) (Signature)

(Signature of Driver)

(Address of Driver)

The following will be completed only when the visual test is conducted by a licensed ophthalmologist or optometrist.

(Date of Examination)

(Name of Ophthalmologist or Optometrist (Print))

(Address of Ophthalmologist or Optometrist)

(Signature of Ophthalmologist or Optometrist)

INSTRUCTIONS ON REVERSE SIDE

(6) Has no current clinical diagnosis of high blood pressure likely to interfere with his ability to operate a motor vehicle safely;

(7) Has no established medical history or clinical diagnosis of rheumatic, arthritic, orthopedic, muscular, neuromuscular, or vascular disease which interferes with his ability to control and operate a motor vehicle safely;

(8) Has no established medical history or clinical diagnosis of epilepsy or any other condition which is likely to cause loss of consciousness or any loss of ability to control a motor vehicle;

(9) Has no mental, nervous, organic or functional disease or psychiatric disorder likely to interfere with his ability to drive a motor vehicle safely;

(10) Has distant visual acuity of at least 20/40 (Snellen) in each eye without corrective lenses or visual acuity separately corrected to 20/40 (Snellen) or better with corrective lenses, distant binocular acuity of at least 20/40 (Snellen) in both eyes with or without corrective lenses, field of vision of at least 70° in the horizontal meridian in each eye, and the ability to recognize the colors of traffic signals and devices showing standard red, green, and amber;

(11) First perceives a forced whispered voice in the better ear at not less than 5 feet with or without the use of a hearing aid or, if tested by use of an audiometric device, does not have an average hearing loss in the better ear greater than 40 decibels at 500 Hz, 1,000 Hz, and 2,000 Hz with or without a hearing aid when the audiometric device is calibrated to American National Standard (formerly ASA Standard) Z24.5—1951.

(12) Does not use a Schedule I drug or other substance identified in Appendix D of this subchapter, an amphetamine, a narcotic, or any other habit-forming drug, except that a driver may use such a substance or drug if the substance or drug is prescribed by a licensed medical practitioner who is familiar with the driver's medical history and assigned duties and who has advised the driver that the prescribed substance or drug will not adversely affect the driver's ability to safely operate a motor vehicle; and

(13) Has no current clinical diagnosis of alcoholism.

INSTRUCTIONS FOR PERFORMING AND RECORDING PHYSICAL EXAMINATIONS

The medical examiner should review these instructions before performing the physical examination. Answer each question yes or no where appropriate.

The medical examiner should be aware of the rigorous physical demands and mental and emotional responsibilities placed on the driver of a commercial motor vehicle. In the interest of public safety, the medical examiner is required to certify that the driver does not have any physical, mental, or organic defect of such a nature as to affect the driver's ability to operate safely a commercial motor vehicle.

tificate by checking the box, "Qualified only when wearing corrective lenses." In recording distance vision use 20 feet as normal. Report all vision as a fraction with 20 as numerator and the smallest type read at 20 feet as denominator. Note ptosis, discharge, visual fields, ocular muscle imbalance, color blindness, corneal scar, exophthalmos, or strabismus, uncorrected by corrective lenses. Monocular drivers are not qualified to operate commercial motor vehicles under existing Federal Motor Carrier Safety Regulations.

If the driver habitually wears contact lenses, or intends to do so while driving, there should be sufficient evidence to indicate that he has good tolerance and is well adapted to their use. The use of contact lenses should be noted on the record.

Ears. Note evidence of mastoid or middle ear disease, discharge, symptoms of aura vertigo, or Meniere's Syndrome. When recording hearing, record distance from patient at which a forced whispered voice can first be heard. If audiometer is used to test hearing, record decibel loss at 500 Hz, 1,000 Hz, and 2,000 Hz.

Throat. Note evidence of disease, irremediable deformities of the throat likely to interfere with eating or breathing, or any laryngeal condition which could interfere with the safe operation of a motor vehicle.

Thorax-heart. Stethoscopic examination is required. Note murmurs and arrhythmias and any past or present history of cardiovascular disease, of a variety known to be accompanied by syncope, dyspnea, collapse, enlarged heart, or congestive heart failures. Electrocardiogram is required when findings so indicate.

Blood pressure. Record with either spring or mercury column type of sphygmomanometer. If the blood pressure is consistently above 160/90 mm. Hg., further tests may be necessary to determine whether the driver is qualified to operate a motor vehicle.

Lungs. If any lung disease is detected, state whether active or arrested; if arrested, your opinion as to how long it has been quiescent.

Gastrointestinal system. Note any diseases of the gastrointestinal system.

Abdomen. Note wounds, injuries, scars, or weakness of muscles of abdominal walls sufficient to interfere with normal function. Any hernia should be noted if present. State how long and if adequately contained by truss.

Abnormal masses. If present, note location, if tender, and whether or not applicant knows how long they have been present. If the diagnosis suggests that the condition might interfere with the control and safe operation of a motor vehicle, more stringent tests must be made before the applicant can be certified.

Tenderness. When noted, state where most pronounced, and suspected cause. If the diagnosis suggests that the condition might interfere with the control and safe operation of a motor vehicle, more stringent tests must be made before the applicant can be certified.

enito-urinary. Urinalysis is required. Acute in-
ns of the genito-urinary tract, as defined by local
State public health laws, indications from urinaly-
f uncontrolled diabetes, symptomatic albumin-
in the urine or other findings indicative of health
itions likely to interfere with the control and safe
ation of a motor vehicle, will disqualify an appli-
from operating a motor vehicle.
eurological. If positive Romberg is reported,
ate degrees of impairment. Pupillary reflexes
ld be reported for both light and accommodation.
jerks are to be reported absent only when not
nable upon reinforcement and as increased when
s actually lifted from the floor following a light
on the patella, sensory vibratory and positional
rmalities should be noted.
xtremities. Carefully examine upper and lower
mities. Record the loss or impairment of leg, foot,
rm, hand, or fingers. Note any and all deformi-
he presence of atrophy, semiparalysis or paraly-
r varicose veins. If a hand or finger deformity
s, determine whether sufficient grasp is present
able the driver to secure and maintain a grip on
eering wheel. If a leg deformity exists, determine
her sufficient mobility and strength exist to en-
the driver to operate pedals properly. Particular
tion should be given to and a record should be
of, any impairment or structural defect which
interfere with the driver's ability to operate a
r vehicle safely.
pine. Note deformities, limitation of motion, or any history of pain, injuries, or disease, past or presently experienced in the cervical or lumbar spine region. If findings so dictate, radiologic and other examinations should be used to diagnose congenital or acquired defects; or spondylolisthesis and scoliosis.

Recto-genital studies. Diseases or conditions causing discomfort should be evaluated carefully to determine the extent to which the condition might be handicapping while lifting, pulling, or during periods of prolonged driving that might be necessary as part of the driver's duties.

Laboratory and other special findings. Urinalysis is required, as well as such other tests as the medical history or findings upon physical examination may indicate are necessary. A serological test is required if the applicant has a history of luetic infection or present physical findings indicate the possibility of latent syphilis. Other studies deemed advisable may be ordered by the medical examiner.

Diabetes. If insulin is necessary to control a diabetic condition, the driver is not qualified to operate a motor vehicle. If mild diabetes is noted at the time of examination, and it is stabilized by use of a hypoglycemic drug and a diet that can be obtained while the driver is on duty, it should not be considered disqualifying. However, the driver must remain under adequate medical supervision.

Controlled Substances Testing. If a test for controlled substances is performed as part of the medical examination, the medical examiner is to check the box next to the statement, "Controlled substance test performed" on the medical examination form. If a test for controlled substances is not performed, the medical examiner is to check the box next to the statement, "Controlled substance test not performed." If a controlled substances test is performed under the requirements of Subpart H of this part, then the medical examiner must also check the box next to the statement, "in accordance with Subpart H," and must obtain information that the results of such test were negative prior to certifying that the driver is otherwise medically qualified. If a controlled substance test is performed, but not in accordance with Subpart H, the medical examiner must also check the box next to the statement, "not in accordance with Subpart H," and ensure that the results of the test were negative prior to certifying that the driver is otherwise medically qualified.

The medical examiner must date and sign his findings upon completion of the examination.

A licensed ophthalmologist or optometrist may perform examinations pertaining to visual acuity, field of vision and ability to recognize colors.

If the medical examiner finds that the person he examined is physically qualified to drive a motor vehicle, he shall complete the Medical Examiner's Certificate and furnish one copy to the person examined and one copy to the motor carrier employer.

FIGURE 1-2 Examination Form (2003)

649-F (6045)

Medical Examination Report
FOR COMMERCIAL DRIVER FITNESS DETERMINATION

1. DRIVER'S INFORMATION Driver completes this section

| Driver's Name (Last, First, Middle) | Social Security No. | Birthdate M / D / Y | Age | Sex ☐ M ☐ F | New Certification ☐ Recertification ☐ Follow-up ☐ | Date of Exam |

| Address | City, State, Zip Code | Work Tel: ( ) Home Tel: ( ) | Driver License No. | License Class ☐ A ☐ B ☐ C ☐ D ☐ Other | State of Issue |

2. HEALTH HISTORY Driver completes this section, but medical examiner is encouraged to discuss with driver.

Yes No
- ☐☐ Any illness or injury in the last 5 years?
- ☐☐ Head/Brain injuries, disorders or illnesses
- ☐☐ Seizures, epilepsy ☐ medication
- ☐☐ Eye disorders or impaired vision (except corrective lenses)
- ☐☐ Ear disorders, loss of hearing or balance
- ☐☐ Heart disease or heart attack; other cardiovascular condition ☐ medication
- ☐☐ Heart surgery (valve replacement/bypass, angioplasty, pacemaker) ☐ medication
- ☐☐ High blood pressure
- ☐☐ Muscular disease
- ☐☐ Shortness of breath

Yes No
- ☐☐ Lung disease, emphysema, asthma, chronic bronchitis
- ☐☐ Kidney disease, dialysis
- ☐☐ Liver disease
- ☐☐ Digestive problems
- ☐☐ Diabetes or elevated blood sugar controlled by: ☐ diet ☐ pills ☐ insulin
- ☐☐ Nervous or psychiatric disorders, e.g., severe depression medication
- ☐☐ Loss of, or altered consciousness

Yes No
- ☐☐ Fainting, dizziness
- ☐☐ Sleep disorders, pauses in breathing while asleep, daytime sleepiness, loud snoring
- ☐☐ Stroke or paralysis
- ☐☐ Missing or impaired hand, arm, foot, leg, finger, toe
- ☐☐ Spinal injury or disease
- ☐☐ Chronic low back pain
- ☐☐ Regular, frequent alcohol use
- ☐☐ Narcotic or habit forming drug use

For any YES answer, indicate onset date, diagnosis, treating physician's name and address, and any current limitation. List all medications (including over-the-counter medications) used regularly or recently.

I certify that the above information is complete and true. I understand that inaccurate, false or missing information may invalidate the examination and my Medical Examiner's Certificate.

Driver's Signature _____   Date _____

Medical Examiner's Comments on Health History (The medical examiner must review and discuss with the driver any "yes" answers and potential hazards of medications, including over-the-counter medications, while driving. This discussion must be documented below.)

FIGURE 1-2 Examination Form (2003), continued

TESTING (Medical Examiner completes Section 3 through 7)
Name: Last, _____ First, _____ Middle, _____

3. VISION

Standard: At least 20/40 acuity (Snellen) in each eye with or without correction. At least 70 degrees peripheral in horizontal meridian measured in each eye. The use of corrective lenses should be noted on the Medical Examiner's Certificate.

INSTRUCTIONS: When other than the Snellen chart is used, give test results in Snellen-comparable values. In recording distance vision, use 20 feet as normal. Report visual acuity as a ratio with 20 as numerator and the smallest type read at 20 feet as denominator. If the applicant wears corrective lenses, these should be worn while visual acuity is being tested. If the driver habitually wears contact lenses, or intends to do so while driving, sufficient evidence of good tolerance and adaptation to their use must be obvious. *Monocular drivers are not qualified.*

Numerical readings must be provided.

ACUITY	UNCORRECTED	CORRECTED	HORIZONTAL FIELD OF VISION	
Right Eye	20/	20/	Right Eye	°
Left Eye	20/	20/	Left Eye	°
Both Eyes	20/	20/		

Applicant can recognize and distinguish among traffic control signals and devices showing standard red, green, and amber colors ?   ☐ Yes ☐ No

Applicant meets visual acuity requirement only when wearing:
☐ Corrective Lenses

Monocular Vision: ☐ Yes ☐ No

Complete next line only if vision testing is done by an opthalmologist or optometrist

Date of Examination _____ Name of Ophthalmologist or Optometrist (print) _____ Tel. No. _____ License No./ State of Issue _____ Signature _____

4. HEARING

Standard: a) Must first perceive forced whispered voice ≥ 5 ft., with or without hearing aid, or b) average hearing loss in better ear ≤ 40 dB
☐ Check if hearing aid used for tests.   ☐ Check if hearing aid required to meet standard.

INSTRUCTIONS: To convert audiometric test results from ISO to ANSI, -14 dB from ISO for 500Hz, -10dB for 1,000 Hz, -8.5 dB for 2000 Hz. To average, add the readings for 3 frequencies tested and divide by 3.

Numerical readings must be recorded.

a) Record distance from individual at which forced whispered voice can first be heard.	Right ear	Left Ear	
	\Feet	\Feet	

b) If audiometer is used, record hearing loss in decibels. (acc: to ANSI Z24.5-1951)

	Right Ear				Left Ear		
	500 Hz	1000 Hz	2000 Hz		500 Hz	1000 Hz	2000 Hz
Average:				Average:			

5. BLOOD PRESSURE/ PULSE RATE.

Numerical readings must be recorded. Medical Examiner should take at least two readings to confirm BP.

Blood Pressure	Systolic	Diastolic	Reading	Category	Expiration Date	Recertification
			140-159/90-99	Stage 1	1 year	1 year if ≤140/90. One-time certificate for 3 months if 141-159/91-99.
Driver qualified if ≤140/90.			160-179/100-109	Stage 2	One-time certificate for 3 months.	1 year from date of exam if ≤140/90
Pulse Rate: ☐ Regular ☐ Irregular			>180/110	Stage 3	6 months from date of exam if ≤140/90	6 months if ≤ 140/90
Record Pulse Rate:						

6. LABORATORY AND OTHER TEST FINDINGS   **Numerical readings must be recorded.**

Urinalysis is required. Protein, blood or sugar in the urine may be an indication for further testing to rule out any underlying medical problem.
Other Testing (Describe and record)

URINE SPECIMEN	SP. GR.	PROTEIN	BLOOD	SUGAR

FIGURE 1-2 Examination Form (2003), continued

| 7. | PHYSICAL EXAMINATION | Height: _____ (in.) Weight: _____ (lbs.) | Name: Last, _____ First, _____ Middle, _____ |

The presence of a certain condition may not necessarily disqualify a driver, particularly if the condition is controlled adequately, is not likely to worsen or is readily amenable to treatment. Even if a condition does not disqualify a driver, the medical examiner may consider deferring the driver temporarily. Also, the driver should be advised to take the necessary steps to correct the condition as soon as possible particularly if the condition, if neglected, could result in more serious illness that might affect driving.

Check YES if there are any abnormalities. Check NO if the body system is normal. Discuss any YES answers in detail in the space below, and indicate whether it would affect the driver's ability to operate a commercial motor vehicle safely. Enter applicable item number before each comment. If organic disease is present, note that it has been compensated for. See *Instructions to the Medical Examiner* for guidance.

BODY SYSTEM	CHECK FOR:	YES*	NO	BODY SYSTEM	CHECK FOR:	YES*	NO
1. General Appearance	Marked overweight, tremor, signs of alcoholism, problem drinking, or drug abuse.			7. Abdomen and Viscera	Enlarged liver, enlarged spleen, masses, bruits, hernia, significant abdominal wall muscle weakness.		
2. Eyes	Pupillary equality, reaction to light, accommodation, ocular motility, ocular muscle imbalance, extraocular movement, nystagmus, exophthalmos. Ask about retinopathy, cataracts, aphakia, glaucoma, macular degeneration and refer to a specialist if appropriate.			8. Vascular System	Abnormal pulse and amplitude, carotid or arterial bruits, varicose veins.		
				9. Genito-urinary System	Hernias.		
3. Ears	Scarring of tympanic membrane, occlusion of external canal, perforated eardrums.			10. Extremities- Limb impaired. Driver may be subject to SPE certificate if otherwise qualified.	Loss or impairment of leg, foot, toe, arm, hand, finger. Perceptible limp, deformities, atrophy, weakness, paralysis, clubbing, edema, hypotonia. Insufficient grasp and prehension in upper limb to maintain steering wheel grip. Insufficient mobility and strength in lower limb to operate pedals properly.		
4. Mouth and Throat	Irremediable deformities likely to interfere with breathing or swallowing.						
5. Heart	Murmurs, extra sounds, enlarged heart, pacemaker, implantable defibrillator.			11. Spine, other musculoskeletal	Previous surgery, deformities, limitation of motion, tenderness.		
6. Lungs and chest, not including breast examination	Abnormal chest wall expansion, abnormal respiratory rate, abnormal breath sounds including wheezes or alveolar rales, impaired respiratory function, cyanosis. Abnormal findings on physical exam may require further testing such as pulmonary tests and/ or xray of chest.			12. Neurological	Impaired equilibrium, coordination or speech pattern, asymmetric deep tendon reflexes, sensory or positional abnormalities, abnormal patellar and Babinit's reflexes, ataxia.		

*COMMENTS:

_____

_____

_____

_____

Note certification status here. See *Instructions to the Medical Examiner* for guidance.

☐ Meets standards in 49 CFR 391.41; qualifies for 2 year certificate
☐ Does not meet standards
☐ Meets standards, but periodic monitoring required due to _____
☐ Driver qualified only for: ☐3 months ☐6 months ☐1 year ☐ Other _____

☐ Wearing corrective lense
☐ Wearing hearing aid
☐ Accompanied by a _____ waiver/ exemption. Driver must present exemption at time of certification.
☐ Skill Performance Evaluation (SPE) Certificate
☐ Driving within an exempt intracity zone (See 49 CFR 391.62)
☐ Qualified by operation of 49 CFR 391.64

Temporarily disqualified due to (condition or medication): _____

Return to medical examiner's office for follow up on _____

Medical Examiner's signature _____
Medical Examiner's name _____
Address _____
Telephone Number _____

| If meets standards, complete a Medical Examiner's Certificate as stated in 49 CFR 391.43(h). (Driver must carry certificate when operating a commercial vehicle.) |

FIGURE 1-2 Examination Form (2003), continued

49 CFR 391.41 Physical Qualifications for Drivers

THE DRIVER'S ROLE

Responsibilities, work schedules, physical and emotional demands, and lifestyles among commercial drivers vary by the type of driving that they do. Some of the main types of drivers include the following: turn around or short relay (drivers return to their home base each evening); long relay (drivers drive 9-11 hours and then have at least a 10-hour off-duty period), straight through haul (cross country drivers); and team drivers (drivers share the driving by alternating their 5-hour driving periods and 5-hour rest periods.)

The following factors may be involved in a driver's performance of duties: abrupt schedule changes and rotating work schedules, which may result in irregular sleep patterns and a driver beginning a trip in a fatigued condition; long hours; extended time away from family and friends, which may result in lack of social support; tight pickup and delivery schedules, with irregularity in work, rest, and eating patterns, adverse road, weather and traffic conditions, which may cause delays and lead to hurriedly loading or unloading cargo in order to compensate for the lost time; and environmental conditions such as excessive vibration, noise, and extremes in temperature. Transporting passengers or hazardous materials may add to the demands on the commercial driver.

There may be duties in addition to the driving task for which a driver is responsible and needs to be fit. Some of these responsibilities are: coupling and uncoupling trailer(s) from the tractor, loading and unloading trailer(s) (sometimes a driver may lift a heavy load or unload as much as 50,000 lbs. of freight after sitting for a long period of time without any stretching period); inspecting the operating condition of tractor and/or trailer(s) before, during and after delivery of cargo; lifting, installing, and removing heavy tire chains; and, lifting heavy tarpaulins to cover open top trailers. The above tasks demand agility, the ability to bend and stoop, the ability to maintain a crouching position to inspect the underside of the vehicle, frequent entering and exiting of the cab, and the ability to climb ladders on the tractor and/or trailer(s).

In addition, a driver must have the perceptual skills to monitor a sometimes complex driving situation, the judgment skills to make quick decisions, when necessary, and the manipulative skills to control an oversize steering wheel, shift gears using a manual transmission, and maneuver a vehicle in crowded areas.

§391.45 PHYSICAL QUALIFICATIONS FOR DRIVERS

(a) A person shall not drive a commercial motor vehicle unless he is physically qualified to do so and, except as provided in §391.67, has on his person the original, or a photographic copy, of a medical examiner's certificate that he is physically qualified to drive a commercial motor vehicle.

(b) A person is physically qualified to drive a motor vehicle if that person:

(1) Has no loss of a foot, a leg, a hand, or an arm, or has been granted a Skill Performance Evaluation (SPE) Certificate (formerly Limb Waiver Program) pursuant to §391.49.

(2) Has no impairment of: (i) A hand or finger which interferes with prehension or power grasping; or (ii) An arm, foot, or leg which interferes with the ability to perform normal tasks associated with operating a commercial motor vehicle; or any other significant limb defect or limitation which interferes with the ability to perform normal tasks associated with operating a commercial motor vehicle; or has been granted a SPE Certificate pursuant to §391.49.

(3) Has no established medical history or clinical diagnosis of diabetes mellitus currently requiring insulin for control;

(4) Has no current clinical diagnosis of myocardial infarction, angina pectoris, coronary insufficiency, thrombosis, or any other cardiovascular disease of a variety known to be accompanied by syncope, dyspnea, collapse, or congestive cardiac failure.

(5) Has no established medical history or clinical diagnosis of a respiratory dysfunction likely to interfere with his ability to control and drive a commercial motor vehicle safely.

(6) Has no current clinical diagnosis of high blood pressure likely to interfere with his ability to operate a commercial motor vehicle safely.

(7) Has no established medical history or clinical diagnosis of rheumatic, arthritic, orthopedic, muscular, neuromuscular, or vascular disease which interferes with his ability to control and operate a commercial motor vehicle safely.

(8) Has no established medical history or clinical diagnosis of epilepsy or any other condition which is likely to cause loss of consciousness or any loss of ability to control a commercial motor vehicle;

(9) Has no mental, nervous, organic, or functional disease or psychiatric disorder likely to interfere with his ability to drive a commercial motor vehicle safely;

(10) Has distant visual acuity of at least 20/40 (Snellen) in each eye without corrective lenses or visual acuity separately corrected to 20/40 (Snellen) or better with corrective lenses, distant binocular acuity of at least 20/40 (Snellen) in both eyes with or without corrective lenses, field of vision of at least 70 degrees in the horizontal meridian in each eye, and the ability to recognize the colors of traffic signals and devices showing standard red, green and amber;

(11) First perceives a forced whispered voice in the better ear not less than 5 feet with or without the use of a hearing aid, or, if tested by use of an audiometric device, does not have an average hearing loss in the better ear greater than 40 decibels at 500 Hz, 1,000 Hz and 2,000 Hz with or without a hearing device when the audiometric device is calibrated to the American National Standard (formerly ASA Standard) Z24.5-1951;

(12) (i) Does not use a controlled substance identified in 21 CFR 1308.11 Schedule I, an amphetamine, a narcotic, or any other habit-forming drug. (ii) Exception: A driver may use such a substance or drug, if the substance or drug is prescribed by a licensed medical practitioner who: (A) Is familiar with the driver's medical history and assigned duties; and (B) Has advised the driver that the prescribed substance or drug will not adversely affect the driver's ability to safely operate a commercial motor vehicle; and

(13) Has no current clinical diagnosis of alcoholism.

INSTRUCTIONS TO THE MEDICAL EXAMINER

General Information

The purpose of this examination is to determine a driver's physical qualification to operate a commercial motor vehicle (CMV) in interstate commerce according to the requirements in 49 CFR 391.41-49. Therefore, the medical examiner must be knowledgeable of these requirements and guidelines developed by the FMCSA to assist the medical examiner in making the qualification determination. The medical examiner should be familiar with the driver's responsibilities and work environment and is referred to the section on the form, **The Driver's Role**.

In addition to reviewing the **Health History** section with the driver and conducting the physical examination, the medical examiner should discuss common prescriptions and over-the-counter medications relative to the side effects and hazards of these medications while driving. Educate the driver to read warning labels on all medications. History of certain conditions may be cause for rejection, particularly if required by regulation, or may indicate the need for additional laboratory tests or more stringent examination perhaps by a medical specialist. These decisions are usually made by the medical examiner in light of the driver's job responsibilities, work schedule and potential for the conditions to render the driver unsafe.

Medical conditions should be recorded even if they are not cause for denial, and they should be discussed with the driver to encourage appropriate remedial care. This advice is especially needed when a condition, if neglected, could develop into a serious illness that could affect driving.

If the medical examiner determines that the driver is fit to drive and is also able to perform non-driving responsibilities as may be required, the medical examiner signs the medical certificate which the driver must carry with his/her license. The certificate must be dated. **Under current regulations, the certificate is valid for two years, unless the driver has a medical condition that does not prohibit driving but does require more frequent monitoring**. In such situations, the medical certificate should be issued for a shorter length of time. The physical examination should be done carefully and at least as complete as is indicated by the attached form. Contact the FMCSA at (202) 366-1790 for further information (a vision exemption, qualifying drivers under 49 CFR 391.64, etc.).

Interpretation of Medical Standards

Since the issuance of the regulations for physical qualifications of commercial drivers, the Federal Motor Carrier Safety Administration (FMCSA) has published recommendations called Advisory Criteria to help medical examiners in determining whether a driver meets the physical qualifications for commercial driving. These recommendations have been condensed to provide information to medical examiners that (1) is directly relevant to the physical examination and (2) is not already included in the medical examination form. The specific regulation is printed in italics and it's reference by section is highlighted.

Federal Motor Carrier Safety Regulations
-Advisory Criteria-

Loss of Limb:
§391.41(b)(1)
A person is physically qualified to drive a commercial motor vehicle if that person:
Has no loss of a foot, leg, hand or an arm, or has been granted a Skill Performance Evaluation (SPE) Certificate pursuant to Section 391.49.

Limb Impairment:
§391.41(b)(2)
A person is physically qualified to drive a commercial motor vehicle if that person:
Has no impairment of: (i) A hand or finger which interferes with prehension or power grasping; or (ii) An arm, foot, or leg which interferes with the ability to perform normal tasks associated with operating a commercial motor vehicle; or (iii) Any other significant limb defect or limitation which interferes with the ability to perform normal tasks associated with operating a commercial motor vehicle; or (iv) Has been granted a Skill Performance Evaluation (SPE) Certificate pursuant to Section 391.49.

A person who suffers loss of a foot, leg, hand or arm or whose limb impairment in any way interferes with the safe performance of normal tasks associated with operating a commercial motor vehicle is subject to the Skill Performance Evaluation Certification Program pursuant to section 391.49, assuming the person is otherwise qualified.

With the advancement of technology, medical aids and equipment modifications have been developed to compensate for certain disabilities. The SPE Certification Program (formerly the Limb Waiver Program) was designed to allow persons with the loss of a foot or limb or with functional impairment to qualify under the Federal Motor Carrier Safety Regulations (FMCSRs) by use of prosthetic devices or equipment modifications which enable them to safely operate a commercial motor vehicle. Since there are no medical aids equivalent to the original body or limb, certain risks are still present, and thus restrictions may be included on individual SPE certificates when a State Director for the FMCSA determines they are necessary to be consistent with safety and public interest.

If the driver is found otherwise medically qualified (391.41(b)(3) through (13)), the medical examiner must check on the medical certificate that the driver is qualified only if accompanied by a SPE certificate. The driver and the employing motor carrier are subject to appropriate penalty if the driver operates a motor vehicle in interstate or foreign commerce without a curent SPE certificate for his/her physical disability.

Diabetes
§391.41(b)(3)
A person is physically qualified to drive a commercial motor vehicle if that person:
Has no established medical history or clinical diagnosis of diabetes mellitus currently requiring insulin for control.

Diabetes mellitus is a disease which, on occasion, can result in a loss of consciousness or disorientation in time and space. Individuals who require insulin for control have conditions which can get out of control by the use of too much or too little insulin, or food intake not consistent with the insulin dosage. Incapacitation may occur from symptoms of hyperglycemic or hypoglycemic reactions (drowsiness, semiconsciousness, diabetic coma or insulin shock).

The administration of insulin is, within itself, a complicated process requiring insulin, syringe, needle, alcohol sponge and a sterile technique. Factors related to long-haul commercial motor vehicle operations, such as fatigue, lack of sleep, poor diet, emotional conditions, stress, and concomitant illness, compound the dangers, the FMCSA has consistently held that a diabetic who uses insulin for control does not meet the minimum physical requirements of the FMCSRs.

Hypoglycemic drugs, taken orally, are sometimes prescribed for diabetic individuals to help stimulate natural body production of insulin. If the condition can be controlled by the use of oral medication and diet, then an individual may be qualified under the present rule. CMV drivers who do not meet the Federal diabetes standard may call (202) 366-1790 for an application for a diabetes exemption.
(See Conference Report on Diabetic Disorders and Commercial Drivers and Insulin-Using Commercial Motor Vehicle Drivers at:
http://www.fmcsa.dot.gov/rulesregs/medreports.htm)

Cardiovascular Condition
§391.41(b)(4)
A person is physically qualified to drive a commercial motor vehicle if that person:
Has no current clinical diagnosis of myocardial infarction, angina pectoris, coronary insufficiency, thrombosis or any other cardiovascular disease of a variety known to be accompanied by syncope, dyspnea, collapse or congestive cardiac failure.

The term "has no current clinical diagnosis of" is specifically designed to encompass: "*a clinical diagnosis of*" (1) a current cardiovascular condition, or (2) a cardiovascular condition which has not fully stabilized regardless of the time limit The term "*known to be*

FIGURE 1-2 Examination Form (2003), continued

accompanied by" is designed to include a clinical diagnosis of a cardiovascular disease (1) which is accompanied by symptoms of syncope, dyspnea, collapse or congestive cardiac failure; and/or (2) which is likely to cause syncope, dyspnea, collapse or congestive cardiac failure.

It is the intent of the FMCSRs to render unqualified, a driver who has a current cardiovascular disease which is accompanied by and/or likely to cause symptoms of syncope, dyspnea, collapse, or congestive cardiac failure. However, the subjective decision of whether the nature and severity of an individual's condition will likely cause symptoms of cardiovascular insufficiency is on an individual basis and qualification rests with the medical examiner and the motor carrier. In those cases where there is an occurrence of cardiovascular insufficiency (myocardial infarction, thrombosis, etc.), it is suggested before a driver is certified that he or she have a normal resting and stress electrocardiogram (ECG), no residual complications and no physical limitations, and is taking no medication likely to interfere with safe driving.

Coronary artery bypass surgery and pacemaker implantation are remedial procedures and thus, not unqualifying. Implantable cardioverter defibrillators are disqualifying due to risk of syncope. Coumadin is a medical treatment which can improve the health and safety of the driver and should not, by its use, medically disqualify the commercial driver. The emphasis should be on the underlying medical condition(s) which require treatment and the general health of the driver. The FMCSA should be contacted at (202) 366-1790 for additional recommendations regarding the physical qualification of drivers on coumadin.
(See Cardiovasular Advisory Panel Guidelines for the Medical examination of Commercial Motor Vehicle Drivers at: http://www.fmcsa.dot.gov/rulesregs/medreports.htm)

Respiratory Dysfunction
§391.41(b)(5)
A person is physically qualified to drive a commercial motor vehicle if that person:
Has no established medical history or clinical diagnosis of a respiratory dysfunction likely to interfere with ability to control and drive a commercial motor vehicle safely.

Since a driver must be alert at all times, any change in his or her mental state is in direct conflict with highway safety. Even the slightest impairment in respiratory function under emergency conditions (when greater oxygen supply is necessary for performance) may be detrimental to safe driving.

(See Conference on Pulmonary/Respiratory Disorders and Commercial Drivers at:
http://www.fmcsa.dot.gov/rulesregs/medreports.htm

Hypertension
§391.41(b)(6)
A person is physically qualified to drive a commercial motor vehicle if that person:
Has no current clinical diagnosis of high blood pressure likely to interfere with ability to operate a commercial motor vehicle safely.

Hypertension alone is unlikely to cause sudden collapse; however, the likelihood increases when target organ damage, particularly cerebral vascular disease, is present. This regulatory criteria is based on FMCSA's Cardiovascular Advisory Guidelines for the Examination of CMV Drivers, which used the Sixth Report of the Joint National Committee on Detection, Evaluation, and Treatment of High Blood Pressure (1997).

Stage 1 hypertension corresponds to a systolic BP of 140-159 mmHg and/or a diastolic BP of 90-99 mmHg. The driver with a BP in this range is at low risk for hypertension-related acute incapacitation and may be medically certified to drive for a one-year period. Certification examinations should be done annually thereafter and should be at or less than 140/90. If less than 160/100, certification may be extended one time for 3 months.

A blood pressure of 160-179 systolic and/or 100-109 diastolic is considered Stage 2 hypertension, and the driver is not necessarily unqualified during evaluation and institution of treatment. The driver is given a one time certification of three months to reduce his or her blood pressure to less than or equal to 140/90. A blood pressure in this range is an absolute indication for anti-hypertensive drug therapy. Provided treatment is well tolerated and the driver demonstrates a BP value of 140/90 or less, he or she may be certified for one year from date of the initial exam. The driver is certified annually thereafter.

A blood pressure at or greater than 180 (systolic) and 110 (diastolic) is considered Stage 3, high risk for an acute BP-related event. The driver may **not** be qualified, even temporarily, until reduced to 140/90 or less and treatment is well tolerated. The driver may be certified for 6 months and biannually (every 6 months) thereafter if at recheck BP is 140/90 or less.

Annual recertification is recommended if the medical examiner does not know the severity of hypertension prior to treatment.

on maximal or near-maximal doses of 2-3 pharmacologic agents. Some causes of secondary hypertension may be amenable to surgical intervention or specific pharmacologic disease.
(See Cardiovascular Advisory Panel Guidelines for the Medical Examination of Commercial Motor Vehicle Drivers at:
http://www.fmcsa.dot.gov/rulesregs/medreports.htm)

Rheumatic, Arthritic, Orthopedic, Muscular, Neuromuscular or Vascular Disease §391.41(b)(7)
A person is physically qualified to drive a commercial motor vehicle if that person:
Has no established medical history or clinical diagnosis of rheumatic, arthritic, orthopedic, muscular, neuromuscular or vascular disease which interferes with the ability to control and operate a commercial motor vehicle safely.

Certain diseases are known to have acute episodes of transient muscle weakness, poor muscular coordination (ataxia), abnormal sensations (paresthesia), decreased muscular tone (hypotonia), visual disturbances and pain which may be suddenly incapacitating. With each recurring episode, these symptoms may become more pronounced and remain for longer periods of time. Other diseases have more insidious onsets and display symptoms of muscle wasting (atrophy), swelling and paresthesia which may not suddenly incapacitate a person but may restrict his/her movements and eventually interfere with the ability to safely operate a motor vehicle. In many instances these diseases are degenerative in nature or may result in deterioration of the involved area.

Once the individual has been diagnosed as having a rheumatic, arthritic, orthopedic, muscular, neuromuscular or vascular disease, then he/she has an established history of that disease. The physician, when examining an individual, should consider the following: (1) the nature and severity of the individual's condition (such as sensory loss or loss of strength); (2) the degree of limitation present (such as range of motion); (3) the likelihood of progressive limitation (not always present initially but may manifest itself over time); and (4) the likelihood of sudden incapacitation. If severe functional impairment exists, the driver does not qualify. In cases where more frequent monitoring is required, a certificate for a shorter period of time may be issued. (See Conference on Neurological Disorders and Commercial Drivers at:
http://www.fmcsa.dot.gov/rulesregs/medreports.htm)

Epilepsy
§391.41(b)(8)
A person is physically qualified to drive a commercial motor vehicle if that person:
Has no established medical history or clinical diagnosis of epilepsy or any other condition which is likely to cause loss of consciousness or any loss of ability to control a motor vehicle.

Epilepsy is a chronic functional disease characterized by seizures or episodes that occur without warning, resulting in loss of voluntary control which may lead to loss of consciousness and/or seizures. Therefore, the following drivers cannot be qualified: (1) a driver who has a medical history of epilepsy; (2) a driver who has a current clinical diagnosis of epilepsy; or (3) a driver who is taking antiseizure medication.

If an individual has had a sudden episode of a nonepileptic seizure or loss of consciousness of unknown cause which did not require antiseizure medication, the decision as to whether that person's condition will likely cause loss of consciousness or loss of ability to control a motor vehicle is made on an individual basis by the medical examiner in consultation with the treating physician. Before certification is considered, it is suggested that a 6 month waiting period elapse from the time of the episode. Following the waiting period, it is suggested that the individual have a complete neurological examination. If the results of the examination are negative and antiseizure medication is not required, then the driver may be qualified.

In those individual cases where a driver has a seizure or an episode of loss of consciousness that resulted from a known medical condition (e.g., drug reaction, high temperature, acute infectious disease, dehydration or acute metabolic disturbance), certification should be deferred until the driver has fully recovered from that condition and has no existing residual complications, and not taking antiseizure medication.

Drivers with a history of epilepsy/seizures off antiseizure medication **and** seizure-free for 10 years may be qualified to drive a CMV in interstate commerce. Interstate drivers with a history of a single unprovoked seizure may be qualified to drive a CMV in interstate commerce if seizure-free **and** off antiseizure medication for a 5-year period or more.
(See Conference on Neurological Disorders and Commercial Drivers at:
http://www.fmcsa.dot.gov/rulesregs/medreports.htm)

Mental Disorders
§391.41(b)(9)
A person is physically qualified to drive a commercial motor vehicle if that person:
Has no mental, nervous, organic or functional disease or psychiatric disorder likely to interfere with ability to drive a motor vehicle safely.

Emotional or adjustment problems contribute directly to an individual's level of memory, reasoning, attention, and judgment. These problems often underlie physical disorders. A variety of functional disorders can cause drowsiness, dizziness, confusion, weakness or paralysis that may lead to incoordination, inattention, loss of functional control and susceptibility to accidents while driving. Physical fatigue, headache, impaired coordination, recurring physical ailments and chronic "nagging" pain may be present to such a degree that certification for commercial driving is inadvisable. Somatic and psychosomatic complaints should be thoroughly examined when determining an individual's overall fitness to drive. Disorders of a periodically incapacitating nature, even in the early stages of development, may warrant disqualification.

Many bus and truck drivers have documented that "nervous trouble" related to neurotic, personality, or emotional or adjustment problems is responsible for a significant fraction of their preventable accidents. The degree to which an individual is able to appreciate, evaluate and adequately respond to environmental strain and emotional stress is critical when assessing an individual's mental alertness and flexibility to cope with the stresses of commercial motor vehicle driving.

When examining the driver, it should be kept in mind that individuals who live under chronic emotional upsets may have deeply ingrained maladaptive or erratic behavior patterns. Excessively antagonistic, instinctive, impulsive, openly aggressive, paranoid or severely depressed behavior greatly interfere with the driver's ability to drive safely. Those individuals who are highly susceptible to frequent states of emotional instability (schizophrenia, affective psychoses, paranoia, anxiety or depressive neuroses) may warrant disqualification. Careful consideration should be given to the side effects and interactions of medications in the overall qualification determination. See Psychiatric Conference Report for specific recommendations on the use of medications and potential hazards for driving.
(See Conference on Psychiatric Disorders and Commercial Drivers at:
http://www.fmcsa.dot.gov/rulesregs/medreports.htm)

Vision
§391.41(b)(10)
A person is physically qualified to drive a commercial motor vehicle if that person:
Has distant visual acuity of at least 20/40 (Snellen) in each eye with or without corrective lenses or visual acuity separately corrected to 20/40 (Snellen) or better with corrective lenses, distant binocular acuity of at least 20/40 (Snellen) in both eyes with or without corrective lenses, field of vision of at least 70 degrees in the horizontal meridian in each eye, and the ability to recognize the colors of traffic signals and devices showing standard red, green, and amber.

The term "ability to recognize the colors of" is interpreted to mean if a person can recognize and distinguish among traffic control signals and devices showing standard red, green and amber, he or she meets the minimum standard, even though he or she may have some type of color perception deficiency. If certain color perception tests are administered, (such as Ishihara, Pseudoisochromatic, Yarn) and doubtful findings are discovered, a controlled test using signal red, green and amber may be employed to determine the driver's ability to recognize these colors.

Contact lenses are permissible if there is sufficient evidence to indicate that the driver has good tolerance and is well adapted to their use. Use of a contact lens in one eye for distance visual acuity and another lens in the other eye for near vision is not acceptable, nor telescopic lenses acceptable for the driving of commercial motor vehicles.

If an individual meets the criteria by the use of glasses or contact lenses, the following statement shall appear on the Medical Examiner's Certificate: "Qualified only if wearing corrective lenses."

CMV drivers who do not meet the Federal vision standard may call (202) 366-1790 for an application for a vision exemption.
(See Visual Disorders and Commercial Drivers at:
http://www.fmcsa.dot.gov/rulesregs/medreports.htm)

Hearing
§391.41(b)(11)
A person is physically qualified to drive a commercial motor vehicle if that person:
First perceives a forced whispered voice in the better ear at not less than 5 feet with or without the use of a hearing aid, or, if tested by use of an audiometric device, does not have an average hearing loss in the better ear greater than 40 decibels at 500 Hz, 1,000 Hz, and 2,000 Hz with or without a hearing aid when the audiometric device is calibrated to American National Standard (formerly ADA Standard) Z24.5-1951.

Since the prescribed standard under the FMCSRs is the

23, etc. The examiner should not use only sibilants (s sounding materials). The opposite ear should be tested in the same manner. If the individual fails the whispered voice test, the audiometric test should be administered.

If an individual meets the criteria by the use of a hearing aid, the following statement must appear on the Medical Examiner's Certificate "Qualified only when wearing a hearing aid."
(See Hearing Disorders and Commercial Motor Vehicle Drivers at:
http://www/fmcsa.dot.gov/rulesregs/medrports.htm)

Drug Use
§391.41(b)(12)
A person is physically qualified to drive a commercial motor vehicle if that person:
Does not use a controlled substance identified in 21 CFR 1308.II.
Schedule I, an amphetamine, a narcotic, or any other habit-forming drug.
Exception: A driver may use such a substance or drug, if the substance or drug is prescribed by a licensed medical practitioner who is familiar with the driver's medical history and assigned duties; and has advised the driver that the prescribed substance or drug will not adversely affect the driver's ability to safely operate a commercial motor vehicle.

This exception does not apply to methadone. The intent of the medical certification process is to medically evaluate a driver to ensure that the driver has no medical condition which interferes with the safe performance of driving tasks on a public road. If a driver uses a Schedule I drug or other substance, an amphetamine, a narcotic, or any other habit-forming drug, it may be cause for the driver to be found medically unqualified. Motor carriers are encouraged to obtain a practitioner's written statement about the effects on transportation safety of the use of a particular drug.

A test for controlled substances is not required as part of this biennial certification process. The FMCSA or the driver's employer should be contacted directly for information on controlled substances and alcohol testing under Part 382 of the FMCSRs.

The term "uses" is designed to encompass instances of prohibited drug use determined by a physician through established medical means. This may or may not involve body fluid testing. If body fluid testing takes place, positive test results should be confirmed by a second test of greater specificity. The term "habit-forming" is intended to include any drug or medication generally recognized as capable of becoming habitual, and which may impair the user's ability to operate a commercial motor vehicle safely.

The driver is medically unqualified for the duration of the prohibited drug(s) use and until a second examination shows the driver is free from the prohibited drug(s) use. Recertification may involve a substance abuse evaluation, the successful completion of a drug rehabilitation program, and a negative drug test result. Additionally, given that the certification period is normally two years, the examiner has the option to certify for a period of less than 2 years if this examiner determines more frequent monitoring is required.
(See Conference on Neurological Disorders and Commercial Drivers and Conference on Psychiatric Disorders and Commercial Drivers at:
http://www.fmcsa.dot.gov/rulesregs/medreports.htm)

Alcoholism
§391.41(b)(13)
A person is physically qualified to drive a commercial motor vehicle if that person:
Has no current clinical diagnosis of alcoholism.

The term "current clinical diagnosis of" is specifically designed to encompass a current alcoholic illness or those instances where the individual's physical condition has not fully stabilized, regardless of the time element. If an individual shows signs of having an alcohol-use problem, he or she should be referred to a specialist. After counseling and/or treatment, he or she may be considered for certification.

There have been plans to merge the CDL and the medical qualification documentation since the early 1990s when feasibility studies and a pilot program were conducted. A negotiated rulemaking committee was formed in 1996[53] and charged with identifying a method for merging the CDL process with the medical qualification process. At that time, one of the identified needs was to improve the quality of the medical examinations. "Doctor shopping" and the lack of understanding by many examiners of the regulations and supporting material were identified as significant problems. Several proposals were discussed to enhance consistency among health care providers performing commercial driver medical examinations. The proposals ranged from requiring examiners to sign a statement indicating that they understand the regulations and agree to follow them to an extensive certification course. The final meeting of the committee occurred in November 1997.

This change in process had not moved forward until late 2006, when an NPRM was published that would require interstate CDL holders subject to the medical requirements of the FMCSRs to provide proof of a current medical examiner's certificate to their State Driver Licensing Agency (SDLA).[54] In 2008, the final rule[55] merging the CDL and the medical certificate was published. This rule covers only interstate CDL holders; thus, interstate operators of vehicles with a gross vehicle weight rating between 10,000 and 26,000 pounds who require medical examination but not CDLs would not be included. Covered drivers will be required to provide a current original or copy of their medical examiner's certificates to their SDLA that records their certification status in the Commercial Driver Licensing Information System (CDLIS) within 10 days. Once a certificate expires, the record will be modified to indicate that the driver is "not certified," and the CDL would be downgraded within 60 days of expiration of the medical certification. Rather than maintaining a copy of the medical certificate, motor carriers would obtain and place in the driver qualification file the driver's CDLIS motor vehicle record documenting the medical certification status prior to permitting the driver to operate a CMV. The date-stamped copy of the medical certificate could be used for 15 days from the date stamped. Drivers will no longer be required to carry a copy of the medical certificate but will continue to be required to carry any Skill Performance Evaluation (SPE) Certificate or exemptions documentation. Drivers who are not required to hold a CDL will continue to be required to provide a copy of the medical certificate to their employers and carry a copy while operating the CMV. This rule added a new definition to §390.5, "medical variance." This includes the SPE and exemptions. It does not include waivers, as these are issued for shorter periods of time. Medical examiners are now required to provide a copy of the medical certificate to the driver and are permitted to provide a copy to the motor carrier. The examiners are required to maintain the certification and the Medical Examination Report for 3 years or consistent with state medical record retention statutes. The effective date of this rule was January 30, 2009, with state compliance required by January 30, 2012 and January 30, 2014 for existing CDL holders subject to this rule. All CDL holders are required to report to their state whether they are involved in interstate or intrastate only (if any interstate commerce, they must declare as interstate) commerce and whether excepted (not required to meet state or federal medical standards) or non-excepted (required to meet state or federal medical requirements). Proposed additional steps to merge the CDL and the medical certification were announced in May 2013.[56] This would require examiners to upload certification determinations on drivers by close of business on the day of examination; FMCSA would then forward to the state the medical status of any interstate CDL holder. It also included a new medical examination reporting form that would be significantly shorter than the form in use at that time. It would eliminate the driver's role, instructions to examiners, and other information that should be covered in the NRCME training (see discussion on the NRCME later in this chapter). It also proposed significantly decreasing the number of health history questions to only 38. Some other significant proposed changes to the form included the following: deleting the question, "any illness or injury in the past 5 years" and adding, "other health condition(s) not described above"; and questions were added on high cholesterol, ever or currently use tobacco, used an illegal substance in the past 2 years or failed a drug test. There are also now questions on whether the driver ever had a sleep study, spent a night in the hospital, or had a broken bone. The testing section would include optional neck circumference and body mass index (BMI) measurements.

The Final Rule was published on April 23, 2015[57] with a revised form that removed the "temporary disqualified" option and added "determination pending" and "incomplete examination" choices. A "final" version of the form was distributed to medical examiners in a *Bulletin to Examiners* in October 2015[58] and a minor revision was made in 2016, when the privacy statement was removed.[59]

For many years, there were plans to update FMCSA medical standards and guidelines, and the planned development processes are available. The first, Overview of Methodologies to Develop Medical Standards and Guidelines for Commercial Motor Vehicle Drivers,[60] describes how the process uses systematic review and meta-analysis to evaluate the relationship between medical conditions and crash risk. Overview of the FMCSA Medical Standards and Guidelines Development Process[61] outlines the steps taken to review and update the standards and guidelines. The DRIVE Act[62] requires a review of guidance every five years. The MRB began review of the Act at their October 2016 meeting.

Probably the most significant requirement of SAFETEA-LU was for the establishment of the NRCME.[63] While Congress would require training and certification, it did allow the potential for self-certification, but FMCSA indicated that it would require a full examination. A Role Delineation Study[64] was conducted to create a task list of components of the commercial driver medical examination, and a survey of medical examiners was distributed.[65-66] From this information, the core curriculum for medical examiner training as well as the medical examiner certification test was developed.

The long-awaited NPRM on the NRCME[1] was published on December 1, 2008. In the proposed rule, FMCSA would develop the core curriculum and distribute it to private sector training providers certified by a nationally recognized accrediting organization. The core training would be anticipated to take one day, but training providers would be able to expand the training to meet the needs of participants. Training could be either through the traditional classroom method, other methods, or a combination. Retraining would be provided by FMCSA at least every three years with complete retraining to be required every 12 years. In the proposed rule, after completing training, medical examiners would be required to pass the FMCSA medical examiner certification test. Recertification would be required every six years to continue to be listed on the NRCME. Once the medical examiner completes training and testing requirements, FMCSA would issue a unique identification number and list the examiner and the examiner's contact information on the NRCME website.

The Final Rule for the NRCME[2] was published in the *Federal Register* on April 20, 2012 with an effective date of May 21, 2012. Once fully implemented, on May 21, 2014, only those examiners who have completed the required curriculum and any required testing would be permitted to perform commercial driver medical examinations. Training organizations were not credentialed or approved by FMCSA but were expected to cover at least the specified core curriculum. Training programs are required to be accredited by a nationally recognized medical profession accrediting organization to provide continuing medical education (CME) units, although they are not required to grant CME for the training. Testing organizations are required to use a test provided by FMCSA. Testing could be either in person or online but, if online, would be subject to specific security and privacy requirements due to the nature of the test and the need for authentication and security of the test. An examiner could only take the certification examination once every 30 days and must take it no more than three years after completing the training. The final rule requires a medical examiner whose certification has not lapsed to recertify every 10 years (but not earlier than nine years) with periodic training every five years (not sooner than four years) and no requirement to complete the initial training. As part of the NRCME process, FMCSA prepared and posted a Medical Examiner Handbook,[67] but it was removed for revision in late 2014 and has not been updated. Additional discussion on the examination process under the NRCME can be found in Chapter 2.

It was hoped that the NRCME would address many of the current concerns of the medical certification program. There was hope that updating the standards and guidance and ongoing maintenance of the ME Handbook would standardize how the examinations are performed. Unfortunately, with the ME Handbook down at this writing and inconsistencies in whether examiners are going strictly by what was in the Handbook or basing their determination on current evidence-based review, the same driver can have very different outcomes on one's examination depending on the driver's examiner. There will continue to be changes in the examination process; as examiners, it is important that we stay abreast of new developments and research. Watch for *Federal Register* announcements that affect the medical qualification process. You can sign up for updates through FMCSA's NRCME listserv.[68] The American College of Occupational and Environmental Medicine (ACOEM)[69] publishes a quarterly newsletter that reviews recent or pending modifications in the examination process.

References

1. National Registry of Certified Medical Examiners, Notice of proposed rule-making, request for comments. Federal Motor Carrier Safety Administration (FMCSA), DOT. *Fed Reg* Vol. 73, No. 231. Monday, December 1, 2008;73129–73147. https://www.gpo.gov/fdsys/pkg/FR-2008-12-01/pdf/E8-28172.pdf.
2. National Registry of Certified Medical Examiners. Final Rule. Federal Motor Carrier Safety Administration (FMCSA), DOT. *Fed Reg* Vol 77, No. 77. April 20, 2012; 24104–24135. https://www.gpo.gov/fdsys/pkg/FR-2012-04-20/pdf/2012-9034.pdf.
3. Zywokarte S. Former Team Leader, Driver Medical Standards, FHWA. Personal communication, October 1996.
4. Qualification of drivers. *Fed Reg* 1969;34(June 7):9080–9085.
5. Qualification of drivers of commercial motor vehicles. *Fed Reg* 1970;35 (April 22):6458–6467.
6. Harmonizing Schedule I Drug Requirements: Final Rule. DOT. FMCSA — *Fed Reg* Jan 30, 2012. https://www.gpo.gov/fdsys/pkg/FR-2012-01-30/pdf/2012-1905.pdf
7. Organization and delegation of powers and duties: Redelegation to the director. Office of Motor Carrier Safety. *Fed Reg* 1999;64(Oct. 29):56270–56271.
8. Commercial driver's license program and controlled substances and alcohol use and testing: Conforming and technical amendments. *Fed Reg* 1997;62(July 11):37150–37153.
9. Qualification of drivers: Medical examination. *Fed Reg* 1992;57(July 28):33276.
10. Federal Motor Carrier Safety Regulations; Technical amendments; Final rule; Technical amendment. *Fed Reg* 2000;65(May 1):25285–25290. https://www.gpo.gov/fdsys/pkg/FR-2000-05-01/pdf/00-10700.pdf.
11. Qualification of drivers: Waiver applications — vision. *Fed Reg* 1992;57 (March 25):10295–10297.
12. Qualification of drivers: Waivers — diabetes. *Fed Reg* 1993;58(July 29):40690–40697.
13. Qualification of drivers: Vision deficiencies — waivers. *Fed Reg* 1994;59 (Nov. 17):39386–39390.
14. Qualification of drivers: Vision and diabetes — limited exemptions. *Fed Reg* 1996;61(Jan. 8):606–611.
15. Qualification of drivers: Vision and diabetes — limited exemptions. *Fed Reg* 1996;61(March 26):13338–13347.
16. Qualification of drivers: Waiver application — vision. *Fed Reg* 1998;63(Jan. 8):1524–1537.
17. Federal Motor Carrier Safety Regulations: Interim final rule, Request for comments. Waivers, exemptions, and pilot programs — rules and procedures. *Fed Reg* 1998;63(Dec. 8):67600–67612.
18. Federal Motor Carrier Safety Administration, US Department of Transportation. Final rule: Waivers, exemptions, and pilot programs. *Fed Reg* 2004;69(Aug. 20):51589–51598. https://www.gpo.gov/fdsys/pkg/FR-2004-08-20/pdf/04-19155.pdf.
19. A report to Congress on the feasibility of a program to qualify individuals with insulin treated diabetes mellitus to operate commercial motor vehicles in

interstate commerce as directed by the Transportation Equity Act for the 21st century. July 2000. https://www.fmcsa.dot.gov/regulations/medical/medical-reports-archive.

20. Notice of intent to issue exemptions and request for comments; Qualification of drivers; Exemption applications; Diabetes. *Fed Reg* 2001;66(July 31): 39548–39553.

21. Department of Transportation, Federal Motor Carrier Safety Administration. Qualification of drivers: Exemption applications: Diabetes. Notice of final dispositions. *Fed Reg* 2003;68(Sept. 3):52441–52452.

22. Department of Transportation, Federal Motor Carrier Safety Administration. Qualification of drivers: Exemption applications: Diabetes. *Fed Reg* 2005;70 (Sept. 2):52465–52467.

23. Safe, Accountable, Flexible, Efficient Transportation Equity Act: A Legacy for Users 2005. www.fhwa.dot.gov/safetealu/legis.htm.

24. Federal Motor Carrier Safety Administration, US Department of Transportation. Notice of revised final disposition. Qualification of drivers; Eligibility criteria and applications; Diabetes exemption. *Fed Reg* 2005;70(Nov. 8):67777–67781. https://www.gpo.gov/fdsys/pkg/FR-2005-11-08/pdf/05-22264.pdf.

25. Federal Motor Carrier Safety Administration, US Department of Transportation. Advance notice of proposed rulemaking request for comments. Qualifications of drivers; Diabetes standard. *Fed Reg* 2006;71(March 17): 13801–13805.

26. Qualifications of Drivers; Diabetes Standard. Notice of proposed rulemaking. Federal Motor Carrier Safety. *Fed Reg* May 4, 2015;80(85):25260–25272. https://www.gpo.gov/fdsys/pkg/FR-2015-05-04/pdf/2015-09993.pdf.

27. Federal Motor Carrier Safety Administration, US Department of Transportation. Medical Review Board Task Report on Insulin Treated Diabetes Mellitus and Commercial Motor Vehicle Drivers. Request for Comments. *Fed Reg* September 9, 2016;62448–62450. https://www.gpo.gov/fdsys/pkg/FR-2016-09-09/pdf/2016-21724.pdf.

28. Federal Motor Carrier Safety Administration, US Department of Transportation. Physical Qualification of Drivers; Standards; Changes to Vision Exemption Program Criteria. *Fed Reg* December 18, 2013;78(243): 76590–76592. https://www.gpo.gov/fdsys/pkg/FR-2013-12-18/pdf/2013-29651.pdf.

29. Federal Motor Carrier Safety Administration FAQs. https://www.fmcsa.dot.gov/faq/Medical-Requirements.

30. Qualification of drivers: Hearing deficiencies — waivers. *Fed Reg* 1993;58(Dec. 15):65638–65643.

31. Qualification of drivers: Application for Exemptions; National Association of the Deaf. Notice of applications for exemptions; request for comments. Federal Motor Carrier Safety Administration, DOT. *Fed Reg* 77(102), May 25, 2012; 31423–31427. https://www.gpo.gov/fdsys/pkg/FR-2012-05-25/pdf/2012-12636.pdf.

32. Qualification of drivers: Application for Exemptions; National Association of the Deaf. Federal Motor Carrier Safety Administration: Notice [Docket No. FMCSA–2012–0154]. *Fed Reg* Vol. 78, No. 22; February 1, 2013. https://www.gpo.gov/fdsys/pkg/FR-2013-02-01/pdf/2013-02266.pdf.

33. Federal Motor Carrier Safety Administration, US Department of Transportation. Qualification of drivers: Exemption requests; Epilepsy and seizure disorders, Notice of applications for exemptions, request for comments. *Fed Reg* 2006;71(Oct. 13):60606–60607. https://www.gpo.gov/fdsys/pkg/FR-2006-10-13/pdf/E6-17032.pdf.
34. Federal Motor Carrier Safety Administration, US Department of Transportation. Qualification of drivers: Exemption applications; Epilepsy and seizure disorders. Applications for exemption, request for comments. *Fed Reg* 2007;72 (Aug 9): 44916–44918. https://www.gpo.gov/fdsys/pkg/FR-2007-08-09/pdf/E7-15495.pdf.
35. Federal Motor Carrier Safety Administration, US Department of Transportation. Qualification of drivers: Exemption applications; Epilepsy and seizure disorders. Applications for exemption, request for comments. *Fed Reg* 2008;73 (Dec 10): 75165–75167. https://www.gpo.gov/fdsys/pkg/FR-2008-12-10/pdf/E8-29188.pdf.
36. Qualification of drivers: Exemption Applications; Epilepsy and Seizure Disorders. Notice of applications for exemption, request for comments. Federal Motor Carrier Safety Administration, US Department of Transportation. *Fed Reg* January 5, 2012;537–539. http://www.gpo.gov/fdsys/pkg/FR-2012-01-05/pdf/2011-33781.pdf.
37. Qualification of drivers: Exemption Applications; Epilepsy and Seizure Disorders, Notice. Federal Motor Carrier Safety Administration, US Department of Transportation. *Fed Reg* January 15, 2013; 78(10):3069–3077. https://www.gpo.gov/fdsys/pkg/FR-2013-01-15/pdf/2013-00709.pdf.
38. Department of Transportation. Federal Motor Carrier Safety Administration (FMCSA). Qualification of drivers: Exemption Applications; Implantable Cardioverter Defibrillators. Notice of denials of exemption applications. *Fed Reg* October 26, 2015;80(76);22259–22261. http://www.gpo.gov/fdsys/pkg/FR-2015-10-26/pdf/2015-27210.pdf.
39. Federal Motor Carrier Safety Administration, US Department of Transportation. Qualification of drivers: Exemption Applications; Narcolepsy. Notice of denial of exemption applications. *Fed Reg* 2015;80(158):49301–49302. https://www.gpo.gov/fdsys/pkg/FR-2015-08-17/pdf/2015-20187.pdf.
40. Medical Review Board, Federal Motor Carrier Safety Administration Website. https://www.fmcsa.dot.gov/mrb.
41. Hegmann KT, Andersson GBJ, Greenberg MI, Phillips B, Rizzo M. FMCSA's Medical Review Board: five years of progress in commercial driver medical examinations. *J Occup Environ Med* 2012;54(4):424-30.
42. Federal Motor Carrier Safety Regulations: Definitions of commercial motor vehicle — interim final rule; Federal Motor Carrier Safety Regulations: Requirements for operators of small passenger-carrying commercial motor vehicles — proposed rule. *Fed Reg* 1999;64(Sept. 3):48510–48517.
43. Federal Motor Carrier Safety Regulations, DOT: Safety requirements for operators of small passenger-carrying commercial motor vehicles used in interstate commerce — final rule. *Fed Reg* 2003;68(Aug. 12):47860–47875.

44. Federal Motor Carrier Safety Regulations, DOT: Safety requirements for operators of small passenger-carrying commercial motor vehicles used in interstate commerce — final rule. *Fed Reg* 2010;75(Feb 1):4996–5002.
45. Interstate school bus safety; Advanced notice of proposed rulemaking; Request for comments. *Fed Reg* 2001;66(Oct. 22):53373–53376.
46. Federal Motor Carrier Safety Administration, US Department of Transportation. Interstate school bus safety; Withdrawal. *Fed Reg* 2004;60(March 24): 13803–13805.
47. National Transportation Safety Board. Highway accident report: Motorcoach Run-off-the-road. New Orleans, Louisiana, May 9, 1999:HAR-01-01, 08/28/2001 NTIS Report No. PB2001–916201. http://www.ntsb.gov/ investigations/AccidentReports/Reports/HAR0101.pdf.
48. Certification Process for Drivers with Serious Medical Conditions. Full Report. GAO-08-826, June 30, 2008. http://www.gao.gov/products/GAO-08-826.
49. Committee on Transportation and Infrastructure. Challenges in verifying the authenticity of commercial drivers' medical certificates.
50. Physical qualification of drivers: Medical examination — certificate. *Fed Reg* 1998;63(Aug. 5):41769–41781.
51. Federal Motor Carrier Safety Administration, US Department of Transportation. Physical qualification of drivers; Medical examination; Final rule. *Fed Reg* 2000;65(Oct. 5):59363–59380. https://www.gpo.gov/fdsys/pkg/FR-2000-10-05 /pdf/00-25337.pdf.
52. Federal Motor Carrier Safety Administration, US Department of Transportation. Motor Carrier Safety Regulations, Miscellaneous technical amendments. *Fed Reg* 2003;68(Sept. 30):56196–56208. https://www.gpo.gov/fdsys/pkg/FR -2003-09-30/pdf/03-24736.pdf.
53. Commercial driver physical qualifications as a part of the commercial driver's license process. *Fed Reg* 1996;61(April 29):18713–18717.
54. Medical Certification Requirements as Part of the CDL. Notice of proposed rulemaking (NPRM); Request for comments. Federal Motor Carrier Safety Administration (FMCSA), DOT. *Fed Reg* 2006;71(Nov. 16):66723–66748. https://www.gpo.gov/fdsys/pkg/FR-2006-11-16/pdf/E6-19246.pdf.
55. Medical Certification Requirements as Part of the CDL. Final Rule. Federal Motor Carrier Safety Administration. US Department of Transportation. *Fed Reg* 2008;73(Dec. 1, 2008): 73095–73128. https://www.gpo.gov/fdsys/pkg/FR -2008-12-01/pdf/E8-28173.pdf.
56. Medical Examiner's Certification Integration. Notice of proposed rulemaking, DOT, FMCSA. Docket No. FMCSA–2012–0178. *Fed Reg* May 10, 2013. 78 (91);27343–27363. http://www.gpo.gov/fdsys/pkg/FR-2013-05-10/pdf/2013 -11080.pdf.
57. Medical Examiner's Certification Integration. Final Rule, DOT, FMCSA. *Fed Reg* April 23, 2015;80(78):22790–22825. https://www.gpo.gov/fdsys/pkg/FR -2015-04-23/pdf/2015-09053.pdf.
58. Bulletin to Medical Examiners. October 2015. https://nationalregistry .fmcsa.dot.gov/Resource-Center/documents/FMCSA-emails/ MedicalExaminer'sCertificationIntegrationRuleformsOctober2015.pdf.

59. Federal Motor Carrier Safety Administration, US Department of Trans-portation. General Technical, Organizational, Conforming, and Correcting Amendments to the Federal Motor Carrier Safety Regulations. Final Rule. *Fed Reg* October 4, 2016; 68336–68359. https://www.gpo.gov/fdsys/pkg/FR-2016-10 -04/pdf/2016-22996.pdf.

60. Federal Motor Carrier Safety Administration, US Department of Transporta-tion. TechBrief: Overview of methodologies to develop medical standards and guidelines for commercial motor vehicle drivers. July 2008;FMCSA-PSP-08-002.

61. Federal Motor Carrier Safety Administration, US Department of Transporta-tion. TechBrief: Overview of the FMCSA medical standards and guidelines development process. July 2008; FMCSA-PSP 08-001.

62. Developing a Reliable and Innovative Vision for the Economy (DRIVE) Act. https://www.congress.gov/bill/114th-congress/senate-bill/1647.

63. National Registry of Certified Medical Examiners Website. https://nationalregistry.fmcsa.dot.gov/NRPublicUI/home.seam.

64. Role Delineation Study. http://www.ntl.bts.gov/lib/30000/30100/30121/RDS _Report_Appendices_41008.pdf.

65. Notice of intent to survey medical examiners who certify the physical quali-fications of commercial motor vehicle drivers. *Fed Reg* 2006;71(July 13): 39697–39698.

66. Notice of intent to survey medical examiners who certify the physical quali-fications of commercial motor vehicle drivers. *Fed Reg* 2005;70(Sept. 29): 56964–56965.

67. Federal Motor Carrier Safety Administration. US Department of Transporta-tion. Medical Examiners Handbook. Currently down for revision. https://www .fmcsa.dot.gov/regulations/medical/fmcsa-medical-examiner-handbook.

68. National Registry of Certified Medical Examiners listserv. https://nrcme.fmcsa .dot.gov/contact.aspx.

69. CDME Review. American College of Occupational and Environmental Medicine. www.acoem.org/ACOEMNewsletters.aspx.

CHAPTER 2

The Examination and the National Registry of Certified Medical Examiners

NATALIE P. HARTENBAUM, MD, MPH, FACOEM

Since the prior edition of this book, the Commercial Driver Medical Examiner (CDME) processes have undergone significant changes, mostly related to the National Registry of Certified Medical Examiners (NRCME). In 2014, the Federal Motor Carrier Safety Administration Medical Examiner Handbook (ME Handbook) was taken off the Federal Motor Carrier Safety Administration (FMCSA) website for update and revision. As this edition is being prepared, examiners still should consider guidance from the prior handbook, as that is what is being taught in the training programs, but should base their final decision on current best medical practice remembering that our ultimate responsibility is to ensure the safety of the motoring public to the extent reasonably possible. Chapters will include information from the most recent ME Handbook, Medical Expert Panel (MEP) reports, and Medical Review Board (MRB) recommendations as well as other relevant reports and literature.

This is one area in which clarifications and modifications are issued on a regular basis. As this manuscript is being prepared, FMCSA has scheduled several webinars to address ongoing questions on the Medical Examination Report Form (for Commercial Driver Medical Certification; MER). Examiners should be sure to keep their email address current as FMCSA will send out bulletins clarifying issues, announcing changes in process, or announcing webinars to explain confusing issues.

As significant changes occur, they will be noted at the end of each chapter in the online version of this book at least twice a year.

This chapter assumes that the examiner has completed the training provided by the NRCME and is able to perform a comprehensive physical examination, understands abnormal physical findings, and is able to review and interpret additional studies such as laboratory results or stress tests. Rather than include the information on how to perform an examination or repeat what should have been part of the training, the focus of this chapter will be on clarifying areas of confusion on the form or process. To the extent possible, this chapter will be organized by topic, a sort of "mega FAQ," with most of the information derived from the NRCME Frequently Asked Questions, webinars, or direct communication with FMCSA.

A. Who Needs FMCSA Commercial Driver Medical Examination?

One area in which there has always been a great deal of confusion is which drivers are required to meet the medical criteria of the Federal Motor Carrier Safety Regulations (FMCSRs), which drivers are required to have drug testing under the Department of Transportation, and which need a commercial driver's license (CDL). Although almost all drivers who require drug and alcohol testing and a CDL are also required to meet FMCSA medical criteria, there are many who will require the examination but not drug testing or carrying a CDL. For the purpose of the medical examination, a commercial motor vehicle (CMV) is defined by 49 CFR 390.5 as follows:

COMMERCIAL MOTOR VEHICLE (CMV) means any self-propelled or towed vehicle used on public highways in interstate commerce to transport passengers or property when:

(a) The vehicle has a gross weight rating or gross combination of 10,001 pounds or more; or

(b) The vehicle is designed or used to transport more than 8 passengers (including the driver) for compensation; or

(c) Is designed or used to transport more than 15 passengers, including the driver, and is not used to transport passengers for compensation; or

(d) Is used in the transporting of materials found by the Secretary of Transportation to be hazardous under 49 CFR U.S.C. 5103 and transporting in a quantity requiring placarding under regulations prescribed by the Secretary under 49 CFR, subtitle B, chapter I, subchapter C.

Most states have adopted the medical criteria for their intrastate commercial drivers, primarily those that require a CDL (in general, operating vehicles above 26,000 pounds). Some states will grandfather in or grant exemptions for some drivers who do not meet the federal medical standards and operate solely in *intra*state commerce. Whether the driver crosses state lines is *not* the determining factor for *intra*state versus *inter*state commerce; it is the property being transported that matters. 49 CFR 390.5 defines interstate and intrastate commerce as follows:

INTERSTATE COMMERCE means trade, traffic, or transportation in the United States—

(1) Between a place in a State and a place outside of such State (including a place outside of the United States);
(2) Between two places in a State through another State or a place outside of the United States; or
(3) Between two places in a State as part of trade, traffic, or transportation originating or terminating outside the State or the United States.

INTRASTATE COMMERCE means any trade, traffic, or transportation in any State which is not described in the term "interstate commerce."

Drivers now need to report into which category they fall when applying for or renewing their CDL or changing the class of CDL.
- **Interstate non-excepted:** Interstate driver and must meet the Federal DOT medical card requirements.
- **Interstate excepted:** Interstate driver and do not have to meet the Federal DOT medical card requirements.
- **Intrastate non-excepted:** Intrastate driver and are required to meet the medical requirements for your State.
- **Intrastate excepted:** You are an Intrastate driver and do not have to meet the medical requirements for your State.

Distinguishing whether the commerce is *inter*state or *intra*state is further explained in the FAQs for CDLs,[1] in which it states that *inter*state commerce is also when the driver operates "between two places within a State, but the cargo or passengers are part of a trip that began or will end in another State or foreign country." If drivers are involved in both *inter*state and *intra*state, they must declare as *inter*state.

There are several categories of *inter*state drivers that are not required to submit their federal medical certification. They would be considered to operate in **excepted *inter*state commerce** if they drive a CMV in *inter*state commerce only for the following excepted activities:
- To transport schoolchildren and/or school staff between home and school
- As federal, state, or local government employees

- To transport human corpses or sick or injured persons
- Fire truck or rescue vehicle drivers during emergencies and other related activities
- Primarily in the transportation of propane winter heating fuel when responding to an emergency condition requiring immediate response such as damage to a propane gas system after a storm or flooding
- In response to a pipeline emergency condition requiring immediate response, such as a pipeline leak or rupture
- In custom harvesting on a farm or to transport farm machinery and supplies used in the custom harvesting operation to and from a farm or to transport custom harvested crops to storage or market
- Beekeeper in the seasonal transportation of bees
- Controlled and operated by a farmer, but is not a combination vehicle (power unit and towed unit), and is used to transport agricultural products, farm machinery, or farm supplies (no placard-able hazardous materials) to and from a farm and within 150 air-miles of the farm
- As a private motor carrier of passengers for nonbusiness purposes
- To transport migrant workers

Drivers are considered non-excepted *intra*state if they operate a CMV only in *intra*state commerce and are required to meet their state of licensure's medical certification requirements (which may be 49 CFR 391.41); if not required to meet state medical requirements, they would be *intra*state excepted.

A detailed explanation to determine which drivers must meet the Federal medical standards is available through FMCSA's Commercial Drivers License webpage.[2]

A medical FAQ[3] uses the example of a FedEx or UPS driver who only operates within a single state but the property the driver is transporting is part of *inter*state commerce, and thus would be considered an *inter*state non-excepted driver.

FAQs[3] indicate that examiners should ask the driver if they are involved in *inter*state or *intra*state commerce to determine whether a driver who does not meet federal medical criteria may be appropriate to be qualified "in accordance with the FMCSRs with any applicable State variance." While all drivers in *inter*state commerce are required to be examined by an examiner on the NRCME, for *intra*state drivers (based not where they drive but where what they transport travels) that is up to the state. If an examiner completes the *state* portion of the examination form, the examiner *must* be aware of the medical requirements in that state and ensure that they are met by that driver.

Since implementation of the North American Free Trade Agreement (NAFTA),[4] drivers from Mexico or Canada may operate CMVs within the United States. There is a reciprocity agreement with both Canada and Mexico that permits drivers who meet medical criteria in their home countries to operate in the United States with some limitations. Canadian or Mexican drivers who are insulin-using diabetics, who have epilepsy, or who are hearing or vision impaired are not authorized to drive CMVs in the United States. Canadian drivers who do not meet the medical fitness provisions of the Canadian National Safety Code for Motor Carriers or Mexican drivers who do not meet the medical fitness provision of the Licencia Federal de Conductor but have been issued a waiver are not qualified to drive CMVs in the United States.[5]

It had been discovered that some Canadian drivers may not have had a medical assessment.[6] Similar to drivers in the United States, many Canadian drivers who operate vehicles between 10,001 and 26,000 pounds are not required to hold a CDL but, unlike the United States, they are not required to meet medical criteria in some Canadian provinces. This was required to be corrected by April 1, 2016, with three possible options:

- Submit a completed FMCSA Medical Report form
- Upgrade to a license class for which a medical report is required
- Seek the services of a certified FMCSA medical examiner and be issued a medical certificate

The NRCME reporting system had been updated to allow entry of Canadian addresses. Drivers with a CDL in Canada are not required to obtain an examination consistent with the NRCME.

B. When Is an Examination Required?

While there is no confusion that a driver without a current valid medical certificate would need a new medical examination, many carriers are unaware that even a driver with a current medical certificate is required to be examined if the "ability to perform his/her normal duties has been impaired by a physical or mental injury or disease".[7] While the medical examiner is responsible for determining whether the driver meets the medical criteria, the employer is responsible to ensure that the driver is medically fit and may require any driver returning from injury or illness to undergo a medical examination.[8] For a new driver, the carrier may accept a driver's current medical certificate or may require the driver to complete an examination by an examiner chosen by the carrier,[8] although one of the expectations with the NRCME was that employers would be more likely to accept prior medical certificates if they had confidence that the examiner was properly trained and certified.

A new complete examination is also required whenever a prior certification determination was made, for example, if the driver was given a 30-, 60-, or 90-day certificate. There is no longer the option to "update" the certificate. The only time that a determination can be amended is when the driver had been placed in the "Determination Pending" status (more on this later).

C. Who Can Perform the Commercial Driver Medical Examination?

For many years, the examination could be performed by "a person who is licensed, certified, and/or registered, in accordance with applicable State laws and regulations, to perform physical examinations. The term includes, but is not limited to, doctors of medicine, doctors of osteopathy, physician assistants, advanced practice nurses, and doctors of chiropractic." In 2008, FMCSA published a Notice of Proposed Rulemaking (NPRM) on the NRCME[9] that would require examiners to be trained and certified in order to conduct the commercial driver medical examination. Finally, in 2012, the final rule was published[10] limiting the examiner pool to only those who have completed the training and certification requirements but not changing the criteria for types of licensed health care professional.

While all drivers in *inter*state non-excepted commerce are required to be examined by an examiner on the NRCME, for *intra*state drivers (based not where they drive but where what they transport travels) that is up to the state.

The FAQs[11] related to the National Registry and examiners follow (with comments, if applicable, in bold italics):

FREQUENTLY ASKED QUESTIONS

Who is eligible to become a medical examiner?

Currently, healthcare professionals who are licensed, certified, and/or registered in accordance with applicable State laws and regulations to perform physical examinations, may perform medical examinations for CMV drivers. This includes, but is not limited to, doctors of medicine, doctors of osteopathy, physician assistants, advanced practice nurses, and doctors of chiropractic.

(Comment: FMCSA has recently begun reviewing scope of practice in some states to determine if the performance of the physical examination is only to initiate a specific treatment for a specific condition, such as physical therapy for a musculoskeletal condition, and not to diagnose and treat a broad range of medical conditions that the examiner will be required to evaluate.)

How do I become a certified medical examiner on the National Registry?

To become a certified medical examiner, you must register through the National Registry website at https://nationalregistry.fmcsa.dot.gov to receive a unique identification number (National Registry Number). You will then need to complete accredited training and pass the Federal Motor Carrier Safety Administration Medical Examiner Certification Test. You may become certified after the compliance date, but you must not issue medical certificates for interstate truck and bus drivers on or after May 21, 2014, until you have completed the certification process.

Do I have to pay for the training and testing to become a certified medical examiner?

Yes. You are responsible for paying any fees charged by the private sector training and testing organizations. FMCSA neither establishes nor regulates the schedules of fees established and collected by private sector training or testing organizations and does not receive any monies collected by these organizations or providers.

How do I find training organizations?

FMCSA posts contact information on the National Registry website for training organizations. However, FMCSA does not approve or endorse training providers or courses.

To access the list of training providers who offer National Registry training, follow these steps:

1. Visit the National Registry website at https://nationalregistry.fmcsa.dot.gov.
2. Select the "Medical Examiners and Assistants" link at the top of the page.
3. Select "Find a Training Organization" from the menu on the left.

How can I determine whether a training provider's program meets all of the National Registry requirements?

Prospective medical examiners may visit the National Registry website at https://nationalregistry.fmcsa.dot.gov to obtain the regulatory requirements for training, including the eight topics (the core curriculum) that must be covered by the training. The training organization must be accredited by a nationally recognized medical profession accrediting organization that provides continuing education units, and the training must include all of the topics outlined in the final rule. The training organization must provide training participants with proof of participation.

How can I find a testing organization?

To find a testing organization near you, follow these steps:

1. Visit the National Registry website at https://nationalregistry.fmcsa.dot.gov
2. Select the "Medical Examiners and Assistants" link at the top of the page.
3. Select "Search for Testing Locations" from the menu on the left. Then select "Find a Testing Organization" to search by testing organization name, city and state, or zip code.
4. Select a test center and click the website link.
5. Follow the instructions on the test organization website to schedule your test appointment.

NOTE: Please be sure to read all the policies and procedures provided by the test organization before you submit your payment; some test organization fees are nonrefundable.

How long will it take to obtain my certification after I pass the test?

You will receive email notification of your certification credential approximately 1 to 2 business days after you pass the certification test. At that time, your information will be available via the National Registry website's Public Search link. Make sure all the information in your National Registry account is up to date. Missing or inconsistent information or expired credentials can cause delays in receiving your certification.

What should I do if it has been longer than expected, and I have not received my certification?

Review the information in your National Registry account to make sure it is up to date. Check to make sure the name you entered exactly matches the name on your medical license. If you have not done so, you must enter your training information and make sure your medical licensing information is not expired by following these steps:

1. Go to the National Registry website at https://nationalregistry.fmcsa.dot.gov
2. Select "Login" in the blue bar at the top of the screen.
3. Enter your username and password and click "Login."
4. Select "View and Add Training Information" under "My Certification and Training" in the blue bar across the top of the screen.
5. Select "Add Training" and enter your training information.
6. Click "Save Changes."

NOTE: The system cannot certify your account until your training information has been entered.

If I don't pass the certification test, can I retake it?

Yes. However, you must wait at least 30 days before taking the test.

Comment: *An NPRM[12] published on December 1, 2016 considered eliminating the 30-day wait, as there is no requirement for any action in the 30-day interval.*

Prior to taking the examination, the FMCSA Complete Guide to Medical Examiner Certification should be reviewed for information on the process and examination.[13]

There are several requirements for examiners to continue to be listed on the NRCME.[14] They must:

- Submit Form MCSA-5850 for each driver examined electronically every month via the National Registry website. If no exams were performed during the month, that must also be reported.
- Submit to periodic monitoring and audits.
- Submit any changes in the application information to FMCSA within 30 days of the change.
- Report to FMCSA any information related to any termination, suspension, or withdrawal of your license, registration, or certificate under State law.
- Maintain documentation of state licensing, registration, or certification and completion of all required training.
- Retain original completed Medical Examination Reports for all drivers examined and a copy or electronic version of the driver's medical examiner's certificate for at least 3 years from the date of the examination.
- Provide copies of Medical Examination Reports and medical examiner's certificates to FMCSA upon request.
- Follow all FMCSA administrative requirements.
- Maintain certification by completing periodic training every 5 years and recertify by passing the ME certification exam every 10 years.

Examiners *must* comply with these requirements—FMCSA can and *has* removed medical examiners from the registry for not complying. This includes providing copies of the MER to FMCSA and other agencies upon request.

With many examiners having been certified in 2012, they are now due for refresher training. In a recent bulletin,[15] FMCSA indicated that refresher training should be available shortly.

Examiners should regularly review the NRCME Resource Center[16] for updates to the NRCME process. FMCSA utilizes email as its primary means to communicate with medical examiners; thus, it is important to keep one's email in the registry current. FMCSA pointed out in a recent webinar that it will only send emails if the information is essential for the examiner to read, in other words, read the email from FMCSA—do not hit delete. The CDME Review[17] newsletter from the American College of Occupational and Environmental Medicine (ACOEM) also provides updates on the NRCME and other aspects of commercial driver medical certification, such as recommendations from the MRB, recent relevant literature, and related litigation.

D. What Versions of the Forms May I Use and Can the Examiner Modify the Form?

There are three forms used in the CDME process:

- Medical Examination Report Form, MCSA-5875 (MER)
- Medical Examiner's Certificate, Form MCSA-5876 (MEC)
- CMV Driver Medical Examination Results Form, MCSA-5850 (electronic only)

FMCSA has provided the MER and MEC, in a downloadable and fillable format in the Resource Center.[16]

These forms have been approved by the Office of Management and Budget (OMB) and, as examiners were reminded in a December 2016 Bulletin to Examiners,[18] *"must be used as prescribed in the regulation. If MEs are using any forms with alterations that are outside of the permissible changes below, they must stop using these forms to be in compliance with the Federal Motor Carrier Safety Regulations."* Except for the following permissible changes, altered forms will not be accepted by State Driver Licensing Agencies (SDLA).

Permissible changes to the MER Form, MCSA-5875 are:

1. A bar code may be added to the form for purposes of forms management in the ME's office, as long as it does not obscure any of the content.
2. The instructions may be resized, as long as they are legible.
3. The instructions may be made available to the driver and the ME separately from the form.
4. The form can be filed/stored without the instructions.
5. The form may be printed in black and white.

Permissible changes to the MEC, Form MCSA-5876 are:

1. The form may be reduced in size, as long as ALL the content is legible.
2. The form may be printed in black and white.

There have been several updates to the MER and MEC since the initial Final Rule. The key change in the most recent version eliminated the privacy statement that had been on earlier forms and the addition of a disclaimer. There have been several communications to examiners on which version of the forms can be used, with the most recent change published in the *Federal Register*[19] and a communication sent to examiners.[20] Only versions of the forms listed here will be accepted by an SDLA.

October and November 2015
- *Posted samples of forms on National Registry website based on delays in posting fillable and downloadable PDF forms*
- *Forms manufacturers began producing and selling*
- *Acceptable until stocks are depleted*
- *In offices where these forms have been programmed into an electronic system that will require IT programming, the current approved versions of the forms should be programmed as soon as practicable.*

December 2015
- *Posted fillable and downloadable PDF forms on FMCSA and National Registry websites*
- *Acceptable until stocks are depleted*
- *In offices where these forms have been programmed into an electronic system that will require IT programming, the current approved versions of the forms should be programmed as soon as practicable.*

April 2016
- *Posted OMB approved versions on the FMCSA and National Registry websites with nonsubstantive changes approved on April 7, 2016.*
  - *Nonsubstantive changes can be seen at the following link by selecting "Justification of Nonmaterial/Non-substantive Change": http://www.reginfo.gov/public/do/PRAViewDocument?ref_nbr =201604-2126-006.*
- *Acceptable until stocks depleted*
- *In offices where these forms have been programmed into an electronic system that will require IT programming, the current approved versions of the forms should be programmed as soon as practicable.*

September 2016
- *Posted OMB approved versions on FMCSA and National Registry websites with nonsubstantive changes below approved on September 6, 2016.*

- *Removal of the Privacy Act statement from the MER Form, MCSA-5875 at the direction of the DOT Chief Privacy Officer*
- *Addition of a disclaimer statement regarding the protection of sensitive information by Medical Examiners*
- *Current approved versions to be used going forward.*

E. How Do I Conduct the Examination and Complete the Forms?

Examiners should know how to perform a complete physical examination, focusing on those aspects of the examinations that could impact safe performance of *all* duties of the CMV operator, both driving and nondriving tasks. This should have been covered in the examiner's professional training with focus on difference for the commercial driver medical examination as part of the NRCME training.

Instructions on completing the MER are found in 49 CFR 391.43 and are included in Chapter 3 on page 98. An FAQ document on completion of the forms can be found in the Resource section of the NRCME website[6] and is included at the end of this chapter. FMCSA held 2 webinars in March 2017 and will be holding additional ones to review completion of the forms, the MER as well as the MEC, and the online determination submission (MCSA-5850). The slides and recordings of the webinars are anticipated to be available on the NRCME Resource page.[16]

Rather than repeating the instruction on form completion, this section will review those areas on the form where there has been confusion or reasons for rejection of submitted forms.

Both the MER and MEC can be completed online and then printed out, completed online and stored electronically (for the MER) or printed out and manually completed. Fillable versions of the forms are available in the Resource Center.[16] If completing by hand, all entries *must* be legible. All sections and questions where a response is required must be completed or there is a risk that the form could be rejected by an SDLA, an employer, or a third-party administrator reviewing the form for accuracy or completeness. Form rejection is an inconvenience for both the driver and examiner and could delay the driver being able to submit paperwork to maintain the CDL.

FIGURE 2-1 Driver Information—Section 1

	MEDICAL RECORD #
SECTION 1. Driver Information *(to be filled out by the driver)*	_____ *(or sticker)*

PERSONAL INFORMATION

Last Name: _____ First Name: _____ Middle Initial: ___ Date of Birth: _____ Age: ___

Street Address: _____ City: _____ State/Province: _____ Zip Code: _____

Driver's License Number: _____ Issuing State/Province: _____ Phone: _____ Gender: ○ M ○ F

E-mail *(optional)*: _____ CLP/CDL Applicant/Holder*: ○ Yes ○ No

Driver ID Verified By**: _____

Has your USDOT/FMCSA medical certificate ever been denied or issued for less than 2 years? ○ Yes ○ No ○ Not Sure

*CLP/CDL Applicant/Holder: See instructions for definitions.   **Driver ID Verified By: Record what type of photo ID was used to verify the identity of the driver, e.g., CDL, driver's license, passport.

Section 1, Driver Information, Figure 2-1, should be completed by the driver except where the examiner or a member of the examiner's staff must note how the driver's identification is verified. The driver's address should be the current address; PO box numbers are permissible. The address may or may not be the same as the address on the driver's license. When this section is reviewed by the examiner, additional information should be sought when the response to a denied or shortened certificate is "yes" or "not sure." The driver's email address is optional, as is the Medical Record #. The Medical Record # could be any number that the examiner's office might choose to use as part of their record management process. If the driver does not have a driver's license (CDL or regular), the medical examiner should enter "none." Just as for age and English language requirement, which are the responsibility of the employer, the examiner is not required to verify that the driver has a license.

FIGURE 2-2 Driver Health History

DRIVER HEALTH HISTORY	
Have you ever had surgery? If "yes," please list and explain below.	○ Yes ○ No ○ Not Sure
Are you currently taking medications *(prescription, over-the-counter, herbal remedies, diet supplements)*? If "yes," please describe below.	○ Yes ○ No ○ Not Sure

(Attach additional sheets if necessary)

This document contains sensitive information and is for official use only. Improper handling of this information could negatively affect individuals. Handle and secure this information appropriately to prevent inadvertent disclosure by keeping the documents under the control of authorized persons. Properly dispose of this document when no longer required to be maintained by regulatory requirements.

Section 1, Driver Health History, Figure 2-2, is also completed by the driver and reviewed by the examiner. Once again, the main issue with this section is that a "yes" or "not sure" response must be explained and later reviewed by the examiner. Additional information elicited by the examiner should be documented in Section 2 of the form. Whether a procedure at age 2 years should be documented requires some judgment on the part of the driver and examiner. Wisdom teeth removal is probably not relevant but surgery for a congenital heart defect, which could impact safe driving, should be noted. If a driver lists any medications, the examiner reviewing this form must understand the medications listed, the conditions that they treat, potential side effects (especially those that might be impairing), and any interaction with other medications. While the statement at the bottom indicates to "properly dispose of this document when no longer required to be maintained by regulatory requirements," I have confirmed with FMCSA who, in turn, confirmed with the Privacy Office[21] that the examiner is not required to discard after the 3 years required maintenance of the form by FMCSA or the state medical record retention requirement.

FIGURE 2-3 Driver Health History continued and top of Page 2

DRIVER HEALTH HISTORY *(continued)*

Do you have or have you ever had:	Yes	No	Not Sure		Yes	No	Not Sure
1. Head/brain injuries or illnesses *(e.g., concussion)*	O	O	O	16. Dizziness, headaches, numbness, tingling, or memory loss	O	O	O
2. Seizures, epilepsy	O	O	O				
3. Eye problems *(except glasses or contacts)*	O	O	O	17. Unexplained weight loss	O	O	O
4. Ear and/or hearing problems	O	O	O	18. Stroke, mini-stroke (TIA), paralysis, or weakness	O	O	O
5. Heart disease, heart attack, bypass, or other heart problems	O	O	O	19. Missing or limited use of arm, hand, finger, leg, foot, toe	O	O	O
6. Pacemaker, stents, implantable devices, or other heart procedures				20. Neck or back problems	O	O	O
				21. Bone, muscle, joint, or nerve problems	O	O	O
7. High blood pressure	O	O	O	22. Blood clots or bleeding problems	O	O	O
8. High cholesterol	O	O	O	23. Cancer	O	O	O
9. Chronic (long-term) cough, shortness of breath, or other breathing problems	O	O	O	24. Chronic (long-term) infection or other chronic diseases	O	O	O
10. Lung disease *(e.g., asthma)*	O	O	O	25. Sleep disorders, pauses in breathing while asleep, daytime sleepiness, loud snoring	O	O	O
11. Kidney problems, kidney stones, or pain/problems with urination	O	O	O	26. Have you ever had a sleep test *(e.g., sleep apnea)*?	O	O	O
12. Stomach, liver, or digestive problems	O	O	O	27. Have you ever spent a night in the hospital?	O	O	O
13. Diabetes or blood sugar problems	O	O	O	28. Have you ever had a broken bone?	O	O	O
Insulin used	O	O	O	29. Have you ever used or do you now use tobacco?	O	O	O
14. Anxiety, depression, nervousness, other mental health problems	O	O	O	30. Do you currently drink alcohol?	O	O	O
				31. Have you used an illegal substance within the past two years?	O	O	O
15. Fainting or passing out	O	O	O	32. Have you ever failed a drug test or been dependent on an illegal substance?	O	O	O

Other health condition(s) not described above: ○ Yes ○ No ○ Not Sure

Did you answer "yes" to any of questions 1-32? If so, please comment further on those health conditions below.   ○ Yes ○ No ○ Not Sure

(Attach additional sheets if necessary)

The driver's name, date of birth, and the exam date must be entered at the top of Page 2 and each subsequent page. The exam date is the date that the examination is conducted. It may or may not be the date on which a certification determination is made and may or may not be the date from which the expiration date would be calculated.

The second portion of the driver health history (Figure 2-3) is completed by the driver and every question must have a response. The driver should comment on any "yes" or "not sure" responses in the space provided. If upon additional questioning a response is clarified, the medical examiner should not change the driver's answer on the form, as the driver certifies that the information is accurate and complete but should add any supplemental information in the comment section located in Section 2, under the Driver Health History Review.

The medical examiner should also request any additional tests or records that are felt to be necessary to determine whether the driver is medically qualified. If the driver indicates having had events such as a heart attack or a sleep study, results of relevant studies should be reviewed; it should never be assumed that the driver's report that the study was "normal" was accurate.

If the driver checks "yes" to Question 23, cancer, the driver should indicate which type and note any treatment.

One question that has come up with some examiners is how to handle a driver's "yes" response to questions 30 through 32. If a driver is currently using illegal drugs or excessive alcohol they would not meet medical standards. If the examiner has any concerns, they should obtain any additional testing or consultation with a specialist to determine if the driver is safe. This may include referral to a substance abuse professional (not under DOT procedures) or obtaining information from a rehabilitation program. Non-DOT testing for drugs and/or alcohol is permitted. The medical advisory criteria[22] includes the statement that "*The term "uses" is designed to encompass instances of prohibited drug use determined by a physician through established medical means. This may or may not involve body fluid testing.*" The ME Handbook[23] notes that "*Certification may require successful completion of a substance abuse professional (SAP)-required drug rehabilitation program*" and that the examiner should record "*any additional drug abuse or alcohol screening tests and evaluation.*"

FIGURE 2-4 Driver's Signature and Health History Review

CMV DRIVER'S SIGNATURE

I certify that the above information is accurate and complete. I understand that inaccurate, false or missing information may invalidate the examination and my Medical Examiner's Certificate, that submission of fraudulent or intentionally false information is a violation of 49 CFR 390.35, and that submission of fraudulent or intentionally false information may subject me to civil or criminal penalties under 49 CFR 390.37 and 49 CFR 386 Appendices A and B.

Driver's Signature: ____________________ Date: ____________

SECTION 2. Examination Report *(to be filled out by the medical examiner)*

DRIVER HEALTH HISTORY REVIEW

Review and discuss pertinent driver answers and any available medical records. Comment on the driver's responses to the "health history" questions that may affect the driver's safe operation of a commercial motor vehicle (CMV).

(Attach additional sheets if necessary)

One of the more common errors found by FMCSA during audit review was omission of the driver signature (Figure 2-4). This is a very important component as it signifies that the driver is aware of the implications of "fraudulent or intentionally false information."

For many, the space in Section 2 (Figure 2-4) for the examiner to document any responses that may affect operation of the CMV (both driving and nondriving tasks) is insufficient. If other relevant information is obtained, that should be documented. An additional page (or pages) should be used and all documentation must be legible. Examiners should complete the entire form and examination, even if they find a disqualifying condition (except if the driver decides to terminate the examination based on an examiner question or response—more on this when incomplete examinations are discussed). This is another area in which FMCSA has found omissions—lack of examiner comments to "yes" or "not sure" responses.

FIGURE 2-5 Testing

Form MCSA-5875		OMB No. 2126-0006 Expiration Date: 8/31/2018
Last Name: _____	First Name: _____	DOB: _____ Exam Date: _____

TESTING

| Pulse rate: _____ Pulse rhythm regular: ○ Yes ○ No | Height: __ feet __ inches Weight: ____ pounds |

Blood Pressure	Systolic	Diastolic	Urinalysis	Sp. Gr.	Protein	Blood	Sugar
Sitting			Urinalysis is required.				
Second reading (optional)			Numerical readings must be recorded.				
Other testing if indicated			Protein, blood, or sugar in the urine may be an indication for further testing to rule out any underlying medical problem.				

Vision
Standard is at least 20/40 acuity (Snellen) in each eye with or without correction. At least 70° field of vision in horizontal meridian measured in each eye. The use of corrective lenses should be noted on the Medical Examiner's Certificate.

Hearing
Standard: Must first perceive whispered voice at not less than 5 feet OR average hearing loss of less than or equal to 40 dB, in better ear (with or without hearing aid).

Acuity	Uncorrected	Corrected	Horizontal Field of Vision
Right Eye:	20/____	20/____	Right Eye: ____ degrees
Left Eye:	20/____	20/____	Left Eye: ____ degrees
Both Eyes:	20/____	20/____	

Check if hearing aid used for test: ☐ Right Ear ☐ Left Ear ☐ Neither

Whisper Test Results   Right Ear   Left Ear
Record distance (in feet) from driver at which a forced whispered voice can first be heard   ____   ____

OR

	Yes No
Applicant can recognize and distinguish among traffic control signals and devices showing red, green, and amber colors	○ ○
Monocular vision	○ ○
Referred to ophthalmologist or optometrist?	○ ○
Received documentation from ophthalmologist or optometrist?	○ ○

Audiometric Test Results

Right Ear			Left Ear		
500 Hz	1000 Hz	2000 Hz	500 Hz	1000 Hz	2000 Hz
____	____	____	____	____	____

Average (right): _____   Average (left): _____

The driver's name, date of birth, and the exam date must be entered at the top of Page 3 (Figure 2-5). All spaces must be completed unless indicated as optional (e.g., second blood pressure reading). Examiners are also not required to complete the visual acuity corrected *and* uncorrected. If the driver requires corrective lenses, then it is not necessary to enter the uncorrected vision. The urinalysis readings should be numerical if possible, but whatever is measured must be entered (i.e., neg for blood or sugar). For some audited exams in which the urinalysis results were blank, it was discovered that the urinalysis was not done. Either a whisper test or an audiogram is required but not both. Pulse rhythm regular, "yes/no" must be marked, as must a response to each of the four questions under acuity and whether a hearing aid is used for the hearing test. Lack of a response to those questions does *not* signify a "no." During the webinar[16] on the form, FMCSA reminded examiners that incomplete forms could be grounds for removal from the NRCME.

FIGURE 2-6 Physical Examination

PHYSICAL EXAMINATION

The presence of a certain condition may not necessarily disqualify a driver, particularly if the condition is controlled adequately, is not likely to worsen, or is readily amenable to treatment. Even if a condition does not disqualify a driver, the Medical Examiner may consider deferring the driver temporarily. Also, the driver should be advised to take the necessary steps to correct the condition as soon as possible, particularly if neglecting the condition could result in a more serious illness that might affect driving.

Check the body systems for abnormalities.

Body System	Normal	Abnormal	Body System	Normal	Abnormal
1. General	O	O	8. Abdomen	O	O
2. Skin	O	O	9. Genito-urinary system including hernias	O	O
3. Eyes	O	O	10. Back/Spine	O	O
4. Ears	O	O	11. Extremities/joints	O	O
5. Mouth/throat	O	O	12. Neurological system including reflexes	O	O
6. Cardiovascular	O	O	13. Gait	O	O
7. Lungs/chest	O	O	14. Vascular system	O	O

Discuss any abnormal answers in detail in the space below and indicate whether it would affect the driver's ability to operate a CMV. Enter applicable item number before each comment.

(Attach additional sheets if necessary)

Once again, every question in the physical examination section (Figure 2-6) must have a response and *all* abnormal findings should be evaluated as to whether they affect the driver's ability to operate the CMV, and documents with additional legible pages should be included if needed.

The next two sections cover determination. Examiners should complete the federal *or* state section but not both. Examiners are trained and certified to examine interstate drivers and evaluate them under interstate medical criteria. Most states have adopted 49 CFR 391.41 for their CDL drivers; thus, in most cases, examiners would complete the federal section. If the driver does not meet the federal criteria and has declared to be *intra*state non-excepted, the examiner can complete the state section. However, the examiner must be aware of the standards and requirements of the state where the driver is licensed and operating. Some states are using the State Determination section differently; therefore, examiners evaluating *intra*state-only drivers should contact that state to ensure that they are following any state-specific requirement. For example, some states have instructed examiners that if the driver does not meet federal medical standards, even if they are *intra*state only, the examiner should disqualify the driver but then refer the individual to the state for additional processing. Examiners must remember that state only *cannot* be used as a restriction if the driver does not meet federal criteria.

FIGURE 2-7 Determination Federal

Last Name: _____ First Name: _____ DOB: _____ Exam Date: _____

Please complete only one of the following (Federal or State) Medical Examiner Determination sections:

MEDICAL EXAMINER DETERMINATION (Federal)

Use this section for examinations performed in accordance with the Federal Motor Carrier Safety Regulations (49 CFR 391.41-391.49):

○ Does not meet standards *(specify reason)*: _____

○ Meets standards in 49 CFR 391.41; qualifies for 2-year certificate

○ Meets standards, but periodic monitoring required *(specify reason)*: _____

    Driver qualified for: ○ 3 months   ○ 6 months   ○ 1 year   ○ other *(specify)*: _____

☐ Wearing corrective lenses   ☐ Wearing hearing aid   ☐ Accompanied by a waiver/exemption *(specify type)*: _____

☐ Accompanied by a Skill Performance Evaluation (SPE) Certificate   ☐ Qualified by operation of 49 CFR 391.64 *(Federal)*

☐ Driving within an exempt intracity zone *(see 49 CFR 391.62) (Federal)*

The first portion of this section (Figure 2-7) is to indicate whether the driver meets criteria under 49 CFR 491.41 with or without a variance. If the examiner determines that the driver does not meet standards, the first bubble should be marked and the reason provided. The driver should be informed of what steps can be taken to be certified. If the driver is disqualified, any prior medical examiner certificates are invalid. Currently, examiners are not required to submit results (actual examination forms or certificates should never be sent to FMCSA by the examiner or driver) until the end of the month following the examination. Beginning on June 22, 2018, reporting is required by midnight local time of the next calendar day following the examination. Drivers may be working for one company with a current valid medical certificate but have an examination for a new company with a more conservative examiner (more likely to disqualify due to medications, abnormal findings, or lack of recent follow-up than the initial examiner) who may disqualify the driver. That driver would need to stop driving, as the newer determination would take precedence. If the examiner is uncertain whether the driver meets the medical standards (wants to review additional information), the determination pending status can be used, which will be discussed later.

If the examiner determines that the driver does meet the medical standards, the examiner can certify the driver for any duration—2 years; 1 year; or 30, 60, or 90 days; and whether any variance is required. The examiner determines the duration of certification for each examination independently and, if the examiner feels that it is appropriate, can issue more than a one 3-month certification in a row.

If the examiner is indicating that hearing aids or corrective lenses are required, the examiner should be certain that the driver meets the criteria with those aids and not just assume that the driver who left glasses at home and had corrective lenses marked on the last examination still meets the vision standard.

If a driver requires a Skill Performance Evaluation (SPE) certificate or a waiver or exemption, it should be indicated. For the driver who is otherwise medically qualified, the standard that the driver does not meet should be noted, such as insulin, hearing, vision, and so on. An MEC would be issued indicating that the waiver/exemption or SPE is required. Drivers and employers should be reminded that the certificate is not valid until the exemption has been granted. Once a determination is made for any examination, it cannot be amended. For any change in status or expiration date, a new examination is required, including for a short certification, such as 30, 60, or 90 days.

FIGURE 2-8 Determination Federal—Determination Pending and Incomplete

☐ Determination pending *(specify reason)*: _____

   ☐ Return to medical exam office for follow-up on *(must be 45 days or less)*: _____

   ☐ Medical Examination Report amended *(specify reason)*: _____

      (if amended) **Medical Examiner's Signature:** _____ **Date:** _____

☐ Incomplete examination *(specify reason)*: _____

Determination Pending is the one section that may be causing the most confusion for examiners and employers. This is to be used when the examiner believes that the driver is safe to operate a CMV but is unable to make a determination because additional information is required. If the driver does *not* meet standards or the examiner does not believe that the driver is safe to operate a CMV, the "Does not meet standards" item should be selected. A driver who is placed in "determination pending status" may continue to operate a CMV if the individual has a valid medical certificate. Once the prior certificate expires, the driver could no longer work. A driver who does not have a valid medical certificate at the time of being placed into determination pending status cannot operate a CMV until the individual has a valid medical certificate but a new examination would not be required when they do return.

Consider the earlier disqualified driver for a new company. That driver has a valid medical certificate for Company A but the examiner for Company B wants information from the treating provider before issuing a medical certificate. If Examiner B does not want to qualify the driver for 30 days and then have to conduct a completely new examination but believes that the driver is safe, the examiner can use this category. The driver can then continue to work while obtaining the information for Examiner B rather than being disqualified and off the road once reported through the SDLA (which occurs by midnight local time next calendar day following the examination, beginning June 22, 2018).

When a driver is placed in determination pending, the examiner indicates when the driver must return to the office, up to 45 days. At 45 days, FMCSA will consider the examination incomplete, amend the NRMCE system, and notify the driver and examiner that a new examination would be needed. The examiner can require the driver to return in less than 45 days and can inform the driver that not returning will result in entering a disqualified determination. This would prevent a driver from "examiner shopping" during the "determination pending" status and if a "qualified" status is entered into the system shortly after the initial exam, FMCSA would investigate if there are different examiners with different determinations in a short period of time.

When the driver returns with the required information, the MER is amended. The reason for amending it must be entered and, at that point, the examiner signs the MER and MEC and indicates the date that they were signed. It is from the date signed that the expiration date would be calculated. An MEC is not issued when the driver is placed in "determination pending" status. The MER can be amended by a different examiner in the same office, but that second examiner should have access to and review prior documentation.

FMCSA provided the following example[6] of use of the "determination pending" status.

"On 1/1/16, a ME examined a driver and decided that they need more information before they can determine whether or not the driver is medically qualified. On the MER, MCSA-5875, page 4 for the 'Medical Examiner Determination', on the top right corner, the ME enters 1/1/16 as the examination date. The ME selects 'determination pending' and specifies the reason. For example, 'need additional information regarding specific condition.' The ME also selects the box for 'return to medical exam office for follow-up on.' The driver must return within 45 days. The ME must tell the driver that they are in a determination pending status and that unless the ME receives the additional information and/or sees the driver back in their office on or before a qualification determination, the exam will no longer be valid and a new exam must be conducted. The ME may enter a date for the driver to return to their office (follow-up appointment) if that information is available or they may wait until the driver returns to their office and add the date

at that time. On the CMV Driver Medical Examination Results Form, MCSA-5850, the ME selects 'determination pending' and enters the date of the examination as the 1/1/16 date from the top right corner of the MER, MCSA-5875.

On 1/15/16, the driver returns to the ME's office and the ME evaluates the information received and/or performs an examination of the driver if the ME determines it is necessary. The ME now has all the information needed to make a qualification determination. On the MER, MCSA-5875, the ME selects the appropriate qualification determination. The ME also selects 'medical examination report amended' and specifies the specific amendment(s) that are being made. The ME signs and dates the MER, MCSA-5875 with the 1/15/16 date; this is the date that the ME is amending the MER, MCSA-5875, the date in which the driver has returned to the ME's office. If the ME has made the determination that the driver is qualified, the 'Medical Examiner's Certificate Expiration Date' is calculated from the 1/15/16 date, the date that the ME actually signs/issues the MEC, Form MCSA-5876. On the CMV Driver Medical Examination Results Form, MCSA-5850, the ME enters the 1/15/16 date for the date the MEC, Form MCSA-5876 is signed/ issued if medically qualified or enters the 1/15/16 date for the date of examination/determination if medically unqualified. This submission of the driver's examination results takes precedence over the initial examination that placed the driver in a determination pending status.

If the driver does not return on or before the 45-day expiration date and the disposition of determination pending is not updated via the National Registry on or before the 45-day expiration date, the examination is no longer valid. FMCSA will notify the ME and the driver in writing and the driver is required to get a new examination, and in this case, the ME must update the MER, MCSA-5875 for this driver by selecting incomplete examination, specifying the reason, and filing the MER, MCSA-5875 in the driver's record. The ME does not need to submit another CMV Driver Medical Examination Results Form, MCSA-5850 into the National Registry system."

The incomplete examination is used when the driver, for any reason, chooses to terminate the examination. It is not to be used if the examiner chooses to stop the examination because the driver does not meet standards. Drivers may choose to stop the examination if they are aware that they will be disqualified so that the entry indicates "incomplete" and not "disqualified" in the NRCME system. My recommendation to examiners is to conduct the entire examination without indicating what additional information you may require or what your determination would be and, at the conclusion, discuss your findings and requirements.

FIGURE 2-9 Medical Examiner Information

| If the driver meets the standards outlined in 49 CFR 391.41, then complete a Medical Examiner's Certificate as stated in 49 CFR 391.43(h), as appropriate. |

I have performed this evaluation for certification. I have personally reviewed all available records and recorded information pertaining to this evaluation, and attest that to the best of my knowledge, I believe it to be true and correct.

Medical Examiner's Signature: _____

Medical Examiner's Name *(please print or type)*: _____

Medical Examiner's Address: _____ City: _____ State: _____ Zip Code: _____

Medical Examiner's Telephone Number: _____ Date Certificate Signed: _____

Medical Examiner's State License, Certificate, or Registration Number: _____ Issuing State: _____

☐ MD ☐ DO ☐ Physician Assistant ☐ Chiropractor ☐ Advanced Practice Nurse

☐ Other Practitioner *(specify)*: _____

National Registry Number: _____ | Medical Examiner's Certificate Expiration Date: _____

This section, Medical Examiner Information (Figure 2-9), must also be filled out completely. Frequent errors are omission of the examiner's signature (which can be electronic or by hand), the examiner's address and phone number, or type of practitioner. The examiner indicates the date that the MEC is signed, which is when the determination is made. This may or may not be the date the examination was conducted. If the driver is placed in "determination pending," the date of the examination and the date the certificate is signed will be different. The expiration date, calculated from the date the certificate is signed, is entered at the bottom right. This is not the date that the examiner's NRCME certificate expires. The examiner who signs the certificate should be the one who completes this section. This should not be completed prior to the examination, either by staff or a different examiner (except as discussed in determination pending). It is considered fraudulent activity if the MER and MEC are signed by someone other than the examiner who conducted the examination and made the determination. The person conducting the examination *must* be on the NRCME. A supervising physician for a physician assistant who is on the NRCME cannot sign for the PA who conducts the examination but is not listed on the NRCME. If one examiner in an office conducts the examination and uses the determination pending status, an electronic MCSA-5850 would need to be entered by that examiner indicating determination pending. A second examiner in the same office with access to the initial evaluation can amend the determination pending status (the only time that the examination can be amended) and would update and complete the MER, sign the MEC, and submit results via the MCSA–5850 using one's own NRCME number.

FIGURE 2-10 Determination (State)

MEDICAL EXAMINER DETERMINATION (State)

Use this section for examinations performed in accordance with the Federal Motor Carrier Safety Regulations (49 CFR 391.41-391.49) with any applicable State variances (which will only be valid for intrastate operations):

○ Does not meet standards in 49 CFR 391.41 with any applicable State variances *(specify reason):* _____

○ Meets standards in 49 CFR 391.41 with any applicable State variances

○ Meets standards, but periodic monitoring required *(specify reason):* _____

    Driver qualified for: ○ 3 months ○ 6 months ○ 1 year ○ other *(specify):* _____

☐ Wearing corrective lenses ☐ Wearing hearing aid ☐ Accompanied by a waiver/exemption *(specify type):* _____

☐ Accompanied by a Skill Performance Evaluation (SPE) Certificate ☐ Grandfathered from State requirements *(State)*

If the driver meets the standards outlined in 49 CFR 391.41, with applicable State variances, then complete a Medical Examiner's Certificate, as appropriate.

I have performed this evaluation for certification. I have personally reviewed all available records and recorded information pertaining to this evaluation, and attest that to the best of my knowledge, I believe it to be true and correct.

Medical Examiner's Signature: _____

Medical Examiner's Name *(please print or type):* _____

Medical Examiner's Address: _____ City: _____ State: _____ Zip Code: _____

Medical Examiner's Telephone Number: _____ Date Certificate Signed: _____

Medical Examiner's State License, Certificate, or Registration Number: _____ Issuing State: _____

☐ MD ☐ DO ☐ Physician Assistant ☐ Chiropractor ☐ Advanced Practice Nurse

☐ Other Practitioner *(specify):* _____

National Registry Number: [_____]	Medical Examiner's Certificate Expiration Date: _____

As discussed earlier, prior to completing this section, Determination (State) (Figure 2-10), the examiner should be aware of the state requirements and understand if and how the state may be using this section of the MER. There is no "determination pending" option for the state.

FIGURE 2-11 Medical Examiner's Certificate

The Medical Examiner's Certificate form (Form MCSA-5876).

This document, Medical Examiner's Certificate (Figure 2-11), serves as the driver's proof of medical qualification. Most of the information in the determination section is repeated on the MEC. Again, everything must be completed. An incomplete MEC is one of the most common reasons for rejection by the SDLA. This can be completed online and printed or printed and then completed. A paper copy must be given to all drivers until June 22, 2018. After that date, it is not required to give a copy to CDL holders, but all others must continue to have a paper copy of the MEC. A copy must be maintained for at least 3 years by the examiner.

The driver must complete the bottom portion of the MEC. Missing signatures, either examiner or driver, is another common reason for rejection by an SDLA.

FIGURE 2-12 Submission of Determination – MCSA-5850

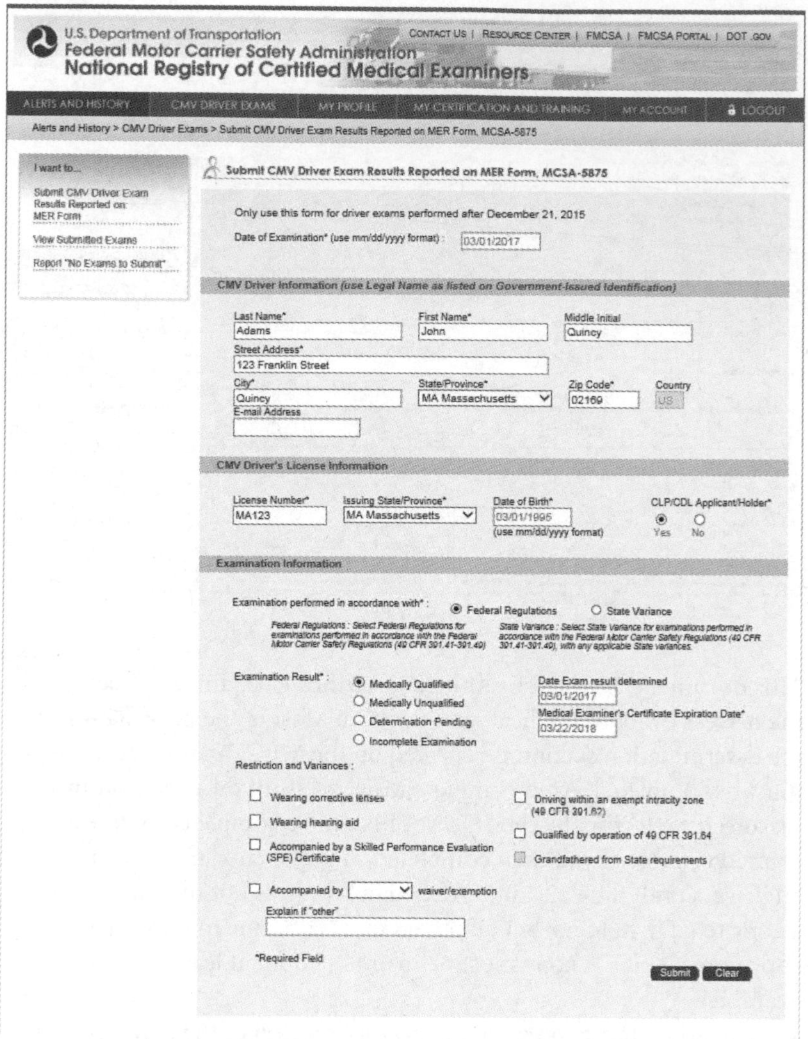
U.S. Department of Transportation
Federal Motor Carrier Safety Administration
National Registry of Certified Medical Examiners

CONTACT US | RESOURCE CENTER | FMCSA | FMCSA PORTAL | DOT.GOV

ALERTS AND HISTORY | CMV DRIVER EXAMS | MY PROFILE | MY CERTIFICATION AND TRAINING | MY ACCOUNT | LOGOUT

Alerts and History > CMV Driver Exams > Submit CMV Driver Exam Results Reported on MER Form, MCSA-5875

I want to...
- Submit CMV Driver Exam Results Reported on MER Form
- View Submitted Exams
- Report "No Exams to Submit"

Submit CMV Driver Exam Results Reported on MER Form, MCSA-5875

Only use this form for driver exams performed after December 21, 2015

Date of Examination* (use mm/dd/yyyy format): 03/01/2017

CMV Driver Information *(use Legal Name as listed on Government-Issued Identification)*

Last Name*: Adams
First Name*: John
Middle Initial: Quincy
Street Address*: 123 Franklin Street
City*: Quincy
State/Province*: MA Massachusetts
Zip Code*: 02169
Country: US
E-mail Address:

CMV Driver's License Information

License Number*: MA123
Issuing State/Province*: MA Massachusetts
Date of Birth*: 03/01/1995 (use mm/dd/yyyy format)
CLP/CDL Applicant/Holder*: (●) Yes ( ) No

Examination Information

Examination performed in accordance with*: (●) Federal Regulations ( ) State Variance

Federal Regulations : Select Federal Regulations for examinations performed in accordance with the Federal Motor Carrier Safety Regulations (49 CFR 391.41-391.49)

State Variance : Select State Variance for examinations performed in accordance with the Federal Motor Carrier Safety Regulations (49 CFR 391.41-391.49), with any applicable State variances.

Examination Result*: (●) Medically Qualified ( ) Medically Unqualified ( ) Determination Pending ( ) Incomplete Examination

Date Exam result determined: 03/01/2017
Medical Examiner's Certificate Expiration Date*: 03/22/2018

Restriction and Variances:

- [ ] Wearing corrective lenses
- [ ] Wearing hearing aid
- [ ] Accompanied by a Skilled Performance Evaluation (SPE) Certificate
- [ ] Accompanied by [ ] waiver/exemption
- [ ] Driving within an exempt intracity zone (49 CFR 391.62)
- [ ] Qualified by operation of 49 CFR 391.64
- [ ] Grandfathered from State requirements

Explain if "other"

*Required Field

Submit | Clear

Examiners would access the online results submission form, Submission of Determination (Figure 2-12), by going to their account and selecting "Submit CMV Driver Exam Results Reported on MER Form." This online form must be submitted when any examination is conducted (whether qualified, unqualified, determination pending, or incomplete) or if there is any change in status (the MER is amended from determination pending), the driver does not return while in determination pending, or if additional information is received that leads the examiner to change the determination (qualified but then information is provided to the examiner prior to expiration of the certificate that disqualified the driver). The most recent 5850 for a driver will take precedence; if there are different determinations from different examiners in a short period of time, FMCSA will evaluate. The driver's email address is optional.

If the driver does have a driver's license, "None" should be entered. An expiration date is required only if the driver is medically qualified.

For now, these must be submitted by the end of the month following the examination. In June 2018, the form will be required by midnight local time the next calendar day following the examination. If no examinations are performed in a given month, examiners are required to enter that in the NRCME system. A process is now in place for batch uploading and examiners can designate third parties or administrative assistants to submit the 5850 on their behalf.

Once an outcome has been submitted, it cannot be edited and a new submission must occur. The only time a MER can be amended is if the driver was in "determination pending" status. If unqualified, incomplete, or a short certificate, a new examination and new submission is required.

As a reminder, the results form—the online MCSA-5850—is the only form that is required to be submitted to FMCSA. Drivers should be reminded that they submit their certificate to the SDLA but not to FMCSA.

F. What Resources Can I Use to Reach a Certification Determination?

There are many resources that the examiner should and may use to reach a certification determination and evaluate the duration of certification. Examiners should always refer to the regulations, interpretations, and FAQs that are included in Chapter 3. The medical advisory criteria, also in Chapter 3[22] are *not* regulatory but rather are guidance. The introduction to the medical advisory criteria explains:

I. Introduction
This appendix contains the Agency's guidelines in the form of Medical Advisory Criteria to help medical examiners assess a driver's physical qualification. These guidelines are strictly advisory and were established after consultation with physicians, States, and industry representatives, and, in some areas, after consideration of recommendations from the Federal Motor Carrier Safety Administration's Medical Review Board and Medical Expert Panels.

II. Interpretation of Medical Standards

Since the issuance of the regulations for physical qualifications of commercial motor vehicle drivers, the Federal Motor Carrier Safety Administration has published recommendations called Advisory Criteria to help medical examiners in determining whether a driver meets the physical qualifications for commercial driving. These recommendations have been condensed to provide information to medical examiners that is directly relevant to the physical examination and is not already included in the Medical Examination Report Form.

The ME Handbook[23] (now down for revision but what is still used as the basis for most NRCME training programs) was mostly derived from medical conference reports. It explained that "guidelines such as advisory criteria, and medical conference reports are recommendations. While not law, the guidelines are intended as best practices for medical examiners." It further recommended that, if not followed, the reason(s) for the variance should be documented. Similarly, the FAQs, in explaining the difference between regulation and guidelines, point out that guidelines are issued "to assist the Medical Examiner to determine if a person is physically qualified to operate a commercial bus or truck. The Medical Examiner may or may not choose to use these guidelines. These guidelines are based on expert review and considered practice standards. The examiner should document the reason(s) for not following the guidelines."

Some of the guidance in the ME Handbook is out of date and not consistent with current best practice or scientific evidence. In addition, there are many medical conditions and treatments that were either not discussed or not in use when the existing guidance was prepared. Examiners should be aware of current literature on medical conditions, their treatment and prognosis, and the risk of the condition or the treatment leading to sudden or gradual impairment or incapacitation. There have been several evidence reviews, MEP recommendations, and recommendations from the MRB or Motor Carrier Safety Advisory Committee (MCSAC) that can be found through the MRB website.[24] In general, these recommendations have *not* been officially adopted by FMCSA (the exception being that FMCSA is utilizing the Seizure MEP recommendation as the criteria to consider whether to grant exemptions to drivers with a seizure disorder), but examiners should be aware of them and consider the science behind the recommendations in making their certification determination. There has been pushback from some examiners and training programs on whether this information should even be mentioned during training. In the Sample Training Manual, which is no longer available, in the respiratory section it reminded examiners that a training program clearly *"distinguishes between what constitutes current FMCSA medical guidance and recommendations by advisory panels, boards, and other stakeholders as to what FMCSA guidance should be."* It also noted that the test uses current guidelines but *"medical examiners may choose to use best practices or other guidelines."*

Table 1-1 in Chapter 1 has the topics discussed at each MRB meeting.

G. What If the Driver Meets the Absolute Medical Standards and the Examiner Believes the Driver Is Safe to Drive but Additional Information Is Required Before Issuing a 1- or 2-Year Certification?

The examiner has a couple of options in this situation. The examiner can either place the driver in the determination pending status (see earlier discussion) or give the driver a shortened certification, either 30, 60, or 90 days. The important thing to remember is that if the driver is placed in determination pending status, the individual *must* return within 45 days or the examination will be considered incomplete and a new examination will be required. If a short certificate is issued, a new examination would be required.

H. What If the Driver Does Not Meet the Absolute Medical Standards but the Examiner Believes the Driver Is Safe and Otherwise Medically Qualified?

FMCSA is currently accepting exemption applications for drivers who do not meet the absolute requirements. There are formal programs for vision, hearing, and insulin-taking diabetics.[25] Exemptions have been granted for drivers who do not meet the seizure criteria and, although applications have been accepted, no exemptions have been granted for drivers with narcolepsy or implantable cardioverter defibrillators (ICD).

If the examiner believes that the driver is otherwise medically qualified (for other conditions and either able to meet FMCSA exemption criteria if they exist or that the condition would not cause the driver to be at risk of sudden or gradual impairment or incapacitation), the examiner should sign the medical examination reporting form and certificate, indicating that it must be accompanied by the required exemption. The expiration date of the certification should be 1 year from the date of the examination or determination. Both the employer and the driver should be made aware that the certificate is not valid until the driver has been granted the exemption, which may take up to 180 days from the date that the complete application is received by FMCSA. This is another area that may change, and the examiner may eventually be responsible for determining whether a driver who requires insulin for control of diabetes meets a predetermined set of criteria.[26]

I. How Long Can Drivers Be Certified?

Drivers can be medically certified for up to 2 years, but there are many circumstances in which the duration should be less, including any medical condition that may not remain stable for 2 years. One FAQ[3] includes the following as examples of conditions for which certification should be shortened to 1 year: hypertension stable on treatment; heart disease; qualified under the 391.64 original diabetes or vision waiver programs; the new insulin or vision exemption program; or driving in exempt intracity zones. It is explained that there should also be a shortened duration of certification if there is a determination by the examiner that a condition requires more frequent monitoring, such as diabetes mellitus or sleep disorders.

During several meetings, FMCSA MRB[27] worked on a Fitness for Duty/Multiple Medical Conditions standard (Table 2-1), which was formally recommended to FMCSA in January 2009. In this proposal, drivers with multiple medical conditions should be medically certified for less than 2 years and those with 4 or more medical conditions should not be qualified until one has been resolved. The MRB also recommended that only physicians (MD/DO) should perform the examination on those drivers with two or more potentially disqualifying conditions. This was *only* a recommendation from the MRB and has not been adopted by FMCSA.

TABLE 2-1 Fitness for Duty/Multiple Medical Conditions

Number of Conditions*	Certification
0 or 1	Maximum 2 years
2**	Maximum 1 year
3**	Maximum 6 months
> 4**	Not eligible until resolution of at least one condition

*Diabetes mellitus requiring medication; cardiovascular disease; hypertension; dysrhythmias; obstructive sleep apnea (OSA); body mass index (BMI) > 35 kg/m2; opioid or benzodiazepine use; renal disease; pulmonary disease with pulmonary function test (PFT) abnormality; epilepsy seizure free for > 10 years; musculoskeletal disease requiring medical, surgical, or prosthetic treatment; requirement for visual exemption; stroke; transient ischemic attack (TIA), major psychiatric illness (as defined pending formal review by the MRB); and other conditions as identified by FMCSA.
**Evaluation to be conducted by a CDME who is a licensed MD or DO.
Recommended by the Medical Review Board, January 22, 2009.

J. May I Give a Copy of the MER to the Employer?

The carrier is required to have a copy of the MEC in the driver qualification file but is *not* required to have a copy of the MER. The employer is not prohibited from obtaining this but a Health Insurance Portability and Accountability Act (HIPAA) compliant release would be required. If the employer does obtain a copy of the medical examination, it must be used and maintained consistent with any state or federal laws regarding personal health information.

FAQS FOR NATIONAL REGISTRY DRIVER EXAMINATION FORMS[6]—JANUARY 24, 2017

General Forms Questions

When are Medical Examiners (MEs) required to use the newly revised driver examination forms (i.e., Medical Examination Report (MER) Form, MCSA-5875 and Medical Examiner's Certificate (MEC), Form MCSA-5876)?

The *Medical Examiner's Certification Integration* final rule requires certified MEs to use the newly revised driver examination forms discussed in the final rule beginning December 22, 2015. However, as a result of the unexpected delays in posting the final versions of the newly revised driver examination forms and recognizing that MEs needed to have access to the forms prior to the effective date for a number of reasons, FMCSA published a Federal Register notice on December 21, 2015, allowing MEs to use both the current and newly revised versions of the MER Form, MCSA-5875 and MEC, Form MCSA- 5876 from December 22, 2015 until April 20, 2016 (80 FR 79273).

Where can the newly revised driver examination forms be found/where can copies of the forms be purchased?

Fillable PDF versions of the MER Form, MCSA-5875 and MEC, Form MCSA-5876 are available on the National Registry and FMCSA websites. These forms can be completed by typing into the electronic PDF form or by printing the form and handwriting information onto the hard copy. FMCSA does not provide the forms for purchase. In addition, the ME has the ability to print the MEC, Form MCSA-5876 from the National Registry system if the information is entered at the time of the examination.

Are the newly revised driver examination forms available as a one page document? Are MEs or forms manufacturers allowed to make changes to the newly revised driver examination forms?

Prior to the *Medical Examiner's Certification Integration* final rule, FMCSA allowed results of examinations performed to be recorded "substantially in accordance with" the examination forms provided in the regulation. As a result of the *Medical Examiner's Certification Integration* final rule, use of the MER Form, MCSA-5875 and MEC, Form MCSA-5876 are required and results of examinations must be recorded on these specific forms. These forms have been approved by the Office of Management and Budget and are published in 49 CFR 391.43(f)(2) and (h)(2), and therefore, must be used "as is." However, there are a few minor changes that are permissible (see below).

Permissible changes to the MER Form, MCSA-5875:

1. A bar code may be added to the MER Form, MCSA-5875 for purposes of forms management in the ME's office, as long as it does not obscure any of the content of the MER Form, MCSA-5875.
2. The instructions may be resized, as long as they are readable.
3. The instructions can be made available to the driver and the ME separately from the MER Form, MCSA-5875.
4. The MER Form, MCSA-5875 can be filed/stored without the instructions.
5. The MER Form, MCSA-5875 can be printed in black and white.

Permissible changes to the MEC, Form MCSA-5876:

1. The MEC, Form MCSA-5876 can be reduced in size, as long as all the content is readable.
2. The MEC, Form MCSA-5876 may be printed in black and white.

These are the only changes allowed. Anything other than what is described above is not allowed including, but not limited to, adding company information or a logo, adding a form number, adding a revision date, rearranging content, etc.

How have the commercial motor vehicle (CMV) driver examination forms, including the CMV Driver Medical Examination Results Form, MCSA-5850, changed?

Specific details regarding changes to all of the driver examination forms are included in the sample forms that are located in the Resource Center of the National Registry website. The sample forms posted in the Resource Center, highlight in yellow, all changes made to the driver examination forms as a result of the *Medical Examiner's Certification Integration* final rule. These changes include the collection of additional driver information, new qualification categories, and the ability to input results from examinations performed in accordance with the Federal Motor Carrier Safety Regulations (FMCSRs) with any applicable State variances (which will be valid for intrastate operations).

There are two different qualification selections on the revised driver examination forms (i.e., in accordance with the FMCSRs and in accordance with the FMCSRs with any applicable State variances), how are these to be used?

Certified MEs are trained and certified to conduct examinations and make qualification determinations of CMV drivers according to the interstate physical qualification standards listed in the FMCSRs and should use the qualification selection of "in accordance with the FMCSRs."

MEs that choose to conduct examinations of intrastate only drivers, some from States that require intrastate drivers to be qualified to a set of standards that also includes applicable State variances from the interstate physical qualification standards listed in the FMCSRs, should use the qualification selection of "in accordance with the FMCSRs with any applicable State variances."

It is the responsibility of the ME to determine which standards they are examining and certifying the driver in accordance with. If the ME is willing to conduct examinations for intrastate only drivers, it is the responsibility of the ME to understand the standards for that particular State which may be different from the Federal physical qualification standards.

For examinations performed in accordance with the FMCSRs with any applicable State variances (which will be valid for intrastate operations), are the only qualification options medically qualified and medically unqualified?
Yes.

Should MEs attempt to certify drivers according to the FMCSRs and if they don't qualify, then attempt to certify them according to the State regulations?
The ME should conduct the examination based on the type of qualification the driver requires. If the ME is willing, and understands the standards for that particular State, they may perform an examination based on the State regulations.

Should MEs ask drivers if they plan to operate in interstate or intrastate commerce?
Yes, the ME conducting the examination should ask the driver what type of qualification they require to determine which standards they need to be examined in accordance with. The driver is required to self- certify with the State Driver's Licensing Agencies (SDLAs) in accordance with 49 CFR 383.71(b)(1) if they are operating in intrastate-only and are subject to the State standards, therefore, they should be able to easily answer this question.

Are MEs expected to know what waivers are available for intrastate drivers?
Certified ME's listed on the National Registry are trained and certified in performing examinations on interstate CMV drivers according to the FMCSRs. However, MEs who choose to perform driver examinations for intrastate only drivers who are licensed in States that have variances from the FMCSRs are required to comply with State regulations and statutes for performing those examinations, to include being knowledgeable of State waivers. If examinations for intrastate only drivers are not conducted according to the State requirements, the SDLA may not accept the MEC, Form MCSA-5876 issued and may require the driver to return to the ME or to get another examination.

Why is the examination date not on the CMV Driver Medical Examination Results Form, MCSA- 5850 or the MEC Form, MCSA-5876?

The examination date is on the data collection screen of the CMV Driver Medical Examination Results Form, MCSA-5850. The date of the examination is not on the MEC, Form MCSA-5876, nor has it ever been, because it is not needed. The purpose of the MEC, Form MCSA-5876 is to indicate the date in which the medical qualification of the driver expires.

What do the revision and expiration dates on the top of the driver examination forms mean? Should the forms be used if a later version is present on the FMCSA website?

The revision date on top of the driver examination forms is used internally by FMCSA and indicates the date in which the form was last updated. The expiration date indicates, to the public, the date the information collection approval for the form expires with the Office of Management and Budget. The driver examination forms found on the National Registry and FMCSA websites are the most recent OMB approved versions. However, all versions of the MER Form, MCSA-5875 and MEC, Form MCSA-5876 with a revision date of August 5, 2015, or later, including those with October, November, and December, 2015, revision dates as well as the current version posted on the National Registry and FMCSA websites without a revision date, are acceptable.

Does the driver's address on the driver examination forms need to match the address on the driver's license?

The driver's address listed on the driver examination forms must be the driver's current address which may be different from the address on the driver's license. The driver's current address is used by FMCSA to contact the driver if situations warrant.

Does the driver's address have to be a street address or is a P.O. Box acceptable?

A P.O. Box is acceptable if it is the driver's current address.

In the State/Province area on the driver examination forms, why is "Province" an option?

The State/Province field was expanded to include Canadian Provinces to allow MEs to report examinations conducted on non-CDL drivers from Canada. FMCSA's reciprocity agreement with Canada allows CDL drivers to operate a CMV in the United States without being examined and certified by a ME listed on the National Registry because they are medically examined as part of obtaining a CDL in Canada. Non-CDL drivers in Canada are not required to complete a medical examination. Therefore, in order for non-CDL drivers from Canada to legally operate a CMV in the United States in interstate commerce, they must be examined by a ME on the National Registry and meet the qualified standard standards outlined in the FMCSRs.

Are MEs required to issue MECs to Canadian or Mexican CDL holders?

MEs are not required to issue MECs to Canadian or Mexican CDL holders because they receive their medical examinations as part of the process of obtaining a CDL in Canada and Mexico.

What is meant by "driving in an exempted intra-city zone" on the new driver examination forms?

"Driving in an exempted intra-city zone" is not a new item on the driver examination forms. An exempt intracity zone is the geographic area of a municipality or the commercial zone of that municipality. For purposes of §391.62, a driver may be considered to operate a CMV wholly within an exempt intracity zone notwithstanding any common control, management, or arrangement for a continuous carriage or shipment to or from a point without such zone.

Can MEs print out the electronic form for the patient to complete and sign or does the patient need to complete an electronic signature as they complete their portion?

Either is acceptable. The driver examination forms must be completed and signed, either electronically or by hand.

Are both interstate and intrastate drivers required to be examined and certified by a ME listed on the National Registry?

All interstate CMV drivers are required to be examined and certified by a ME listed on the National Registry. Each individual State makes the determination as to whether or not intrastate drivers must be examined by a certified ME listed on the National Registry.

If the ME finds a driver to be medically unqualified, can the driver get a second opinion?

Yes, a driver always has the option of getting a second opinion. However, if a driver requests a second opinion for a medical qualification determination, the driver must first seek permission from the employer, the employer has the authority to agree or not to agree.

The driver may be required by the employer to seek the second opinion for a medical qualification determination from an employer-preferred certified ME. In cases where the employer has agreed, the second certified ME must be provided with the all of the health history that was provided to the first ME, and the second ME is made aware the driver is seeking a second opinion for a medical qualification determination.

If a MEC was issued by the first ME and the second ME issues a second MEC, the decision rests with the employer as to which MEC to accept.

CMV Driver Medical Examination Results Form, MCSA-5850

Are MEs required to complete the CMV Driver Medical Examination Results Form, MCSA-5850 as it appears in the sample, or is the sample a representation of what the form looks like on the National Registry website when reporting CMV driver examination results?

The sample located on the National Registry website is a representation of the information being collected. The data entry screen for entering CMV driver examination results will look different, but will ask for the same information.

Does the ME always have to complete the CMV Driver Examination Results Form, MCSA-5850?

Yes, completing the CMV Driver Examination Results Form, MCSA-5850 is a regulatory requirement for all certified MEs listed on the National Registry for each interstate CMV driver examination completed.

What happens if a ME does not report examination results as required by the FMCSRs?

The ME is in violation of the FMCSRs which is grounds for removal from the National Registry.

When is it required for the ME to submit information to the National Registry system that no examinations have been completed for the month?

Beginning on June 22, 2015, if the ME does not perform a medical examination of any driver who is required to be examined by a ME listed on the National Registry during any calendar month, the ME must report that fact to FMCSA, via the National Registry website, by the close of business on the last day of such month.

What happens if a ME does not report that they have not performed any examinations?

If the ME does not report that no examinations have been completed for the month, the ME is in violation of the FMCSRs which is grounds for removal from the National Registry.

Medical Examination Report Form, MCSA-5875

On the MER Form, MCSA-5875, is a medical record number required? If not, are MEs allowed to use that space to record driver identification numbers or social security numbers if that is how the MEs office tracks patient records?

No, the medical record number is not required. This space may be left blank or used by the MEs office to record whatever medical record number that is used by their clinic, employee ID, driver ID, or otherwise.

What does the ME enter on page one of the MER Form, MCSA-5875 where it is labeled "Driver ID verified by***"?**

The ME enters the type of photo ID that the ME used to verify the driver's identity, such as a driver's license or passport.

If the driver answers vital questions with "not sure" (e.g., seizure, methadone use), should the ME investigate and change the responses to "yes" and make appropriate medical decisions?
No, the ME may not change a driver's answer on the form because the driver certifies that the information is accurate and complete. The ME should however, initiate dialog regarding "not sure" answers to determine if record review or additional testing is necessary to determine whether the driver is medically qualified. The ME may add information related to "not sure" responses in the comment section located in Section 2, under the Driver Health History Review.

For the question on the MER Form, MCSA-5875 labeled "What surgery have you ever had," is the driver required to record medical history such as an inguinal hernia repair when they were 3 months old?
The driver is required to fully disclose their medical history and report conditions that the certified ME should be aware of, and consider, in making the individual determination whether to issue a MEC, Form MCSA-5876 to a driver. A complete history provides the ME the opportunity to identify potential issues that may require further assessment or consultation with the treating medical professional before rendering a qualification decision. It is left to the discretion of the ME to identify and comment on the responses that may affect the driver's safe operation of a CMV under the Driver Health History Review.

In the medical examination determination section on pages 4 and 5 of the MER Form, MCSA 5875, it appears that corrective lenses, hearing aid, exemptions, etc. are related to the option for "Meets standards, but periodic monitoring required (specify reason)", is this correct?
No, the restrictions and variances apply when the driver is medically qualified.

When selecting "does not meet standards" on the MER Form, MCSA-5875, how long is this in effect?
"Does not meet standards" means the driver is not medically qualified at the time of the examination. Until a certified ME makes a determination that the driver is medically qualified the driver is not able to operate a CMV in interstate commerce. If the driver returns for a physical examination in the future, the ME is responsible for determining whether or not the driver is qualified.

When should the determination pending qualification category be used?
Determination Pending is used when a ME examines a driver and needs more information to make a qualification decision. Using this category provides the ME with up to 45 days to collect the information needed to make a qualification decision.

How should MEs fill out the MER, MCSA-5875 and submit the results of the examination using the CMV Driver Medical Examination Results Form, MCSA-5850 when the determination pending qualification category is used?

FMCSA has provided the following scenario and directions describing how to fill out the MER, MCSA- 5875 and submit the results of the examination using the CMV Driver Medical Examination Results Form, MCSA-5850 when the determination pending qualification category is used:

> On 1/1/16, a ME examined a driver and decided that they need more information before they can determine whether or not the driver is medically qualified. On the MER, MCSA-5875, page 4 for the "Medical Examiner Determination", on the top right corner, the ME enters 1/1/16 as the examination date. The ME selects "determination pending" and specifies the reason. For example, "need additional information regarding specific condition." The ME also selects the box for "return to medical exam office for follow-up on." The driver must return within 45 days. The ME must tell the driver that they are in a determination pending status and that unless the ME receives the additional information and/or sees the determination, the exam will no longer be valid and a new exam must be conducted. The ME may enter a date for the driver to return to their office (follow-up appointment) if that information is available or they may wait until the driver returns to their office and add the date at that time. On the CMV Driver Medical Examination Results Form, MCSA-5850, the ME selects "determination pending" and enters the date of the examination as the 1/1/16 date from the top right corner of the MER, MCSA-5875.

> On 1/15/16, the driver returns to the MEs office and the ME evaluates the information received and/or performs an examination of the driver if the ME determines it is necessary. The ME now has all the information needed to make a qualification determination. On the MER, MCSA-5875, the ME selects the appropriate qualification determination. The ME also selects "medical examination report amended" and specifies the specific amendment(s) that are being made. The ME signs and dates the MER, MCSA-5875 with the 1/15/16 date; this is the date that the ME is amending the MER, MCSA-5875, the date in which the driver has returned to the ME's office. If the ME has made the determination that the driver is qualified, the "Medical Examiner's Certificate Expiration Date" is calculated from the 1/15/16 date, the date that the ME actually signs/issues the MEC, Form MCSA-5876. On the CMV Driver Medical Examination Results Form, MCSA-5850, the ME enters 1/1/16 for the "date of examination", and 1/15/16 for the "date exam results determined" which is the date that the MEC, Form MCSA-5876 is signed/issued if medically qualified or the date that a medically unqualified decision is made. The "medical examiner's certificate expiration date" is calculated from the "date exam results determined" if the driver is found to be medically qualified. This submission of the driver's examination results takes precedence over the initial examination that placed the driver in a determination pending status.

> If the driver does not return on or before the 45-day expiration date and the disposition of determination pending is not updated via the National Registry

on or before the 45-day expiration date, the examination is no longer valid. The driver is required to get a new examination, and in this case, the ME must update the MER, MCSA-5875 for this driver by selecting incomplete examination, specifying the reason, and filing the MER, MCSA-5875 in the driver's record. The ME does not need to submit another CMV Driver Medical Examination Results Form, MCSA-5850 into the National Registry system.

When is a MER, MCSA-5875 allowed to be amended?

A MER, MCSA-5875 is only allowed to be amended when a driver is in a determination pending status for situations where new information (e.g., test results, etc.) has been received or there has been a change in the driver's medical status since the initial examination, but prior to a final qualification determination. When "MER amended" is selected, the ME must provide the reason for the amendment (e.g., received test results), sign and date the MER, MCSA-5875. A MER, MCSA-5875 cannot be amended after an examination has been in determination pending status for more than 45 days or after a final qualification determination has been made. The driver is required to obtain a new medical examination, and a new MER, MCSA-5875 must be completed.

Are MEs allowed to make the determination pending category a shorter duration than 45 days?

Yes, the ME may require the driver to provide the information sooner than 45 days. The ME should enter the date that the information will be required on the line, "Return to medical exam office for follow-up on (must be 45 days or less)." The ME may amend the certification decision at any time during the 45 days by entering the results into the National Registry via the CMV Driver Medical Examination Results, Form MCSA-5850 as Medically Qualified, Medically Unqualified, or Incomplete Examination. If a shorter duration is used, the ME will need to amend the certification decision prior to the end of the duration. Otherwise, the driver's examination will remain in determination pending until the end of 45 days.

If the ME uses a shorter duration than 45 days for the determination pending category, is the same process followed to report the examination results to the National Registry?

No, the process is not the same. If the duration is shorter than 45 days, a certification decision must be made during that time and the results must be reported via the CMV Driver Medical Examination Results, Form MCSA-5850. If the full 45 days is used, the driver's examination will remain in determination pending until the end of the 45 days when the exam will be considered invalid.

When should a ME use determination pending versus issuing a MEC, Form MCSA-5876 with a short qualification timeframe?

The decision whether to use determination pending versus issuing a MEC, Form MCSA-5876 with a short qualification timeframe is up to the discretion of the ME.

How should the ME address the fact that the driver may have to pay for more than one examination by using the determination pending category?

It is the responsibility of the driver to be examined by a certified ME listed on the National Registry for a determination to be made as to whether or not the driver is physically qualified to operate a CMV in interstate commerce. A second examination for determination pending is no different from a driver needing a second examination because he/she was medically unqualified or received a MEC, Form, MCSA-5876 that is only valid for a short period of time such as a 3-month MEC, Form MCSA-5876. In those instances, the driver would still need to go back to the ME for a qualification determination.

Is the ME required to use the determination pending if the driver's MEC, Form MCSA-5876 expires in two days?

The ME is never required to use the determination pending category. Use of this category is discretionary. If a ME chooses to use the determination pending category and the driver has time left on his/her current MEC, Form MCSA-5876, the driver may continue driving until the driver's MEC, Form MCSA-5876 expires, the ME makes a final qualification determination, or the 45 days in determination pending status expires.

If the ME examines the driver and the condition is something that the ME feels is disqualifying, the ME should not use the determination pending category. Instead, the ME should disqualify the driver.

If the ME determines the driver is safe to operate a CMV based on the initial examination and the driver's MEC, Form MCSA-5876 will expire shortly after the initial examination, the ME may issue a short-term MEC, Form MCSA-5876 rather than using the determination pending category.

When "determination pending" is selected, does the ME issue a MEC, Form MCSA-5876 for up to or including 45 days?

No, the determination pending category is only to be used while waiting for additional information to make a qualification determination. If the driver has a current MEC, Form MCSA-5876, the driver may continue to operate; if not, the driver is not authorized to operate a CMV in interstate commerce.

Is a ME able to put a driver into a determination pending status consecutively?

The FMCSRs do not prohibit the ME from using determination pending more than once. However, if the disposition of determination pending is not updated with a qualification decision via the National Registry on or before the 45-day initial pending determination expiration date, the initial examination is no longer valid and the driver is required to get a new medical examination. Therefore, a driver can be placed into a second pending determination status as the result of a new examination.

When a driver is placed into a determination pending category, can the driver go to another certified ME for a second opinion?
Yes, a driver always has the option of getting a second opinion. However, the driver must disclose an accurate and complete medical history. Also, please note that the employer is not required to accept the second opinion.

If a driver can get a second opinion, does the driver need to reveal that to the second ME that another ME has placed them into a determination pending status?
Federal regulations do not require the driver to reveal it. However, the driver must report a complete and accurate health history.

Does a second medical examination need to be completed when the driver returns within the 45-day determination pending timeframe?
The decision as to whether or not to conduct a second medical examination when the driver returns within the 45-day determination pending timeframe is up to the discretion of the ME.

When a driver is placed in determination pending for further testing, is the driver able to return to a different ME in the same practice?
Yes, the driver may return to the original certified ME that placed the driver in the determination pending category or any certified ME in the same practice for the follow up examination. However, the ME is required to submit a new CMV Driver Medical Examination Results Form, MCSA-5850 through their National Registry account to record the results of the examination.

Can the ME provide a driver with a grace period in which the driver's physical examination is placed on hold?
No, the regulations do not allow for a grace period. However, the determination pending category may be used if the ME examines a driver and needs more information to make a qualification decision. Using this category provides the ME with up to 45 days to collect the information needed to make a qualification decision.

How should the incomplete examination result be used?
Incomplete Examination allows the ME to submit examination results for a driver whose medical evaluation was not completed. This includes a driver that may have decided during the examination that he/she did not want to continue the examination and leaves the MEs office. Submitting this type of examination result alerts FMCSA to the possibility of a driver visiting more than one ME to receive a specific desired examination result.

What are the repercussions to a driver who starts an examination with one ME, does not complete his/her examination, and then goes to a second ME for a second certification examination?
The National Registry will have the capability to flag such exams, identify missing or false information reported by the driver in the Driver Health History section of

the MER Form, MCSA-5875, and make a determination to void the driver's MEC, Form MCSA-5876, if appropriate.

The standard for blood pressure is no longer on the MER Form, MCSA-5875. Has it changed, does the standard still apply? If the driver's blood pressure is one or two points greater than 140/90, can the ME qualify the driver?

The blood pressure guidelines, although previously part of the Medical Examination Report, are now part of the Medical Advisory Criteria. The blood pressure guidelines are not, nor have they ever been, regulatory in nature. FMCSA leaves blood pressure criteria decisions up to the discretion of the ME to determine driver qualification.

The Medical Advisory Criteria for Hypertension provides guidance that the MEC may be extended for 3 months when a driver's blood pressure is less than 160/100. Can a MEC still be extended for 3 months?

The Medical Advisory Criteria is guidance and not regulation. The FMCSRs do not provide an option for an extension of the MEC, Form MCSA-5876. If a 3-month MEC, Form MCSA-5876 is issued, it is considered a short-term MEC, not an extension. The length of time that the MEC, Form MCSA-5876 is issued for is determined by the ME and may be issued for up to 2 years.

Medical Examiner's Certificate, Form MCSA-5876

Is the ME required to complete the MEC, Form MCSA-5876 in addition to the MER Form, MCSA-5875, since the medical examiner determination (State or Federal) section of the MER Form,

Yes, MEs must complete a MER Form, MCSA-5875 for each driver they examine. ME's must also complete and issue the original MEC, Form MCSA-5876, to each qualified driver. The MEC, Form MCSA-5876 is not the same as the medical examiner determination (State or Federal) section on the MER, MCSA-5875.

Is the box on the previous Medical Examiner's Certificate titled "Medical Certificate Expiration Date" and the box on the revised MEC, Form MCSA-5876 titled "Medical Examiner's Certificate Expiration Date" the same thing?

Yes, they are the same. On all forms, this box is intended to capture the expiration date of the Medical Examiner's Certificate that is being issued to the driver. The title on the MEC, Form MCSA-5876 was changed by adding the word "examiner" to make it consistent with the title of the form, which is the "Medical Examiner's Certificate." It is not meant to capture the MEs medical license or National Registry certification expiration date.

Should the ME use the end date of the current MEC, Form MCSA-5876 to calculate the new Medical Examiner's Certificate expiration date?

No, the ME should use the date of issuance of the new MEC, Form MCSA-5876 to calculate the Medical Examiner's Certificate expiration date.

If a driver has been issued a MEC, Form MCSA-5876 for three months, returns to the office just before the MEC, Form MCSA-5876 expires, and the ME completes another medical examination and issues the driver a two year MEC, Form MCSA-5876, is the date used to calculate the expiration date on the new MEC, Form MCSA-5876 the date of the second exam?

Yes. The new examination decision supersedes the previous examination.

Are MEs still allowed to issue a one-time 3-month MEC, Form MCSA-5876?

Yes, the duration of every MEC, Form MCSA-5876 issued is up to the discretion of the ME. Therefore, sequential 3-month MEC, Form MCSA-5876 can be issued if the ME determines it necessary.

If a ME disqualifies a driver or provides a short-term MEC, Form MCSA-5876, is the ME required to conduct a complete examination of the driver when they return?

Yes, each time a qualification decision is made, a medical examination is required to be performed as outlined in 49 CFR 391.43 (f)(2).

If a driver is examined and issued a 3-month MEC, Form MCSA-5876 by one ME, can the driver be examined by a different ME the next time or do they need to go back to the same ME?

MCSA-5875 appears to include the same information as displayed on the MEC, Form MCSA. The driver is able to visit any ME listed on the National Registry for their medical examination.

Once the examination is completed, is the ME required to provide the driver with a copy of the completed electronic form?

The ME must provide the driver with the original paper MEC, Form MCSA-5876 (printed or handwritten). Beginning on June 22, 2018, MEs will no longer be required to issue a paper MEC, Form MCSA-5876 to CLP/CDL applicants/holders. FMCSA will electronically transmit the MEC information to the SDLA for posting to the driver's record. However, for non-CLP/CDL applicants/holders, MEs will continue to issue a paper MEC, Form MCSA-5876.

Definitions

What is the definition of commercial learner's permit (CLP)?

49 CFR 383.5 defines CLP as a permit issued to an individual by a State or other jurisdiction of domicile which, when carried with a valid driver's license issued by the same State or jurisdiction, authorizes the individual to operate a class of a commercial motor vehicle when accompanied by a holder of a valid CDL for purposes of behind-the-wheel training.

What is the definition of commercial driver's license (CDL)?

49 CFR 383.5 defines CDL as a license issued by a State or the District of Columbia which authorizes the individual to operate a class of a CMV. A CMV that requires a CDL is one that:

1. has a gross combination weight rating or gross combination weight of 26,001 pounds or more inclusive of a towed unit with a gross vehicle weight rating (GVWR) or gross vehicle weight (GVW) of more than 10,000 pounds; or
2. has a GVWR or GVW of 26,001 pounds or more; or
3. is designed to transport 16 or more passengers, including the driver; or
4. is used to transport either hazardous materials requiring hazardous materials placards on the vehicle or any quantity of a select agent or toxin.

What is the definition of interstate commerce?

49 CFR 390.5 defines interstate commerce as trade, traffic, or transportation in the United States—

1. Between a place in a State and a place outside of such State (including a place outside of the United States);
2. Between two places in a State through another State or a place outside of the United States; or (3) Between two places in a State as part of trade, traffic, or transportation originating or terminating outside the State or the United States.

What is the definition of intrastate commerce?

49 CFR 390.5 defines intrastate commerce as any trade, traffic, or transportation in any State which is not described in the term "interstate commerce."

References

1. Federal Motor Carrier Safety Administration, U.S. Department of Transportation. Commercial Driver's License FAQs: https://ask.fmcsa.dot.gov/app/answers/list/c/24,29.
2. Federal Motor Carrier Safety Administration, U.S. Department of Transportation. Commercial Driver's License: Medical https://www.fmcsa.dot.gov/registration/commercial-drivers-license/medical
3. Federal Motor Carrier Safety Administration, U.S. Department of Transportation. Medical Frequently Asked Questions. https://www.fmcsa.dot.gov/faq/Medical-Requirements.

4. U.S. Department of Transportation. North American Free Trade Agreement—
   U.S. Department of Transportation Regulations. https://www.fmcsa.dot.gov
   /sites/fmcsa.dot.gov/files/docs/NAFTA_Fact_Sheet_508CLN.pdf.
5. 49 CFR 391.41(a)(1)(i). Physical qualifications for drivers. https://www.ecfr.gov
   /cgi-bin/retrieveECFR?gp=1&ty=HTML&h=L&mc=true&=PART&n=pt49.5
   .391#se49.5.391_141.
6. Federal Motor Carrier Safety Administration, U.S. Department of Transportation. FAQs for National Registry Driver Examination Forms. January 24, 2017.
   https://nationalregistry.fmcsa.dot.gov/ResourceCenter/documents/FAQs
   %20National%20Registry%20Driver%20Examination%20Forms.pdf.
7. Federal Motor Carrier Safety Administration, U.S. Department of Transportation. Guidance for § 391.45: Persons who must be medically examined and
   certified. https://www.fmcsa.dot.gov/regulations/title49/section/391.45.
8. Federal Motor Carrier Safety Administration, U.S. Department of Transportation. Guidance for § 391.41: Physical qualifications for drivers. https://www
   .fmcsa.dot.gov/regulations/title49/section/391.41.
9. National Registry of Certified Medical Examiners, Notice of proposed rulemaking, request for comments. Federal Motor Carrier Safety Administration,
   U.S. Department of Transportation. *Fed Reg.* 2008;73(Dec. 1):73129–73147.
   https://www.fmcsa.dot.gov/regulations/rulemaking/E8-28172.
10. National Registry of Certified Medical Examiners. Final Rule. Federal Motor
    Carrier Safety Administration, U.S. Department of Transportation. *Fed Reg.*
    Vol 77, No. 77. April 20, 2012; 24104-24135. https://www.gpo.gov/fdsys/pkg/FR
    -2012-04-20/pdf/2012-9034.pdf.
11. Federal Motor Carrier Safety Administration, U.S. Department of Transpor-
    tation. National Registry of Certified Medical Examiners Frequently Asked
    Questions. https://nationalregistry.fmcsa.dot.gov/ResourceCenter/documents
    /National_Registry_FAQ.pdf
12. Federal Motor Carrier Safety Administration, U.S. Department of Transporta-
    tion. Process for Department of Veterans Affairs (VA) Physicians to Be Added
    to the National Registry of Certified Medical Examiners. Federal Motor Carrier
    Safety Administration, U.S. Department of Transportation. Notice of pro-
    posed rulemaking. [Docket No. FMCSA–2016–0333]. *Fed Reg.* December 1,
    2016: 86673–86684. https://www.gpo.gov/fdsys/pkg/FR-2016-12-01/pdf/2016
    -28746.pdf.
13. Federal Motor Carrier Safety Administration, U.S. Department of Transpor-
    tation. National Registry of Certified Medical Examiners Complete Guide
    to Medical Examiner Certification. https://nationalregistry.fmcsa.dot.gov
    /ResourceCenter/documents/Complete_Guide_to_ME_Certification.pdf.
14. Federal Motor Carrier Safety Administration, U.S. Department of Transporta-
    tion. Fact Sheet—Medical Examiner. https://nationalregistry.fmcsa.dot.gov
    /ResourceCenter/documents/FactSheetMedical_Examiners.pdf.
15. Federal Motor Carrier Safety Administration, U.S. Department of Transportation.
    National Registry of Certified Medical Examiners. Refresher Training Statement.
    December 19, 2016. https://nationalregistry.fmcsa.dot.gov/ResourceCenter
    /documents/FMCSA-emails/RefresherTrainingStatementemail.pdf.

16. Federal Motor Carrier Safety Administration, U.S. Department of Transportation. National Registry of Certified Medical Examiners Resource Center. https://nationalregistry.fmcsa.dot.gov/ResourceCenter/.
17. American College of Occupational and Environmental Medicine. Continuing Education. https://www.acoem.org/ACOEMNewsletters.aspx.
18. Federal Motor Carrier Safety Administration, U.S. Department of Transportation. National Registry of Certified Medical Examiners. Clarification Regarding Alterations to Driver Examination Forms. December 2, 2016. https://nationalregistry.fmcsa.dot.gov/ResourceCenter/documents/FMCSA -emails/ClarificationRegardingAlterationstoDriverExaminationForms.pdf.
19. Federal Motor Carrier Safety Administration, U.S. Department of Transportation. Physical Qualifications and Examinations: Medical Examination Report and Medical Examiner's Certificate Forms. Federal Motor Carrier Safety Administration, U.S. Department of Transportation. Notice of decision on use of Medical Examination Report and Medical Examiner's Certificate Forms. [Docket FMCSA–2012–0178]. *Fed Reg.* October 27, 2016: 74700- 74711. https://www.gpo.gov/fdsys/pkg/FR-2016-10-27/pdf/2016-25976.pdf.
20. Federal Motor Carrier Safety Administration, U.S. Department of Transportation. National Registry of Certified Medical Examiners. Clarification of Changes to the Driver Examination Forms. November 17, 2016. https://nationalregistry.fmcsa.dot.gov/ResourceCenter/documents/FMCSA -emails/ClarificationofChangestotheDriverExaminationFormsEmail111716.pdf.
21. American College of Occupational and Environmental Medicine. CDME Review (Spring 2017).
22. Appendix A to Part 391—Medical Advisory Criteria. http://www.ecfr.gov/cgi -bin/text-idx?SID=acae60ac272c7c329e4926be905433c5&mc=true&node=pt49 .5.391&rgn=div5#ap49.5.391_171.a.
23. Federal Motor Carrier Safety Administration, U.S. Department of Transportation. Medical Examiner Handbook, currently in the process of revision. https://www.fmcsa.dot.gov/regulations/medical/fmcsa-medical-examiner -handbook.
24. Federal Motor Carrier Safety Administration, U.S. Department of Transportation. Medical Review Board. https://www.fmcsa.dot.gov/mrb.
25. Federal Motor Carrier Safety Administration, U.S. Department of Transportation. Driver Exemption Programs. https://www.fmcsa.dot.gov/medical/driver -medical-requirements/driver-exemption-programs.
26. Federal Motor Carrier Safety Administration, U.S. Department of Transportation. Qualifications of Drivers; Diabetes standard. Advanced notice of proposed rulemaking. Federal Motor Carrier Safety Administration, U.S. Department of Transportation. [Docket FMCSA– 2005–23151]. *Fed Reg.* May 4, 2015: 25260- 25272. https://www.fmcsa.dot.gov/regulations/rulemaking/2015-09993.
27. Federal Motor Carrier Safety Administration, U.S. Department of Transportation. Summary for the January 22, 2009, Medical Review Board Public Meeting. www.mrb.fmcsa.dot.gov/documents/FinalJan122009_MRB_Meeting_Sum _Certified4-22-09.pdf.

CHAPTER 3

Regulations, Advisory Criteria, Interpretations, and Frequently Asked Questions

NATALIE P. HARTENBAUM, MD, MPH, FACOEM

Since the prior edition of this book, the Commercial Driver Medical Examiner (CDME) processes have undergone significant changes, mostly related to the National Registry of Certified Medical Examiners (NRCME). In 2014, the Federal Motor Carrier Safety Administration Medical Examiner Handbook (ME Handbook) was taken off the Federal Motor Carrier Safety Administration (FMCSA) website for update and revision. As this edition is being prepared, examiners still should consider guidance from the prior handbook, as that is what is being taught in the training programs, but should base their final decision on current best medical practice remembering that our ultimate responsibility is to ensure the safety of the motoring public to the extent reasonably possible. Chapters will include information from the most recent ME Handbook, Medical Expert Panel (MEP) reports, and Medical Review Board (MRB) recommendations as well as other relevant reports and literature.

The regulations, guidelines and frequently asked questions in the print version of this book are current as of the date of publication. As significant changes occur, they will be noted at the end of each chapter in the online version of this book at least twice a year.

Since the first edition of this guide was published, the amount of information that the examiner is expected to consider has increased substantially. Prior to around 2000, most examiners thought the only information they needed to know was included on the two-sided, one-sheet examination form. When the form was updated in 2000,[1] it included the driver's role, the advisory criteria, and referenced the conference reports;[2] examiners then became aware of the additional information. Now with the National Registry of Certified Medical Examiners (NRCME), examiners should have been trained on at least the regulations, guidelines, interpretations,[3,4] and other information issued by the Federal Motor Carrier Safety Administration (FMCSA), much of it included in the FMCSA Medical Examiner Handbook,[5] which is currently down for revision. While not required to be considered by examiners, many believe that the Medical Expert Panel reports and recommendations[6] and those of the Medical Review Board[7] constitute current best practice and should at least be considered during the certification determination. With the most recent revision to the medical examination form, the advisory criteria was again removed with the expectation that all examiners were familiar with this information through their NRCME training. FMCSA is currently in the process of a regulatory review, during which many of the frequently asked questions (FAQs) and interpretations may be updated.

This chapter includes most of the regulations relevant to the commercial driver medical certification program. There is guidance for many of the standards on the FMCSA website, which are also included here under the related standard. The Medical Advisory Criteria is now found in Appendix A to 390.41. Medical program FAQs[8] and general FAQs on the NRCME[9] are included in this chapter, while FAQs on the forms are in the Examination chapter.

In the print edition of this book, these are only as current as the most recent print date. The online version will be periodically updated as the information changes.

Most states have adopted FMCSA medical criteria to some extent for their intrastate (commerce within a single state) commercial driver's license (CDL) holders. Some states may have exemptions, waivers, or grandfather programs for some drivers. Examiners must be familiar with the intrastate medical criteria for their state and for surrounding states. The determination of whether the driver is operating in intrastate or interstate (between states) is dependent not on the geographic scope of driving but on whether the commerce (the property being transported) is interstate.

Note that the weight used to define a commercial vehicle in the Federal Motor Carrier Safety Regulations (FMCSRs; which includes the medical requirements) in 49 CFR 390.5 differs from that found in 49 CFR 382 (Controlled Substances and Alcohol Use and Testing) and 383 (Commercial Driver's License). In the sections on controlled substance testing and CDL, a commercial motor vehicle is defined as a motor vehicle or combination of motor vehicles used in commerce to transport passengers or property if the motor vehicle:

(1) has a gross combination weight rating of 11,794 or more kilograms (26,001 or more pounds) inclusive of a towed unit with a gross vehicle weight rating of more than 4,536 kilograms (10,000 pounds); or

(2) has a gross vehicle weight rating of 11,794 or more kilograms (26,001 or more pounds); or

(3) is designed to transport 16 or more passengers, including the driver; or

(4) is of any size and is used in the transportation of materials found to be hazardous for the purposes of the Hazardous Materials Transportation Act (49 U.S.C. 5103(b)) and which require the motor vehicle to be placarded under the Hazardous Materials Regulations (49 CFR part 172, subpart F).

While there is overlap in drivers who require a CDL and drug testing, differences include the weight of the vehicle and the number of passengers the vehicle is designed to transport. The criteria for determining which drivers require a medical examination is found in 49 CFR 390.5 below.

I have only included the most relevant portions of 390.5. "* * *" indicates there are sections that have not been included.[1]

Title 49—Transportation

Chapter III— PART 390—FEDERAL MOTOR CARRIER SAFETY REGULATIONS; GENERAL – Current as of November 9, 2016

§390.3 General applicability.

(a) (1) The rules in subchapter B of this chapter are applicable to all employers, employees, and commercial motor vehicles that transport property or passengers in interstate commerce.

* * *

(d) *Additional requirements.* Nothing in subchapter B of this chapter shall be construed to prohibit an employer from requiring and enforcing more stringent requirements relating to safety of operation and employee safety and health.

* * *

(f) *Exceptions.* Unless otherwise specifically provided, the rules in this subchapter do not apply to—

(1) All school bus operations as defined in §390.5, except for the provisions of §§391.15(e) and (f), 392.80, and 392.82 of this chapter.

(2) Transportation performed by the Federal government, a State, or any political subdivision of a State, or an agency established under a compact between States that has been approved by the Congress of the United States;

(3) The occasional transportation of personal property by individuals not for compensation nor in the furtherance of a commercial enterprise;

(4) The transportation of human corpses or sick and injured persons;

(5) The operation of fire trucks and rescue vehicles while involved in emergency and related operations;

(6) The operation of commercial motor vehicles designed or used to transport between 9 and 15 passengers (including the driver), not for direct compensation, provided the vehicle does not otherwise meet the definition of a commercial motor vehicle, except that motor carriers and drivers operating such vehicles are required to comply with §§390.15, 390.19, 390.21(a) and (b)(2), 391.15(e) and (f), 392.80 and 392.82 of this chapter.

(7) Either a driver of a commercial motor vehicle used primarily in the transportation of propane winter heating fuel or a driver of a motor vehicle used to respond to a pipeline emergency, if such regulations would prevent the driver from responding to an emergency condition requiring immediate response as defined in §390.5.

Guidance for § 390.3: General applicability. (only those related to medical examination)

QUESTION 1: Does the government exception in §390.3(f)(2) apply to motor carriers doing business with the government?

GUIDANCE: No. The exception applies only when the government is the motor carrier.

QUESTION 2: Are the FMCSRs applicable to drivers and CMVs which transport tools, equipment, and supplies across State lines in a CMV?

GUIDANCE: Yes, the FMCSRs are applicable to drivers and CMVs in interstate commerce which transport property. The property in this situation is the tools, equipment, and supplies.

QUESTION 3: Are the operations of a church which provides bus tours to the general public for compensation subject to the FMCSRs as a for-hire motor carrier?

GUIDANCE: Yes, the church is a for-hire motor carrier of passengers subject to the FMCSRs.

QUESTION 4: Are the FMCSRs applicable to the rail movement of trailers and inter modal container chassis that previously or subsequently were moved by highway by a motor carrier in interstate commerce?

GUIDANCE: No. They are only subject when being moved as a motor vehicle by highway by a motor carrier.

QUESTION 5: Are personnel involved in road testing CMVs across a State line subject to the FMCSRs?

GUIDANCE: Yes, any driver (including mechanics, technicians, driver trainees and other personnel) operating a CMV in interstate commerce must be in compliance with the FMCSRs.

QUESTION 6: How does one distinguish between intra- and interstate commerce for the purposes of applicability of the FMCSRs?

GUIDANCE: Interstate commerce is determined by the essential character of the movement, manifested by the shipper's fixed and persistent intent at the time of shipment, and is ascertained from all of the facts and circumstances surrounding the transportation. When the intent of the transportation being performed is interstate in nature, even when the route is within the boundaries of a single State, the driver and CMV are subject to the FMCSRs.

QUESTION 7: Are Red Cross vehicles/drivers subject to the FMCSRs?

GUIDANCE: Red Cross vehicles/drivers used to provide emergency relief under the provisions of §390.23 are not subject to the FMCSRs while providing the relief. However, these vehicles/drivers would be subject when operating at other times, provided they are used in interstate commerce and the vehicles meet the definition of a CMV.

* * *

QUESTION 9: Are the FMCSRs applicable to drivers/vehicles operated by a State or local educational institution which is apolitical subdivision of the State?

GUIDANCE: §390.3(f)(2) specifically exempts transportation performed by a State or a political subdivision including any agency of a State or locality from the FMCSRs. The drivers, however, may be subject to the CDL requirements and/or State laws that are similar to the FMCSRs.

QUESTION 10: Are the FMCSRs applicable to drivers/vehicles operated by a transit authority owned and operated by a State or a political subdivision of the State?

GUIDANCE: §390.3(f)(2) specifically exempts transportation performed by the Federal Government, a State, or any political subdivision of a State from the FMCSRs. However, this exemption does not apply to the CDL requirements in part 383. Also, if governmental entities engage in interstate charter transportation of passengers, they must comply with accident report retention requirements of part 390.

QUESTION 11: Is the interstate transportation of students, teachers and parents to school events such as athletic contests and field trips performed

by municipalities subject to the FMCSRs? If a fee is charged to defer the municipality's expenses, does this affect the applicability of the regulations?

GUIDANCE: §390.3(f)(2) specifically exempts transportation performed by the Federal Government, a State, or any political subdivision of a State from the FMCSRs. Charging a fee to defer governmental costs does not affect this exemption. However, this exemption does not apply to the CDL requirements in part 383. Also, if governmental entities engage in interstate charter transportation of passengers, they must comply with accident report retention requirements of part 390.

* * *

QUESTION 14: What is the applicability of the FMCSRs to motor carriers owning and operating school buses that contract with a municipality to provide pupil transportation services?

GUIDANCE: For the purposes of the FMCSRs, parts 390-399, "school bus operation" means the use of a school bus to transport school children and/or school personnel from home to school and from school to home. A "school bus" is a passenger motor vehicle designed to carry more than 10 passengers in addition to the driver, and used primarily for school bus operations (see §390.5). School bus operations and transportation performed by government entities are specifically exempted from the FMCSRs under §390.3(f).

However, anyone operating school buses under contract with a school is a for-hire motor carrier. When a nongovernment, for-hire motor carrier transports children to school-related functions other than "school bus operation" such as sporting events, class trips, etc., and operates across State lines, its operation must be conducted in accordance with the FMCSRs. This applies to motor carriers that operate CMVs as defined under part 390 which includes vehicles which have a GVWR of 10,001 pounds or more or are designed or used to carry passengers for compensation, except 6-passenger taxicabs not operating on fixed routes.

In certain instances, carriers providing school bus transportation are not subject to the Bus Regulatory Reform Act of 1982 and the minimum financial responsibility requirements (part 387) issued under this Act. Transportation of school children and teachers that is organized, sponsored, and paid for by the school district is not subject to part 387. Therefore, school bus contractors must comply with the FMCSRs for interstate trips such as sporting events and class trips but are not required by Federal regulations to carry a specific level of insurance coverage.

For those operations provided by school bus contractors that are subject to the FMCSRs, the motor carriers must keep driver and vehicle records as required by the regulations. This would include driver qualifications records (part 391), driver records of duty status (part 395), accident report retention (part 390), and inspection, repair, and maintenance records (part 396) for the drivers and vehicles that are used on the trips that are subject to the FMCSRs. These records are not required under the FMCSRs for the other vehicles in the motor carrier's fleet that are not subject to the regulations.

§390.5 Definitions.

* * *

Commercial motor vehicle means any self-propelled or towed motor vehicle used on a highway in interstate commerce to transport passengers or property when the vehicle—

(1) Has a gross vehicle weight rating or gross combination weight rating, or gross vehicle weight or gross combination weight, of 4,536 kg (10,001 pounds) or more, whichever is greater; or

(2) Is designed or used to transport more than 8 passengers (including the driver) for compensation; or

(3) Is designed or used to transport more than 15 passengers, including the driver, and is not used to transport passengers for compensation; or

(4) Is used in transporting material found by the Secretary of Transportation to be hazardous under 49 U.S.C. 5103 and transported in a quantity requiring placarding under regulations prescribed by the Secretary under 49 CFR, subtitle B, chapter I, subchapter C.

Exempt intracity zone means the geographic area of a municipality or the commercial zone of that municipality described in appendix F to subchapter B of this chapter. The term "exempt intracity zone" does not include any municipality or commercial zone in the State of Hawaii. For purposes of §391.62, a driver may be considered to operate a commercial motor vehicle wholly within an exempt intracity zone notwithstanding any common control, management, or arrangement for a continuous carriage or shipment to or from a point without such zone.

* * *

Interstate commerce means trade, traffic, or transportation in the United States—

(1) Between a place in a State and a place outside of such State (including a place outside of the United States);

(2) Between two places in a State through another State or a place outside of the United States; or

(3) Between two places in a State as part of trade, traffic, or transportation originating or terminating outside the State or the United States.

Intrastate commerce means any trade, traffic, or transportation in any State which is not described in the term "interstate commerce."

* * *

Medical examiner means the following:

(1) For medical examinations conducted before May 21, 2014, a person who is licensed, certified, and/or registered, in accordance with applicable State laws and regulations, to perform physical examinations. The term includes but is not limited to, doctors of medicine, doctors of osteopathy, physician assistants, advanced practice nurses, and doctors of chiropractic.

(2) For medical examinations conducted on and after May 21, 2014, an individual certified by FMCSA and listed on the National Registry of Certified Medical Examiners in accordance with subpart D of this part.

Medical variance means a driver has received one of the following from FMCSA that allows the driver to be issued a medical certificate:

(1) An exemption letter permitting operation of a commercial motor vehicle pursuant to part 381, subpart C, of this chapter or §391.64 of this chapter;

(2) A skill performance evaluation certificate permitting operation of a commercial motor vehicle pursuant to §391.49 of this chapter.

* * *

School bus means a passenger motor vehicle which is designed or used to carry more than 10 passengers in addition to the driver, and which the Secretary determines is likely to be significantly used for the purpose of transporting preprimary, primary, or secondary school students to such schools from home or from such schools to home.

School bus operation means the use of a school bus to transport only school children and/or school personnel from home to school and from school to home.

* * *

State means a State of the United States and the District of Columbia and includes a political subdivision of a State.

United States means the 50 States and the District of Columbia.

Guidance for § 390.5: Definitions.

QUESTION 6: Is transporting an empty CMV across State lines for purposes of repair and maintenance considered interstate commerce?

GUIDANCE: Yes. The FMCSRs are applicable to drivers and CMVs in interstate commerce which transport property. The property in this situation is the empty CMV.

* * *

QUESTION 9: Are mobile cranes operating in interstate commerce considered CMVs, and are they subject to the FMCSRs?

GUIDANCE: The definition of CMV encompasses mobile cranes. Unlike the off-road motorized construction equipment discussed in Guidance Questions 7 and 8 above, mobile cranes are readily capable of traveling at highway speeds, over extended distances, and in the mixed traffic of public highways. Although the functions a crane performs are distinct from the transportation provided by a truck, the ready mobility of the crane depends on its permanent integration with a truck chassis. The truck chassis is equipped with wheels, tires, brakes, a suspension system, and other components. The mobile crane itself, like an empty CMV (see Guidance Question 6), is considered property.

Subpart D—National Registry of Certified Medical Examiners

Source: 77 FR 24127, Apr. 20, 2012, unless otherwise noted.

§390.101 Scope.

The rules in this subpart establish the minimum qualifications for FMCSA certification of a medical examiner and for listing the examiner on FMCSA's National Registry of Certified Medical Examiners. The National Registry of Certified Medical Examiners Program is designed to improve highway safety and operator health by requiring that medical examiners be trained and certified to determine effectively whether an operator meets FMCSA physical qualification standards under part 391 of this chapter. One component of the National Registry Program is the registry itself, which is a national database of names and contact information for medical examiners who are certified by FMCSA to perform medical examinations of operators.

§390.103 Eligibility requirements for medical examiner certification.

(a) To receive medical examiner certification from FMCSA a person must:
    (1) Be licensed, certified, or registered in accordance with applicable State laws and regulations to perform physical examinations. The applicant must be an advanced practice nurse, doctor of chiropractic, doctor of medicine, doctor of osteopathy, physician assistant, or other medical professional authorized by applicable State laws and regulations to perform physical examinations.
    (2) Complete a training program that meets the requirements of §390.105.
    (3) Pass the medical examiner certification test provided by FMCSA and administered by a testing organization that meets the requirements of §390.107 and that has electronically forwarded to FMCSA the applicant's completed test and application information no more than three years after completion of the training program required by paragraph (a)(2) of this section. An applicant must not take the test more than once every 30 days.

(b) If a person has medical examiner certification from FMCSA, then to renew such certification the medical examiner must remain qualified under paragraph (a)(1) of this section and complete additional testing and training as required by §390.111(a) (5).

§390.105 Medical examiner training programs.

An applicant for medical examiner certification must complete a training program that:

(a) Is conducted by a training provider that:

(1) Is accredited by a nationally recognized medical profession accrediting organization to provide continuing education units; and

(2) Meets the following administrative requirements:

    (i) Provides training participants with proof of participation.

    (ii) Provides FMCSA point of contact information to training participants.

(b) Provides training to medical examiners on the following topics:

(1) Background, rationale, mission, and goals of the FMCSA medical examiner's role in reducing crashes, injuries, and fatalities involving commercial motor vehicles.

(2) Familiarization with the responsibilities and work environment of commercial motor vehicle operation.

(3) Identification of the operator and obtaining, reviewing, and documenting operator medical history, including prescription and over-the-counter medications.

(4) Performing, reviewing, and documenting the operator's medical examination.

(5) Performing, obtaining, and documenting additional diagnostic tests or medical opinion from a medical specialist or treating physician.

(6) Informing and educating the operator about medications and non-disqualifying medical conditions that require remedial care.

(7) Determining operator certification outcome and period for which certification should be valid.

(8) FMCSA reporting and documentation requirements.

Guidance on the core curriculum specifications for use by training providers is available from FMCSA.

§390.107 Medical examiner certification testing.

An applicant for medical examiner certification or recertification must apply, in accordance with the minimum specifications for application elements established by FMCSA, to a testing organization that meets the following criteria:

(a) The testing organization has documented policies and procedures that:

(1) Use secure protocols to access, process, store, and transmit all test items, test forms, test data, and candidate information and ensure access by authorized personnel only.

(2) Ensure testing environments are reasonably comfortable and have minimal distractions.

(3) Prevent to the greatest extent practicable the opportunity for a test taker to attain a passing score by fraudulent means.

(4) Ensure that test center staff who interact with and proctor examinees or provide technical support have completed formal training, demonstrate competency, and are monitored periodically for quality assurance in testing procedures.

(5) Accommodate testing of individuals with disabilities or impairments to minimize the effect of the disabilities or impairments while maintaining the security of the test and data.

(b) Testing organizations that offer testing of examinees not at locations that are operated and staffed by the organizations but by means of remote, computer-based systems must, in addition to the requirements of paragraph (a) of this section, ensure that such systems:

(1) Provide a means to authenticate the identity of the person taking the test.

(2) Provide a means for the testing organization to monitor the activity of the person taking the test.

(3) Do not allow the person taking the test to reproduce or record the contents of the test by any means.

(c) The testing organization has submitted its documented policies and procedures as defined in paragraph (a) of this section and, if applicable, paragraph (b) of this section to FMCSA and agreed to future reviews by FMCSA to ensure compliance with the criteria listed in this section.

(d) The testing organization administers only the currently authorized version of the medical examiner certification test developed and furnished by FMCSA.

[77 FR 24127, Apr. 20, 2012, as amended at 78 FR 58483, Sept. 24, 2013]

---

§390.109 Issuance of the FMCSA medical examiner certification credential.

Upon compliance with the requirements of §390.103(a) or (b), FMCSA will issue to a medical examiner applicant an FMCSA medical examiner certification credential with a unique National Registry Number and will add the medical examiner's name to the National Registry of Certified Medical Examiners. The certification credential will expire 10 years after the date of its issuance.

---

§390.111 Requirements for continued listing on the National Registry of Certified Medical Examiners.

(a) To continue to be listed on the National Registry of Certified Medical Examiners, each medical examiner must:

(1) Continue to meet the requirements of this subpart and the applicable requirements of part 391 of this chapter.

(2) Report to FMCSA any changes in the application information submitted under §390.103(a)(3) within 30 days of the change.

(3) Continue to be licensed, certified, or registered, and authorized to perform physical examinations, in accordance with the applicable laws and regulations of each State in which the medical examiner performs examinations.

(4) Maintain documentation of State licensure, registration, or certification to perform physical examinations for each State in which the examiner performs examinations and maintain documentation of and completion of all training required by this section and §390.105. The medical examiner must make this documentation available to an authorized representative of FMCSA or an authorized representative of Federal, State, or local government. The medical examiner must provide this documentation within 48 hours of the request for investigations and within 10 days of the request for regular audits of eligibility.

(5) Maintain medical examiner certification by completing training and testing according to the following schedule:

    (i) No sooner than 4 years and no later than 5 years after the date of issuance of the medical examiner certification credential, complete periodic training as specified by FMCSA.

    (ii) No sooner than 9 years and no later than 10 years after the date of issuance of the medical examiner certification credential:

        (A) Complete periodic training as specified by FMCSA; and

        (B) Pass the test required by §390.103(a)(3).

(b) FMCSA will issue a new medical examiner certification credential valid for 10 years to a medical examiner who complies with paragraphs (a)(1) through (4) of this section and who successfully completes the training and testing as required by paragraphs (a)(5)(i) and (ii) of this section.

§390.113 Reasons for removal from the National Registry of Certified Medical Examiners.

FMCSA may remove a medical examiner from the National Registry of Certified Medical Examiners when a medical examiner fails to meet or maintain the qualifications established by this subpart, the requirements of other regulations applicable to the medical examiner, or otherwise does not meet the requirements of 49 U.S.C. 31149. The reasons for removal may include, but are not limited to:

(a) The medical examiner fails to comply with the requirements for continued listing on the National Registry of Certified Medical Examiners, as described in §390.111.

(b) FMCSA finds that there are errors, omissions, or other indications of improper certification by the medical examiner of an operator in either the completed Medical Examination Reports or the medical examiner's certificates.

(c) The FMCSA determines the medical examiner issued a medical examiner's certificate to an operator of a commercial motor vehicle who failed to meet the applicable standards at the time of the examination.

(d) The medical examiner fails to comply with the examination requirements in §391.43 of this chapter.

(e) The medical examiner falsely claims to have completed training in physical and medical examination standards as required by this subpart.

§390.115 Procedure for removal from the National Registry of Certified Medical Examiners.

(a) **Voluntary removal.** To be voluntarily removed from the National Registry of Certified Medical Examiners, a medical examiner must submit a request to the FMCSA Director, Office of Carrier, Driver and Vehicle Safety Standards. Except as provided in paragraph (b) of this section, the Director, Office of Carrier, Driver and Vehicle Safety Standards will accept the request and the removal will become effective immediately. On and after the date of issuance of a notice of proposed removal from the National Registry of Certified Medical Examiners, as described in paragraph (b) of this section, however, the Director, Office of Carrier, Driver and Vehicle Safety Standards will not approve the medical examiner's request for voluntary removal from the National Registry of Certified Medical Examiners.

(b) **Notice of proposed removal.** Except as provided by paragraphs (a) and (e) of this section, FMCSA initiates the process for removal of a medical examiner from the National Registry of Certified Medical Examiners by issuing a written notice of proposed removal to the medical examiner, stating the reasons that removal is proposed under §390.113 and any corrective actions necessary for the medical examiner to remain listed on the National Registry of Certified Medical Examiners.

(c) **Response to notice of proposed removal and corrective action.** A medical examiner who has received a notice of proposed removal from the National Registry of Certified Medical Examiners must submit any written response to the Director, Office of Carrier, Driver and Vehicle Safety Standards no later than 30 days after the date of Issuance of the notice of proposed removal. The response must indicate either that the medical examiner believes FMCSA has relied on erroneous reasons, in whole or in part, in proposing removal from the National Registry of Certified Medical Examiners, as described in paragraph (c)(1) of this section, or that the medical examiner will comply and take any corrective action specified in the notice of proposed removal, as described in paragraph (c)(2) of this section.

    (1) **Opposing a notice of proposed removal.** If the medical examiner believes FMCSA has relied on an erroneous reason, in whole or in part, in proposing removal from the National Registry of Certified Medical Examiners, the medical examiner must explain the basis for his or her belief that FMCSA relied on an erroneous reason in proposing the removal. The Director, Office of Carrier, Driver and Vehicle Safety Standards will review the explanation.

        (i) If the Director, Office of Carrier, Driver and Vehicle Safety Standards finds FMCSA has wholly relied on an erroneous reason for proposing removal from the National Registry of Certified Medical Examiners, the Director, Office of Carrier, Driver and Vehicle Safety Standards will withdraw the notice of proposed removal and notify the medical examiner in writing of the determination. If the Director, Office of Carrier, Driver and Vehicle Safety Standards finds FMCSA has partly relied on an erroneous reason for proposing removal from the National Registry of Certified Medical Examiners, the Director, Office of Carrier, Driver and Vehicle Safety Standards will modify the notice of proposed removal and notify the medical examiner in writing of the determination. No later than 60 days after the date the Director, Office of Carrier, Driver and Vehicle Safety Standards modifies a notice of proposed removal, the medical examiner must comply with this subpart and correct any deficiencies identified in the modified notice of proposed removal as described in paragraph (c)(2) of this section.

(ii) If the Director, Office of Carrier, Driver and Vehicle Safety Standards finds FMCSA has not relied on an erroneous reason in proposing removal, the Director, Office of Carrier, Driver and Vehicle Safety Standards will affirm the notice of proposed removal and notify the medical examiner in writing of the determination. No later than 60 days after the date the Director, Office of Carrier, Driver and Vehicle Safety Standards affirms the notice of proposed removal, the medical examiner must comply with this subpart and correct the deficiencies identified in the notice of proposed removal as described in paragraph (c)(2) of this section.

(iii) If the medical examiner does not submit a written response within 30 days of the date of issuance of a notice of proposed removal, the removal becomes effective and the medical examiner is immediately removed from the National Registry of Certified Medical Examiners.

(2) **Compliance and corrective action.**

(i) The medical examiner must comply with this subpart and complete the corrective actions specified in the notice of proposed removal no later than 60 days after either the date of issuance of the notice of proposed removal or the date the Director, Office of Carrier, Driver and Vehicle Safety Standards affirms or modifies the notice of proposed removal, whichever is later. The medical examiner must provide documentation of compliance and completion of the corrective actions to the Director, Office of Carrier, Driver and Vehicle Safety Standards. The Director, Office of Carrier, Driver and Vehicle Safety Standards may conduct any investigations and request any documentation necessary to verify that the medical examiner has complied with this subpart and completed the required corrective action(s). The Director, Office of Carrier, Driver and Vehicle Safety Standards will notify the medical examiner in writing whether he or she has met the requirements to continue to be listed on the National Registry of Certified Medical Examiners.

(ii) If the medical examiner fails to complete the proposed corrective action(s) within the 60-day period, the removal becomes effective and the medical examiner is immediately removed from the National Registry of Certified Medical Examiners. The Director, Office of Carrier, Driver and Vehicle Safety Standards will notify the person in writing that he or she has been removed from the National Registry of Certified Medical Examiners.

(3) At any time before a notice of proposed removal from the National Registry of Certified Medical Examiners becomes final, the recipient of the notice of proposed removal and the Director, Office of Carrier, Driver and Vehicle Safety Standards may resolve the matter by mutual agreement.

(d) **Request for administrative review.** If a person has been removed from the National Registry of Certified Medical Examiners under paragraph (c)(1)(iii), (c)(2)(ii), or (e) of this section, that person may request an administrative review no later than 30 days after the date the removal becomes effective. The request must be submitted in writing to the FMCSA Associate Administrator for Policy and Program Development. The request must explain the error(s) committed in removing the medical examiner from the National Registry of Certified Medical Examiners, and include a list of all factual, legal, and procedural issues in dispute, and any supporting information or documents.

(1) **Additional procedures for administrative review.** The Associate Administrator may ask the person to submit additional data or attend a conference to discuss the removal. If the person does not provide the information requested, or does not attend the scheduled conference, the Associate Administrator may dismiss the request for administrative review.

(2) **Decision on administrative review.** The Associate Administrator will complete the administrative review and notify the person in writing of the decision. The decision constitutes final Agency action. If the Associate Administrator decides the removal was not valid, FMCSA will reinstate the person and reissue a certification credential to expire on the expiration date of the certificate that was invalidated under paragraph (g) of this section. The reinstated medical examiner must:

(i) Continue to meet the requirements of this subpart and the applicable requirements of part 391 of this chapter.

(ii) Report to FMCSA any changes in the application information submitted under §390.103(a)(3) within 30 days of the reinstatement.

(iii) Be licensed, certified, or registered in accordance with applicable State laws and regulations to perform physical examinations.

(iv) Maintain documentation of State licensure, registration, or certification to perform physical examinations for each State in which the examiner performs examinations and maintains documentation of completion of all training required by §§390.105 and 390.111 of this part. The medical examiner must also make this documentation available to an authorized representative of FMCSA or an authorized representative of Federal, State, or local government. The medical examiner must provide this documentation within 48 hours of the request for investigations and within 10 days of the request for regular audits of eligibility.

(v) Complete periodic training as required by the Director, Office of Carrier, Driver and Vehicle Safety Standards.

(e) **Emergency removal.** In cases of either willfulness or in which public health, interest, or safety requires, the provisions of paragraph (b) of this section are not applicable and the Director, Office of Carrier, Driver and Vehicle Safety Standards may immediately remove a medical examiner from the National Registry of Certified Medical Examiners and invalidate the certification credential issued under §390.109. A person who has been removed under the provisions of this paragraph may request an administrative review of that decision as described under paragraph (d) of this section.

(f) **Reinstatement on the National Registry of Certified Medical Examiners.** No sooner than 30 days after the date of removal from the National Registry of Certified Medical Examiners, a person who has been voluntarily or involuntarily removed may apply to the Director, Office of Carrier, Driver and Vehicle Safety Standards to be reinstated. The person must:

(1) Continue to meet the requirements of this subpart and the applicable requirements of part 391 of this chapter.

(2) Report to FMCSA any changes in the application information submitted under §390.103(a)(3).

(3) Be licensed, certified, or registered in accordance with applicable State laws and regulations to perform physical examinations.

(4) Maintain documentation of State licensure, registration, or certification to perform physical examinations for each State in which the person performs examinations and maintains documentation of completion of all training required by §§390.105 and 390.111. The medical examiner must also make this documentation available to an authorized representative of FMCSA or an authorized representative of Federal, State, or local government. The person must provide this documentation within 48 hours of the request for investigations and within 10 days of the request for regular audits of eligibility.

(5) Complete training and testing as required by the Director, Office of Carrier, Driver and Vehicle Safety Standards.

(6) In the case of a person who has been involuntarily removed, provide documentation showing completion of any corrective actions required in the notice of proposed removal.

(g) **Effect of final decision by FMCSA.** If a person is removed from the National Registry of Certified Medical Examiners under paragraph (c) or (e) of this section, the certification credential issued under §390.109 is no longer valid. However, the removed person's information remains publicly available for 3 years, with an indication that the person is no longer listed on the National Registry of Certified Medical Examiners as of the date of removal.

[77 FR 24127, Apr. 20, 2012, as amended at 80 FR 59074, Oct. 1, 2015]

Subpart E—Physical Qualifications and Examinations

§391.41 Physical qualifications for drivers.

(a) (1) (i) A person subject to this part must not operate a commercial motor vehicle unless he or she is medically certified as physically qualified to do so, and, except as provided in paragraph (a)(2) of this section, when on-duty has on his or her person the original, or a copy, of a current medical examiner's certificate that he or she is physically qualified to drive a commercial motor vehicle.

NOTE: Effective December 29, 1991, the FMCSA Administrator determined that the new Licencia Federal de Conductor issued by the United Mexican States is recognized as proof of medical fitness to drive a CMV. The United States and Canada entered into a Reciprocity Agreement, effective March 30, 1999, recognizing that a Canadian commercial driver's license is proof of medical fitness to drive a CMV. Therefore, Canadian and Mexican CMV drivers are not required to have in their possession a medical examiner's certificate if the driver has been issued, and possesses, a valid commercial driver license issued by the United Mexican States, or a Canadian Province or Territory and whose license and medical status, including any waiver or exemption, can be electronically verified. Drivers from any of the countries who have received a medical authorization that deviates from the mutually accepted compatible medical standards of the resident country are not qualified to drive a CMV in the other countries. For example, Canadian drivers who do not meet the medical fitness provisions of the Canadian National Safety Code for Motor Carriers, but are issued a waiver by one of the Canadian Provinces or Territories, are not qualified to drive a CMV in the United States. In addition, U.S. drivers who received a medical variance from FMCSA are not qualified to drive a CMV in Canada.

(ii) A person who qualifies for the medical examiner's certificate by virtue of having obtained a medical variance from FMCSA, in the form of an exemption letter or a skill performance evaluation certificate, must have on his or her person a copy of the variance documentation when on-duty.

(2) **CDL/CLP exception.** (i)(A) Beginning on January 30, 2015 and ending on the day before June 22, 2018, a driver required to have a commercial driver's license under part 383 of this chapter, and who submitted a current medical examiner's certificate to the State in accordance with 49 CFR 383.71(h) documenting that he or she meets the physical qualification requirements of this part, no longer needs to carry on his or her person the medical examiner's certificate specified at §391.43(h), or a copy, for more than 15 days after the date it was issued as valid proof of medical certification.

(i) Beginning on June 22, 2018, a driver required to have a commercial driver's license or a commercial learner's permit under 49 CFR part 383, and who has a current medical examiner's certificate documenting that he or she meets the physical qualification requirements of this part, is no longer needs to carry on his or her person the medical examiner's certificate specified at §391.43(h).

(ii) Beginning July 8, 2015, a driver required to have a commercial learner's permit under part 383 of this chapter, and who submitted a current medical examiner's certificate to the State in accordance with §383.71(h) of this chapter documenting that he or she meets the physical qualification requirements of this part, no longer needs to carry on his or her person the medical examiner's certificate specified at §391.43(h), or a copy for more than 15 days after the date it was issued as valid proof of medical certification.

(iii) A CDL or CLP holder required by §383.71(h) of this chapter to obtain a medical examiner's certificate, who obtained such by virtue of having obtained a medical variance from FMCSA, must continue to have in his or her possession the original or copy of that medical variance documentation at all times when on-duty.

(3) A person is physically qualified to drive a commercial motor vehicle if:

(i) That person meets the physical qualification standards in paragraph (b) of this section and has complied with the medical examination requirements in §391.43; or

(ii) That person obtained from FMCSA a medical variance from the physical qualification standards in paragraph (b) of this section and has complied with the medical examination requirement in §391.43.

(b) A person is physically qualified to drive a commercial motor vehicle if that person:

(1) Has no loss of a foot, a leg, a hand, or an arm, or has been granted a skill performance evaluation certificate pursuant to §391.49;

(2) Has no impairment of:

(i) A hand or finger which interferes with prehension or power grasping; or

(ii) An arm, foot, or leg which interferes with the ability to perform normal tasks associated with operating a commercial motor vehicle; or any other significant limb defect or limitation which interferes with the ability to perform normal tasks associated with operating a commercial motor vehicle; or has been granted a skill performance evaluation certificate pursuant to §391.49.

(3) Has no established medical history or clinical diagnosis of diabetes mellitus currently requiring insulin for control;

(4) Has no current clinical diagnosis of myocardial infarction, angina pectoris, coronary insufficiency, thrombosis, or any other cardiovascular disease of a variety known to be accompanied by syncope, dyspnea, collapse, or congestive cardiac failure.

(5) Has no established medical history or clinical diagnosis of a respiratory dysfunction likely to interfere with his/her ability to control and drive a commercial motor vehicle safely;

(6) Has no current clinical diagnosis of high blood pressure likely to interfere with his/her ability to operate a commercial motor vehicle safely;

(7) Has no established medical history or clinical diagnosis of rheumatic, arthritic, orthopedic, muscular, neuromuscular, or vascular disease which interferes with his/her ability to control and operate a commercial motor vehicle safely;

(8) Has no established medical history or clinical diagnosis of epilepsy or any other condition which is likely to cause loss of consciousness or any loss of ability to control a commercial motor vehicle;

(9) Has no mental, nervous, organic, or functional disease or psychiatric disorder likely to interfere with his/her ability to drive a commercial motor vehicle safely;

(10) Has distant visual acuity of at least 20/40 (Snellen) in each eye without corrective lenses or visual acuity separately corrected to 20/40 (Snellen) or better with corrective lenses, distant binocular acuity of at least 20/40 (Snellen) in both eyes with or without corrective lenses, field of vision of at least 70° in the horizontal Meridian in each eye, and the ability to recognize the colors of traffic signals and devices showing standard red, green, and amber;

(11) First perceives a forced whispered voice in the better ear at not less than 5 feet with or without the use of a hearing aid or, if tested by use of an audiometric device, does not have an average hearing loss in the better ear greater than 40 decibels at 500 Hz, 1,000 Hz, and 2,000 Hz with or without a hearing aid when the audiometric device is calibrated to American National Standard (formerly ASA Standard) Z24.5—1951.

(12) (i) Does not use any drug or substance identified in 21 CFR 1308.11 Schedule I, an amphetamine, a narcotic, or other habit-forming drug.

   (ii) Does not use any non-Schedule I drug or substance that is identified in the other Schedules in 21 CFR part 1308 except when the use is prescribed by a licensed medical practitioner, as defined in §382.107, who is familiar with the driver's medical history and has advised the driver that the substance will not adversely affect the driver's ability to safely operate a commercial motor vehicle.

(13) Has no current clinical diagnosis of alcoholism.

[35 FR 6460, Apr. 22, 1970]

Guidance for § 391.41: Physical qualifications for drivers.

QUESTION 1: Who is responsible for ensuring that medical certifications meet the requirements?

GUIDANCE: Medical certification determinations are the responsibility of the medical examiner. The motor carrier has the responsibility to ensure that the medical examiner is informed of the minimum medical requirements and the characteristics of the work to be performed. The motor carrier is also responsible for ensuring that only medically qualified drivers are operating CMVs in interstate commerce.

QUESTION 2: Do the physical qualification requirements of the FMCSRs infringe upon a person's religious beliefs if such beliefs prohibit being examined by a licensed doctor of medicine or osteopathy?

GUIDANCE: No. To determine whether a governmental regulation infringes on a person's right to freely practice his religion, the interest served by the regulation must be balanced against the degree to which a person's rights are adversely affected. *Biklen v. Board of Education,* 333 F. Supp. 902 (N.D.N.Y. 1971) aff'd 406 U.S. 951 (1972).

If there is an important objective being promoted by the requirement and the restriction on religious freedom is reasonably adapted to achieving that objective, the requirement should be upheld. *Burgin v. Henderson,* 536 F.2d 501 (2d. Cir. 1976). Based on the tests developed by the courts and the important objective served, the regulation meets Constitutional standards. It does not deny a driver his First Amendment rights.

QUESTION 3: What are the physical qualification requirements for operating a CMV in interstate commerce?

GUIDANCE: The physical qualification regulations for drivers in interstate commerce are found at §391.41. Instructions to medical examiners performing physical examinations of these drivers are found at §391.43. Interpretive guidelines are distributed upon request.

The qualification standards cover 13 areas which directly relate to the driving function. All but four of the standards require a judgment by the medical examiner. A person's qualification to drive is determined by a medical examiner who is knowledgeable about the driver's functions and whether a particular condition would interfere with the driver's ability to operate a CMV safely. In the case of vision, hearing, insulin-using diabetes, and epilepsy, the current standards are absolute, providing no discretion to the medical examiner.

QUESTION 4: Is a driver who is taking prescription methadone qualified to drive a CMV in interstate commerce?

GUIDANCE: Methadone is a habit-forming narcotic which can produce drug dependence and is not an allowable drug for operators of CMVs.

QUESTION 5: May the medical examiner restrict a driver's duties?

GUIDANCE: No. The only conditions a medical examiner may impose upon a driver otherwise qualified involve the use of corrective lenses or hearing aids, securement of a waiver or limitation of driving to exempt intracity zones (see §391.43(g)). A medical examiner who believes a driver has a condition not specified in §391.41 that would affect his ability to operate a CMV safely should refuse to sign the examiner's certificate.

QUESTION 6: If an interstate driver tests positive for alcohol or controlled substances under part 382, must the driver be medically re-examined and obtain a new medical examiner's certificate to drive again?

GUIDANCE: The driver is not required to be medically re-examined or to obtain a new medical examiner's certificate *provided* the driver is seen by an SAP who evaluates the driver, does not make a clinical diagnosis of alcoholism, and provides the driver with documentation allowing the driver to return to work. However, if the SAP determines that alcoholism exists, the driver is not qualified to drive a CMV in interstate commerce. The ultimate responsibility rests with the motor carrier to ensure the driver is medically qualified and to determine whether a new medical examination should be completed.

QUESTION 7: Are drivers prohibited from using CB radios and earphones?

GUIDANCE: No. CB radios and earphones are not prohibited under the regulations, as long as they do not distract the driver and the driver is capable of complying with §391.41(b)(11).

QUESTION 8: Is the use of coumadin, an anticoagulant, an automatic disqualification for drivers operating CMVs in interstate commerce?

GUIDANCE: No. Although the FHWA 1987 "Conference on Cardiac Disorders and Commercial Drivers" recommended that drivers who are taking anticoagulants not be allowed to drive, the agency has not adopted a rule to that effect. The medical examiner and treating specialist may, but are not required to, accept the Conference recommendations. Therefore, the use of coumadin is not an automatic disqualification, but a factor to be considered in determining the driver's physical qualification status.

* * *

---
§391.43 Medical examination; certificate of physical examination.

(a) Except as provided by paragraph (b) of this section, the medical examination must be performed by a medical examiner listed on the National Registry of Certified Medical Examiners under subpart D of part 390 of this chapter.

(b) A licensed optometrist may perform so much of the medical examination as pertains to visual acuity, field of vision, and the ability to recognize colors as specified in paragraph (10) of §391.41(b).

(c) Medical examiners shall:

   (1) Be knowledgeable of the specific physical and mental demands associated with operating a commercial motor vehicle and the requirements of this subpart, including the medical advisory criteria prepared by the FMCSA as guidelines to aid the medical examiner in making the qualification determination; and

   (2) Be proficient in the use of and use the medical protocols necessary to adequately perform the medical examination required by this section.

(d) Any driver authorized to operate a commercial motor vehicle within an exempt intracity zone pursuant to §391.62 of this part shall furnish the examining medical examiner with a copy of the medical findings that led to the issuance of the first certificate of medical examination which allowed the driver to operate a commercial motor vehicle wholly within an exempt intracity zone.

(e) Any driver operating under a limited exemption authorized by §391.64 shall furnish the medical examiner with a copy of the annual medical findings of the endocrinologist, ophthalmologist or optometrist, as required under that section. If the medical examiner finds the driver qualified under the limited exemption in §391.64, such fact shall be noted on the Medical Examiner's Certificate.

(f) The medical examination shall be performed, and its results shall be recorded on the Medical Examination Report Form, MCSA-5875, set out below:

Form MCSA-5875   OMB No. 2126-0006   Expiration Date: 8/31/2018

Public Burden Statement
A Federal agency may not conduct or sponsor, and a person is not required to respond to, nor shall a person be subject to a penalty for failure to comply with a collection of information subject to the requirements of the Paperwork Reduction Act unless that collection of information displays a current valid OMB Control Number. The OMB Control Number for this information collection is 2126-0006. Public reporting for this collection of information is estimated to be approximately 25 minutes per response, including the time for reviewing instructions, gathering the data needed, and completing and reviewing the collection of information. All responses to this collection of information are mandatory. Send comments regarding this burden estimate or any other aspect of this collection of information, including suggestions for reducing this burden to: Information Collection Clearance Officer, Federal Motor Carrier Safety Administration, MC-RRA, 1200 New Jersey Avenue, SE, Washington, D.C. 20590.

U.S. Department of Transportation
Federal Motor Carrier
Safety Administration

Medical Examination Report Form
(for Commercial Driver Medical Certification)

MEDICAL RECORD #
_____
(or sticker)

SECTION 1. Driver Information (to be filled out by the driver)

PERSONAL INFORMATION

Last Name: _____ First Name: _____ Middle Initial: ____ Date of Birth: _____ Age: ___

Street Address: _____ City: _____ State/Province: _____ Zip Code: _____

Driver's License Number: _____ Issuing State/Province: _____ Phone: _____ Gender: ○ M ○ F

E-mail (optional): _____ CLP/CDL Applicant/Holder*: ○ Yes ○ No

Driver ID Verified By**: _____

Has your USDOT/FMCSA medical certificate ever been denied or issued for less than 2 years? ○ Yes ○ No ○ Not Sure

*CLP/CDL Applicant/Holder: See instructions for definitions.   **Driver ID Verified By: Record what type of photo ID was used to verify the identity of the driver, e.g., CDL, driver's license, passport.

DRIVER HEALTH HISTORY

Have you ever had surgery? If "yes," please list and explain below.   ○ Yes ○ No ○ Not Sure

Are you currently taking medications (prescription, over-the-counter, herbal remedies, diet supplements)? If "yes," please describe below.   ○ Yes ○ No ○ Not Sure

(Attach additional sheets if necessary)

This document contains sensitive information and is for official use only. Improper handling of this information could negatively affect individuals. Handle and secure this information appropriately to prevent inadvertent disclosure by keeping the documents under the control of authorized persons. Properly dispose of this document when no longer required to be maintained by regulatory requirements.

OMB No. 2126-0006   Expiration Date: 8/31/2018

Last Name: _____   First Name: _____   DOB: _____   Exam Date: _____

DRIVER HEALTH HISTORY (continued)

Do you have or have you ever had:	Yes	No	Not Sure		Yes	No	Not Sure
1. Head/brain injuries or illnesses (e.g., concussion)	O	O	O	16. Dizziness, headaches, numbness, tingling, or memory loss	O	O	O
2. Seizures, epilepsy	O	O	O	17. Unexplained weight loss	O	O	O
3. Eye problems (except glasses or contacts)	O	O	O	18. Stroke, mini-stroke (TIA), paralysis, or weakness	O	O	O
4. Ear and/or hearing problems	O	O	O	19. Missing or limited use of arm, hand, finger, leg, foot, toe	O	O	O
5. Heart disease, heart attack, bypass, or other heart problems	O	O	O	20. Neck or back problems	O	O	O
6. Pacemaker, stents, implantable devices, or other heart procedures	O	O	O	21. Bone, muscle, joint, or nerve problems	O	O	O
7. High blood pressure	O	O	O	22. Blood clots or bleeding problems	O	O	O
8. High cholesterol	O	O	O	23. Cancer	O	O	O
9. Chronic (long-term) cough, shortness of breath, or other breathing problems	O	O	O	24. Chronic (long-term) infection or other chronic diseases	O	O	O
10. Lung disease (e.g., asthma)	O	O	O	25. Sleep disorders, pauses in breathing while asleep, daytime sleepiness, loud snoring	O	O	O
11. Kidney problems, kidney stones, or pain/problems with urination	O	O	O	26. Have you ever had a sleep test (e.g., sleep apnea)?	O	O	O
12. Stomach, liver, or digestive problems	O	O	O	27. Have you ever spent a night in the hospital?	O	O	O
13. Diabetes or blood sugar problems	O	O	O	28. Have you ever had a broken bone?	O	O	O
Insulin used	O	O	O	29. Have you ever used or do you now use tobacco?	O	O	O
14. Anxiety, depression, nervousness, other mental health problems	O	O	O	30. Do you currently drink alcohol?	O	O	O
				31. Have you used an illegal substance within the past two years?	O	O	O
15. Fainting or passing out	O	O	O	32. Have you ever failed a drug test or been dependent on an illegal substance?	O	O	O

Other health condition(s) not described above: O Yes O No O Not Sure

Did you answer "yes" to any of questions 1-32? If so, please comment further on those health conditions below.   O Yes O No O Not Sure

(Attach additional sheets if necessary)

CMV DRIVER'S SIGNATURE

I certify that the above information is accurate and complete. I understand that inaccurate, false or missing information may invalidate the examination and my Medical Examiner's Certificate, that submission of fraudulent or intentionally false information is a violation of 49 CFR 390.35, and that submission of fraudulent or intentionally false information may subject me to civil or criminal penalties under 49 CFR 390.37 and 49 CFR 386 Appendices A and B.

Driver's Signature: _____   Date: _____

SECTION 2. Examination Report (to be filled out by the medical examiner)

DRIVER HEALTH HISTORY REVIEW

Review and discuss pertinent driver answers and any available medical records. Comment on the driver's responses to the "health history" questions that may affect the driver's safe operation of a commercial motor vehicle (CMV).

(Attach additional sheets if necessary)

Last Name:	First Name:	DOB:	Exam Date:

TESTING

| Pulse rate: | Pulse rhythm regular: ○ Yes ○ No | | Height: __ feet __ inches Weight: ___ pounds |

Blood Pressure	Systolic	Diastolic	Urinalysis	Sp. Gr.	Protein	Blood	Sugar
Sitting			Urinalysis is required. Numerical readings must be recorded.				
Second reading (optional)							
Other testing if indicated			Protein, blood, or sugar in the urine may be an indication for further testing to rule out any underlying medical problem.				

Vision
Standard is at least 20/40 acuity (Snellen) in each eye with or without correction. At least 70° field of vision in horizontal meridian measured in each eye. The use of corrective lenses should be noted on the Medical Examiner's Certificate.

Hearing
Standard: Must first perceive whispered voice at not less than 5 feet OR average hearing loss of less than or equal to 40 dB, in better ear (with or without hearing aid).

Check if hearing aid used for test: ☐ Right Ear ☐ Left Ear ☐ Neither

Acuity	Uncorrected	Corrected	Horizontal Field of Vision
Right Eye:	20/____	20/____	Right Eye: ___ degrees
Left Eye:	20/____	20/____	Left Eye: ___ degrees
Both Eyes:	20/____	20/____	

Whisper Test Results

Right Ear   Left Ear

Record distance *(in feet)* from driver at which a forced whispered voice can first be heard   _____   _____

	Yes	No
Applicant can recognize and distinguish among traffic control signals and devices showing red, green, and amber colors	○	○
Monocular vision	○	○
Referred to ophthalmologist or optometrist?	○	○
Received documentation from ophthalmologist or optometrist?	○	○

OR

Audiometric Test Results

Right Ear			Left Ear		
500 Hz	1000 Hz	2000 Hz	500 Hz	1000 Hz	2000 Hz
_____	_____	_____	_____	_____	_____

Average (right): _____   Average (left): _____

PHYSICAL EXAMINATION

The presence of a certain condition may not necessarily disqualify a driver, particularly if the condition is controlled adequately, is not likely to worsen, or is readily amenable to treatment. Even if a condition does not disqualify a driver, the Medical Examiner may consider deferring the driver temporarily. Also, the driver should be advised to take the necessary steps to correct the condition as soon as possible, particularly if neglecting the condition could result in a more serious illness that might affect driving.

Check the body systems for abnormalities.

Body System	Normal	Abnormal	Body System	Normal	Abnormal
1. General	○	○	8. Abdomen	○	○
2. Skin	○	○	9. Genito-urinary system including hernias	○	○
3. Eyes	○	○	10. Back/Spine	○	○
4. Ears	○	○	11. Extremities/joints	○	○
5. Mouth/throat	○	○	12. Neurological system including reflexes	○	○
6. Cardiovascular	○	○	13. Gait	○	○
7. Lungs/chest	○	○	14. Vascular system	○	○

Discuss any abnormal answers in detail in the space below and indicate whether it would affect the driver's ability to operate a CMV. Enter applicable item number before each comment.

(Attach additional sheets if necessary)

Form MCSA-5875   OMB No. 2126-0006   Expiration Date: 8/31/2018

Last Name: _____ First Name: _____ DOB: _____ Exam Date: _____

Please complete only one of the following (Federal or State) Medical Examiner Determination sections:

MEDICAL EXAMINER DETERMINATION (Federal)

Use this section for examinations performed in accordance with the Federal Motor Carrier Safety Regulations (49 CFR 391.41-391.49):

○ Does not meet standards *(specify reason)*: _____

○ Meets standards in 49 CFR 391.41; qualifies for 2-year certificate

○ Meets standards, but periodic monitoring required *(specify reason)*: _____

   Driver qualified for: ○ 3 months   ○ 6 months   ○ 1 year   ○ other *(specify)*: _____

☐ Wearing corrective lenses   ☐ Wearing hearing aid   ☐ Accompanied by a waiver/exemption *(specify type)*: _____

☐ Accompanied by a Skill Performance Evaluation (SPE) Certificate   ☐ Qualified by operation of 49 CFR 391.64 *(Federal)*

☐ Driving within an exempt intracity zone *(see 49 CFR 391.62) (Federal)*

☐ Determination pending *(specify reason)*: _____

   ☐ Return to medical exam office for follow-up on *(must be 45 days or less)*: _____

   ☐ Medical Examination Report amended *(specify reason)*: _____

     (if amended) Medical Examiner's Signature: _____ Date: _____

☐ Incomplete examination *(specify reason)*: _____

> **If the driver meets the standards outlined in 49 CFR 391.41, then complete a Medical Examiner's Certificate as stated in 49 CFR 391.43(h), as appropriate.**

I have performed this evaluation for certification. I have personally reviewed all available records and recorded information pertaining to this evaluation, and attest that to the best of my knowledge, I believe it to be true and correct.

Medical Examiner's Signature: _____

Medical Examiner's Name *(please print or type)*: _____

Medical Examiner's Address: _____ City: _____ State: _____ Zip Code: _____

Medical Examiner's Telephone Number: _____ Date Certificate Signed: _____

Medical Examiner's State License, Certificate, or Registration Number: _____ Issuing State: _____

☐ MD ☐ DO ☐ Physician Assistant ☐ Chiropractor ☐ Advanced Practice Nurse

☐ Other Practitioner *(specify)*: _____

National Registry Number: _____ | Medical Examiner's Certificate Expiration Date: _____

Form MCSA-5875   OMB No. 2126-0006   Expiration Date: 8/31/2018

Last Name: _____ First Name: _____ DOB: _____ Exam Date: _____

MEDICAL EXAMINER DETERMINATION (State)

Use this section for examinations performed in accordance with the Federal Motor Carrier Safety Regulations (49 CFR 391.41-391.49) with any applicable State variances (which will only be valid for intrastate operations):

○ Does not meet standards in 49 CFR 391.41 with any applicable State variances *(specify reason)*: _____

○ Meets standards in 49 CFR 391.41 with any applicable State variances

○ Meets standards, but periodic monitoring required *(specify reason)*: _____

   Driver qualified for: ○ 3 months   ○ 6 months   ○ 1 year   ○ other *(specify)*: _____

☐ Wearing corrective lenses   ☐ Wearing hearing aid   ☐ Accompanied by a waiver/exemption *(specify type)*: _____

☐ Accompanied by a Skill Performance Evaluation (SPE) Certificate   ☐ Grandfathered from State requirements *(State)*

> **If the driver meets the standards outlined in 49 CFR 391.41, with applicable State variances, then complete a Medical Examiner's Certificate, as appropriate.**

I have performed this evaluation for certification. I have personally reviewed all available records and recorded information pertaining to this evaluation, and attest that to the best of my knowledge, I believe it to be true and correct.

Medical Examiner's Signature: _____

Medical Examiner's Name *(please print or type)*: _____

Medical Examiner's Address: _____ City: _____ State: _____ Zip Code: _____

Medical Examiner's Telephone Number: _____ Date Certificate Signed: _____

Medical Examiner's State License, Certificate, or Registration Number: _____ Issuing State: _____

☐ MD ☐ DO ☐ Physician Assistant ☐ Chiropractor ☐ Advanced Practice Nurse

☐ Other Practitioner *(specify)*: _____

National Registry Number: _____ | Medical Examiner's Certificate Expiration Date: _____

Instructions for Completing the Medical Examination Report Form (MCSA-5875)

I. Step-By-Step Instructions

Driver:

Section 1: Driver Information

- **Personal Information:** Please complete this section using your name as written on your driver's license, your current address and phone number, your date of birth, age, gender, driver's license number and issuing state.

  o **CLP/CDL Applicant/Holder:** Check "yes" if you are a commercial learner's permit (**CLP**) or commercial driver's license (**CDL**) holder, or are applying for a CLP or CDL. CDL means a license issued by a State or the District of Columbia which authorizes the individual to operate a class of a commercial motor vehicle (**CMV**). A CMV that requires a CDL is one that: (1) has a gross combination weight rating or gross combination weight of 26,001 pounds or more inclusive of a towed unit with a gross vehicle weight rating (**GVWR**) or gross vehicle weight (**GVW**) of more than 10,000 pounds; or (2) has a GVWR or GVW of 26,001 pounds or more; or (3) is designed to transport 16 or more passengers, including the driver; or (4) is used to transport either hazardous materials requiring hazardous materials placards on the vehicle or any quantity of a select agent or toxin.

  o **Driver ID Verified By:** The Medical Examiner/staff completes this item and notes the type of photo ID used to verify the driver's identity such as, commercial driver's license, driver's license, or passport, etc.

  o **Question: Has your USDOT/FMCSA medical certificate ever been denied or issued for less than two years?** Please check the correct box "yes" or "no" and if you aren't sure check the "not sure" box.

- **Driver Health History:**

  o **Have you ever had surgery:** Please check "yes" if you have ever had surgery and provide a written explanation of the details (type of surgery, date of surgery, etc.)

  o **Are you currently taking medications (prescription, over-the-counter, herbal remedies, diet supplements):** Please check "yes" if you are taking any diet supplements, herbal remedies, or prescription or over the counter medications. In the box below the question, indicate the name of the medication and the dosage.

  o **#1-32:** Please complete this section by checking the "yes" box to indicate that you have, or have ever had, the health condition listed or the "No" box if you have not. Check the "not sure" box if you are unsure.

  o **Other Health Conditions not described above:** If you have, or have had, any other health conditions not listed in the section above, check "Yes" and in the box provided and list those condition(s).

  o **Any yes answers to questions #1-32 above:** If you have answered "yes" to any of the questions in the Driver Health History section above, please explain your answers further in the box below the question. For example, if you answered "yes" to question #5 regarding heart disease, heart attack, bypass, or other heart problem, indicate which type of heart condition. If you checked "yes" to question #23 regarding cancer, indicate the type of cancer. Please add any information that will be helpful to the Medical Examiner.

- **CMV Driver Signature and Date:** Please read the certification statement, sign and date it, indicating that the information you provided in Section 1 is accurate and complete.

Medical Examiner:

Section 2: Examination Report

- **Driver Health History Review:** Review answers provided by the driver in the driver health history section and discuss any "yes" and "not sure" responses. In addition, be sure to compare the medication list to the health history responses ensuring that the medication taken matches the medical conditions noted. Explore with the driver any answers that seem unclear. Record any information that the driver omitted. As the Medical Examiner conducting the driver's physical examination you are required to complete the entire medical examination even if you detect a medical condition that you consider disqualifying, such as deafness. Medical Examiners are expected to determine the driver's physical qualification for operating a commercial vehicle safely. Thus, if you find a disqualifying condition for which a driver may receive a Federal Motor Carrier Safety Administration medical exemption, please record that on the driver's Medical Examiner's Certificate, Form MCSA-5876, as well as on the Medical Examination Report Form, MCSA-5875.

- **Testing:**

  o **Pulse rate and rhythm, height, and weight:** record these as indicated on the form.

  o **Blood Pressure:** record the blood pressure (systolic and diastolic) of the driver being examined. A second reading is optional and should be recorded if found to be necessary.

  o **Urinalysis:** record the numerical readings for the specific gravity, protein, blood and sugar.

  o **Vision:** The current vision standard is provided on the form. When other than the Snellen chart is used, give test results in Snellen-comparable values. When recording distance vision, use 20 feet as normal. Record the vision acuity results and indicate if the driver can recognize and distinguish among traffic control signals and devices showing red, green, and amber colors; has monocular vision; has been referred to an ophthalmologist or optometrist; and if documentation has been received from an ophthalmologist or optometrist.

  o **Hearing:** The current hearing standard is provided on the form. Hearing can be tested using either a whisper test or audiometric test. Record the test results in the corresponding section for the test used.

- **Physical Examination:** Check the body systems for abnormalities and indicate normal or abnormal for each body system listed. Discuss any abnormal answers in detail in the space provided and indicate whether it would affect the driver's ability to safely operate a commercial motor vehicle.

In this next section, you will be completing either the Federal or State determination, not both.

- **Medical Examiner Determination (Federal):** Use this section for examinations performed in accordance with the FMCSRs (49 CFR 391.41-391.49). Complete the medical examiner determination section completely. When determining a driver's physical qualification, please note that English language proficiency (49 CFR part 391.11: General qualifications of drivers) is not factored into that determination.

  o **Does not meet standards:** Select this option when a driver is determined to be not qualified and provide an explanation of why the driver does not meet the standards in 49 CFR 391.41.

  o **Meets standards in 49 CFR 391.41; qualifies for 2-year certification:** Select this option when a driver is determined to be qualified and will be issued a 2-year Medical Examiner's Certificate.

  o **Meets standards, but periodic monitoring is required:** Select this option when a driver is determined to be qualified but needs periodic monitoring and provide an explanation of why periodic monitoring is required. Select the corresponding time frame that the driver is qualified and if selecting other, specify the time frame.

  - **Determination that driver meets standards:** Select all categories that apply to the driver's certification (e.g., wearing corrective lenses, accompanied by a waiver/exemption, driving within an exempt intracity zone, etc.)

  o **Determination pending:** Select this option when more information is needed to make a qualification decision and specify a date, on or before the 45 day expiration date, for the driver to return to the medical exam office for follow-up. This will allow for a delay of the qualification decision for as many as 45 days. If the disposition of the pending examination is not updated via the National Registry on or before the 45 day expiration date, FMCSA will notify the examining medical examiner and the driver in writing that the examination is no longer valid and that the driver is required to be re-examined.

  - **MER amended:** A Medical Examination Report Form (MER), MCSA-5875, may only be amended while in determination pending status for situations where new information (e.g., test results, etc.) has been received or there has been a change in the driver's medical status since the initial examination, but prior to a final qualification determination. Select this option when a Medical Examination Report Form, MCSA-5875, is being amended; provide the reason for the amendment, sign and date. In addition, initial and date any changes made on the Medical Examination Report Form, MCSA-5875. A Medical Examination Report Form, MCSA-5875, cannot be amended after an examination has been in determination pending status for more than 45 days or after a final qualification determination has been made. The driver is required to obtain a new physical examination and a new Medical Examination Report Form, MCSA-5875, be completed.

  o **Incomplete examination:** Select this when the physical examination is not completed for any reason (e.g., driver decides they do not want to continue with the examination and leaves) other than situations outlined under determination pending.

  o **Medical Examiner information, signature and date:** Provide your name, address, phone number, occupation, license, certificate, or registration number and issuing state, national registry number, signature and date.

  o **Medical Examiner's Certificate Expiration Date:** Enter the date the driver's Medical Examiner's Certificate (MEC) expires.

- **Medical Examiner Determination (State):** Use this section for examinations performed in accordance with the FMCSRs (49 CFR 391.41-391.49) and any applicable State variances (which will only be valid for intrastate operations). Complete the medical examiner determination section completely.

  o **Does not meet standards in 49 CFR 391.41 with any applicable State variances:** Select this option when a driver is determined to be not qualified and provide an explanation of why the driver does not meet the standards in 49 CFR 391.41 with any applicable State variances.

  o **Meets standards in 49 CFR 391.41 with any applicable State variances:** Select this option when a driver is determined to be qualified and will be issued a 2-year Medical Examiner's Certificate.

  o **Meets standards, but periodic monitoring is required:** Select this option when a driver is determined to be qualified but needs periodic monitoring and provide an explanation of why periodic monitoring is required. Select the corresponding time frame that the driver is qualified and if selecting other, specify the time frame.

  - **Determination that driver meets standards:** Select all categories that apply to the driver's certification (e.g., wearing corrective lenses, accompanied by a waiver/exemption, etc.).

  o **Medical Examiner information, signature and date:** Provide your name, address, phone number, occupation, license, certificate, or registration number and issuing state, national registry number, signature and date.

  o **Medical Examiner's Certificate Expiration Date:** Enter the date the driver's Medical Examiner's Certificate (MEC) expires.

- **II.** If updating an existing exam, you must resubmit the new exam results, via the Medical Examination Results Form, MCSA-5850, to the National Registry, and the most recent dated exam will take precedence.

- **III.** To obtain additional information regarding this form go to the Medical Program's page on the Federal Motor Carrier Safety Administration's website at http://www.fmcsa.dot.gov/regulations/medical.

(g) Upon completion of the medical examination required by this subpart:

   (1) The medical examiner must date and sign the Medical Examination Report and provide his or her full name, office address, and telephone number on the Report.

   (2) (i) Before June 22, 2018, if the medical examiner finds that the person examined is physically qualified to operate a commercial motor vehicle in accordance with §391.41(b), he or she must complete a certificate in the form prescribed in paragraph (h) of this section and furnish the original to the person who was examined. The examiner must provide a copy to a prospective or current employing motor carrier who requests it.

   (ii) Beginning June 22, 2018, if the medical examiner identifies that the person examined will not be operating a commercial motor vehicle that requires a commercial driver's license or a commercial learner's permit and finds that the driver is physically qualified to operate a commercial motor vehicle in accordance with §391.41(b), he or she must complete a certificate in the form prescribed in paragraph (h) of this section and furnish the original to the person who was examined. The examiner must provide a copy to a prospective or current employing motor carrier who requests it.

   (3) Beginning June 22, 2018, if the medical examiner finds that the person examined is not physically qualified to operate a commercial motor vehicle in accordance with §391.41(b), he or she must inform the person examined that he or she is not physically qualified, and that this information will be reported to FMCSA. All medical examiner's certificates previously issued to the person are not valid and no longer satisfy the requirements of §391.41(a).

   (4) Beginning December 22, 2015, if the medical examiner finds that the determination of whether the person examined is physically qualified to operate a commercial motor vehicle in accordance with §391.41(b) should be delayed pending the receipt of additional information or the conduct of further examination in order for the medical examiner to make such determination, he or she must inform the person examined that the additional information must be provided or the further examination completed within 45 days, and that the pending status of the examination will be reported to FMCSA.

   (5) (i) (A) Once every calendar month, beginning May 21, 2014 and ending on June 22, 2018, the medical examiner must electronically transmit to the Director, Office of Carrier, Driver and Vehicle Safety Standards, via a secure Web account on the National Registry, a completed CMV Driver Medical Examination Results Form, MCSA-5850. The Form must include all information specified for each medical examination conducted during the previous month for any driver who is required to be examined by a medical examiner listed on the National Registry of Certified Medical Examiners.

   (B) Beginning June 22, 2018 by midnight (local time) of the next calendar day after the medical examiner completes a medical examination for any driver who is required to be examined by a medical examiner listed on the National Registry of Certified Medical Examiners, the medical examiner must electronically transmit to the

Director, Office of Carrier, Driver and Vehicle Safety Standards, via a secure FMCSA-designated Web site, a completed CMV Driver Medical Examination Results Form, MCSA-5850. The Form must include all information specified for each medical examination conducted for each driver who is required to be examined by a medical examiner listed on the National Registry of Certified Medical Examiners in accordance with the provisions of this subpart E, and should also include information for each driver who is required by a State to be examined by a medical examiner listed on the National Registry of Certified Medical Examiners in accordance with the provisions of this subpart E and any variances from those provisions adopted by such State.

(ii) Beginning on June 22, 2015, if the medical examiner does not perform a medical examination of any driver who is required to be examined by a medical examiner listed on the National Registry of Certified Medical Examiners during any calendar month, the medical examiner must report that fact to FMCSA, via a secure FMCSA-designated Web site, by the close of business on the last day of such month.

(h) The medical examiner's certificate shall be completed in accordance with the following Form MCSA-5876, Medical Examiner's Certificate:

Form MCSA-5876   OMB No. 2126-0006   Expiration Date: 8/31/2018

Public Burden Statement
A Federal agency may not conduct or sponsor, and a person is not required to respond to, nor shall a person be subject to a penalty for failure to comply with a collection of information subject to the requirements of the Paperwork Reduction Act unless that collection of information displays a current valid OMB Control Number. The OMB Control Number for this information collection is 2126-0006. Public reporting for this collection of information is estimated to be approximately 1 minute per response, including the time for reviewing instructions, gathering the data needed, and completing and reviewing the collection of information. All responses to this collection of information are mandatory. Send comments regarding this burden estimate or any other aspect of this collection of information, including suggestions for reducing this burden to: Information Collection Clearance Officer, Federal Motor Carrier Safety Administration, MC-RRA, 1200 New Jersey Avenue, SE, Washington, D.C. 20590.

U.S. Department of Transportation
Federal Motor Carrier
Safety Administration

Medical Examiner's Certificate
(for Commercial Driver Medical Certification)

I certify that I have examined **Last Name:** _____ **First Name:** _____ in accordance with (please check only one):

○ the Federal Motor Carrier Safety Regulations (49 CFR 391.41-391.49) and, with knowledge of the driving duties, I find this person is qualified, and, if applicable, only when (check all that apply) **OR**
○ the Federal Motor Carrier Safety Regulations (49 CFR 391.41-391.49) with any applicable State variances (which will only be valid for intrastate operations), and, with knowledge of the driving duties, I find this person is qualified, and, if applicable, only when (check all that apply):

☐ Wearing corrective lenses ☐ Accompanied by a _____ waiver/exemption ☐ Driving within an exempt intracity zone (49 CFR 391.62) (Federal)
☐ Wearing hearing aid ☐ Accompanied by a Skill Performance Evaluation (SPE) Certificate ☐ Qualified by operation of 49 CFR 391.64 (Federal)
                                                  ☐ Grandfathered from State requirements (State)

The information I have provided regarding this physical examination is true and complete. A complete Medical Examination Report Form, MCSA-5875, with any attachments embodies my findings completely and correctly, and is on file in my office.

Medical Examiner's Certificate Expiration Date
_____

Medical Examiner's Signature   **Medical Examiner's Telephone Number**   **Date Certificate Signed**

Medical Examiner's Name (please print or type)   ○ MD ○ Physician Assistant ○ Advanced Practice Nurse
                                             ○ DO ○ Chiropractor ○ Other Practitioner (specify) _____

Medical Examiner's State License, Certificate, or Registration Number   **Issuing State**   **National Registry Number**

Driver's Signature   **Driver's License Number**   **Issuing State/Province**

Driver's Address   **CLP/CDL Applicant/Holder**
Street Address: _____ City: _____ State/Province: _____ Zip Code: _____ ○ Yes ○ No

This document contains sensitive information and is for official use only. Improper handling of this information could negatively affect individuals. Handle and secure this information appropriately to prevent inadvertent disclosure by keeping the documents under the control of authorized persons. Properly dispose of this document when no longer required to be maintained by regulatory requirements.

(i)   Each original (paper or electronic) completed Medical Examination Report and a copy or electronic version of each medical examiner's certificate must be retained on file at the office of the medical examiner for at least 3 years from the date of examination. The medical examiner must make all records and information in these files available to an authorized representative of FMCSA or an authorized Federal, State, or local enforcement agency representative, within 48 hours after the request is made.

[35 FR 6460, Apr. 22, 1970]

EDITORIAL NOTE: For Federal Register citations affecting §391.43, see the List of CFR Sections Affected, which appears in the Finding Aids section of the printed volume and at www.fdsys.gov.

Guidance for § 391.43: Medical examination; certificate of physical examination.

QUESTION 1: May a motor carrier, for the purposes of §391.41, or a State driver licensing agency, for the purposes of §383.71, accept the results of a medical examination performed by a foreign medical examiner?

GUIDANCE: Yes. Foreign drivers operating in the U.S. with a driver's license recognized as equivalent to the CDL may be medically certified in accordance with the requirements of part 391, subpart E, by a medical examiner in the driver's home country who is licensed, certified, and/or registered to perform physical examinations in that country. *However,* U.S. drivers operating in interstate commerce within the U.S. must be medically certified in accordance with part 391, subpart E, by a medical examiner licensed, certified, and/or registered to perform physical examinations in the U.S.

QUESTION 2: May a urine sample collected for purposes of performing a subpart H test be used to test for diabetes as part of a driver's FHWA-required physical examination?

GUIDANCE: In general, no. However, the DOT has recognized an exception to this general policy whereby, after 60 milliliters of urine have been set aside for subpart H testing, any remaining portion of the sample may be used for other nondrug testing, but only if such other nondrug testing is required by the FHWA (under part 391, subpart E) such as testing for glucose and protein levels.

QUESTION 3: Is a chest x-ray required under the minimum medical requirements of the FMCSRs?

GUIDANCE: No, but a medical examiner may take an x-ray if appropriate.

QUESTION 4: Does §391.43 of the FMCSRs require that physical examinations of applicants for employment be conducted by medical examiners employed by or designated by the carrier?

GUIDANCE: No.

QUESTION 5: Does a medical certificate displaying a facsimile of a medical examiner's signature meet the "signature of examining health care professional" requirement?

GUIDANCE: Yes.

QUESTION 6: The driver's medical exam is part of the Mexican Licencia Federal. If a roadside inspection reveals that a Mexico-based driver has not had the medical portion of the Licencia Federal re-validated, is the driver considered to be without a valid medical certificate or without a valid license?

GUIDANCE: The Mexican Licencia Federal is issued for a period of 10 years but must be re-validated every 2 years. A condition of re-validation is that the driver must pass a new physical examination. The dates for each re-validation are on the Licencia Federal and must be stamped at the completion of each physical. This constitutes documentation that the driver is medically qualified. Therefore, if the Licencia Federal is not re-validated every 2 years as specified by Mexican law, the driver's license is considered invalid.

QUESTION 7: If a motor carrier sends a potential interstate driver to a medical examiner to have both a pre-employment medical examination and a pre-employment controlled substances test performed, how must the medical examiner conduct the medical examination including the certification the driver meets the physical qualifications of §391.41(b)?

GUIDANCE: The medical examiner must complete the physical examination first without collecting the Part 382 controlled substances urine specimen. If the potential driver meets the requirements of Part 391, Subpart E [especially §391.41(b)] and the medical examiner chooses to certify the potential driver as qualified to operate commercial motor vehicles (CMV) in interstate commerce, the medical examiner may prepare the medical examiner's certificate.

After the medical examiner has completed the medical examiner's certificate and provided a copy to the potential driver and to the motor carrier who will use the potential driver's services, the medical examiner may collect the specimen for the 49 CFR Part 382 pre-employment controlled substances test. The motor carrier is held fully responsible for ensuring the potential driver is not used to operate CMVs until the carrier receives a verified negative controlled substances test result from the medical review officer. A Department of Transportation pre-employment controlled substances test is not a medical examination test.

§391.45 Persons who must be medically examined and certified.

The following persons must be medically examined and certified in accordance with §391.43 of this subpart as physically qualified to operate a commercial motor vehicle:

(a) Any person who has not been medically examined and certified as physically qualified to operate a commercial motor vehicle;

(b) (1) Any driver who has not been medically examined and certified as qualified to operate a commercial motor vehicle during the preceding 24 months; or

(2) Any driver authorized to operate a commercial motor vehicle only with an exempt intracity zone pursuant to §391.62, or only by operation of the exemption in §391.64, if such driver has not been medically examined and certified as qualified to drive in such zone during the preceding 12 months;

(c) Any driver whose ability to perform his/her normal duties has been impaired by a physical or mental injury or disease; and

(d) Beginning June 22, 2018, any person found by a medical examiner not to be physically qualified to operate a commercial motor vehicle under the provisions of paragraph (g)(3) of §391.43.

[35 FR 6460, Apr. 22, 1970, as amended at 36 FR 223, Jan. 7, 1971; 54 FR 12202, Mar. 24, 1989; 61 FR 13347, Mar. 26, 1996; 80 FR 22821, Apr. 23, 2015; 80 FR 59075, Oct. 1, 2015]

Guidance for § 391.45: Persons who must be medically examined and certified.

QUESTION 1: Is it intended that the words "person" and "driver" be used interchangeably in §391.45?
GUIDANCE: Yes.

QUESTION 2: Do the FMCSRs require applicants, possessing a current medical certificate, to undergo a new physical examination as a condition of employment?
GUIDANCE: No. However, if a motor carrier accepts such a currently valid certificate from a driver subject to part 382, the driver is subject to additional controlled substance testing requirements unless otherwise excepted in subpart H.

QUESTION 3: Must a driver who is returning from an illness or injury undergo a medical examination even if his current medical certificate has not expired?
GUIDANCE: The FMCSRs do not require an examination in this case unless the injury or illness has impaired the driver's ability to perform his/her normal duties. However, the motor carrier may require a driver returning from any illness or injury to take a physical examination. But, in either case, the motor carrier has the obligation to determine if an injury or illness renders the driver medically unqualified.

§391.47 Resolution of conflicts of medical evaluation.

(a) **Applications.** Applications for determination of a driver's medical qualifications under standards in this part will only be accepted if they conform to the requirements of this section.

(b) **Content.** Applications will be accepted for consideration only if the following conditions are met.

  (1) The application must contain the name and address of the driver, motor carrier, and all physicians involved in the proceeding.

  (2) The applicant must submit proof that there is a disagreement between the physician for the driver and the physician for the motor carrier concerning the driver's qualifications.

  (3) The applicant must submit a copy of an opinion and report including results of all tests of an impartial medical specialist in the field in which the medical conflict arose. The specialist should be one agreed to by the motor carrier and the driver.

    (i) In cases where the driver refuses to agree on a specialist and the applicant is the motor carrier, the applicant must submit a statement of his/her agreement to submit the matter to an impartial medical specialist in the field, proof that he/she has requested the driver to submit to the medical specialist, and the response, if any, of the driver to his/her request.

    (ii) In cases where the motor carrier refuses to agree on a medical specialist, the driver must submit an opinion and test results of an impartial medical specialist, proof that he/she has requested the motor carrier to agree to submit the matter to the medical specialist and the response, if any, of the motor carrier to his/her request.

  (4) The applicant must include a statement explaining in detail why the decision of the medical specialist identified in paragraph (b)(3) of this section, is unacceptable.

  (5) The applicant must submit proof that the medical specialist mentioned in paragraph (b)(3) of this section was provided, prior to his/her determination, the medical history of the driver and an agreed-upon statement of the work the driver performs.

  (6) The applicant must submit the medical history and statement of work provided to the medical specialist under paragraph (b)(5) of this section.

  (7) The applicant must submit all medical records and statements of the physicians who have given opinions on the driver's qualifications.

  (8) The applicant must submit a description and a copy of all written and documentary evidence upon which the party making application relies in the form set out in 49 CFR 386.37.

  (9) The application must be accompanied by a statement of the driver that he/she intends to drive in interstate commerce not subject to the commercial zone exemption or a statement of the carrier that he/she has used or intends to use the driver for such work.

(10) The applicant must submit three copies of the application and all records.

(c) **Information**. The Director, Office of Carrier, Driver and Vehicle Safety Standards (MC-PS) may request further information from the applicant if he/she determines that a decision cannot be made on the evidence submitted. If the applicant fails to submit the information requested, the Director may refuse to issue a determination.

(d) (1) **Action**. Upon receiving a satisfactory application the Director, Office of Carrier, Driver and Vehicle Safety Standards (MC-PS) shall notify the parties (the driver, motor carrier, or any other interested party) that the application has been accepted and that a determination will be made. A copy of all evidence received shall be attached to the notice.

(2) **Reply**. Any party may submit a reply to the notification within 15 days after service. Such reply must be accompanied by all evidence the party wants the Director, Office of Carrier, Driver and Vehicle Safety Standards (MC-PS) to consider in making his/her determination. Evidence submitted should include all medical records and test results upon which the party relies.

(3) **Parties**. A party for the purposes of this section includes the motor carrier and the driver, or anyone else submitting an application.

(e) **Petitions to review, burden of proof.** The driver or motor carrier may petition to review the Director's determination. Such petition must be submitted in accordance with §386.13(a) of this chapter. The burden of proof in such a proceeding is on the petitioner.

(f) **Status of driver.** Once an application is submitted to the Director, Office of Carrier, Driver and Vehicle Safety Standards (MC-PS), the driver shall be deemed disqualified until such time as the Director, Office of Carrier, Driver and Vehicle Safety Standards (MC-PS) makes a determination, or until the Director, Office of Carrier, Driver and Vehicle Safety Standards (MC-PS) orders otherwise.

[42 FR 18081, Apr. 5, 1977, as amended at 42 FR 53966, Oct. 4, 1977; 60 FR 38746, July 28, 1995; 78 FR 58483, Sept. 24, 2013; 80 FR 59075, Oct. 1, 2015]

Guidance for § 391.47: Resolution of conflicts of medical evaluation.

QUESTION 1: Does the FHWA issue formal medical decisions as to the physical qualifications of drivers on an individual basis?

GUIDANCE: No, except upon request for resolution of a conflict of medical evaluations.

§391.49 Alternative physical qualification standards for the loss or impairment of limbs.

(a) A person who is not physically qualified to drive under §391.41(b)(1) or (b)(2) and who is otherwise qualified to drive a commercial motor vehicle, may drive a commercial motor vehicle, if the Division Administrator, FMCSA, has granted a Skill Performance Evaluation (SPE) Certificate to that person.

(b) **SPE certificate**—(1) **Application.** A letter of application for an SPE certificate may be submitted jointly by the person (driver applicant) who seeks an SPE certificate and by the motor carrier that will employ the driver applicant, if the application is accepted.

    (2) **Application address.** The application must be addressed to the applicable field service center, FMCSA, for the State in which the co-applicant motor carrier's principal place of business is located. The address of each, and the States serviced, are listed in §390.27 of this chapter.

    (3) **Exception.** A letter of application for an SPE certificate may be submitted unilaterally by a driver applicant. The application must be addressed to the field service center, FMCSA, for the State in which the driver has legal residence. The driver applicant must comply with all the requirements of paragraph (c) of this section except those in (c)(1)(i) and (iii). The driver applicant shall respond to the requirements of paragraphs (c)(2)(i) to (v) of this section, if the information is known.

(c) A letter of application for an SPE certificate shall contain:

    (1) Identification of the applicant(s):

        (i)   Name and complete address of the motor carrier coapplicant;

        (ii) Name and complete address of the driver applicant;

        (iii) The U.S. DOT Motor Carrier Identification Number, if known; and

        (iv) A description of the driver applicant's limb impairment for which SPE certificate is requested.

    (2) Description of the type of operation the driver will be employed to perform:

        (i)   State(s) in which the driver will operate for the motor carrier coapplicant (if more than 10 States, designate general geographic area only);

        (ii) Average period of time the driver will be driving and/or on duty, per day;

        (iii) Type of commodities or cargo to be transported;

        (iv) Type of driver operation (i.e., sleeper team, relay, owner operator, etc.); and

        (v)   Number of years experience operating the type of commercial motor vehicle(s) requested in the letter of application and total years of experience operating all types of commercial motor vehicles.

    (3) Description of the commercial motor vehicle(s) the driver applicant intends to drive:

        (i)   Truck, truck tractor, or bus make, model, and year (if known);

        (ii) Drive train;

    (A) Transmission type (automatic or manual—if manual, designate number of forward speeds);

    (B) Auxiliary transmission (if any) and number of forward speeds; and

    (C) Rear axle (designate single speed, 2 speed, or 3 speed).

  (iii) Type of brake system;

  (iv) Steering, manual or power assisted;

  (v) Description of type of trailer(s) (i.e., van, flatbed, cargo tank, drop frame, lowboy, or pole);

  (vi) Number of semitrailers or full trailers to be towed at one time;

  (vii) For commercial motor vehicles designed to transport passengers, indicate the seating capacity of commercial motor vehicle; and

  (viii) Description of any modification(s) made to the commercial motor vehicle for the driver applicant; attach photograph(s) where applicable.

(4) Otherwise qualified:

  (i) The coapplicant motor carrier must certify that the driver applicant is otherwise qualified under the regulations of this part;

  (ii) In the case of a unilateral application, the driver applicant must certify that he/she is otherwise qualified under the regulations of this part.

(5) Signature of applicant(s):

  (i) Driver applicant's signature and date signed;

  (ii) Motor carrier official's signature (if application has a coapplicant), title, and date signed. Depending upon the motor carrier's organizational structure (corporation, partnership, or proprietorship), the signer of the application shall be an officer, partner, or the proprietor.

(d) The letter of application for an SPE certificate shall be accompanied by:

(1) A copy of the results of the medical examination performed pursuant to §391.43;

(2) A copy of the medical certificate completed pursuant to §391.43(h);

(3) A medical evaluation summary completed by either a board qualified or board certified physiatrist (doctor of physical medicine) or orthopedic surgeon. The coapplicant motor carrier or the driver applicant shall provide the physiatrist or orthopedic surgeon with a description of the job-related tasks the driver applicant will be required to perform;

  (i) The medical evaluation summary for a driver applicant disqualified under §391.41(b)(1) shall include:

    (A) An assessment of the functional capabilities of the driver as they relate to the ability of the driver to perform normal tasks associated with operating a commercial motor vehicle; and

    (B) A statement by the examiner that the applicant is capable of demonstrating precision prehension (e.g., manipulating knobs and switches) and power grasp prehension (e.g., holding and maneuvering the steering wheel) with each upper limb separately. This requirement does not apply to an individual who was granted a waiver, absent a prosthetic device, prior to the publication of this amendment.

(ii) The medical evaluation summary for a driver applicant disqualified under §391.41(b)(2) shall include:

   (A) An explanation as to how and why the impairment interferes with the ability of the applicant to perform normal tasks associated with operating a commercial motor vehicle;

   (B) An assessment and medical opinion of whether the condition will likely remain medically stable over the lifetime of the driver applicant; and

   (C) A statement by the examiner that the applicant is capable of demonstrating precision prehension (*e.g.*, manipulating knobs and switches) and power grasp prehension (*e.g.*, holding and maneuvering the steering wheel) with each upper limb separately. This requirement does not apply to an individual who was granted an SPE certificate, absent an orthotic device, prior to the publication of this amendment.

(4) A description of the driver applicant's prosthetic or orthotic device worn, if any;

(5) Road test:

   (i) A copy of the driver applicant's road test administered by the motor carrier coapplicant and the certificate issued pursuant to §391.31(b) through (g); or

   (ii) A unilateral applicant shall be responsible for having a road test administered by a motor carrier or a person who is competent to administer the test and evaluate its results.

(6) Application for employment:

   (i) A copy of the driver applicant's application for employment completed pursuant to §391.21; or

   (ii) A unilateral applicant shall be responsible for submitting a copy of the last commercial driving position's employment application he/she held. If not previously employed as a commercial driver, so state.

(7) A copy of the driver applicant's SPE certificate of certain physical defects issued by the individual State(s), where applicable; and

(8) A copy of the driver applicant's State Motor Vehicle Driving Record for the past 3 years from each State in which a motor vehicle driver's license or permit has been obtained.

(e) **Agreement.** A motor carrier that employs a driver with an SPE certificate agrees to:

(1) File promptly (within 30 days of the involved incident) with the Medical Program Specialist, FMCSA service center, such documents and information as may be required about driving activities, accidents, arrests, license suspensions, revocations, or withdrawals, and convictions which involve the driver applicant. This applies whether the driver's SPE certificate is a unilateral one or has a coapplicant motor carrier;

   (i) A motor carrier who is a coapplicant must file the required documents with the Medical Program Specialist, FMCSA for the State in which the carrier's principal place of business is located; or

(ii) A motor carrier who employs a driver who has been issued a unilateral SPE certificate must file the required documents with the Medical Program Specialist, FMCSA service center, for the State in which the driver has legal residence.

(2) Evaluate the driver with a road test using the trailer the motor carrier intends the driver to transport or, in lieu of, accept a certificate of a trailer road test from another motor carrier if the trailer type(s) is similar, or accept the trailer road test done during the Skill Performance Evaluation if it is a similar trailer type(s) to that of the prospective motor carrier. Job tasks, as stated in paragraph (e)(3) of this section, are not evaluated in the Skill Performance Evaluation;

(3) Evaluate the driver for those nondriving safety related job tasks associated with whatever type of trailer(s) will be used and any other nondriving safety related or job related tasks unique to the operations of the employing motor carrier; and

(4) Use the driver to operate the type of commercial motor vehicle defined in the SPE certificate only when the driver is in compliance with the conditions and limitations of the SPE certificate.

(f) The driver shall supply each employing motor carrier with a copy of the SPE certificate.

(g) The Division Administrator/State Director, FMCSA, may require the driver applicant to demonstrate his or her ability to safely operate the commercial motor vehicle(s) the driver intends to drive to an agent of the Division Administrator/State Director, FMCSA. The SPE certificate form will identify the power unit (bus, truck, truck tractor) for which the SPE certificate has been granted. The SPE certificate forms will also identify the trailer type used in the Skill Performance Evaluation; however, the SPE certificate is not limited to that specific trailer type. A driver may use the SPE certificate with other trailer types if a successful trailer road test is completed in accordance with paragraph (e)(2) of this section. Job tasks, as stated in paragraph (e)(3) of this section, are not evaluated during the Skill Performance Evaluation.

(h) The Division Administrator/State Director, FMCSA, may deny the application for SPE certificate or may grant it totally or in part and issue the SPE certificate subject to such terms, conditions, and limitations as deemed consistent with the public interest. The SPE certificate is valid for a period not to exceed 2 years from date of issue, and may be renewed 30 days prior to the expiration date.

(i) The SPE certificate renewal application shall be submitted to the Medical Program Specialist, FMCSA service center, for the State in which the driver has legal residence, if the SPE certificate was issued unilaterally. If the SPE certificate has a coapplicant, then the renewal application is submitted to the Medical Program Specialist, FMCSA field service center, for the State in which the coapplicant motor carrier's principal place of business is located. The SPE certificate renewal application shall contain the following:

(1) Name and complete address of motor carrier currently employing the applicant;

(2) Name and complete address of the driver;

(3) Effective date of the current SPE certificate;

(4) Expiration date of the current SPE certificate;

(5) Total miles driven under the current SPE certificate;

(6) Number of accidents incurred while driving under the current SPE certificate, including date of the accident(s), number of fatalities, number of injuries, and the estimated dollar amount of property damage;

(7) A current medical examination report;

(8) A medical evaluation summary pursuant to paragraph (d)(3) of this section, if an unstable medical condition exists. All handicapped conditions classified under §391.41(b)(1) are considered unstable. Refer to paragraph (d)(3)(ii) of this section for the condition under §391.41(b)(2) which may be considered medically stable.

(9) A copy of driver's current State motor vehicle driving record for the period of time the current SPE certificate has been in effect;

(10) Notification of any change in the type of tractor the driver will operate;

(11) Driver's signature and date signed; and

(12) Motor carrier coapplicant's signature and date signed.

(j) (1) Upon granting an SPE certificate, the Division Administrator/State Director, FMCSA, will notify the driver applicant and co-applicant motor carrier (if applicable) by letter. The terms, conditions, and limitations of the SPE certificate will be set forth. A motor carrier shall maintain a copy of the SPE certificate in its driver qualification file. A copy of the SPE certificate shall be retained in the motor carrier's file for a period of 3 years after the driver's employment is terminated. The driver applicant shall have the SPE certificate (or a legible copy) in his/her possession whenever on duty.

(2) Upon successful completion of the skill performance evaluation, the Division Administrator/State Director, FMCSA, for the State where the driver applicant has legal residence, must notify the driver by letter and enclose an SPE certificate substantially in the following form:

Skill Performance Evaluation Certificate

Name of Issuing Agency _____

Agency Address _____

Telephone Number _____

Issued Under 49 CFR 391.49, subchapter B of the Federal Motor Carrier Safety Regulations

Driver's Name _____

Effective Date _____

Social Security Number _____

Date of Birth_____

Expiration Date _____

Address _____

Driver Disability_____

Check One: ☐ New ☐ Renewal

Driver's License (State) (Number) _____

In accordance with 49 CFR 391.49, subchapter B of the Federal Motor Carrier Safety Regulations (FMCSRs), the driver application for a skill performance evaluation (SPE) certificate is hereby granted authorizing the above-named driver to operate in interstate or foreign commerce under the provisions set forth below. This certificate is granted for the period shown above, not to exceed 2 years, subject to periodic review as may be found necessary. This certificate may be renewed upon submission of a renewal application. Continuation of this certificate is dependent upon strict adherence by the above-named driver to the provisions set forth below and compliance with the FMCSRs. Any failure to comply with provisions herein may be cause for cancellation.

CONDITIONS: As a condition of this certificate, reports of all accidents, arrests, suspensions, revocations, withdrawals of driver licenses or permits, and convictions involving the above-named driver shall be reported in writing to the Issuing Agency by the **employing motor carrier** within 30 days after occurrence.

LIMITATIONS:

1. Vehicle Type (power unit):* _____

2. Vehicle modification(s): _____

3. Prosthetic or Orthotic device(s) (Required to be Worn While Driving): _____

4. Additional Provision(s): _____

NOTICE: To all **motor carriers** employing a driver with an SPE certificate. This certificate is granted for the operation of the *power unit only.* It is the responsibility of the employing motor carrier to evaluate the driver with a road test using the trailer type(s) the motor carrier intends the driver to transport, or in lieu of, accept the trailer road test done during the SPE if it is a similar trailer type(s) to that of the prospective motor carrier. Also, it is the responsibility of the employing motor carrier to evaluate the driver for those non-driving safety-related job tasks associated with the type of trailer(s) utilized, as well as, any other non-driving safety-related or job-related tasks unique to the operations of the employing motor carrier. The SPE of the above named driver was given by a Skill Performance Evaluation Program Specialist. It was successfully completed utilizing the above named power unit and _____ (trailer, if applicable). The tractor or truck had a _____ transmission.

Please read the *NOTICE* paragraph above.

Name _____

Signature _____

Title _____

Date _____

(k) The Division Administrator/State Director, FMCSA, may revoke an SPE certificate after the person to whom it was issued is given notice of the proposed revocation and has been allowed a reasonable opportunity to appeal.

(l) Falsifying information in the letter of application, the renewal application, or falsifying information required by this section by either the applicant or motor carrier is prohibited.

[65 FR 25287, May 1, 2000, as amended at 65 FR 59380, Oct. 5, 2000; 67 FR 61824, Oct. 2, 2002; 78 FR 58483, Sept. 24, 2013]

Guidance for § 391.49: Alternative physical qualification standards for the loss or impairment of limbs.

QUESTION 1: Since 49 CFR 391.49 does not mandate a Skill Performance Evaluation, does the term "performance standard" mean that the State must give a driving test or other Skill Performance Evaluation to the driver for every waiver issued or does this term mean that, depending upon the medical condition, the State may give some other type of performance test? For example, in the case of a vision waiver, would a vision examination suffice as a performance standard?

GUIDANCE: Under the Tolerance Guidelines, Appendix C, Paragraph 3(j), each State that creates a waiver program for intrastate drivers is responsible for determining what constitutes "sound medical judgment," as well as determining the performance standard. In the example used above, a vision examination would suffice as a performance standard. It is the responsibility of each State establishing a waiver program to determine what constitutes an appropriate performance standard.

391.64 Grandfathering for certain drivers participating in vision and diabetes waiver study programs.

(a) The provisions of §391.41(b)(3) do not apply to a driver who was a participant in good standing on March 31, 1996, in a waiver study program concerning the operation of commercial motor vehicles by insulin-controlled diabetic drivers;=*provided:*

    (1) The driver is physically examined every year, including an examination by a board-certified/eligible endocrinologist attesting to the fact that the driver is:

        (i)   Otherwise qualified under §391.41;

    (ii) Free of insulin reactions (an individual is free of insulin reactions if that individual does not have severe hypoglycemia or hypoglycemia unawareness, and has less than one documented, symptomatic hypoglycemic reaction per month);

    (iii) Able to and has demonstrated willingness to properly monitor and manage his/her diabetes; and

    (iv) Not likely to suffer any diminution in driving ability due to his/her diabetic condition.

(2) The driver agrees to and complies with the following conditions:

    (i) A source of rapidly absorbable glucose shall be carried at all times while driving;

    (ii) Blood glucose levels shall be self-monitored one hour prior to driving and at least once every four hours while driving or on duty prior to driving using a portable glucose monitoring device equipped with a computerized memory;

    (iii) Submit blood glucose logs to the endocrinologist or medical examiner at the annual examination or when otherwise directed by an authorized agent of the FMCSA;

    (iv) Provide a copy of the endocrinologist's report to the medical examiner at the time of the annual medical examination; and

    (v) Provide a copy of the annual medical certification to the employer for retention in the driver's qualification file and retain a copy of the certification on his/her person while driving for presentation to a duly authorized Federal, State or local enforcement official.

(b) The provisions of §391.41(b)(10) do not apply to a driver who was a participant in good standing on March 31, 1996, in a waiver study program concerning the operation of commercial motor vehicles by drivers with visual impairment in one eye; *provided:*

(1) The driver is physically examined every year, including an examination by an ophthalmologist or optometrist attesting to the fact that the driver:

    (i) Is otherwise qualified under §391.41; and

    (ii) Continues to measure at least 20/40 (Snellen) in the better eye.

(2) The driver provides a copy of the ophthalmologist or optometrist report to the medical examiner at the time of the annual medical examination.

(3) The driver provides a copy of the annual medical certification to the employer for retention in the driver's qualification file and retains a copy of the certification on his/her person while driving for presentation to a duly authorized federal, state or local enforcement official.

[61 FR 13346, Mar. 26, 1996]

Appendix A to Part 391—Medical Advisory Criteria

I. INTRODUCTION

This appendix contains the Agency's guidelines in the form of Medical Advisory Criteria to help medical examiners assess a driver's physical qualification. These guidelines are strictly advisory and were established after consultation with physicians, States, and industry representatives, and, in some areas, after consideration of recommendations from the Federal Motor Carrier Safety Administration's Medical Review Board and Medical Expert Panels.

II. INTERPRETATION OF MEDICAL STANDARDS

Since the issuance of the regulations for physical qualifications of commercial motor vehicle drivers, the Federal Motor Carrier Safety Administration has published recommendations called Advisory Criteria to help medical examiners in determining whether a driver meets the physical qualifications for commercial driving. These recommendations have been condensed to provide information to medical examiners that is directly relevant to the physical examination and is not already included in the Medical Examination Report Form.

A. Loss of Limb: §391.41(b)(1)

A person is physically qualified to drive a commercial motor vehicle if that person: Has no loss of a foot, leg, hand or an arm, or has been granted a Skills Performance Evaluation certificate pursuant to §391.49.

B. Limb Impairment: §391.41(b)(2)

1. A person is physically qualified to drive a commercial motor vehicle if that person: Has no impairment of:
   (i) A hand or finger which interferes with prehension or power grasping; or
   (ii) An arm, foot, or leg which interferes with the ability to perform normal tasks associated with operating a commercial motor vehicle; or
   (iii) Any other significant limb defect or limitation which interferes with the ability to perform normal tasks associated with operating a commercial motor vehicle; or
   (iv) Has been granted a Skills Performance Evaluation certificate pursuant to §391.49.

2. A person who suffers loss of a foot, leg, hand or arm or whose limb impairment in any way interferes with the safe performance of normal tasks associated with operating a commercial motor vehicle is subject to the Skills Performance Evaluation Certificate Program pursuant to §391.49, assuming the person is otherwise qualified.

3. With the advancement of technology, medical aids and equipment modifications have been developed to compensate for certain disabilities. The Skills Performance Evaluation Certificate Program (formerly the Limb Waiver Program) was designed to allow persons with the loss of a

foot or limb or with functional impairment to qualify under the Federal Motor Carrier Safety Regulations by use of prosthetic devices or equipment modifications which enable them to safely operate a commercial motor vehicle. Since there are no medical aids equivalent to the original body or limb, certain risks are still present, and thus restrictions may be included on individual Skills Performance Evaluation certificates when a State Director for the Federal Motor Carrier Safety Administration determines they are necessary to be consistent with safety and public interest.

4. If the driver is found otherwise medically qualified (§391.41(b)(3) through (13)), the medical examiner must check on the Medical Examiner's Certificate that the driver is qualified only if accompanied by a Skills Performance Evaluation certificate. The driver and the employing motor carrier are subject to appropriate penalty if the driver operates a motor vehicle in interstate or foreign commerce without a current Skill Performance Evaluation certificate for his/her physical disability.

C. Diabetes: §391.41(b)(3)

1. A person is physically qualified to drive a commercial motor vehicle if that person: Has no established medical history or clinical diagnosis of diabetes mellitus currently requiring insulin for control.

2. Diabetes mellitus is a disease which, on occasion, can result in a loss of consciousness or disorientation in time and space. Individuals who require insulin for control have conditions which can get out of control by the use of too much or too little insulin, or food intake not consistent with the insulin dosage. Incapacitation may occur from symptoms of hyperglycemic or hypoglycemic reactions (drowsiness, semi consciousness, diabetic coma or insulin shock).

3. The administration of insulin is, within itself, a complicated process requiring insulin, syringe, needle, alcohol sponge and a sterile technique. Factors related to long-haul commercial motor vehicle operations, such as fatigue, lack of sleep, poor diet, emotional conditions, stress, and concomitant illness, compound the dangers, the Federal Motor Carrier Safety Administration has consistently held that a diabetic who uses insulin for control does not meet the minimum physical requirements of the Federal Motor Carrier Safety Regulations.

4. Hypoglycemic drugs, taken orally, are sometimes prescribed for diabetic individuals to help stimulate natural body production of insulin. If the condition can be controlled by the use of oral medication and diet, then an individual may be qualified under the present rule. Commercial motor vehicle drivers who do not meet the Federal diabetes standard may call (202) 366-4001 for an application for a diabetes exemption.

D. Cardiovascular Condition: §391.41(b)(4)

1. A person is physically qualified to drive a commercial motor vehicle if that person: Has no current clinical diagnosis of myocardial infarction, angina pectoris, coronary insufficiency, thrombosis or any other cardiovascular

disease of a variety known to be accompanied by syncope, dyspnea, collapse or congestive cardiac failure.

2. The term "has no current clinical diagnosis of" is specifically designed to encompass: "a clinical diagnosis of" a current cardiovascular condition, or a cardiovascular condition which has not fully stabilized regardless of the time limit. The term "known to be accompanied by" is designed to include a clinical diagnosis of a cardiovascular disease which is accompanied by symptoms of syncope, dyspnea, collapse or congestive cardiac failure; and/or which is s likely to cause syncope, dyspnea, collapse or congestive cardiac failure.

3. It is the intent of the Federal Motor Carrier Safety Regulations to render unqualified, a driver who has a current cardiovascular disease which is accompanied by and/or likely to cause symptoms of syncope, dyspnea, collapse, or congestive cardiac failure. However, the subjective decision of whether the nature and severity of an individual's condition will likely cause symptoms of cardiovascular insufficiency is on an individual basis and qualification rests with the medical examiner and the motor carrier. In those cases where there is an occurrence of cardiovascular insufficiency (myocardial infarction, thrombosis, etc.), it is suggested before a driver is certified that he or she have a normal resting and stress electrocardiogram, no residual complications and no physical limitations, and is taking no medication likely to interfere with safe driving.

4. Coronary artery bypass surgery and pacemaker implantation are remedial procedures and thus, not medically disqualifying. Implantable cardioverter defibrillators are disqualifying due to risk of syncope. Coumadin is a medical treatment which can improve the health and safety of the driver and should not, by its use, medically disqualify the commercial motor vehicle driver. The emphasis should be on the underlying medical condition(s) which require treatment and the general health of the driver. The Federal Motor Carrier Safety Administration should be contacted at (202) 366-4001 for additional recommendations regarding the physical qualification of drivers on coumadin.

E. **Respiratory Dysfunction: §391.41(b)(5)**
1. A person is physically qualified to drive a commercial motor vehicle if that person: Has no established medical history or clinical diagnosis of a respiratory dysfunction likely to interfere with ability to control and drive a commercial motor vehicle safely.

2. Since a driver must be alert at all times, any change in his or her mental state is in direct conflict with highway safety. Even the slightest impairment in respiratory function under emergency conditions (when greater oxygen supply is necessary for performance) may be detrimental to safe driving.

3. There are many conditions that interfere with oxygen exchange and may result in incapacitation, including emphysema, chronic asthma, carcinoma, tuberculosis, chronic bronchitis and sleep apnea. If the medical

examiner detects a respiratory dysfunction, that in any way is likely to interfere with the driver's ability to safely control and drive a commercial motor vehicle, the driver must be referred to a specialist for further evaluation and therapy. Anticoagulation therapy for deep vein thrombosis and/or pulmonary thromboembolism is not medically disqualifying once optimum dose is achieved, provided lower extremity venous examinations remain normal and the treating physician gives a favorable recommendation.

F. Hypertension: §391.41(b)(6)

1. A person is physically qualified to drive a commercial motor vehicle if that person: Has no current clinical diagnosis of high blood pressure likely to interfere with ability to operate a commercial motor vehicle safely.

2. Hypertension alone is unlikely to cause sudden collapse; however, the likelihood increases when target organ damage, particularly cerebral vascular disease, is present. This regulatory criteria is based on the Federal Motor Carrier Safety Administration's Cardiovascular Advisory Guidelines for the Examination of commercial motor vehicle Drivers, which used the Sixth Report of the Joint National Committee on Detection, Evaluation, and Treatment of High Blood Pressure (1997).

3. Stage 1 hypertension corresponds to a systolic blood pressure of 140-159 mmHg and/or a diastolic blood pressure of 90-99 mmHg. The driver with a blood pressure in this range is at low risk for hypertension-related acute incapacitation and may be medically certified to drive for a one-year period. Certification examinations should be done annually thereafter and should be at or less than 140/90. If less than 160/100, certification may be extended one time for 3 months.

4. A blood pressure of 160-179 systolic and/or 100-109 diastolic is considered Stage 2 hypertension, and the driver is not necessarily unqualified during evaluation and institution of treatment. The driver is given a one-time certification of three months to reduce his or her blood pressure to less than or equal to 140/90. A blood pressure in this range is an absolute indication for anti-hypertensive drug therapy. Provided treatment is well tolerated and the driver demonstrates a blood pressure value of 140/90 or less, he or she may be certified for one year from date of the initial exam. The driver is certified annually thereafter.

5. A blood pressure at or greater than 180 (systolic) and 110 (diastolic) is considered Stage 3, high risk for an acute blood pressure-related event. The driver may not be qualified, even temporarily, until reduced to 140/90 or less and treatment is well tolerated. The driver may be certified for 6 months and biannually (every 6 months) thereafter if at recheck blood pressure is 140/90 or less.

6. Annual recertification is recommended if the medical examiner does not know the severity of hypertension prior to treatment. An elevated

blood pressure finding should be confirmed by at least two subsequent measurements on different days.

7. Treatment includes nonpharmacologic and pharmacologic modalities as well as counseling to reduce other risk factors. Most antihypertensive medications also have side effects, the importance of which must be judged on an individual basis. Individuals must be alerted to the hazards of these medications while driving. Side effects of somnolence or syncope are particularly undesirable in commercial motor vehicle drivers.

8. Secondary hypertension is based on the above stages. Evaluation is warranted if patient is persistently hypertensive on maximal or near-maximal doses of 2-3 pharmacologic agents. Some causes of secondary hypertension may be amenable to surgical intervention or specific pharmacologic disease.

G. **Rheumatic, Arthritic, Orthopedic, Muscular, Neuromuscular or Vascular Disease: §391.41(b)(7)**

1. A person is physically qualified to drive a commercial motor vehicle if that person: Has no established medical history or clinical diagnosis of rheumatic, arthritic, orthopedic, muscular, neuromuscular or vascular disease which interferes with the ability to control and operate a commercial motor vehicle safely.

2. Certain diseases are known to have acute episodes of transient muscle weakness, poor muscular coordination (ataxia), abnormal sensations (paresthesia), decreased muscular tone (hypotonia), visual disturbances and pain which may be suddenly incapacitating. With each recurring episode, these symptoms may become more pronounced and remain for longer periods of time. Other diseases have more insidious onsets and display symptoms of muscle wasting (atrophy), swelling and paresthesia which may not suddenly incapacitate a person but may restrict his/her movements and eventually interfere with the ability to safely operate a motor vehicle. In many instances these diseases are degenerative in nature or may result in deterioration of the involved area.

3. Once the individual has been diagnosed as having a rheumatic, arthritic, orthopedic, muscular, neuromuscular or vascular disease, then he/she has an established history of that disease. The physician, when examining an individual, should consider the following: The nature and severity of the individual's condition (such as sensory loss or loss of strength); the degree of limitation present (such as range of motion); the likelihood of progressive limitation (not always present initially but may manifest itself over time); and the likelihood of sudden incapacitation. If severe functional impairment exists, the driver does not qualify. In cases where more frequent monitoring is required, a certificate for a shorter period of time may be issued.

H. Epilepsy: §391.41(b)(8)

1. A person is physically qualified to drive a commercial motor vehicle if that person: Has no established medical history or clinical diagnosis of epilepsy or any other condition which is likely to cause loss of consciousness or any loss of ability to control a motor vehicle.
2. Epilepsy is a chronic functional disease characterized by seizures or episodes that occur without warning, resulting in loss of voluntary control which may lead to loss of consciousness and/or seizures. Therefore, the following drivers cannot be qualified:
    (i) A driver who has a medical history of epilepsy;
    (ii) A driver who has a current clinical diagnosis of epilepsy; or
    (ii) A driver who is taking antiseizure medication.
3. If an individual has had a sudden episode of a nonepileptic seizure or loss of consciousness of unknown cause which did not require antiseizure medication, the decision as to whether that person's condition will likely cause loss of consciousness or loss of ability to control a motor vehicle is made on an individual basis by the medical examiner in consultation with the treating physician. Before certification is considered, it is suggested that a 6 month waiting period elapse from the time of the episode. Following the waiting period, it is suggested that the individual have a complete neurological examination. If the results of the examination are negative and antiseizure medication is not required, then the driver may be qualified.
4. In those individual cases where a driver has a seizure or an episode of loss of consciousness that resulted from a known medical condition (*e.g.,* drug reaction, high temperature, acute infectious disease, dehydration or acute metabolic disturbance), certification should be deferred until the driver has fully recovered from that condition and has no existing residual complications, and not taking antiseizure medication.
5. Drivers with a history of epilepsy/seizures off antiseizure medication and seizure-free for 10 years may be qualified to drive a commercial motor vehicle in interstate commerce. Interstate drivers with a history of a single unprovoked seizure may be qualified to drive a commercial motor vehicle in interstate commerce if seizure-free and off antiseizure medication for a 5-year period or more.

I. Mental Disorders: §391.41(b)(9)

1. A person is physically qualified to drive a commercial motor vehicle if that person: Has no mental, nervous, organic or functional disease or psychiatric disorder likely to interfere with ability to drive a motor vehicle safely.
2. Emotional or adjustment problems contribute directly to an individual's level of memory, reasoning, attention, and judgment. These problems often underlie physical disorders. A variety of functional disorders can cause drowsiness, dizziness, confusion, weakness or paralysis that

may lead to incoordination, inattention, loss of functional control and susceptibility to accidents while driving. Physical fatigue, headache, impaired coordination, recurring physical ailments and chronic "nagging" pain may be present to such a degree that certification for commercial driving is inadvisable. Somatic and psychosomatic complaints should be thoroughly examined when determining an individual's overall fitness to drive. Disorders of a periodically incapacitating nature, even in the early stages of development, may warrant disqualification.

3. Many bus and truck drivers have documented that "nervous trouble" related to neurotic, personality, or emotional or adjustment problems is responsible for a significant fraction of their preventable accidents. The degree to which an individual is able to appreciate, evaluate and adequately respond to environmental strain and emotional stress is critical when assessing an individual's mental alertness and flexibility to cope with the stresses of commercial motor vehicle driving.

4. When examining the driver, it should be kept in mind that individuals who live under chronic emotional upsets may have deeply ingrained maladaptive or erratic behavior patterns. Excessively antagonistic, instinctive, impulsive, openly aggressive, paranoid or severely depressed behavior greatly interfere with the driver's ability to drive safely. Those individuals who are highly susceptible to frequent states of emotional instability (schizophrenia, affective psychoses, paranoia, anxiety or depressive neuroses) may warrant disqualification. Careful consideration should be given to the side effects and interactions of medications in the overall qualification determination.

J. Vision: §391.41(b)(10)

1. A person is physically qualified to drive a commercial motor vehicle if that person: Has distant visual acuity of at least 20/40 (Snellen) in each eye with or without corrective lenses or visual acuity separately corrected to 20/40 (Snellen) or better with corrective lenses, distant binocular acuity of at least 20/40 (Snellen) in both eyes with or without corrective lenses, field of vision of at least 70 degrees in the horizontal meridian in each eye, and the ability to recognize the colors of traffic signals and devices showing standard red, green, and amber.

2. The term "ability to recognize the colors of" is interpreted to mean if a person can recognize and distinguish among traffic control signals and devices showing standard red, green and amber, he or she meets the minimum standard, even though he or she may have some type of color perception deficiency. If certain color perception tests are administered, (such as Ishihara, Pseudoisochromatic, Yarn) and doubtful findings are discovered, a controlled test using signal red, green and amber may be employed to determine the driver's ability to recognize these colors.

3. Contact lenses are permissible if there is sufficient evidence to indicate that the driver has good tolerance and is well adapted to their use. Use

of a contact lens in one eye for distance visual acuity and another lens in the other eye for near vision is not acceptable, nor telescopic lenses acceptable for the driving of commercial motor vehicles.

4. If an individual meets the criteria by the use of glasses or contact lenses, the following statement shall appear on the Medical Examiner's Certificate: "Qualified only if wearing corrective lenses." commercial motor vehicle drivers who do not meet the Federal vision standard may call 202-366-4001 for an application for a vision exemption.

K. Hearing: §391.41(b)(11)

1. A person is physically qualified to drive a commercial motor vehicle if that person: First perceives a forced whispered voice in the better ear at not less than 5 feet with or without the use of a hearing aid, or, if tested by use of an audiometric device, does not have an average hearing loss in the better ear greater than 40 decibels at 500 Hz, 1,000 Hz, and 2,000 Hz with or without a hearing aid when the audiometric device is calibrated to American National Standard (formerly ADA Standard) Z24.5-1951.

2. Since the prescribed standard under the Federal Motor Carrier Safety Regulations is from the American National Standards Institute, formerly the American Standards Association, it may be necessary to convert the audiometric results from the International Organization for Standardization standard to the American National Standards Institute standard. Instructions are included on the Medical Examination Report Form.

3. If an individual meets the criteria by using a hearing aid, the driver must wear that hearing aid and have it in operation at all times while driving. Also, the driver must be in possession of a spare power source for the hearing aid.

4. For the whispered voice test, the individual should be stationed at least 5 feet from the medical examiner with the ear being tested turned toward the medical examiner. The other ear is covered. Using the breath which remains after a normal expiration, the medical examiner whispers words or random numbers such as 66, 18, 3, etc. The medical examiner should not use only sibilants (s sounding materials). The opposite ear should be tested in the same manner.

5. If the individual fails the whispered voice test, the audiometric test should be administered. If an individual meets the criteria by the use of a hearing aid, the following statement must appear on the Medical Examiner's Certificate "Qualified only when wearing a hearing aid."

L. Drug Use: §391.41(b)(12)

1. A person is physically qualified to drive a commercial motor vehicle if that person does not use any drug or substance identified in 21 CFR 1308.11, an amphetamine, a narcotic, or other habit-forming drug. A driver may use a non-Schedule I drug or substance that is identified in the other Schedules in 21 CFR part 1308 if the substance or drug is prescribed by a licensed medical practitioner who:

     (i)   Is familiar with the driver's medical history, and assigned duties; and

     (ii) Has advised the driver that the prescribed substance or drug will not adversely affect the driver's ability to safely operate a commercial motor vehicle.

2. This exception does not apply to methadone. The intent of the medical certification process is to medically evaluate a driver to ensure that the driver has no medical condition which interferes with the safe performance of driving tasks on a public road. If a driver uses an amphetamine, a narcotic or any other habit-forming drug, it may be cause for the driver to be found medically unqualified. If a driver uses a Schedule I drug or substance, it will be cause for the driver to be found medically unqualified. Motor carriers are encouraged to obtain a practitioner's written statement about the effects on transportation safety of the use of a particular drug.

3. A test for controlled substances is not required as part of this biennial certification process. The Federal Motor Carrier Safety Administration or the driver's employer should be contacted directly for information on controlled substances and alcohol testing under Part 382 of the FMCSRs.

4. The term "uses" is designed to encompass instances of prohibited drug use determined by a physician through established medical means. This may or may not involve body fluid testing. If body fluid testing takes place, positive test results should be confirmed by a second test of greater specificity. The term "habit-forming" is intended to include any drug or medication generally recognized as capable of becoming habitual, and which may impair the user's ability to operate a commercial motor vehicle safely.

5. The driver is medically unqualified for the duration of the prohibited drug(s) use and until a second examination shows the driver is free from the prohibited drug(s) use. Recertification may involve a substance abuse evaluation, the successful completion of a drug rehabilitation program, and a negative drug test result. Additionally, given that the certification period is normally two years, the medical examiner has the option to certify for a period of less than 2 years if this medical examiner determines more frequent monitoring is required.

M. Alcoholism: §391.41(b)(13)

1. A person is physically qualified to drive a commercial motor vehicle if that person: Has no current clinical diagnosis of alcoholism.

2. The term "current clinical diagnosis of" is specifically designed to encompass a current alcoholic illness or those instances where the individual's physical condition has not fully stabilized, regardless of the time element. If an individual shows signs of having an alcohol-use problem, he or she should be referred to a specialist. After counseling and/or treatment, he or she may be considered for certification.

[80 FR 22822, Apr. 23, 2015]

FMCSA Frequently Asked Questions Medical

(Editor's Note: I have copied the FAQs essentially directly from the website, and have added bullets in some places for ease of reading. I have tried to group them by topic. Many are now out of date; the FMCSA is in the process of review of all guidance.)

How will enforcement officials know that a limb-impaired Canadian driver has demonstrated their ability to driver a commercial motor vehicle in accordance with the NSC?

The fact that the driver possesses a valid Canadian commercial driver's license, with the proper class for the vehicle configuration being operated, is proof that the driver demonstrated his/her ability to drive a commercial motor vehicle.

Will Canadian drivers with limb impairments be required to obtain a waiver from FMCSA to drive in the United States?

No, the National Safety Code (NSC) Medical Standards for Drivers and the FMCSR have been deemed equivalent with respect to limb impairments contained in 49 CFR 391.49. To obtain a Canadian provincial/territorial license, such drivers must be fitted with a prosthetic device as appropriate, and must have demonstrated their ability to operate the vehicle.

Can a Canadian driver apply for a Skill Performance Evaluation (SPE) certificate to drive in the United States?

The reciprocity agreement between the United States and Canada does not permit drivers who do not meet the medical fitness requirements of Canada to drive in the United States. Both countries agree that Canadian drivers who do not meet the medical provisions in the National Safety Code of Canada but have a waiver by one of the Canadian Provinces or territories would not be qualified to operate a CMV in the United States. The National Safety Code states that a driver must wear a prosthesis and demonstrate his/her ability in an on-road test. Some of the Canadian provinces have not adopted the National Safety Code. If a driver has no prosthesis when entering the United States, the driver is not qualified to operate here.

It is not necessary for a Canadian driver to apply for a Skill Performance Evaluation certificate to drive in the United States. A valid commercial driver's license issued by a Canadian Province or Territory is proof of medical fitness to drive. If a Canadian driver is required to wear a prosthesis, the driver must wear the prosthesis while operating a commercial vehicle in the U.S. If a driver has no prosthesis when entering the U.S., the driver is not qualified to operate here.

What happens if a driver is not truthful about his/her health history on the medical examination form?

The FMCSA medical certification process is designed to ensure drivers are physically qualified to operate commercial vehicles safely. Each driver is required to complete the Health History section on the first page of the examination report and certify that the responses are complete and true. The driver must also certify that he/she understands that inaccurate, false or misleading information may invalidate the examination and medical examiner's certificate.

FMCSA relies on the medical examiner's clinical judgment to decide whether additional information should be obtained from the driver's treating physician. Deliberate omission or falsification of information may invalidate the examination and any certificate issued based on it. A civil penalty may also be levied against the driver under 49 U.S.C. 521(b)(2)(b), either for making a false statement or for concealing a disqualifying condition.

What tests are used to determine if a driver has adequate hearing to drive safely?
The tests are either the forced whisper test or audiometry. For the whispered voice test, the driver should be 5 feet from the examiner with the ear being tested turned toward the examiner. The other ear is covered. Using the breath which remains after a forced expiration, the examiner whispers words or random numbers such as 66,18.23. The examiner should not use only sibilants (s-sounding test materials). If the individual fails the whisper test, the audiometric test should be administered.

What is the Medical Review Board?
The Medical Review Board (MRB) is a nationally recognized standing board of licensed physicians established by FMCSA to provide expert advice to the Secretary of Transportation on matters related to physical qualifications of drivers, medical standards and guidelines, materials for training medical examiners, functional tests for drivers with multiple disabilities and identifying risks of sudden incapacitation.

How can I get more information or apply to serve on the Medical Review Board (MRB)?
Contact the MRB staff on (202) 366-4001 or fmcsamrb@fmcsa.dot.gov

Are motor carriers legally obligated to provide air conditioning in commercial motor vehicles?
The FMCSRs do not address this issue.

Is the employer legally responsible for paying for the DOT medical examination?
The FMCSRs do not address this issue.

Does the FMCSA set any guidelines for Medical Examiner fees associated with conducting medical examinations?
No. There is no fee schedule.

Is there a "grandfathering" provision for the Vision and Diabetes standards?
Section 391.41(b)(10) does not apply to a driver who was a participant in good standing on March 31, 1996, in a waiver study program concerning the operation of CMVs by drivers with visual impairment in one eye; provided: (1) The driver is physically examined every year, including examination by an ophthalmologist or optometrist attesting to the fact that the driver: (i) Is otherwise qualified under

391.41; and (ii) Continues to measure at least 20/40 (Snellen) in the better eye. (2) The driver provides a copy of the ophthalmologist or optometrist report to the Medical Examiner at the time of the annual medical examination. (3) The driver provides a copy of the annual medical certification to the employer for retention in the driver's qualification file and retains a copy of the certification on his/her person while driving for presentation to an authorized federal, state or local law enforcement official. The grandfathering provision is no longer available.

Who can give a waiver or exemption?

The Medical Examiner cannot grant waivers or exemptions. Only the FMCSA grants waivers or exemptions for certain medical conditions if the individual is otherwise qualified to drive. Section 381.205 of the FMCSRs allow the driver to request a waiver if one or more of the FMCSRs prevent the driver from operating a CMV or make it unreasonably difficult to do so, during a unique, non-emergency event that will take no more than three months to complete.

What is a waiver? An exemption?

A waiver is temporary regulatory relief from one or more of the FMCSRs given to a person subject to the regulations, or a person who intends to engage in an activity that would be subject to the regulations. A waiver provides the person with relief from the regulation for up to three months. 49 CFR 391.64 provides waivers to CMV drivers who were in the initial vision and insulin programs in the early 1990's.

An exemption is a temporary regulatory relief from one of more of the FMCSRs given to a person or class of persons subject to the regulations, or who intend to engage in an activity that would make them subject to the regulation. An exemption provides the person or class of persons with relief from the regulations for up to two years, but may be renewed.

Who should I contact if I have questions about the information I am required to submit to the FMCSA to obtain a waiver or exemption?

You should contact the Office of Bus and Truck Standards and Operations, Federal Motor Carrier Safety Administration, 1200 New Jersey Avenue SE, Washington, DC 20590.

The telephone number is 703-448-3094.

Can I apply for an exemption from the hypertension standard?

A CMV driver may apply for an exemption from any of the standards. Exemptions are granted only in those instances where the driver can show that safety would not be diminished by granting the exemption. 49 CFR 381.300

Can I get a waiver if I have had a single unprovoked seizure?

Drivers who have had one unprovoked seizure by definition do not have epilepsy (2 or more unprovoked seizures). Drivers who are seizure-free and off anticonvulsant medication(s) for at least 5 years after a single unprovoked seizure can be certified. Earlier return to work may be considered for drivers with a normal

EEG who have no epileptic-form activity and normal examination by a neurologist specializing in epilepsy.

Is it possible to get exemptions for some medical conditions?

Under 49 United States Code 31315 and 31136(e), the FMCSA may grant an exemption from the FMCSRs if the agency determines it is in the public interest and would likely achieve a level of safety equivalent to, or greater than, the level that would be achieved by complying with the safety regulation. Sections 381.300 through 381.330 of the FMCSRs describe procedures applicants must follow to apply for exemptions and can be viewed at 49 CFR 381.330. FMCSA currently has exemption programs for vision and insulin-treated diabetes mellitus, and offers a certificate program for drivers with limb impairments. FMCSA also has a special certification program for drivers with missing and/or impaired limbs (49 CFR 391.41(b)(1).

When may I request a waiver/exemption?

You may request a waiver if one or more of the FMCSRs would prevent you from using or operating CMVs or make it unreasonably difficult to do so, during a unique, non-emergency event that will take no more than three months to complete. You may apply for an exemption if one or more FMCSRs prevents you from implementing more efficient or effective operations that would maintain a level of safety equivalent to or greater than the level achieved without the exemption.

Who should I contact if I have questions about the status of my application for a Vision or Diabetes exemption?

You should contact the Office of Bus and Truck Standards and Operations, Federal Motor Carrier Safety Administration, 1200 New Jersey Avenue SE, Washington, DC 20590.

The telephone number is 1-703-448-3094.

Where may I obtain an application for an epilepsy waiver?

A CMV driver may apply for an exemption from any of the standards. Exemptions are granted only in those instances where the driver can show that safety would not be diminished by granting the exemption. 49 CFR 381.300

How do I request a waiver/exemption?

For exemptions from Federal standards other than Diabetes or Vision, please refer to the FMCSRs in Sections 381.210 and 391.310.

How long will it take the agency to respond to my request for a waiver?

The agency will issue a final decision within 180 days of the date it receives your completed application. However, if you leave out required information, it takes longer to complete your application.

What will the FMCSA do after the agency receives my request for a waiver?

After the application is complete, the FMCSA will review the request and make a recommendation to the Administrator. The final decision whether to grant or deny the application for waiver is made by the Administrator.

What am I required to do if the FMCSA grants my exemption?
You must comply with the terms and conditions of the exemption. This information is provided to you.

What is a pilot program?
A pilot program collects specific data to evaluate alternatives to the regulations or innovative approaches to safety while ensuring that the safety performance goals of the regulations are satisfied.

In a pilot program, temporary regulatory relief from one or more FMCSR is given to a person or class of persons subject to the regulations or to a person or class of persons who intend to engage in an activity that would be subject to the regulations.

The number of participants in the pilot program must be large enough to ensure statistically valid findings. 381.400

NOTE: FMCSA is not conducting medical pilot programs at this time.

Who determines if a pilot program should be initiated?
Generally, pilot programs are initiated by the FMCSA when the agency determines that there may be an effective alternative to one or more of the requirements in the FMCSRs, but does not have sufficient research data to support the development of a notice of proposed rulemaking to change the regulation. 381.400

What should I do if I have an idea or suggestion for a pilot program?
You may send a written statement to the Federal Motor Carrier Safety Administration, U.S. Department of Transportation, Office of Bus & Truck Standards and Operations, 1200 New Jersey Avenue SE, Washington, DC 20590. 381.400

I operate a CMV in the United States but reside outside of the United States. Can I use my foreign medical certificate?
Yes, if you are a resident of Mexico or Canada. Drivers certified in Canada are certified to drive in the United States, providing they meet U.S. requirements. For Mexican drivers, the medical examination is part of the Licencia Federal. It is not necessary for Mexican drivers to carry a separate medical certifying document.

A CMV operator from Canada or Mexico who has been issued a valid commercial driver's license by a Canadian Province or the Mexican Licencia Federal is no longer required to have a medical certificate. The driver's medical exam is part of the driver's license process and is proof of medical fitness to drive in the United States. However, Canadian and Mexican drivers who are insulin-using diabetics, who have epilepsy, or who are hearing-and-vision impaired are not qualified to drive CMVs in the United States. Furthermore, Canadian drivers who do not meet the medical fitness provisions of the Canadian National Safety Code for Motor Carriers but who have been issued a waiver by one of the Canadian Provinces or Territories are not qualified to drive CMVs in the United States. Similarly, Mexican drivers who do not meet the medical fitness provision of The Licencia Federal de

Conductor but who have been issued a waiver by The Licencia Federal de Conductor are not qualified to drive CMVs in the United States.

Are government employees exempt from routine/yearly physical examinations?
Transportation performed by the Federal government, a State, or any political subdivision of a State, or an agency established under a compact between states that has been approved by the Congress of the United States are exempt from the FMCSRs, if the political entity chooses.

If a driver has had surgery for Meniere's Disease, is the condition disqualifying?
There is surgery for Meniere's Disease. The FMCSA is now reviewing this issue in relation to certification.

Is Meniere's Disease disqualifying?
Meniere's Disease: a condition associated with severe and unpredictable bouts of dizziness (vertigo) is disqualifying. This recommendation can be found in the Conference on Neurological Disorders and Commercial Drivers.

What is the ANSI Standard?
When the audiometric device is calibrated to the American National Standard (formerly the American Standard Association (ASA) Z24.5-11951. Since the prescribed standard under the FMCSRs is the American National Standards Institute (ANSI), it may be necessary to convert the audiometric results from the ISO standard to the ANSI standard. Instructions are included on the Medical Examination Report form.

Are CMV Drivers required to be CPR certified?
No. There is no regulation that requires CMV drivers to be CPR certified.

Does my driving record affect my eligibility for a medical certificate?
No.

What is the basis of FMCSA's recommendations regarding high blood pressure?
FMCSA medical guidelines for hypertension are based on the Sixth Report of the Joint National Committee on Prevention, Detection, Evaluation and Treatment of High Blood Pressure (JNC 6–1997). The prior cardiovascular guidelines were based on an earlier JNC report.

The medical standard (49 CFR 391.41 (b) (6) permits qualification of CMV drivers if the driver has no current clinical diagnosis of high blood pressure likely to interfere with his/her ability to operate a motor vehicle safely. FMCSA provides guidelines to assist the Medical Examiner in determining if a person is physically qualified to operate a motor vehicle.

What is the effect on driver certification based on FMCSA hypertension stages?
A driver with a diagnosis of hypertension on treatment should have at least an annual certification.

A CMV driver with a Blood pressure (BP) 140/90 may be certified for 2 years.

- First time BP elevated:
  - Stage 1—BP 140-159/90-99 Certification Period 1 year
  - Stage 2—BP 160-179/100-109 Certification Period 3 months as one time certification. Within the 3 months, if the blood pressure is below 140/90, the driver may receive 1 year certification.
  - Stage 3—BP Reading >180/110 Disqualified. When the blood pressure is less than 140/90, the driver can be certified at 6 month intervals.

If a driver with hypertension has lowered his blood pressure to normal range, lost weight, and is off medications, can he/she be certified for 2 years?
This is the Medical Examiner's decision.

Why are the diagnosis and treatment of hypertension important?
These criteria are important because there is strong prospective, randomized clinical-trial evidence that hypertension markedly increases the risk of cardiovascular disease and that effective treatment reduces cardiovascular morbidity and mortality. To be certified to drive, the driver should have ongoing hypertension management and be free of side effects that may impair safe driving.

Am I required to have a medical certificate if I only operate a CMV in my home State (intrastate commerce)?
Intrastate drivers are subject to the physical qualification regulations of their States. All 50 States have adapted their regulations based on some of the Federal requirements. Many states grant waivers for certain medical conditions.

NOTE: FedEx, UPS and DHL drivers usually do not leave the state but are subject to interstate regulations.

Can I report a driver operating without a medical certificate? What protection can I expect as a whistleblower and to whom would I report it?
Yes. Guidelines for reporting a driver operating a CMV without a medical certificate issued by a Medical Examiner and whistleblower protections, i.e., Motor Carrier Employee Whistle Blower Protection (49 United States Code 31105 and 29 Code of Federal Regulations 1978).

Is the driver required to provide a copy to the employer?
Yes, the motor carrier (employer) is required to keep a copy of the medical card (certificate) on file and the driver is required to keep the medical certificate (and supporting documents as required) with him while driving.

As a Medical Examiner, can I disclose the results of my medical evaluation to a CMV driver's employer?
49 CFR 391.43 "Instructions to the Medical Examiner" do not address or prohibit the sharing of medical information. Refer to the HIPAA regulations for guidance. http://www.hhs.gov/ocr/hipaa.

Is a release form required to be completed in order for the employer to legally keep the medical certification card on file?

No. The Medical Examiner is required to provide a copy of the Medical Examiner's Certificate (49 Code of Federal Regulations (CFR) 391.43(g)) to the motor carrier that employs the driver. A release form is not required. The motor carrier is required to keep a copy of the certificate in the driver qualification file (49 CFR 391.51(b)(7)).

Who is required to have a copy of the Medical Certificate?

Section 391.43(g) requires the Medical Examiner to give a copy of the medical certificate to the driver and the motor carrier (employer), if the driver passes the medical examination.

Will my employer have access to my medical evaluation?

Although the FMCSRs do not require the Medical Examiner to give a copy of the Medical Examination Report to the employer, the FMCSA does not prohibit employers from obtaining copies of the medical examination form (long form). Medical Examiners should have a release form signed by the driver if the employer wishes to obtain a copy of the medical examination form (long form).

Employers must comply with applicable State and Federal laws regarding the privacy and maintenance of employee medical information. For information about the provisions of the Standards for Privacy of Individually Identifiable Health Information (the Privacy Rule) that was mandated by the Health Insurance Portability & Accountability Act of 1996 (HIPAA) (Public Law 104-191), contact the U.S. Department of Health & Human Services at the HIPAA Web site of the Office of Civil Rights. Their toll-free information line is: 1-866-627-7748.

Do drivers need to carry the medical certification when driving a CMV?

As of January 30, 2015, Class A, B, or C commercial drivers which certify as "non-exempted interstate" drivers are no longer required to carry their Medical Examiner Certificate in their possession.

May a driver who has non-insulin treated diabetes mellitus (treated with oral medication) be certified for 2 years?

In all cases, clinical judgment is required. The Medical Examiner decides if the driver's diabetes is adequately controlled, which determines certification, length of certification or disqualification. FMCSA guidelines recommend performing annual examination for vision, neurological function and cardiovascular disease, including hypertension. In general, the diabetic driver should have annual re-certification examinations.

Where can I find the FMCSRs?

All of the FMCSRs are listed numerically on the FMCSA's Web site at http://www.fmcsa.dot.gov/rules-regulations/administration/fmcsr/fmcsrguide.asp?section_type=A.

Can I still get a medical certificate if I have a medical condition that is being treated by a physician?

The decision is made by the Medical Examiner. The examiner may request information about the driver's condition from their treating doctor. In general, certification is permitted if the driver does not have a condition, use medication or receive treatment that impairs safe driving.

Can a driver be qualified if he/she is having recurring episodes of ventricular tachycardia?

Drivers with sustained ventricular tachycardia (lasting > 15 seconds) should be disqualified. Drivers experiencing non-sustained V-TACH should be evaluated by a cardiologist to determine the effect on the driver's ability to drive safely, treatment, and if the underlying cause of the ventricular tachycardia is disqualifying (see cardiovascular guidelines for complete review).

How soon may a driver be certified after coronary artery bypass grafting (CABG) surgery?

The driver should not return to driving sooner than 3 months after CABG, to allow the sternal incision to heal. The driver should meet all the following criteria:

- Clearance by physician (usually cardiologist)
- Resting echocardiogram with an LVEF >40% after CABG
- Asymptomatic status with no angina

Can a driver who takes nitroglycerine for angina be certified?

Yes. Nitroglycerine use is not disqualifying. The Medical Examiner may require an evaluation by the treating Cardiologist to make sure that the driver's angina is stable.

If a driver had a Myocardial Infarction (MI), followed by coronary artery bypass graft (CABG) several months ago, should he have an ETT (exercise tolerance test) as recommended in the MI guidelines but not in the CABG guidelines?

Medical Examiners should follow the most current clinical guidelines; therefore after an MI, drivers should obtain an ejection fraction and ETT before returning to work and because of the CABG keeping the driver off work 3 months (not 2 as for MI) to allow time for sternal wound healing.

Can I drive a commercial vehicle after having angioplasty/stents inserted into my heart?

Yes. Drivers who have uncomplicated, elective Percutaneous Coronary Intervention (PCI), with or without stenting, to treat stable angina may return to work as soon as one week after the procedure. Criteria for return to work after PCI include:

- Examination and approval by the treating cardiologist;
- Asymptomatic;
- No injury to the vascular access site;
- ETT three to six months post PCI.

- In the CMV driver this requires exercising to workload capacity of at least six METS (through Bruce Stage II or equivalent), attaining a heart rate >85% of predicted maximum (unless on beta blockers), a rise in SBP >20mmHg without angina, and having no significant ST segment depression or elevation. Stress radionuclide or echocardiography imaging should be performed for symptomatic individuals, individuals with an abnormal resting echocardiogram, or those drivers who fail to obtain the minimal standards required from the standard ETT;
- Annual medical qualification examination;
- Negative ETT at least every other year (criteria above) and tolerance of all cardiovascular medication. The driver should not experience orthostatic symptoms, including light-headedness; a resting SBP <95mmHg systolic; or a systolic blood pressure decline >20mmHg upon standing.

What is a satisfactory exercise tolerance test?

A satisfactory ETT requires exercising to a workload capacity of at least six METS (through Bruce Stage II or equivalent) attaining a heart rate of >85% of predicted maximum (unless on beta blockers), a rise in SBP >20mmHg without angina, and having no significant ST segment depression or elevation.

Stress radionuclide or exercise echocardiogram should be performed for symptomatic individuals, individuals with an abnormal resting electrocardiogram, or individuals who fail to meet the ETT requirements.

My medical certificate is still valid. Am I prohibited from operating a CMV if I have a medical condition that developed after my last medical certificate was issued?

FMCSA regulations prohibit a driver from beginning or continuing to drive if their ability and/or alertness is impaired by: fatigue, illness, or any cause that makes it unsafe to begin (continue) to drive a commercial vehicle.

Even if a driver currently has a valid medical certificate, the driver is prohibited from driving a CMV with any medical condition that would be disqualifying or may interfere with the safe operation of a CMV. Once a disqualifying medical condition is resolved, and before resuming operation of CMVs, a driver is responsible for obtaining re-certification from a Medical Examiner. 391.45

How long does it take to get my medical certificate once my medical examination is complete?

The FMCSRs do not specify that the Medical Examiner must give a copy of the Medical Examiner's Certificate to the driver immediately following the examination. The Medical Examiner may require additional medical tests or reports from your treating physician.

What are the differences between the medical standards and the medical advisory criteria and the medical guidelines?

The Medical Examiner must follow the standards found in 49 CFR 391.41. In the case of vision, hearing, epilepsy and diabetes requiring any use of insulin, the FMCSRs standards are absolute and allow no discretion by the Medical Examiner.

FMCSA also provides medical advisory criteria and medical guidelines to assist the Medical Examiner determine if a person is physically qualified to operate a commercial bus or truck. The Medical Examiner may or may not choose to use these guidelines. These guidelines are based on expert review and considered practice standards. The examiner should document the reason(s) for not following the guidelines.

Can carriers set their own standards for CMV drivers who operate in interstate commerce?

49 CFR Section 390.3(d) gives employers the right to adopt stricter medical standards. Motor Carriers (companies) cannot set less restrictive standards. In addition, the employer can require the driver to perform ancillary duties as a condition of employment.

What does the medical examination involve?

The driver must be medically examined and certified in accordance with Section 391.43 of the FMCSRs.

What medical criteria are required to obtain a medical certificate?

The physical qualification regulations for CMV drivers in interstate commerce are found at Section 391.41(b) of the FMCSRs. Instructions to Medical Examiners performing physical examinations are found at Section 391.43. Advisory criteria under 391.41 are recommendations. They are accessible on the FMCSA's Web site at http://www.fmcsa.dot.gov/rules-regulations/administration/medical.htm. FMCSA has published medical conference reports as recommendations to assist Medical Examiners determine whether a driver is qualified under Section 391.41(b). The conference reports may be accessed on the FMCSA Web site.

Are holders of Class 3 pilot licenses required to have another physical for commercial driving?

Drivers of CMV who operate in interstate commerce must be medically qualified in accordance with 49 CFR 391.41.

If I am a medically certified pilot, can I legally operate a CMV?

Section 391.43(g) requires the Medical Examiner to give a copy of the medical certificate to the driver and the motor carrier (employer), if the driver passes the medical examination.

How do Medical Examiners differ from Medical Review Officers?

A Medical Review Officer (MRO) is a licensed physician responsible for receiving and reviewing laboratory results generated by an employer's drug testing program and evaluating medical explanations for test results. More information on MROs is available online at http://www.dot.gov/ost/dapc/mro.html. Medical Examiner means a person who is licensed, certified, or registered, in accordance with applicable State laws and regulations to perform physical examinations. This includes but is not limited to doctors of medicine, doctors of osteopathy, physician assistants, advanced practice nurses and doctors of chiropractic.

May a Medical Examiner qualify a driver who has blood in his urine?

The Medical Examiner decides to certify, time-limit or disqualify. The decision to certify a driver is determined by whether the examiner believes that the blood in the urine affects the ability of the commercial driver to drive safely. Regardless of whether the CMV driver is certified, the Medical Examiner should document referral to a specialist or the driver's Primary Care Provider.

For how long is my medical certificate valid?

The certificate is valid for 2 years. In addition, drivers with specific medical conditions require more frequent certification:

- Hypertension (high blood pressure) stable on treatment 1 year
- Heart disease 1 year
- Qualified under 391.64 the original diabetes and vision waiver program 1 year
- New insulin and vision exemption program 1 year
- Driving in exempt intra-city zone 1 year
- Determination by examiner that condition requires more frequent monitoring, such as diabetes mellitus or sleep disorders.

Are there duties related to the FMCSA medical certification?

No, the FMCSA does not have duties. The Medical Examiner is required to know the FMCSA driver physical qualification standards, medical guidelines, and advisory criteria. The examiner should understand the mental and physical demands of operating a CMV.

What information should the Medical Examiner have available to decide if a driver is medically qualified?

Medical Examiners who perform FMCSA medical examinations should understand: (1) Specific physical and mental demands associated with operating a CMV, (2) Physical qualification standards specified by 49 CFR 391.41 (b) (1-13), (3) FMCSA advisory criteria and other criteria prepared by the FMCSA, and (4) FMCSA medical guidelines to assess the CMV driver's medical condition.

Why is the DOT physical examination important?

The FMCSA physical examination is required to help ensure that a person is medically qualified to safely operate a CMV. In the interest of public safety, CMV drivers are held to higher physical, mental and emotional standards than passenger car drivers.

Are the DOT medical examinations covered by HIPAA?

Regulatory requirements take precedence over the Health Insurance Portability and Accountability Act (HIPAA) of 1996. There are potential subtle interpretations that can cause significant problems for the Medical Examiner. What information must or can be turned over to the carrier is a legal issue, and if in doubt, the examiner should obtain a legal opinion. Federal Motor Carrier Safety Regulation 391.43 does not address or prohibit the sharing of medical information by Medical Examiners. http://www.hhs.gov/ocr/hipaa

How can I get a copy of my medical evaluation file?

You can contact the Medical Examiner that conducted your evaluation for a copy of your medical certification examination.

Can a driver on oxygen therapy be qualified to drive in interstate commerce?

In most cases, the use of oxygen therapy while driving is disqualifying. Concerns include oxygen equipment malfunction, risk of explosion, and the presence of significant underlying disease that is disqualifying, such as pulmonary hypertension. The driver must be able to pass a Pulmonary Function Test (PFT).

What is the Federal Motor Carrier Safety Administration?

The Motor Carrier Safety Improvement Act of 1999 created the Federal Motor Carrier Safety Administration (FMCSA) as a separate administration within the U.S. Department of Transportation on January 1, 2000. The primary mission of FMCSA is to reduce crashes, injuries, and fatalities involving large trucks and buses. FMCSA is headquartered in Washington, D.C., and employs more than 1,000 individuals in all 50 States, the District of Columbia, and Puerto Rico. For more information, go to About Us section on the FMCSA Web site.

May I request reconsideration if I am found not qualified for a medical certificate?

The decision to qualify a driver to operate a CMV in interstate commerce is the sole responsibility of the Medical Examiner. The driver may discuss the basis for the disqualification with the Medical Examiner and explore options for reconsideration.

Who signs the medical certificate?

The Medical Examiner who performs the medical examination must sign the Medical Certificate.

What is the protocol if the Medical Examiner's Certificate gets damaged, lost or unreadable?

A copy of the Medical Examiner's Certificate should be kept on file in the Medical Examiner's office. The driver may request a replacement copy of the certificate from the Medical Examiner or get a copy of the certificate from the motor carrier.

What if the certifying doctor is no longer available?

If the original Medical Examiner is not available, the physician or Medical Examiner in the office may sign the replacement certificate. The advisory criteria states that the original may be copied and given to the driver. Some physicians may require the driver to undergo a new physical examination.

What medications disqualify a CMV driver?

A driver cannot take a controlled substance or prescription medication without a prescription from a licensed practitioner.

If a driver uses a drug identified in 21 CFR 1308.11 (391.42(b)(12)) or any other substance such as amphetamine, a narcotic, or any other habit forming drug, the driver is medically unqualified.

There is an exception: the prescribing doctor can write that the driver is safe to be a commercial driver while taking the medication. In this case, the Medical Examiner may, but does not have to, certify the driver.

- Any anti-seizure medication used for the prevention of seizures is disqualifying.
- Methadone use is disqualifying.

The Medical Examiner has 2 ways to determine if any medication a driver uses will adversely affect safe operation of a CMV:

1. Review each medication—prescription, non-prescription and supplement
2. Request a letter from the prescribing doctor

Can a CMV driver be disqualified for using a legally prescribed drug?
Although the driver has a legal prescription, he/she may be disqualified if the medication could adversely affect the driver's ability to drive a CMV safely.

Can a driver be qualified if he is taking Methadone?
No. CMV drivers taking Methadone cannot be qualified.

Can a driver be qualified if taking prescribed medical marijuana?
No. Drivers taking medical marijuana cannot be certified.

Can CMV drivers be qualified while being prescribed Provigil (Modafinil)?
Provigil (Modafinil) is a medication used to treat excessive sleepiness caused by certain sleep disorders. These sleep disorders are narcolepsy, obstructive sleep apnea/hypopnea syndrome and shift work sleep disorders. Provigil has several concerning side effects such as chest pain, dizziness, difficulty breathing, heart palpitations, irregular and/or fast heartbeat, increased blood pressure, tremors or shaking movements, anxiety, nervousness, rapidly changing mood, problems with memory, blurred vision or other vision changes to name a few. Many drugs interact with Provigil which include over-the-counter medications, prescription medications, nutritional supplements, herbal products, alcohol containing beverages and caffeine. The use of Provigil needs careful supervision. Provigil may affect concentration, function or may hide signs that an individual is tired. It is recommended that until an individual knows how Provigil affects him/her, they may not drive, use machinery or do any activity that requires mental alertness.

Who can serve as a Medical Examiner and perform DOT physical exams?
Federal Motor Carrier Safety Regulations define Medical Examiner as a person who is licensed, certified and/or registered in accordance with applicable State laws and regulations to perform physical examinations. The term includes but is not limited to doctors of medicine, doctors of osteopathy, physician assistants, advanced practice nurses and doctors of chiropractic.

Is Proteinuria disqualifying?

Depending on the amount, protein in the urine (Proteinuria) may indicate significant renal disease. The Medical Examiner may certify, time limit, or disqualify a
commercial driver with Proteinuria. The decision is based on whether the examiner
believes that Proteinuria may adversely affect safe driving regardless of the examiner's decision. The driver should be referred for follow-up.

Is Narcolepsy disqualifying?

The guidelines recommend disqualifying a CMV driver with a diagnosis of Narcolepsy,
regardless of treatment, because of the likelihood of excessive daytime somnolence.

When is audiometry required?

A medical examiner may require a driver to have an audiometry test. If the driver
fails the whisper test, the driver must pass an audiometer test to be qualified to
drive a CMV.

Office audiometry is not able to test a person with a hearing aid. The person needs
to be referred for accurate testing.

Can a driver receive a hearing waiver?

Currently, there is no waiver program for hearing.

What are the hearing requirements for CMV drivers?

A person is physically qualified to drive a CMV if that person: First perceives a
forced whispered voice in the better ear at not less than five feet with or without
the use of a hearing aid or if tested by use of an audiometric device, does not
have an average hearing loss in the better ear greater than 40 decibels at 500Hz,
1000Hz and 2,000 Hz with or without a hearing aid when the audiometric device is
calibrated to the American National Standard Z24.5-1951.

Are CMV drivers who operate in interstate commerce required to have a medical certificate?

Drivers are required to have a DOT Medical Certificate:

- If they operate a motor vehicle with a gross vehicle weight rating (GVWR),
  gross combination weight rating (GCWR), gross vehicle weight (GCW), or gross
  combination weight (GCW) of 4,536 kilograms or more in interstate commerce.
- If they operate a motor vehicle designed or used to transport more than 15
  passengers (including the driver) in interstate commerce.
- If they operate a motor vehicle designed or used to transport between 9 and
  15 passengers, for direct compensation, beyond 75 air miles from the driver's
  normal work-reporting location, in interstate commerce.
- If they transport hazardous materials, in a quantity requiring placards, in
  interstate commerce.

Is getting a medical certificate mandatory for all CMV drivers in the United States?

In general, all CMV drivers driving in interstate commerce within the United States
must obtain medical certification from a Medical Examiner. CMV drivers from
Canada and Mexico can be medically qualified in their countries.

What is the age requirement for operating a CMV in interstate commerce?
A person must be at least 21 years old to drive a CMV in interstate commerce.

What medical conditions disqualify a commercial bus or truck driver?
The truck driver must be medically qualified to not only drive the vehicle safely, but also to do pre and post trip safety inspections, secure the load and make sure it has not shifted. Bus drivers have different demands.

By regulation, Specific Medically Disqualifying Conditions Found Under 49 CFR 391.41 are Hearing Loss, Vision Loss, Epilepsy and Insulin Use.

Drivers who require a Diabetes or Vision exemption to safely drive a CMV in addition to those pre-printed on the certification form are disqualified until they receive such an exemption.

Is the certification limited to current employment or job duties?
When a Medical Examiner grants medical certification, he/she certifies the driver to perform any job duty required of a commercial driver, not just the driver's current job duties.

If the driver admits to regular alcohol use, and based on responses on the driver history, further questioning or additional tools such as CAGE, AUDIT or TWEAK assessments, may the examiner require further evaluation prior to signing the medical certificate?
Yes. Except where absolute criteria exist, the final determination as to whether the driver meets the FMCSA medical standards is to be made by the medical examiner. The examiner should use whatever tools or additional assessments they feel are necessary. Under 391.43, Instructions to the Medical Examiner -Laboratory and "Other Testing," support is provided to the examiner if they believe that "Other test(s) may be indicated based upon the medical history or findings of the physical examination."

Further supporting the need for additional evaluation is the medical advisory criteria for 391.41(b) 13 which notes that "if an individual shows signs of having an alcohol-use problem, he or she should be referred to a specialist. After counseling and/or treatment, he or she may be considered for certification."

While not regulation, the medical advisory criteria are provided by the FMCSA to assist the Medical Examiner in determining if a person is physically qualified to operate a CMV. The Medical Examiner may or may not choose to use these guidelines. These guidelines are based on expert review and considered practice standards. The examiner should document the reason(s) for not following the guidelines.

General Frequently Asked Questions to the National Registry of Certified Medical Examiners.

What is the National Registry of Certified Medical Examiners?

The National Registry of Certified Medical Examiners (National Registry) is a new Federal Motor Carrier Safety Administration (FMCSA) program that establishes minimum training and testing requirements for all State-licensed healthcare professionals who perform physical qualification examinations for truck and bus drivers. Beginning May 21, 2014, all drivers who need a new medical certificate must see an examiner on the National Registry. Medical certificates issued prior to May 21, 2014 remain valid until the expiration date.

Why did FMCSA establish the National Registry?

FMCSA issued the rule in response to the statutory requirements in the Safe, Accountable, Flexible, Efficient Transportation Equity Act: A Legacy for Users (SAFETEA-LU), the surface transportation reauthorization legislation enacted in 2005. The final rule will improve safety by ensuring that medical examiners have completed training and testing concerning FMCSA's physical qualifications standards and only issue medical certificates to individuals who meet those standards.

Commercial Motor Vehicle (CMV) Drivers

Do I have to have a new physical examination with a medical examiner on the National Registry on May 21, 2014, even if my certificate is not yet expired?

No. Medical certificates issued prior to May 21, 2014, are valid until the expiration date on the certificate. Any interstate CMV driver seeking a medical certificate on or after May 21, 2014, must obtain it from an examiner listed on the National Registry website located at https://nationalregistry.fmcsa.dot.gov.

Will the physical qualifications standards change on May 21, 2014, as a result of the National Registry deadline?

No. The physical qualifications standards for CMV drivers will not change. What may happen is that some examiners who have completed the mandatory training and testing may conduct more thorough examinations and subsequently, identify drivers who were not supposed to receive unrestricted 2-year medical certificates.

How do I find a certified medical examiner?

Certified medical examiners are listed on the National Registry website at https://nationalregistry.fmcsa.dot.gov.

I prefer going to my doctor for my commercial motor vehicle physical exam. Can I still use him/her after May 21, 2014?

Yes. You can still use your doctor provided he/she is listed as a certified medical examiner on the National Registry. If not, you will have to use a certified medical examiner who is listed on the National Registry website at https://nationalregistry.fmcsa.dot.gov.

Will the medical examiner inform the State driver licensing agency that I have passed the physical examination?

No. Commercial driver's license (CDL) holders are still required to provide proof of medical certification to the State agency issuing the license. Contact your State driver licensing agency for information about how to provide proof of your medical certificate.

Do I have to send a copy of my medical certificate to FMCSA?

No. Your medical certificate information will be transmitted electronically to FMCSA by your medical examiner.

Will the medical examination reports be entered into the National Registry?

No. FMCSA will not collect or store medical examination reports (i.e., the long form).

Motor Carriers

Are motor carriers required to verify that a driver's medical card issued on or after May 21, 2014, was issued by a healthcare professional on the National Registry?

Yes. The regulations require that motor carriers check the National Registry website to verify that the medical examiner is certified. However, motor carriers are not required to contact the medical examiner to verify that he/she signed the document.

May a motor carrier accept a medical certificate issued prior to May 21, 2014, from a person applying for a job as an interstate driver?

Yes. Medical certificates issued before May 21, 2014, remain valid until the expiration date, even if the certificates were issued by a healthcare professional who is not listed on the National Registry. The new National Registry requirements are applicable only to medical examinations performed on or after May 21, 2014. For example, if a driver has a 2-year medical certificate issued on May 1, 2014, that medical certificate is valid through May 1, 2016. Therefore, the driver would not be required to obtain a medical certificate from an examiner on the National Registry until he/she renews the medical certificate.

May motor carriers that have preferred examiners continue to rely on those individuals to perform medical examinations for their drivers?

Yes. They can use preferred examiners provided those individuals are listed on the National Registry. The regulations allow healthcare professionals who are licensed by a State to perform physical examinations, and who have completed FMCSA's training and testing requirements for the National Registry, to issue medical certificates. Therefore, if the examiner has completed all of the training and testing requirements prior to issuing any new medical certificates on or after May 21, 2014, FMCSA will accept the newly issued certificates. And, any medical certificates issued before May 21, 2014, will remain valid until the expiration date, regardless of whether the examiner enrolls in the National Registry.

If a driver receives a medical certificate from a medical examiner who is later removed from the National Registry for inappropriate activities, is the medical certificate still valid?

Yes. However, FMCSA may exercise its authority to review the medical examiner's report (long form) and, if necessary, discuss the matter with the driver to make an individual determination whether the driver may need to obtain a new medical certificate.

Medical Examiners

Who is eligible to become a medical examiner?

Currently, healthcare professionals who are licensed, certified, and/or registered in accordance with applicable State laws and regulations to perform physical examinations, may perform medical examinations for CMV drivers. This includes, but is not limited to, doctors of medicine, doctors of osteopathy, physician assistants, advanced practice nurses, and doctors of chiropractic.

How do I become a certified medical examiner on the National Registry?

To become a certified medical examiner, you must register through the National Registry website at https://nationalregistry.fmcsa.dot.gov to receive a unique identification number (National Registry Number). You will then need to complete accredited training and pass the Federal Motor Carrier Safety Administration Medical Examiner Certification Test. You may become certified after the compliance date, but you must not issue medical certificates for interstate truck and bus drivers on or after May 21, 2014, until you have completed the certification process.

Do I have to pay for the training and testing to become a certified medical examiner?

Yes. You are responsible for paying any fees charged by the private sector training and testing organizations. FMCSA neither establishes nor regulates the schedules of fees established and collected by private sector training or testing organizations and does not receive any monies collected by these organizations or providers.

How do I find training organizations?

FMCSA posts contact information on the National Registry website for training organizations. However, FMCSA does not approve or endorse training providers or courses.

To access the list of training providers who offer National Registry training, follow these steps:

1. Visit the National Registry website at https://nationalregistry.fmcsa.dot.gov.
2. Select the "Medical Examiners and Assistants" link at the top of the page.
3. Select "Find a Training Organization" from the menu on the left.

How can I determine whether a training provider's program meets all of the National Registry requirements?

Prospective medical examiners may visit the National Registry website at https:// nationalregistry.fmcsa.dot.gov to obtain the regulatory requirements for training, including the eight topics (the core curriculum) that must be covered by the training. The training organization must be accredited by a nationally recognized medical profession accrediting organization that provides continuing education units, and the training must include all of the topics outlined in the final rule. The training organization must provide training participants with proof of participation.

How can I find a testing organization?

To find a testing organization near you, follow these steps:

1. Visit the National Registry website at https://nationalregistry.fmcsa.dot.gov
2. Select the "Medical Examiners and Assistants" link at the top of the page
3. Select "Search for Testing Locations" from the menu on the left. Then select "Find a Testing Organization" to search by testing organization name, city and state, or zip code.
4. Select a test center and click the website link.
5. Follow the instructions on the test organization website to schedule your test appointment.

NOTE: Please be sure to read all the policies and procedures provided by the test organization before you submit your payment; some test organization fees are non-refundable.

How long will it take to obtain my certification after I pass the test?

You will receive email notification of your certification credential approximately 1 to 2 business days after you pass the certification test. At that time, your information will be available via the National Registry website's Public Search link. Make sure all the information in your National Registry account is up to date. Missing or inconsistent information or expired credentials can cause delays in receiving your certification.

What should I do if it has been longer than expected, and I have not received my certification?

Review the information in your National Registry account to make sure it is up to date. Check to make sure the name you entered exactly matches the name on your medical license. If you have not done so, you must enter your training information and make sure your medical licensing information is not expired by following these steps:

1. Go to the National Registry website at https://nationalregistry.fmcsa.dot.gov
2. Select "Login" in the blue bar at the top of the screen.
3. Enter your username and password and click "Login."
4. Select "View and Add Training Information" under "My Certification and Training" in the blue bar across the top of the screen.
5. Select "Add Training" and enter your training information.
6. Click "Save Changes."

NOTE: The system cannot certify your account until your training information has been entered.

If I don't pass the certification test, can I retake it?
Yes. However, you must wait at least 30 days before taking the test.

How do I submit the monthly report of medical certificates to FMCSA?
The CMV Driver Medical Examination Results, Form MCSA-5850, is a secure, online form that is only available through your National Registry account. FMCSA will not accept submissions by any other means.

Certified medical examiners may submit the CMV Driver Medical Examination Results by following these steps:

1. Go to the National Registry website at https://nationalregistry.fmcsa.dot.gov
2. Login to your National Registry account.
3. Select "CMV Driver Exams" from the blue bar at the top of the screen.
4. Select "Submit CMV Driver Exam Results."
5. Enter driver information and exam data, click "Submit."

Be sure to submit a form for each driver exam you have completed during the previous month. If you have not completed any exams during the previous month, select the box next to "No exams completed during this period" on the CMV Driver Examination Results page.

When do I have to begin submitting CMV Driver Examination Results?
You must submit exam results for all driver examinations you perform on or after May 21, 2014. This must be done by the end of the following month. For example, if you perform a driver exam on May 21, you must report that exam by June 30, 2014. You may, but are not required to, submit CMV Driver Examination Results for exams performed before May 21, 2014.

State Commercial Driver Licensing Agencies

Are State agencies that issue CDLs required to verify the validity of the medical certificate?
No. State licensing agencies are required to enter the medical certificate information, including the National Registry identification number, onto interstate CDL holders' driving record, accessible through the Commercial Driver's License Information System (CDLIS), but they are not required to verify the accuracy of the medical certificate.

FMCSA anticipates publishing and implementing a final rule that would provide a means for the Agency to receive the medical certificates from certified examiners. The Agency would then transmit the medical certificate information directly to the State licensing agency to reduce the possibility of falsification of medical certificates.

Enforcement (Roadside Inspectors)

Are roadside inspectors required to verify that medical certificates are issued by examiners on the National Registry?

No. As part of the North American Standard Inspection procedure, roadside inspectors will verify that interstate drivers subject to the physical qualifications standards have a medical certificate (e.g., a paper or electronic copy with e-signature or, in the case of a CDL holder, a paper or electronic copy or proof on the CDL driving record). However, inspectors are not required to verify that examiners are listed on the National Registry. If an inspector wants to verify the identity of an examiner, and has internet access at the inspection site, he/she may visit and search the registry to verify the examiner identified on the certificate is listed on the National Registry.

References

1. Federal Motor Carrier Safety Administration, Department of Transportation. Physical qualification of drivers; Medical examination; Final rule. *Fed Reg* 2000;65(Oct. 5):59363–59380. https://www.gpo.gov/fdsys/pkg/FR-2000-10-05 /pdf/00-25337.pdf.
2. Federal Motor Carrier Safety Administration Medical Conference Reports – now archived. https://www.fmcsa.dot.gov/regulations/medical/medical-reports -archive
3. Title 49, Subtitle B, Chapter, Part 360. eCFR. http://www.ecfr.gov/cgi-bin /retrieveECFR?gp=1&ty=HTML&h=L&mc=true&=PART&n=pt49.5.390.
4. Interpretations to Title 49, Subtitle B, Chapter, Part 360. https://www.fmcsa.dot .gov/regulations/title49/b/5/3/list?filter=Driver
5. Federal Motor Carrier Safety Administration Medical Examiner Handbook. https://www.fmcsa.dot.gov/regulations/medical/fmcsa-medical-examiner -handbook. Currently under revision.
6. Medical Expert Panel Reports. https://www.fmcsa.dot.gov/regulations /medical/reports-how-medical-conditions-impact-driving
7. Proceedings of the FMCSE Medical Review Board. https://www.fmcsa.dot .gov/medical-review-board-mrb-proceedings
8. Federal Motor Carrier Safety Administration Medical Frequently Asked Questions. https://www.fmcsa.dot.gov/faq/Medical-Requirements.
9. Federal Motor Carrier Safety Administration National Registry of Certified Medical Examiners Frequently Asked Questions. https://nationalregistry.fmcsa .dot.gov/ResourceCenter/documents/National_Registry_FAQ.pdf

PART II

Specific Medical Conditions

Most of the regulations that are used to determine whether a commercial driver should be medically qualified are intentionally left vague. While there are four criteria that are considered to be absolute (although the driver may be eligible for an exemption)—vision, hearing, use of insulin, and use of medications to control seizures—the others are intentionally left to the discretion of the medical examiner. When the regulations state that a person should not be certified if a disease "of a variety known to be accompanied by_____" is present, should the examiner refuse to qualify anyone with a medical diagnosis for which one of the possible outcomes is listed? Or should certification be acceptable unless the risk of sudden incapacitation is almost inevitable?

The intent of these regulations is to balance risk to the public and risk of taking a driver out of service who is at low risk of a specific event—the inability to operate a commercial motor vehicle safely. Many medical conditions can have an impact on driving ability, but usually drivers have sufficient warning to pull their vehicles to the side of the road and prevent an accident.

One component of risk is exposure. Although noncommercial drivers often spend less than 3 hours per day behind the wheel, the individuals we are asked to evaluate under 49 CFR 391.41 may be on the road more than 10 hours daily. A neurologic event that has a 1 in 10 chance of occurring during the time a driver of a private vehicle is behind the wheel may have 3 to 4 times the likelihood of occurring while a commercial driver is driving. One long accepted acceptable risk is from the Canadian Cardiovascular Society, which uses a 1 percent annual risk of an accident as the defining point at which a commercial driver should not be medically qualified.[1]

Although the functional status resulting from a chronic disease may not significantly increase the risk for a noncommercial driver, a commercial driver has additional stressors with which to contend (*see* Part III). The following factors may be involved in a driver's performance of duties: abrupt schedule changes and rotating work schedules, which may result in irregular sleep patterns and a driver beginning a trip in a fatigued condition; long hours; extended time away from family and friends, which may result in lack of social support; tight pickup and delivery schedules, with irregularity in work, rest, and eating patterns; adverse road, weather, and traffic conditions, which may cause delays and lead to hurriedly loading or unloading cargo in order to compensate for the lost time; and environmental conditions such as excessive vibration, noise, and extremes in temperature. Transporting passengers or hazardous materials may add to the demands on the commercial driver.

Also:

- Hours-of-service regulations
- Pay by the mile
- Lack of parking facilities
- Poor food choices available at truck stops
- Scheduling problems
- Long hours
- Delays at loading docks
- Proper sleep
- Lack of available health care
- Prolonged sitting
- Intermittent intense exercise during loading, tarping, tying down, etc.
- Vibration

Chronic medical problems also may interfere with many of the nondriving tasks of a commercial driver. Musculoskeletal or neurologic impairments may impede the driver's ability to manipulate load-secure-ment devices or maneuver the steering wheel. Most important is the fact that the medical condition may not be present in isolation. A driver with currently stable heart disease and noninsulin-requiring diabetes should be evaluated differently from a driver with only a single disease process. It also is very important to obtain information from all treating health care providers to assess compliance with treatment and stability of the medical condition(s). If the examiner believes that the driver currently meets the criteria and is safe to operate a commercial vehicle but is uncertain of long-term status, the driver should be certified for less than 2 years to monitor medical status.

Several references are available to guide the examiner in the decision-making process. The first resource must be the regulations and instructions to examiners, both of which are reproduced in this book (*see* Chapter 3). The medical advisory criteria by the Federal Motor Carrier Safety Administration (FMCSA)—also included in this book—provide guidance and, until recently, were included on the examination form. The Medical Examiner Handbook (ME Handbook), although down for update, still provides a valuable resource for a *starting point* for reaching certification determinations. Another resource is the Frequently Asked Questions. While not official FMCSA recommendations, examiners should review evidence-based reviews, Medical Expert Panel reports, and recommendations from the Medical Review Board. While these are not *required* to be followed, examiners should always be considering current knowledge and best practice in evaluating the risk for sudden or gradual impairment or incapacitation of a commercial motor vehicle operator.

In this section, the attempt was to compile as much available information on specific medical conditions as possible. The intent was to separate the guidance that had been provided by FMCSA (and while provided by FMCSA, it is still *guidance*) and other sources. Updates as they become available will be posted in the online version of this book.

Examiners must remember that they are responsible for making the ultimate certification determination (although they should always obtain information from all treating providers). Their decision must be based on good medical judgment, knowledge of disease processes, and an understanding of the driver's roles and responsibilities. Remember that what is included here is *guidance*, not requirements.

Reference

1. Canadian Cardiovascular Society Consensus Conference 2003. Assessment of the Cardiac Patient for Fitness to Drive and Fly. http://www.ccs.ca/images/Guidelines/Guidelines_POS_Library/DF_CC_2003.pdf

CHAPTER 4
Cardiovascular Disorders

NATALIE P. HARTENBAUM, MD, MPH, FACOEM

Since the prior edition of this book, the Commercial Driver Medical Examiner (CDME) processes have undergone significant changes, mostly related to the National Registry of Certified Medical Examiners (NRCME). In 2014, the Federal Motor Carrier Safety Administration Medical Examiner Handbook (ME Handbook) was taken off the Federal Motor Carrier Safety Administration (FMCSA) website for update and revision. As this edition is being prepared, examiners still should consider guidance from the prior handbook, as that is what is being taught in the training programs, but should base their final decision on current best medical practice remembering that our ultimate responsibility is to ensure the safety of the motoring public to the extent reasonably possible. Chapters will include information from the most recent ME Handbook, Medical Expert Panel (MEP) reports, and Medical Review Board (MRB) recommendations as well as other relevant reports and literature.

While there have been recommendations on cardiovascular conditions presented to FMCSA since 2007, none has been adopted as formal guidance by FMCSA.

As significant changes occur, they will be noted at the end of each chapter in the online version of this book at least twice a year.

Cardiovascular conditions are one of the more common conditions an examiner will be asked to consider during the certification process. It is difficult to determine the increased risk that cardiovascular conditions play in commercial motor vehicle (CMV) crashes. In a 1989 study of 189 fatal-to-driver heavy truck accidents, 10 percent of the accidents were at least in part attributed to medical problems and, of those, 90 percent were cardiac in origin.[1] The 2007 *Evidence Report on Cardiovascular Disease and Commercial Motor Vehicle Driver Safety* and the Medical Expert Panel[2,3] found inconclusive evidence as to whether commercial drivers with cardiovascular disease (CVD) were at an increased risk of motor vehicle crash (MVC). In evaluating the general driving population with CVD, an increased risk of crash was found as well as a similarly increased risk for private drivers with hypertension.

Due to insufficient data, it was inconclusive whether coronary artery disease (CAD), arrhythmias, or other CVDs specifically increased the risk for MVC. A recent study found that commercial drivers with a high cardiovascular risk score had a higher likelihood of crash even after controlling for confounders.[4]

The regulations covering CVDs and hypertension are contained in:

---

49 CFR 391.41(b) (4 and 6): *A person is physically qualified to drive a commercial motor vehicle if that person;*

(4) *Has no current clinical diagnosis of myocardial infarction, angina pectoris, coronary insufficiency, thrombosis, or any other cardiovascular disease of a variety known to be accompanied by syncope, dyspnea, collapse, or congestive cardiac failure;*

(6) *Has no current clinical diagnosis of high blood pressure likely to interfere with his/her ability to operate a motor vehicle safely.*

The advisory criteria[5] for the evaluation of commercial drivers that had been included on the prior version of the medical examination form can now be found in Appendix A to 49 CFR 391.41. It is explained that the term "has no current clinical diagnosis of" is intended to include a current condition or one that has not fully stabilized. The "accompanied by" term would include a condition for which there are or there is likely to be symptoms of syncope, dyspnea, collapse, or congestive cardiac failure. The criteria suggest that before they are certified, those drivers with a history of coronary insufficiency should have a normal resting and stress electrocardiogram (ECG), no residual complications, no physical limitations, and should be taking no medication likely to interfere with safe driving. It is noted that coronary artery bypass grafting (CABG) and pacemakers are not automatically disqualifying while implantable cardioverter defibrillators would be. With Coumadin (warfarin), the focus should be on the underlying condition.

Details on current FMCSA guidance on blood pressure (BP) were removed from the examination form with the implementation of the NRCME but are still included in the advisory criteria and will be reviewed later.

There are a few frequently asked questions[6] that address cardiac conditions, which mostly repeat what was in the ME Handbook. One question is a reminder that medical certificates should only be valid 1 year for those drivers with heart disease or those with hypertension who are stable on medication.

There are currently four questions on the Medical Examination Report Form that pertain to cardiovascular disease, asking whether the driver has the following:

- Heart disease, heart attack, bypass, or other heart problems
- Pacemaker, stents, implantable devices, or other heart procedures
- High blood pressure
- High cholesterol

When performing a medical examination for a commercial driver, the medical examiner should ask the same cardiac questions as for any other patient. Responses on the history portion of the examination form should be reviewed with the driver. These include whether the driver has the following:

- A current clinical diagnosis of myocardial infarction, angina pectoris, coronary insufficiency, or thrombosis?
- Syncope, dyspnea, or collapse?
- Heart failure?
- A history of heart disease or acute myocardial infarction?
- A history of other heart conditions?
- A history of heart surgery (valve replacement/bypass, angioplasty, ICD, pacemaker)?
- Use cardiovascular medications that effectively control a condition without side effects that interfere with safe driving?

If the driver indicates having any type of CVD, the examiner should obtain the onset date and diagnosis, any current medication or other treatment, any potential negative impacts of the treatment or medication, and any limitations due to the condition.

The physical evaluation should include whether the driver has murmurs, extra heart sounds, or arrhythmias; an enlarged heart; abnormal pulse and amplitude; distended neck veins; carotid or arterial bruits; or varicose veins. Other findings that might suggest cardiac disease are rales, ascites, or peripheral edema.

A driver who has any abnormal physical findings that have not already been evaluated should be referred for additional assessment. For most conditions, the recommendations would suggest that the examiner review any objective tests or specialist evaluations. While not specific FMCSA guidance, I would suggest that the examiner review the actual objective studies and not just the note from the health care provider that the driver is "safe to drive." The examiner must remember that signing the medical certificate indicates that the examiner has fully evaluated the driver and believes that the driver meets the medical criteria and is at low risk of sudden or gradual impairment or incapacitation on the date the certificate is signed.

Cardiac Conditions

The remainder of this chapter represents what had been in the ME Handbook[7] unless otherwise noted. For many years, examiners relied on the report from the Conference on Cardiac Disorders and Commercial Drivers.[8] In 2002, guidance was updated by the Cardiovascular Advisory Panel Guidelines for the Medical Examination of Commercial Motor Vehicle Drivers (referred to simply as advisory panel in the text to follow).[9] With few exceptions, this was utilized by FMCSA for the cardiovascular section of the ME Handbook. While the ME Handbook has been removed from the FMCSA website for update, the cardiovascular recommendation tables that summarized almost all cardiac conditions and were most recently updated in 2009 are still available through the FMCSA website[10] and are reproduced here with the applicable cardiovascular condition.

As an introduction to the tables, FMCSA explained:

"As part of its review process, FMCSA considers medical evidence reports, medical expert panel (MEP) opinion, and Medical Review Board (MRB) recommendations. FMCSA also considers other factors such as feasibility and impact.

These tables do not include recommendations that have been submitted to FMCSA for consideration but not adopted by FMCSA. However, FMCSA posts copies of the medical evidence report executive summaries and MEP recommendations on the FMCSA Web page Reports—How Medical Conditions Impact Driving found at https://www.fmcsa.dot.gov/regulations /medical/reports-how-medical-conditions-impact-driving. Reports of MRB proceedings are posted on the MRB Web site at https://www.fmcsa.dot.gov /medical-review-board-mrb-proceedings."

In April 2007, the Medical Expert Panel on Cardiovascular Disease and Commercial Motor Vehicle Safety (referred to as the MEP in the text to follow) presented their findings and recommendations to the FMCSA Medical Review Board.[2] The recommended changes are included in the text that follows and in Table 4-22. The recommendations of the MEP were mostly accepted by the Medical Review Board (MRB),[11] but FMCSA has not yet determined which, if any, of these recommendations will be incorporated into FMCSA guidance.

While examiners should start with the most recent guidance issued by FMCSA, they should document their rationale for their determination.

Examiners may wish to review criteria from other countries or organizations for comparison.[12–14]

Cardiac Tests

There are several cardiovascular studies that FMCSA had included in the ME Handbook with recommended acceptable criteria. Examiners were reminded to not base their decisions solely on the measurements from cardiovascular tests, as some could have a component of subjective interpretation. Good clinical judgment and an understanding of the test and its limitations must be understood.

Echocardiogram – An acceptable echocardiogram was described as having a left ventricular ejection fraction (LVEF ≥40%) with no pulmonary hypertension. They defined pulmonary hypertension as pulmonary artery pressure greater than 50% of systemic systolic blood as determined by echocardiography or cardiac catheterization.

Exercise Tolerance Test (ETT) – For the driver to meet ETT criteria, the driver should be able to exercise to a workload capacity greater than 6 Metabolic Equivalents (METs; Bruce protocol stage II or equivalent) and attain a heart rate greater than or equal to 85% of maximal predicted heart rate (unless on beta blockers). During the test, the driver should have a rise in systolic BP greater than or equal to 20 mm Hg without angina and no significant ST segment depression.

The 2007 panel[2] recommended that the definition of abnormal ETT be an inability to exceed 6 METs without reference to the protocol used.

Hypertension

It is important to measure BP accurately; in those cases in which white-coat hypertension may be a concern, 24-hour ambulatory monitoring may be useful.

The advisory criteria explain that it is understood that hypertension itself is unlikely to cause collapse; however, the concern is on potential end-organ damage and its consequences. Prior to identifying a driver as hypertensive, the BP should be confirmed by two separate readings on subsequent days.

The BP criteria many of us are familiar with was based on the *Sixth Report of the Joint National Committee* (JNC VI),[15] but the Medical Expert Panel (MEP) on Cardiovascular Disease[2] recommended that this be updated to be consistent with JNC VII[16] (of course, JNC VIII[17] has been released since the MEP recommendations).

The Advisory Criteria and recommendation table suggest that drivers with Stage 1 hypertension are at low risk for hypertension-related acute incapacitation and could be medically certified to drive for a 1-year period with annual recertification if the BP was less than 140/90. If greater than 140/90 but less than 160/100 on a subsequent examination, certification could be extended one time for 3 months. Drivers with Stage 2 hypertension could be given one 3-month certification to reduce the BP to less than or equal to 140/90. After that 3-month period, if the driver can show that therapy is well tolerated and the BP value is less than or equal to 140/90, the driver could be certified for 1 year from the date of the initial exam and then recertified annually.

A BP greater than or equal to 180 (systolic) and 110 (diastolic) was considered Stage 3, high risk for an acute BP-related event. The driver should not be qualified, even temporarily, until reduced to less than or equal to 140/90 and treatment is well tolerated. The driver may be certified for 6 months and biannually (every 6 months) thereafter if, at recheck, BP is less than or equal to 140/90.

Evaluation is warranted if the patient is persistently hypertensive on maximal or near-maximal doses of two to three pharmacologic agents. Some causes of secondary hypertension may be amenable to surgical intervention or specific pharmacologic therapy.

The most recent official recommendations for hypertension that had been on the form and are described in the advisory criteria are included in the 2009 Update Cardiovascular Recommendation Table on Hypertension (Table 4-1).

TABLE 4-1 Cardiovascular Recommendation Table on Hypertension

Diagnosis	Physiology/Functional	Certification	Recertification
Essential Hypertension	Evaluate for other clinical CVD including TOD.* Presence of TOD, CVD, or diabetes may affect therapy selected.	Yes, if asymptomatic. Rarely disqualifying alone.	Biennial
Stage 1 (140–159/ 90–99 mm Hg)	Usually asymptomatic. Low risk for near-term incapacitating event.	Yes. Rarely disqualifying alone.	Annual BP <140/90 at annual exam. If not, but <160/100, certification extended one time for 3 months.
Stage 2 (160–179/ 100–109 mm Hg)	Low risk for incapacitating event. Risk increased in presence of TOD. Indication for pharmacologic therapy.	Yes. One time certification for 3 months. Yes, at recheck if: BP ≤140/90 mm Hg; certify for 1 year from date of initial exam.	Annual BP ≤140/90.
Stage 3 (≥180/110 mm Hg)	High risk for acute hypertension-related event.	No. Immediately disqualifying. Yes, at recheck if: BP ≤140/90 mm Hg; treatment is well tolerated; certify for 6 months from date of initial exam.	Every 6 months BP ≤140/90.
Secondary Hypertension	Evaluation warranted if persistently hypertensive on maximal or near-maximal doses of 2–3 pharmacologic agents. May be amenable to surgical/specific therapy.	Based on above stages. Yes if: Stage 1 or nonhypertensive; at least 3 months after surgical correction.	Annual BP ≤140/90.

BP = blood pressure; CVD = cardiovascular disease; TOD = target organ damage.
* TOD: Heart Failure, Stroke or Transient Ischemic Attack, Peripheral Artery Disease, Retinopathy, Left Ventricular Hypertrophy, Nephropathy. Examiner may disqualify a driver if TOD significantly impairs driver's work capacity. Driver should have no excess sedation or orthostatic change in BP. From the 2009 Update to the Cardiovascular Recommendation Tables.[10]

A FAQ[6] on duration of certification for the hypertensive driver indicates that it is up to the examiner whether to certify a driver for 2 years who had hypertension but has now lost weight, is off medication, and BP is now in an acceptable range.

There has been a good deal of confusion as to whether the "one additional 3-month" is a lifetime or single episode guidance. A response from FMCSA[18] indicated that this is guidance and would not prohibit an examiner from issuing another 3-month certification "if the examiner believes the medical condition does not prohibit driving but does require more frequent monitoring."

In the past, if the examiner issued a three-month certification for hypertension and the driver returned within that 3-month period, it was at the discretion of the examiner whether the entire examination needed to be repeated. With the current process, if the driver is placed in the determination pending status (see Chapter 2 on the examination to review determination pending status) and returns within the 45 days, a new examination would not be needed; the Medical Examiner Report can just be amended. If the driver had been issued a medical certificate—as an example, for 3 months—this evaluation cannot be amended and there is little reason for the driver to return much before the certificate expires. At that time, the examiner would conduct a new evaluation, complete a new form, and enter a new determination in the NRCME system. The extent of the examination is up to the examiner; however, the examiner, upon signing the new medical certificate, indicates that the driver meets all medical criteria, not just the recently checked BP. The FAQs for National Registry Driver Examination Forms[19] explains that the examiner is not bound by the BP guidelines as the "Medical Advisory Criteria is guidance and not regulation. FMCSA leaves BP criteria decisions up to the discretion of the ME to determine driver qualification." The response to whether the certification can be extended explains that the "FMCSRs do not provide an option for an extension of the MEC, Form MCSA-5876. If a 3-month MEC, Form MCSA-5876 is issued, it is considered a short-term MEC, not an extension. The length of time that the MEC, Form MCSA-5876 is issued for is determined by the ME and may be issued for up to 2 years."

The 2007 MEP[2] made several significant recommendations (Table 4-2) to modify FMCSA guidance on hypertension.

TABLE 4-2 MEP Recommended Changes to Cardiovascular Disease Guidelines—Presented to FMCSA January 25, 2007—Section 3: CMV drivers with hypertension

1) The MEP recommends that a series of statements explaining the general principles of certification of individuals with hypertension be added to the current CVD guidelines. These general principles are as follows:

    a) Certification and recertification of individuals with hypertension should be based on a combination of factors: blood pressure, the presence of target organ damage, and co-morbidities.

    b) To provide consistency in certification, blood pressure recorded at the certification (or recertification) examination should be used to determine blood pressure stage. The certifying examiner may decide on the length of certification for drivers with elevated blood pressure despite treatment.

    c) All CMV drivers should be referred to their personal physician for therapy, education, and long-term management.

2) The MEP recommends that text be added to the current FMCSA guidelines in this section noting that there is an expectation throughout this section that blood pressure has been measured appropriately.

3) The MEP recommends that text be added to the current FMCSA guidelines in this section noting that there is an expectation throughout this section that blood pressure medication has been titrated appropriately. The target blood pressure for titration should be <140/<90.

4) The MEP recommends that text be added to the current FMCSA guidelines included in this section noting that medical examiners should ensure that individuals with hypertension are properly educated about the importance of making appropriate changes in lifestyle and proper compliance with medication.

5) The MEP recommends the current guidelines be clarified so that current ambiguity about thresholds that define hypertension stage in the existing guidelines be eliminated. The panel recommends that updated guidelines note that the hypertension stages used in updated guidelines are consistent with those recommended by the Joint National Committee (VII) on Prevention, Detection, Evaluation, and Treatment of High Blood Pressure.[13]

CMV = commercial motor vehicles; CVD = cardiovascular disease; FMCSA = Federal Motor Carrier Safety Administration; MEP = Medical Expert Panel

* From Expert Panel Recommendations. Cardiovascular Disease and Commercial Motor Vehicle Driver Safety.[2]

Ischemic Heart Disease

Next to hypertension, one of the most common cardiovascular conditions encountered in commercial driver medical examinations is ischemic heart disease (IHD). Although most deaths from CAD are sudden, in most cases, the driver would have enough warning to pull over to the side of the road to avert an accident. However, one concern would be the occurrence of an arrhythmia in conjunction with the ischemic event, which could be suddenly incapacitating.

The evaluation of a driver with CAD should take into account the driver's functional reserve, symptoms, risk for arrhythmias, and severity of disease. A complete medical history and physical examination must be performed, with special attention given to heart size, rhythm, and rate, as well as the presence or absence of abnormal murmurs, gallops, or pulses. EKGs are not routinely recommended as part of the examination but should be obtained if clinically indicated. There is some suggestion that commercial drivers have an increased number of risk factors for coronary heart disease (CHD).[4,20,21]

The examiner should obtain information about risk factors by taking a history, from the driver's physician, or through additional testing. Multiple risk factors alone should not drive the certification decision. It had been recommended that asymptomatic drivers older than 45 years with multiple risk factors for CHD or others considered as high risk for a CHD event should not be certified if they have an abnormal ETT, ischemic changes on EKG, or functional incapacitation. High risk is defined as the presence of diabetes mellitus or peripheral vascular disease (considered to be CHD risk equivalents) or with a Framingham CHD risk for nonfatal myocardial infarction (MI) or CHD death of greater than 20 percent for 10 years.

The recommendation tables for CMV drivers without known heart disease (Table 4-3) did not specifically recommend for or against an ETT in asymptomatic individuals based on risk factors alone but did note that for those that are high risk, the ETT should be normal. The U.S. Preventive Services Task Force does not recommend routine screening by exercise testing for all individuals. They do point out the following: "For persons in certain occupations, such as pilots and heavy equipment operators for whom sudden incapacitation or sudden death may endanger the safety of others, considerations other than the health benefit to the individual patient may influence the decision to screen for CHD".[22]

TABLE 4-3 Cardiovascular Recommendation Table—Without Known Coronary Heart Disease (CHD)

Diagnosis	Physiology/Functional	Certification	Recertification
Asymptomatic, healthy	Low CHD event risk. Assess for clinically apparent risk factors. Use, when possible, Framingham risk score model to predict 10-year CHD event risk. Increasing age is a surrogate marker for increasing atherosclerotic plaque burden.	Yes, if asymptomatic; rarely disqualifying alone.	Biennial
Asymptomatic, high-risk person (as designated by CHD risk-equivalent condition)* Asymptomatic, high-risk person >45 years with multiple risk factors for CHD	Subclinical coronary atherosclerosis is a concern. High-risk status requires close physician follow-up and aggressive comprehensive risk factor management.	Yes if: asymptomatic. No if: Abnormal ETT;** ischemic changes on ECG;† functional incapacitation by one of conditions.	Annual

* CHD risk equivalent is defined as presence of diabetes mellitus, peripheral vascular disease, or Framingham risk score predicting a 20% CHD event risk over the next 10 years.

** Abnormal Exercise Tolerance Test (ETT) is defined by an inability to exceed 6 metabolic equivalents (METS); beyond completion of Stage II, or 6 minutes) on a standard Bruce protocol or the presence of ischemic symptoms and/or signs (e.g., characteristic angina pain or 1 mm ST depression or elevation in 2 or more leads), inappropriate systolic blood pressure (SBP) and/or heart rate responses (e.g., inability in the maximal heart rate to meet or exceed 85% of age-predicted maximal heart rate), or ventricular dysrhythmia.

† Ischemic ECG changes are defined by the presence of new 1 mm ST-segment elevation or depression and/or marked T wave abnormality. From the 2009 Update to the Cardiovascular Recommendation Tables.[10]

After a **myocardial infarction,** there should be a 2-month wait and an evaluation by a cardiologist prior to returning to commercial driving. An echocardiogram, measuring ejection fraction (EF) is recommended to assess ventricular function. This could be performed while still in the hospital, but it should demonstrate an EF of greater than 40 percent. An ETT should be performed 4 to 6 weeks after the MI, and it should be repeated at least every 2 years, more often if indicated. The driver also should not have any side effects from medication, including orthostatic symptoms. Upon returning to work, the driver who has had an MI should be examined annually and should be asymptomatic.

Angina pectoris usually is caused by narrowing or spasm in one or more coronary arteries. It can be either stable or unstable. If there has not been angina at rest and symptoms have been stable without a change in the pattern of the angina for at least 3 months, the driver can be qualified after examination and clearance from the treating provider, ideally a cardiologist. The driver should have an annual qualification examination and an ETT performed at least every 2 years with normal results. In addition, it is recommended that the individual have stable angina, be asymptomatic both from the disease and from the medications (no light-headedness), and tolerate medications. Unstable angina was defined as pain occurring at rest and changes in pattern or decreased response to medication. The MEP[2] recommended removing the asymptomatic criteria, with the sole criterion being that the driver should have a stable pattern of angina.

Percutaneous coronary interventions (PCIs) can be performed in either the acute (MI or unstable angina) or chronic coronary insufficiency setting. If the PCI is performed electively to treat stable angina and there is no damage to the vascular site, the driver could return to work after 1 week with examination and approval of the treating cardiologist but should be certified for no longer than 6 months. An ETT is recommended 3 to 6 months after the procedure, with an appropriate result as defined previously. Those drivers who are symptomatic, have an abnormal resting ECG, or are unable to meet the minimum ETT standards should have stress radionuclide or echocardiogram performed. Drivers who have undergone PCIs should have annual medical qualification examinations and a negative ETT at least every 2 years. In addition, it is recommended that they be asymptomatic both from the disease and from the medications (no light-headedness), no resting systolic BP less than 95 mm Hg, and no systolic BP decline greater than 20 mm Hg upon standing. If the PCI is performed because of an MI or unstable angina, the recommended waiting period for those conditions should apply. The MEP[2] recommended eliminating the requirement for an ETT 3 to 6 months following a PCI as the American College of Cardiology, American Heart Association, and Society for Cardiovascular and Angiography Interventions[23,24] were no longer recommending testing 6 to 9 months after PCI.

A waiting period of 3 months is recommended prior to returning to work as a CMV operator after **coronary artery bypass grafting** (CABG). This is to allow for sufficient time for sternal wound healing. Examination and approval by a cardiologist should precede return to work, and the driver should undergo annual medical certification examinations. The driver should also tolerate any cardiovascular medications without orthostatic symptoms and an LVEF greater than or equal to 40%. ETTs were not recommended prior to return to work, and there was no specific recommendation as to the frequency of ETTs within 5 years of CABG. When an ETT is performed, the driver should be able to meet the earlier criteria and should not have any ventricular dysrhythmias. The examiner should have a low threshold for requiring radionuclide stress testing or echocardiographic myocardial imaging in these individuals. These are indicated if the driver cannot meet the ETT criteria, has a dysrhythmia, or has an abnormal ECG. A resting echocardiogram is recommended at or prior to the first qualifying examination after the procedure (in-hospital after CABG is acceptable), and the driver's EF should not be less than 40 percent. For consistency, the MEP[2] recommended changing the frequency of ETT beginning 5 years after the CABG to every 2 years, as is recommended for drivers who have had an MI or have angina pectoris. They also recommended that all drivers with known heart disease have their medications titrated to the optimal dose.

TABLE 4-4 Cardiovascular Recommendation Table—With Known Coronary Heart Disease (CHD)

Diagnosis	Physiology/ Functional	Certification	Recertification
Post-Myocardial Infarction (MI)	Risk of recurrent major cardiac event highest within the first months post-MI. Drivers in a rehabilitation program can receive comprehensive secondary prevention therapy.	Yes if: At least 2 months post-MI; cleared by cardiologist; no angina; post-MI ejection fraction ≥40% (by echocardiogram or ventriculogram); tolerance to current cardiovascular medications. No if: Recurrent angina symptoms; post-MI ejection fraction <40% (by echocardiogram or ventriculogram); abnormal ETT demonstrated prior to planned work return; ischemic changes on rest ECG; poor tolerance to current cardiovascular medications.	Annual Biennial ETT at minimum (If test positive or inconclusive, imaging stress test may be indicated). Cardiologist examination recommended.
Angina Pectoris	Lower end of spectrum among CHD patients for risk of adverse clinical outcomes. Condition usually implies that at least one coronary artery has hemodynamically significant narrowing.	Yes, if asymptomatic. No if: Rest angina or change in angina pattern within 3 months of examination; abnormal ETT; ischemic changes on rest ECG; intolerance to cardiovascular therapy.	Annual Biennial ETT at minimum (If test positive or inconclusive, imaging stress test may be indicated.) Cardiologist examination recommended.
Post-Percutaneous Coronary Intervention (PCI)	Rapid recovery for elective PCIs for stable angina. Delayed re-stenosis is the major PCI limitation and requires intensive secondary prevention.	Yes if: At least 1 week after procedure; approval by cardiologist; tolerance to medications. ETT 3 to 6 months after PCI. No if: Incomplete healing or complication at vascular access site; rest angina; ischemic ECG changes.	Annual Recommend cardiologist examination. Biennial ETT at minimum (If test positive or inconclusive, imaging stress test may be indicated.)

TABLE 4-4 continued

Diagnosis	Physiology/ Functional	Certification	Recertification
Post-Coronary Artery Bypass Surgery (CABG)	Delay in return to work to allow sternal incision healing. Because of increasing risk of graft closure over time, ETT is obtained.	Yes if: At least 3 months after CABG; LVEF ≥40% post-CABG; approval by cardiologist; asymptomatic; tolerance to medications.	Annual After 5 years: Annual ETT. Imaging stress test may be indicated.

ECG = electrocardiogram; ETT = exercise tolerance test; LVEF = left ventricular ejection fraction.
From the 2009 Update to the Cardiovascular Recommendation Tables.[10]

Valvular Heart Disease

Individuals with valvular heart disease will have varying degrees of disability, ranging from none to severe impairment. Examiners should be able to distinguish the murmur severity (Table 4-5). Additional evaluation would generally be recommended if the murmurs are systolic, grade I or II, and the driver has signs or symptoms of heart disease; systolic and grade III or higher; holosystolic or late systolic or diastolic or continuous. Certification decisions should be based on the severity of the diagnosis, symptoms and cardiac function. Evaluation should be by a cardiologist, with the initial evaluation including a history, physical examination, and ECG, and in many patients a chest X-ray. Depending on the specific diagnosis, ECG or ETT may be indicated. For detailed recommendations see Tables 4-6 through 4-10.

TABLE 4-5 Murmur Severity from the Medical Examiner Handbook

- Grade I – Must strain to hear a murmur.
- Grade II – Can hear a faint murmur without straining.
- Grade III – Can easily hear a moderately loud murmur.
- Grade IV – Can easily hear a moderately loud murmur that has a thrill.
- Grade V – Can hear the murmur when only part of the stethoscope is in contact with the skin.
- Grade VI – Can hear the murmur with the stethoscope close to the skin; it does not have to be in contact with the skin to detect the murmur.

Mitral Stenosis. Certification decisions should be based on valve area and symptoms. Concerns would include episodes of angina, syncope, fatigue, and the ability to perform tasks that require exertion. In addition to the standard initial evaluation, two-dimensional Doppler echocardiography should be performed. Stress testing may be indicated to assess exercise tolerance and functional capacity. Symptoms—the presence of atrial fibrillation or systolic embolization—also should be considered in addition to valve area. Drivers with either mild or moderate mitral stenosis can be certified annually if they are asymptomatic. They should be evaluated annually by a cardiologist, and a two-dimensional Doppler echocardiography usually would be appropriate. Drivers should be disqualified if their symptoms place them in New York Heart Association Class II or higher, have paroxysmal or established atrial fibrillation, or they have a history of systolic embolization. Additional recommendations are in Table 4-6.

TABLE 4-6 Cardiovascular Recommendation Table—Mitral Stenosis

Diagnosis	Physiology/Functional	Certification	Recertification
Mild Mitral Stenosis MVA ≥1.6 cm²	In the presence of symptoms consistent with moderate to severe mitral stenosis but a calculated valve area suggesting mild mitral stenosis, the severity of the stenosis should be reassessed and an alternative explanation for symptoms should be considered.	Yes, if asymptomatic.	Annual
Moderate Mitral Stenosis MVA 1.0–1.6 cm²		Yes, if asymptomatic.	Annual
Severe Mitral Stenosis MVA ≤1.0 cm²		Yes if: At least 4 weeks post-percutaneous balloon mitral valvotomy; at least 3 months postsurgical commissurotomy; clearance by cardiologist. No if: NYHA Class II or higher; atrial fibrillation; pulmonary artery pressure >50% of systemic pressure; inability to exercise for >6 METs on Bruce protocol (Stage II).	Annual Annual evaluation by a cardiologist.

METs = metabolic equivalents; MVA = mitral valve area; NYHA = New York Heart Association.
From the 2009 Update to the Cardiovascular Recommendation Tables.[10]

Mitral Regurgitation. The standard initial evaluation is a chest X-ray and a two-dimensional Doppler echocardiogram. Stress testing should be obtained if needed to assess effort tolerance and symptomatic status if unclear. In some cases, transesophageal echocardiography may be appropriate. Drivers with severe mitral regurgitation who are symptomatic or have reduced effort tolerance, ruptured chordae or flail leaflet, atrial fibrillation, or thromboembolism should be disqualified. Other recommendations can be found in Table 4-7.

TABLE 4-7 Recommendation Table—Mitral Regurgitation

Diagnosis	Physiology/ Functional	Certification	Recertification
Mild Mitral Regurgitation		Yes, if: Asymptomatic; normal LV size and function;* normal PAP.	Annual Annual echo not necessary.
Moderate Mitral Regurgitation		Yes, if: Asymptomatic; normal LV size and function;* normal PAP.	Annual Annual echocardiogram.
Severe Mitral Regurgitation		Yes, if: asymptomatic.	Annual Echocardiogram every 6–12 months. Exercise testing may be helpful to assess symptoms.
		Yes if: At least 3 months postsurgery; Asymptomatic; cleared by cardiologist.	Annual
		No if: Symptomatic; inability to achieve >6 METs on Bruce protocol; ruptured chordae or flail leaflet; atrial fibrillation; LV dysfunction;* thromboembolism; pulmonary artery pressure >50% of systolic arterial pressure.	

EF = ejection fraction; LV = left ventricular; LVEDD = left ventricular end-diastolic dimension; LVESD = left ventricular end-systolic dimension; PAP = pulmonary artery pressure.
*Measures include: LVEF <60%; LVESD ≥45mm; LVEDD ≥70mm.
From the 2009 Update to the Cardiovascular Recommendation Tables.[10]

Aortic Stenosis. Patients with aortic stenosis tend to do well initially but once symptoms of angina, syncope, or congestive heart failure develop, prognosis is poor. Sudden death has been seen in some patients with aortic stenosis who were asymptomatic. The initial evaluation should include the history and physical examination, ECG, and two-dimensional Doppler echocardiography to assess gradient, valve area, and severity of left ventricular hypertrophy. Cardiac catheterization and coronary angiography may be needed, and ETT is occasionally required to assess symptoms, effort tolerance, and prognosis. Table 4-8 contains the recommendations for the commercial driver with aortic stenosis.

TABLE 4-8 Cardiovascular Recommendation Table—Aortic Stenosis

Diagnosis	Physiology/Functional	Certification	Recertification
Mild Aortic Stenosis (AVA >1.5 cm)^2	If symptoms are consistent with aortic stenosis but calculated valve area suggests mild aortic stenosis, the severity of the stenosis and an alternative explanation for symptoms needs to be reassessed.	Yes, if asymptomatic.	Annual Echocardiogram every 5 years.
Moderate Aortic Stenosis (AVA ≥1.0-1.5 cm)^2		Yes, if asymptomatic. Yes if at least 3 months after surgery. No if: angina, heart failure, syncope; atrial fibrillation; LV dysfunction with EF <50%; thromboembolism.	Annual Echocardiogram every 1 to 2 years Annual
Severe Aortic Stenosis (AVA <1.0 cm)^2		Yes, if at least 3 months after surgery. No, irrespective of symptoms or LV function.	Annual

AVA = aortic valve area; EF = ejection fraction; LV = left ventricular.

From the 2009 Update to the Cardiovascular Recommendation Tables.[10]

Aortic Regurgitation. In addition to the standard evaluation, chest X-ray and two-dimensional echocardiography should be obtained. ETT may be useful for those who are sedentary or if symptoms are equivocal. Drivers with severe aortic regurgitation should be disqualified if they are symptomatic or unable to meet ETT criteria. For details, refer to Table 4-9. After valve repair, there should be a 3-month waiting period, clearance by a cardiologist, and no thromboembolic complications.

TABLE 4-9 Cardiovascular Recommendation Table—Aortic Regurgitation

Diagnosis	Physiology/ Functional	Certification	Recertification
Mild Aortic Regurgitation		Yes, if asymptomatic.	Annual Echocardiogram every 2–3 years.
Moderate Aortic Regurgitation		Yes, if: normal LV function; no or mild LV enlargement.	Annual Echocardiogram every 2 to 3 years.
Severe Aortic Regurgitation		Yes if: asymptomatic; normal LV function (EF = 50%); LV dilatation (LVEDD <60mm, LVESD <50mm).	Every 6 months Echocardiogram every 6–12 months.
		If LVEDD = 60 mm or LVESD = 50 mm.	Every 4–6 months Echocardiogram every 4–6 months if no surgery performed.
		No if: Symptoms; Unable to complete Bruce protocol Stage II; reduced EF <50%, LV dilatation LVEDD >70mm or LVESD >55mm.	
		Yes if: Valve surgery and at least 3 months postsurgery; asymptomatic; cleared by cardiologist	Annual

EF = ejection fraction; LVEDD = left ventricular end-diastolic dimension; LVESD = left ventricular end-systolic dimension.
From the 2009 Update to the Cardiovascular Recommendation Tables.[10]

Valve Repair. After valve repair with a mechanical prosthetic valve, if is recommended that commercial drivers could return to work after at least a 3-month wait and clearance by a cardiologist—provided they are asymptomatic. They should not be qualified if they have left ventricular dysfunction (EF <40%), thromboembolic complications postprocedure, or pulmonary hypertension, or if they are unable to maintain adequate anticoagulation. If a biologic prosthetic valve is used, the same criteria should be used except that anticoagulation is not necessary if there is no history of emboli or a hypercoagulable state. Additional recommendations are in Table 4-10.

The MEP[2] did not offer any recommended changes for drivers with valvular heart disease.

TABLE 4-10 Cardiovascular Recommendation Table—Valve Replacement

Diagnosis	Physiology/ Functional	Certification	Recertification
Mechanical Valves		Yes if: at least 3 months postop; asymptomatic; cleared by cardiologist. No if: symptomatic; LV dysfunction– EF <40%; thromboembolic complication postprocedure; pulmonary hypertension; unable to maintain adequate anticoagulation (based on monthly INR checks).	Annual Recommend evaluation by cardiologist.*
Prosthetic Valve Dysfunction		No Yes if: surgically corrected; at least 3 months postop; asymptomatic; cleared by cardiologist.	Annual Recommend evaluation by cardiologist.*
	Atrial fibrillation.	Yes if: anticoagulated adequately for at least 1 month and monitored by at least monthly INR, rate/rhythm control adequate; cleared by cardiologist.	Annual
Biologic Prostheses	Anticoagulant therapy not necessary in patients in sinus rhythm (after initial 3 months), in absence of prior emboli or hypercoagulable state.	Yes if: at least 3 months postop; asymptomatic; none of above disqualifying criteria for mechanical valves; cleared by cardiologist.	Annual Recommend evaluation by cardiologist.*

EF = ejection fraction; INR = international normalized ratio; LV = left ventricular.
*The role of annual echocardiography in stable patients is controversial.
From the 2009 Update to the Cardiovascular Recommendation Tables.[10]

Myocardial Disease

Since the publication of the *Cardiovascular Advisory Panel Report*[9] and the ME Handbook, the classifications of cardiomyopathies have changed.[25] Although many of the recommendations based on prior categories of cardiomyopathy are still applicable, the MEP[2] recommended updating the classifications to reflect the new guidelines.

Based on the 2002 Advisory Panel,[9] the ME Handbook recommended that drivers with echocardiographically diagnosed hypertrophic cardiomyopathy (HCM) not be qualified, and this was included in the ME Handbook. Those with borderline HCM, hypertensive HCM, or other similar diagnoses could be qualified but should be reevaluated annually.

With the current recognition that not all patients with HCM are at high risk of sudden incapacitation, the MEP[2] recommended that, since the individuals who meet the following criteria are at lower risk of sudden death,[26] they could be medically certified although followed closely.

- No history of cardiac arrest
- No spontaneous sustained ventricular tachycardia (VT)
- Normal exercise BP (e.g., no decrease at maximal exercise)
- No nonsustained VT
- No family history of premature sudden death
- No syncope
- Left ventricular septum thickness < 30 mm

Guidance on drivers with congestive cardiac failure or idiopathic dilated cardiomyopathy states that those with an EF of less than 40 percent should be disqualified. If a subsequent evaluation demonstrates an improved EF, greater than or equal to 40 percent or more, the driver can be recertified if asymptomatic. Evaluation should include two-dimensional Doppler echocardiography to assess EF, left ventricular size, and whether valvular heart disease is present. Radionuclide ventriculography or ETT may be indicated in some patients. Drivers should not be qualified if they have symptomatic congestive cardiac function. If they are asymptomatic with an EF of less than 50 percent but with either sustained or nonsustained ventricular tachycardia or symptomatic palpitations, they should not be qualified. Drivers can be considered for certification after disqualification if symptoms resolve, they do not have ventricular arrhythmia, and the EF improves to greater than or equal to 40 percent. If certified, these drivers should be evaluated annually with echocardiography and Holter monitoring.

The MEP[2] recommended modifying the criteria to clarify that drivers who have sustained ventricular arrhythmia for 30 seconds or more *or* if intervention is required *or* if the LVEF is less than 40 percent should not be qualified.

The guidance had been that, due to a poor prognosis, drivers with restrictive cardiomyopathy should be disqualified and the MEP did not recommend any modification.

TABLE 4-11 Cardiovascular Recommendation Table - Cardiomyopathies and Congestive Heart Failure

Diagnosis	Physiology/ Functional	Certification	Recertification
Hypertrophic Cardiomyopathy		No.	
Idiopathic Dilated Cardiomyopathy and Congestive Heart Failure		No, if symptomatic CHF. No if: asymptomatic; ventricular arrhythmias present; LVEF ≤50%. No if: asymptomatic; no ventricular arrhythmias; LVEF <40%. Yes if: asymptomatic; no ventricular arrhythmias; LVEF 40%–50%.	Annual Requires annual cardiology evaluation, including echocardiography and Holter monitoring.
Restrictive Cardiomyopathy		No	

CHF = congestive heart failure; LVEF = left ventricular ejection fraction

From the 2009 Update to the Cardiovascular Recommendation Tables.[10]

Cardiac Arrhythmias, Pacemakers, and Implantable Defibrillators

Arrhythmias are the cardiac disorder most likely to suddenly impair a driver. Driving generally is safe for most individuals with arrhythmias, but incapacitation can occur suddenly and unpredictably. The initial evaluation should include a medical history and a review of records, physical examination, and additional testing as indicated. A good review on the effect of arrhythmias on consciousness and the impact on public safety is by the American Heart Association (AHA) and the North American Society of Pacing and Electrophysiology (NAS) and an update by the same groups.[27,28]

The ME Handbook indicated that the prognosis in drivers with arrhythmias is mostly based on the underlying disease. The examiners should consider the following:

- Is the underlying heart disease disqualifying?
- What is the risk for sudden death?
- What is the risk for cerebral hypoperfusion and loss of consciousness?

Supraventricular Tachycardias

Some patients are at increased risk of stroke with atrial fibrillation. It had been recommended that those at risk of stroke be adequately anticoagulated for at least one month with at least monthly monitoring of the INR and annual certification. The 2007 MEP[2] recommended providing details on how examiners should evaluate risk of stroke from embolization from atrial fibrillation. They suggested that the CHADS2 (Cardiac Failure, Hypertension, Age, Diabetes, Stroke and Transient Ischemic Attack)[29] model would be the most appropriate.

The MEP[2] recommended for drivers with atrial fibrillation that if warfarin is used, the INR should be between 2.0 and 3.0 with the target 2.5, except in those with a mechanical valve, for whom the target should be greater than 2.5. Those patients, who are anticoagulated, should be adequately anticoagulated for at least 1 month and monitored monthly by INR, with annual recertification. Their rate and rhythm should be adequately controlled, determined preferably by a cardiologist.

The ME Handbook also recommended that if the fibrillation occurs following thoracic surgery, the drivers also should be controlled on anticoagulants for at least one month and followed monthly by INR, with clearance by a cardiologist. Recertification should be annually. Drivers who are asymptomatic with atrioventricular nodal reentrant tachycardia, atrioventricular reentrant tachycardia, and Wolff-Parkinson-White (WPW) syndrome or atrial tachycardia or junctional tachycardia can be certified after a one-month wait, as could drivers who have atrial flutter and have undergone isthmus ablation. Drivers who have been resuscitated from an episode of sudden death or who have compromised cerebral function should not be certified. The recommendation table also recommends against qualifying those drivers with WPW and atrial fibrillation.

Drivers with multifocal atrial tachycardia can be medically qualified provided that they are asymptomatic or the symptoms are controlled and the multifocal atrial tachycardia is not associated with another condition that is disqualifying, such as severe pulmonary disease. Recertification should be annual. Other details on supraventricular arrhythmias from the recommendation tables are in Table 14-12.

Updates to the ACC/AHA Guidelines for the Management of Patients with Atrial Fibrillation were issued in 2007[30] and again in 2014.[31]

TABLE 4-12 Cardiovascular Recommendation on Supraventricular Tachycardias

Diagnosis	Physiology/ Functional	Certification	Recertification
Atrial Fibrillation			
Lone Atrial Fibrillation	Good prognosis and low risk for stroke.	Yes	Annual
Atrial fibrillation as cause of or a risk for stroke	Risk for stroke decreased by anticoagulation.	Yes if: anticoagulated adequately for at least 1 month; anticoagulation monitored by at least monthly INR; rate/rhythm control deemed adequate (recommend assessment by cardiologist).	Annual
Atrial fibrillation following thoracic surgery	Good prognosis and duration usually limited.	In atrial fibrillation at time of return to work; Yes if: anticoagulated adequately for at least 1 month; anticoagulation monitored by at least monthly INR; rate/rhythm control deemed adequate (recommend assessment by cardiologist).	Annual

TABLE 4-12 continued

Diagnosis	Physiology/ Functional	Certification	Recertification
Atrial Flutter	Same as for atrial fibrillation.	Same as for atrial fibrillation. Yes if: isthmus ablation performed and at least 1 month after procedure; arrhythmia successfully treated; cleared by electrophysiologist.	Same as for atrial fibrillation. Annual
Multifocal Atrial Tachycardia	Often associated with comorbidities, such as lung disease, that may impair prognosis.	Yes if: asymptomatic, unless associated condition is disqualifying. No, if symptomatic. Yes if: symptoms controlled and secondary cause is not exclusionary.	Annual Annual
Atrioventricular Nodal Reentrant Tachycardia (AVNRT) Atrioventricular Reentrant Tachycardia (AVRT) and Wolff-Parkinson-White (WPW) Syndrome Atrial Tachycardia Junctional Tachycardia	Prognosis generally excellent, but may rarely have syncope or symptoms of cerebral hypoperfusion. For those with WPW, pre-excitation presents risk for death or syncope if atrial fibrillation develops.	No if: symptomatic; WPW with atrial fibrillation. Yes if: asymptomatic; treated and asymptomatic for at least 1 month and assessed and cleared by expert in cardiac arrhythmias.	Annual Recommend consultation with cardiologist.

WPW = Wolff-Parkinson-White.
From the 2009 Update to the Cardiovascular Recommendation Tables.[10]

Ventricular Arrhythmias

Ventricular arrhythmias carry a higher risk of sudden incapacitation and may be the cause of the majority of sudden cardiac deaths. General recommendations are to consider the LVEF and whether the driver has sustained or nonsustained VT, as well as whether the driver is compliant with treatment recommendations. In general, there should be a one-month waiting period after initiation of therapy or any other treatment for ventricular arrhythmias associated with CHD, right ventricular outflow abnormality, or idiopathic VT. Drivers must be asymptomatic and have clearance from a cardiovascular specialist. They should be recertified at least annually with annual evaluation by a cardiovascular specialist. The guidance suggested that drivers with ongoing sustained VT; nonsustained ventricular tachycardia (NSVT) with an EF of less than 40%; or a diagnosis of HCM, Long QT syndrome, or Brugada syndrome should not be certified. With a diagnosis of dilated cardiomyopathy, the driver should not be certified if sustained ventricular tachycardia, NSVT with an EF less than or equal to 40 percent, or episodes of syncope or near syncope occur.

Bundle branch block can progress, leading to third-degree heart block. Drivers who are symptomatic should not be certified. If the individual is asymptomatic and the risk from any underlying heart disease is acceptable, the driver can be certified for up to 2 years. If the driver is currently under treatment for a disease that has been symptomatic, has no underlying cardiac disease, and is cleared by a cardiologist, the individual can be certified but should be recertified annually.

TABLE 4-13 Ventricular Arrhythmia

Diagnosis	Physiology/Functional	Certification	Recertification
Coronary Heart Disease (CHD)	Sustained VT: Poor prognosis and high risk.	No	Annual Cardiology examination required.
	NSVT, LVEF <0.40: Unfavorable prognosis.	No	
	NSVT, LVEF ≥0.40: Generally considered to have good prognosis.	No, if symptomatic. Yes if: asymptomatic; at least 1 month after drug or other therapy is successful; cleared by cardiologist.	
Dilated Cardiomyopathy	NSVT (LVEF ≤0.40).	No	
	Sustained VT, any LVEF.	No	
	Syncope/near syncope, any LVEF: High risk.	No	
Hypertrophic Cardiomyopathy	Variable but uncertain prognosis.		

TABLE 4-13 continued

Diagnosis	Physiology/Functional	Certification	Recertification
Right Ventricular Outflow VT	Low risk for syncope.	No, if symptomatic.	
		Yes, if asymptomatic.	Annual Recommend evaluation by cardiologist.
		Yes if: at least 1 month after drug or other therapy successful; asymptomatic; cleared by electrophysiologist	Annual Evaluation by cardiologist required.
Idiopathic Left Ventricular VT	Favorable prognosis and low risk for syncope	No, if symptomatic	
		Yes, if asymptomatic.	Annual Recommend evaluation by cardiologist.
		Yes if: at least 1 month after successful drug therapy or ablation; cleared by electrophysiologist.	Annual Evaluation by cardiologist required.
Long QT Interval Syndrome	High risk for ventricular arrhythmic death.	No	
Brugada Syndrome	High risk for ventricular arrhythmic death.	No	
Bundle Branch Block Axis Deviation	Progression of disease in the conduction system can lead to third degree heart block with total loss of electrical connection between the atria and ventricles, causing syncope or sudden death.	Yes if: asymptomatic (depends on risk from underlying heart disease.) Yes, if treated for symptomatic disease (see pacemaker); No disqualifying heart disease; cleared by cardiologist. No, if symptomatic.	Every 2 years Annual

LVEF = left ventricular ejection fraction; NSVT = nonsustained ventricular tachycardia; VT = ventricular tachycardia.
From the 2009 Update to the Cardiovascular Recommendation Tables.[10]

Pacemakers and Syncope

The regulations clearly state that a driver with a cardiovascular condition that may be accompanied by syncope should not be qualified to drive but there is little guidance on the driver with a single syncopal episode, especially when the etiology is unknown. Examiners are advised that they should distinguish between pre-syncope (i.e., dizziness, lightheadedness) and true syncope (i.e., loss of consciousness). The medications used by drivers should not predispose them to precipitous declines in blood pressure, syncope, fatigue, or electrolyte shifts and imbalances.

The MEP[2] recommended that the examiner should be provided with sufficient documentation to distinguish cardiogenic syncope from syncope due to other causes. Evaluation of the patient with syncope should begin with a detailed history and physical examination, ECG, and review of medications. History should focus on factors that can differentiate cardiac from noncardiac causes such as an aura, prodrome, postictal confusion, or focal neurologic deficits. Tonic-clonic movement can be seen with both cardiac and neurologic syncopal episodes. The presence or absence of orthostatic hypotension, carotid bruits, or neurologic abnormalities should be noted. If these are normal, the next steps should be an echocardiogram, exercise test, and evaluation for ischemia. A good review on the evaluation of syncope is from the AHA/ACCF (American College of Cardiology Foundation).[32]

With sinus node dysfunction or atrioventricular block, the driver should not be certified until at least 1 month after pacemaker insertion, provided that underlying heart disease is not disqualifying. Recertification should be annual, with documented pacemaker checks. The MEP[2] recommended that the current guideline pertaining to the use of pacemakers in individuals with neurocardiogenic syncope be revised; they recommended no longer accepting a pacemaker as definitive treatment for neurocardiogenic syncope.

TABLE 4-14 Cardiovascular Recommendation Table—Pacemaker

Diagnosis	Physiology/Functional	Certification	Recertification
Sinus Node Dysfunction	Variable long-term prognosis depending on underlying disease, but cerebral hypoperfusion corrected by support of heart rate by pacemaker.	No Yes if: 1 month after pacemaker implantation; documented correct function by pacemaker center; underlying disease is not disqualifying.	Annual Documented pacemaker checks.
Atrioventricular (AV) Block	Variable long-term prognosis depending on underlying disease, but cerebral hypoperfusion corrected by support of heart rate by pacemaker.	No Yes if: 1 month after pacemaker implantation and documented correct function by pacemaker center; underlying disease is not disqualifying.	Annual Documented pacemaker checks.
Neurocardiogenic Syncope	Excellent long-term survival prognosis, but there is risk for syncope that may be due to cardioinhibitory (slowing heart rate) or vasodepressor (drop in blood pressure) components, or both. Pacemaker will affect only cardioinhibitory component, but will lessen effect of vasodepressor component.	No, with symptoms. Yes if: 3 months* after pacemaker implantation; documented correct function by pacemaker center; absence of symptom recurrence.	Annual Documented pacemaker checks. Absence of symptom recurrence.
Hypersensitive Carotid Sinus with Syncope	Excellent long-term survival prognosis, but there is risk for syncope that may be due to cardioinhibitory (slowing heart rate) or vasodepressor (drop in blood pressure) components, or both. Pacemaker will affect only cardioinhibitory component, but will lessen effect of vasodepressor component.	No, with symptoms. Yes if: 3 months* after pacemaker implantation; documented correct function by pacemaker center; absence of symptom recurrence.	Annual Documented regular pacemaker checks. Absence of symptom recurrence.

* Three months recommended due to possible vasodepressor component of syndrome not necessarily treated by pacing.

From the 2009 Update to the Cardiovascular Recommendation Tables.[10]

Implantable cardioverter defibrillators (ICDs) are now increasingly being used in patients for both primary and secondary prevention. They do not prevent arrhythmias but attempt to terminate the arrhythmia once it occurs. After a ventricular arrhythmia occurs, it may take 20 seconds for an ICD to discharge; during this time, a driver may lose consciousness. Drivers who have had an ICD implanted after cardiac arrest or hemodynamically significant ventricular tachycardia should not be certified. Drivers who have an ICD placed for primary prevention are believed to be at sufficient risk of sudden death that they should not be operating commercial motor vehicles [27, 28]. In the majority of these patients, the cardiac function LVEF will be less than 40 percent, which by itself is a disqualifying condition. The 2007 MEP[2] recommended upholding the prohibition of the medical certification of drivers with ICDs.

An evidence review, *Implantable Cardioverter Defibrillators and Cardiac Resynchronization Therapy (CRT): Implications for Driving a CMV*,[33] was presented to the MRB in July 2009. The findings from this review indicated that those individuals who met the clinical criteria for implantation of CRT devices with or without the defibrillator would not meet the guidelines of the cardiovascular MEP and the MRB on that topic. Whether the device is turned on or off is relevant. The clinical indications for the CRT included the following:

- Moderate to severe chronic heart failure (NYHA Functional Class III or IV)
- Symptomatic despite stable, optimal heart failure drug therapy
- LVEF less than 35%
- QRS duration greater than 120 ms

FMCSA has since begun accepting applications for exemptions from drivers with implantable defibrillators, but none have been granted.

TABLE 4-15 Cardiovascular Recommendation Table – Implantable Cardioverter Defibrillator

Diagnosis	Physiology/Functional	Certification	Recertification
Primary Prevention	Patient has high risk for death and sudden incapacitation.	No	
Secondary Prevention	Patient demonstrated to have high risk for death and sudden incapacitation.	No.	

From the 2009 Update to the Cardiovascular Recommendation Tables.[10]

Vascular Disease

Examiners should ensure that drivers with a history of vascular disease do not also have associated CAD or cerebrovascular disease.

The ME Handbook recommended that all drivers with abdominal aortic aneurysms (AAAs) greater than 5 cm should be disqualifying due to the high risk of rupture. The 2007 MEP recommended that this be increased to 5.5 cm.[2] Based on recent literature, they also recommended that if the AAA is between 4.0 and 5.4 cm, drivers could be certified if asymptomatic and cleared by a vascular surgeon who indicates that surgery is not needed. If surgery is not planned and there are no symptoms, the driver could be qualified annually and the size of the aneurysm followed by ultrasound. It had been recommended that drivers with aneurysms of the thoracic aorta be disqualified if the aneurysm diameter is greater than 3.5 cm; this was recommended to be increased to 5.0 cm.

Drivers who have undergone surgery for repair of abdominal aortic aneurysm, thoracic aortic aneurysm, or aneurysm of another vessel should not be cleared for commercial driving for at least 3 months and should obtain clearance from a cardiovascular specialist.

TABLE 4-16 Cardiovascular Recommendation Tables—Aneurysm

Diagnosis	Physiology/Functional	Certification	Recertification
Abdominal Aortic Aneurysm (AAA)	Evaluate for associated cardiovascular diseases.		
	Aneurysm <4.0 cm.	Yes, if asymptomatic.	Annual
	Aneurysm 4.0 to <5.0 cm.	Yes if: asymptomatic; cleared by vascular specialist.	Annual Ultrasound for change in size.
	Ultrasound to identify change in size.	No, if: symptomatic; surgery recommended by vascular specialist.	
		Yes if: at least 3 months after surgical repair; cleared by cardiovascular specialist.	Annual
	Aneurysm >5.0 cm.	No.	
		Yes if: at least 3 months after surgical repair; cleared by cardiovascular specialist.	Annual
Thoracic Aneurysm	Evaluate for associated cardiovascular diseases.	No, if >3.5 cm.	
		Yes if: at least 3 months after surgical repair; cleared by cardiovascular specialist.	Annual
Aneurysms of Other Vessels	Assess for risk of rupture and for associated cardiovascular diseases.	No	
		Yes if: at least 3 months after surgical repair; cleared by cardiovascular specialist.	Annual

From the 2009 Update to the Cardiovascular Recommendation Tables.[10]

Peripheral vascular disease (PVD) may present with intermittent claudication. If there are no other disqualifying cardiovascular conditions, the driver can be certified but should be recertified annually. It had been recommended that the driver with pain at rest be disqualified from operating commercial vehicles. There should be at least a 3-month wait after surgery or angioplasty for PVD, and these drivers should be recertified annually. The 2007 MEP recommended that drivers with PVD should only be disqualified if pain occurs at rest.[2]

Deep venous thrombosis (DVT) can result in local complications as well as pulmonary emboli, a cause of sudden incapacitation. DVTs should be disqualifying until the driver is adequately treated. This includes no residual acute DVT and, if on warfarin (Coumadin), regulated for at least 1 month, with the international normalized ratio (INR) monitored at least monthly.

The MEP[2] recommended clarifying this to include the following:

- Active DVT should disqualify an individual from driving a CMV.
- Individuals who have experienced DVT that has resolved should be maintained on anticoagulation with a vitamin K antagonist for a minimum of 3 months (preferably 6 months) following resolution.
- If on a vitamin K antagonist such as warfarin (Coumadin), drivers need to be regulated at least 1 month prior to certification (or recertification) and have their INR monitored at least monthly thereafter.
- International normalized ratio should be maintained within the target range: 2.0–3.0.
- Individuals treated with subcutaneous heparin or low molecular weight heparin may be certified (or recertified) to drive a CMV as soon as the DVT has resolved.

If there were pulmonary emboli, drivers should not be certified for at least 3 months from a pulmonary embolus. They should be on appropriate long-term therapy and, if Coumadin is used, the dosage should be regulated for at least 1 month, with follow-up INR at least monthly. These drivers should be recertified at least annually.

Varicose veins and superficial thrombophlebitis do not carry a significant risk of embolism. Individuals with these problems can be medically qualified if no other disqualifying abnormalities are found.

TABLE 4-17 Cardiovascular Recommendation Table—Peripheral Vascular and Venous Disease

Diagnosis	Physiology/ Functional	Certification	Recertification
Peripheral Vascular Disease (PVD)	Evaluate for associated cardiovascular diseases	Yes, if no other disqualifying cardiovascular condition.	Annual
Intermittent Claudication	Most common presenting manifestation of occlusive arterial disease.	Yes if: at least 3 months after surgery; relief of symptoms; no other disqualifying cardiovascular disease.	Annual
	Rest pain	No, if symptoms	
		Yes if: at least 3 months after surgery; relief of symptoms and signs; no other disqualifying cardiovascular disease.	Annual
Acute Deep Vein Thrombosis (DVT)		No, if symptoms.	
		Yes if: no residual acute deep venous thrombosis; if on Coumadin: regulated for at least 1 month; INR monitored at least monthly.	Annual
Superficial Phlebitis		Yes if: DVT ruled out; no other disqualifying cardiovascular disease.	Biennial
Pulmonary Embolus		No, if symptoms.	
		Yes if: no pulmonary embolism for at least 3 months; on appropriate long-term treatment; if on Coumadin: regulated for at least 1 month; INR monitored at least monthly; no other disqualifying cardiovascular disease.	Annual
Chronic Thrombotic Venous Disease		Yes, if no symptoms.	Biennial
Varicose veins		Yes, if no complications.	Biennial
Coumadin	Use of INR required.	Yes if: stabilized for 1 month; INR monitored at least monthly.	Annual

From the 2009 Update to the Cardiovascular Recommendation Tables.[10]

Heart Transplantation

Commercial drivers who have had a heart transplantation and want to return to work can be considered after a 1-year wait. They should be asymptomatic, cleared by a cardiologist, and stable on medications. In addition, there should be no signs of rejection. Drivers should be recertified every 6 months after an evaluation by a cardiologist.

TABLE 4-18 Cardiovascular Recommendation Table—Heart Transplantation

Diagnosis	Physiology/ Functional	Certification	Recertification
Heart Transplantation	Special attention to: accelerated atherosclerosis, transplant rejection, general health.	Yes if: at least 1 year post-transplant; asymptomatic; stable on medications; no rejection; consent from cardiologist to drive commercially.	Biannual Clearance by cardiologist required.

From the 2009 Update to the Cardiovascular Recommendation Tables.[10]

Congenital Heart Disease

Most drivers with symptom-limiting congenital heart disease will select themselves out of the commercial driver pool. With improvements in medical and surgical treatment, however, the examiner may see an increasing number of drivers with congenital heart disease. The decision to qualify should be based on the specific diagnosis, current symptoms, and the natural history of the disease, including early and late complications. The evaluation should include a medical history and a complete review of all pertinent medical records, a complete history and physical examination, a chest X-ray, and a comprehensive two-dimensional Doppler echocardiogram. In drivers in whom cardiac arrhythmias are a concern, ambulatory monitoring at rest and during exercise should be done. In some cases, an ETT also would be useful. For drivers who had recently undergone surgery, at least a 3-month wait and clearance by a cardiologist knowledgeable in adult congenital heart disease is recommended. Drivers with congenital heart disease, whether having undergone surgical repair or followed medically, should be recertified annually with evaluation by a cardiologist knowledgeable in adult congenital heart disease. For recommendations on specific conditions, see Tables 4-19 to 4-21, FMCSA Cardiovascular Recommendation Tables for drivers with congenital heart disease.

TABLE 4-19 Cardiovascular Recommendation Table—Aortic Congenital Heart Disease

Diagnosis	Physiology/ Functional	Certification	Recertification
Bicuspid Aortic Valve	May result in aortic stenosis or regurgitation (see section on Valvular Diseases), aortic root enlargement, aortic aneurysm formation, and aortic rupture.	See section on Valvular Diseases. No if: aortic transverse diameter >5.5 cm. Yes if: surgical intervention successfully performed.	See section on Valvular Diseases. Annual
Subvalvular Aortic Stenosis	Mild = favorable. Has potential for progression. Moderate or severe = unfavorable.	Yes if: aortic; no valvular abnormality or hypertrophic cardiomyopathy. No if: symptomatic and mean pressure gradient >30 mm Hg. Yes if: at least 3 months after successful surgical resection when cleared by cardiologist knowledgeable in congenital heart disease.	Annual Evaluation by cardiologist knowledgeable in adult congenital heart disease is required. Annual Evaluation by cardiologlst knowledgeable in adult congenital heart disease required, including echocardiogram.
Discrete Supravalvular Aortic Stenosis	Unfavorable prognosis due to associated coronary and aortic disorder.	No, unless surgery. Yes if: At least 3 months postsurgical intervention; Cleared by cardiologist knowledgeable in adult congenital heart disease.	Annual Evaluation by cardiologist knowledgeable in adult congenital heart disease is recommended.

TABLE 4-19 continued

Diagnosis	Physiology/ Functional	Certification	Recertification
Marfan Syndrome	Cardiovascular disorders are the major cause of morbidity and mortality, including risk of sudden death.	Yes if: no cardiovascular involvement. No if: any aortic root enlargement; moderate or more severe aortic regurgitation; > mild mitral regurgitation related to mitral valve prolapse; LV dysfunction with EF <40% and no associated valve disease.	Annual Evaluation by cardiologist knowledgeable in adult congenital heart disease required, including aortic root imaging and echocardiography.

EF = ejection fraction; LV = left ventricular.

From the 2009 Update to the Cardiovascular Recommendation Tables.[10]

TABLE 4-20 Cardiovascular Recommendation Table—Atrial Septal Defects

Diagnosis	Physiology/ Functional	Certification	Recertification
Atrial Septal Defect (ASD): Ostium Secundum	Small ASD = favorable.	Yes if asymptomatic.	Annual Evaluation by cardiologist knowledgeable in congenital heart disease, including echocardiogram.
	Moderate to large ASD = unfavorable.	No if: symptoms of dyspnea, palpitations or a paradoxical embolus; pulmonary hypertension; right-to-left shunt; pulmonary to systemic flow ratio >1.5:1.	
		Yes if: at least 3 months after surgery or at least 4 weeks after device closure; asymptomatic and clearance by cardiologist knowledgeable in adult congenital heart disease.	Annual Evaluation by cardiologist knowledgeable in adult congenital heart disease every 2 years.

TABLE 4-20 continued

Diagnosis	Physiology/Functional	Certification	Recertification
ASD: Ostium Primum	Small ASD = favorable prognosis.	Yes if asymptomatic.	Annual Evaluation by cardiologist knowledgeable in adult congenital heart disease required, including echocardiogram.
	Moderate to large ASD = unfavorable prognosis.	No if: symptoms of dyspnea, palpitations or a paradoxical embolus; Echo-Doppler demonstrates pulmonary artery pressure >50% systemic; Echo-Doppler demonstrates right-to-left shunt; Pulmonary to systemic flow ratio >1.5:1 heart block on an electrocardiogram; more than mild mitral valve regurgitation; left ventricular outflow tract obstruction with a gradient >30 mm Hg.	
		Yes if: at least 3 months after surgical intervention if none of the above disqualifying criteria; no symptomatic arrhythmia and no significant residual shunt; cleared by cardiologist knowledgeable in adult congenital heart disease.	Annual Evaluation by cardiologist knowledgeable in adult congenital heart disease.

From the 2009 Update to the Cardiovascular Recommendation Tables.[10]

TABLE 4-21 Cardiovascular Recommendation Tables – Congenital Heart Disease

Diagnosis	Physiology/ Functional	Certification	Recertification
Sinus Venosus Atrial Septal Defect (ASD)	Usually associated with anomalous pulmonary venous connection. Prognosis depends on size of ASD. Commonly associated with sinus node dysfunction, particularly after surgery.	Yes if: small shunt and hemodynamically insignificant. No if: symptoms of dyspnea, palpitations or a paradoxical embolus; Echo-Doppler examination demonstrating pulmonary artery pressure >50% systemic; Echo-Doppler examination demonstrating a right-to-left shunt; pulmonary to systemic flow ratio >1.5:1; Heart block or sinus node dysfunction on an electrocardiogram	Annual Evaluation by cardiologist knowledgeable in adult congenital heart disease.
		Yes if: at least 3 months after surgical intervention; hemodynamics are favorable; cleared by cardiologist knowledgeable in adult congenital heart disease.	Annual Evaluation by cardiologist knowledgeable in adult congenital heart disease, including Holter monitor.
Patent Ductus Arteriosus (PDA)	Small = favorable. Moderate to large = Unfavorable.	Yes, if small shunt. No if: symptoms of dyspnea or palpitations; pulmonary hypertension; right-to-left shunt; progressive LV enlargement or decreased systolic function.	Annual
		Yes if: at least 3 months after surgery or 1 month after device closure; none of the above disqualifying criteria; cleared by cardiologist knowledgeable in adult congenital heart disease.	Annual Should have evaluation by cardiologist knowledgeable in adult congenital heart disease.

TABLE 4-21 continued

Diagnosis	Physiology/ Functional	Certification	Recertification
Coarctation of the Aorta	Mild = favorable.	Yes if: mild and unoperated; BP controlled; no associated disqualifying disease.	Annual Evaluation by cardiologist knowledgeable in adult congenital heart disease recommended.
	Moderate or severe = unfavorable prognosis.	No	
Coarctation of the Aorta after Intervention	Unfavorable prognosis with persistent risk of cardiovascular events.	Yes, if: perfect repair.	Annual Evaluation by cardiologist knowledgeable in adult congenital heart disease required.
Pulmonary Valve Stenosis (PS)	Mild and moderate = favorable.	Yes, if mild or moderate.	Annual Evaluation by cardiologist knowledgeable in adult congenital heart disease.
	Severe PS may be unfavorable, associated with arrhythmias and, rarely, sudden death.	No if: symptoms of dyspnea, palpitations or syncope; pulmonary valve peak gradient >50 mm Hg with normal output; RV pressure >50% systemic pressure; >mild RVH; >mild RV dysfunction; >moderate pulmonary valve regurgitation; main pulmonary artery >5 cm.	
		Yes if: 3 months after surgical valvotomy or 1 month after balloon valvuloplasty; none of the above disqualifying criteria; cleared by cardiologist knowledgeable in adult congenital heart disease.	Annual Recommend evaluation by cardiologist knowledgeable in adult congenital heart disease.

TABLE 4-21 continued

Diagnosis	Physiology/ Functional	Certification	Recertification
Other Causes of Right Ventricular Outflow Obstruction in Persons with Congenital Heart Disease	Double chambered right ventricle. Infundibular pulmonary stenosis. Supravalvar pulmonary stenosis. Pulmonary artery stenosis.	Yes if: hemodynamic data and criteria similar to individuals with isolated pulmonary valve stenosis who are eligible for certification.	Annual Recommend evaluation by cardiologist knowledgeable in adult congenital heart disease.
Ebstein Anomaly	Mild = favorable.	Yes if: mild; asymptomatic; no intracardiac lesions; no shunt; no symptomatic arrhythmia or accessory conduction; only mild cardiac enlargement; only mild RV dysfunction.	Annual Evaluation by cardiologist knowledgeable in adult congenital heart disease.
	Moderate and severe variants = unfavorable.	Yes if: at least 3 months postsurgical intervention; none of the above disqualifying features.	Annual Echocardiogram and evaluation by cardiologist knowledgeable in adult congenital heart disease required.
Tetralogy of Fallot	Unfavorable in the unrepaired state.	No, if uncorrected.	
	Repaired = variable prognosis.	Yes if: excellent result obtained from surgery; asymptomatic; no significant pulmonary or tricuspid valve regurgitation; no pulmonary stenosis; no history of arrhythmias; no residual shunt.	Annual Evaluation by cardiologist knowledgeable in adult congenital heart disease required, including ECG, 24-hour Holter monitor, exercise testing, Doppler echocardiogram.

TABLE 4-21 continued

Diagnosis	Physiology/ Functional	Certification	Recertification
Transposition of the Great Vessels	Unfavorable if uncorrectable.	No	
	Atrial switch repair (Mustard or Senning procedures). Unfavorable long-term prognosis.	No	
	After Rastelli repair.	Yes if: asymptomatic and excellent result obtained from surgery.	Annual Evaluation by cardiologist knowledgeable in adult congenital heart disease.
	After arterial switch repair, prognosis appears favorable.	No (data currently not sufficient to support qualification in this group).	
Congenitally Corrected Transposition	95% have associated intracardiac lesions. Conduction system is inherently abnormal.	Yes if: none of the following disqualifying criteria.	Annual Required annual evaluation by cardiologist knowledgeable in adult congenital heart disease includes echocardiography and 24-hour Holter Monitor.

TABLE 4-21 continued

Diagnosis	Physiology/ Functional	Certification	Recertification
Congenitally Corrected Transposition (continued)		No if: symptoms of dyspnea, palpitations, syncope or paradoxical embolus; intracardiac lesion, such as ventricular septal defect (VSD); >moderate pulmonary stenosis with a pulmonary ventricular pressure >50% systemic; >mild RV or LV enlargement or dysfunction; Moderate or greater tricuspid valve (systemic atrioventricular valve) regurgitation; history of atrial or ventricular arrhythmia; ECG with heart block; Right-to-left shunt or significant residual left-to-right shunt. Yes if: at least 3 months after surgery; none of the above disqualifying criteria; prosthetic valve–must meet requirements for that valve; cleared by cardiologist knowledgeable in adult congenital heart disease.	Annual Evaluation by cardiologist knowledgeable in adult congenital heart disease.

TABLE 4-21 continued

Diagnosis	Physiology/ Functional	Certification	Recertification
Ventricular Septal Defect (VSD)	Small = favorable.	Yes, if small shunt.	Annual Evaluation by cardiologist knowledgeable in adult congenital heart disease recommended.
	Moderate to large VSD has effect on pulmonary pressure and ventricular size and function.	No if: Moderate to large VSD; symptoms of dyspnea, palpitations or syncope; pulmonary artery hypertension; right-to-left shunt, LV enlargement or reduced function; Pulmonary to systemic flow ratio >1.5:1.	
		Yes if: at least 3 months after surgery; none of the above disqualifying criteria; no serious dysrhythmia on 24-hour Holter monitoring; QRS interval <120 ms (if right ventricle conduction delay >120 ms on ECG, can be certified if invasive His bundle studies show no infra-His block or other serious electrophysiologic disorder); cleared by cardiologist knowledgeable in adult congenital heart disease.	Annual Evaluation by cardiologist knowledgeable in adult congenital heart disease, including 24-hour Holter monitoring.

LV = left ventricular; RV = right ventricular; RVH = right ventricular hypertrophy.
From the 2009 Update to the Cardiovascular Recommendation Tables[10][0]

Cardiovascular Medications

With the exception of anticoagulants discussed earlier, cardiovascular medications are not specifically addressed in the medical examination. The medical examiner should review all medications and any potential side effects. Reviewing medications also can provide the examiner with information on a diagnosis that may not have been identified on the history questions. When it is discovered that a driver is on a cardiovascular medication, two main issues need to be addressed. First, what condition is the medication treating? Second, are there significant side effects from the medication? Frequently, an individual will deny medical problems, and when the use of a medication is discovered, the individual will claim to no longer have the medical problem because of the medication.

Some of the side effects that should be addressed by an examiner performing a commercial driver medical examination are somnolence, fatigue, impaired judgment, impaired reflexes, neurologic dysfunction, and orthostatic changes.

TABLE 4-22 Recommended Changes to Cardiovascular Disease Guidelines – Presented to the Federal Motor Carrier Safety Administration (FMCSA) April 25, 2007

Section 1: Drivers without known heart disease
1   The Medical Expert Panel (MEP) recommends that the currently used definition for abnormal exercise tolerance testing (ETT) should be revised so that it is defined as an inability to exceed 6 METs (metabolic equivalents) on ETT.

Section 2: CMV drivers with known chronic heart disease
1   The MEP recommends that it be made clear that for all guidelines in this section, there is an expectation that individuals with known CHD will have had all of their medications titrated to the optimal dose.
2   The current FMCSA guideline states that individuals with angina pectoris may be qualified for certification if they are rendered asymptomatic. The MEP recommended that CMV drivers with angina pectoris may be qualified for certification to drive a CMV if the pattern of angina is stable.
3   Current FMCSA guidelines state that an individual with angina pectoris who has undergone a percutaneous coronary intervention (PCI) may be qualified to drive if he or she meets all the following conditions:
    •   At least one week has passed since the procedure
    •   The treating cardiologist provides approval
    •   The individual has demonstrated tolerance to medications
    •   The individual has a normal ETT 3 to 6 months following PCI
4   The MEP recommended removing the last of these conditions (normal ETT 3 to 6 months following PCI).
5   Current FMCSA guidelines state that individuals who have undergone coronary artery bypass surgery that meet the requirements for certification should be recertified on an annual basis for five years. After this time, such individuals should undergo an exercise tolerance test annually. The MEP recommended extending the time between exercise tolerance tests to two years.

TABLE 4-22 continued

Section 3: CMV drivers with hypertension

The MEP recommended several changes to the guideline statements in Section 3.

1 The MEP recommends that a series of statements explaining the general principles of certification of individuals with hypertension be added to the current CVD guidelines. These general principles are as follows:

   á Certification and recertification of individuals with hypertension should be based on a combination of factors: blood pressure, the presence of target organ damage, and co-morbidities.

   b To provide consistency in certification, blood pressure recorded at the certification (or recertification) examination should be used to determine blood pressure stage. The certifying examiner may decide on the length of certification for drivers with elevated blood pressure despite treatment.

   c All CMV drivers should be referred to their personal physician for therapy, education, and long-term management.

2 The MEP recommends that text be added to the current FMCSA guidelines in this section noting that there is an expectation throughout this section that blood pressure has been measured appropriately.

3 The MEP recommends that text be added to the current FMCSA guidelines in this section noting that there is an expectation throughout this section that blood pressure medication has been titrated appropriately. The target blood pressure for titration should be <140/<90.

4 The MEP recommends that text be added to the current FMCSA guidelines included in this section noting that medical examiners should ensure that individuals with hypertension are properly educated about the importance of making appropriate changes in lifestyle and proper compliance with medication.

5 The MEP recommends the current guidelines be clarified so that current ambiguity about thresholds that define hypertension stage in the existing guidelines be eliminated. The panel recommends that updated guidelines note that the hypertension stages used in updated guidelines are consistent with those recommended by the Joint National Committee on Prevention, Detection, Evaluation, and Treatment of High Blood Pressure.

Section 4: CMV drivers with supraventricular tachycardias

1 The MEP recommends that the current ambiguity associated with "lone atrial fibrillation" be resolved by making it clear that the diagnosis refers to individuals with atrial fibrillation with no identifiable underlying disease. This is usually diagnosed in younger persons.

2 The MEP recommends that FMCSA provide details of how risk for stroke from embolization among individuals with atrial fibrillation should be determined. The panel recommends that the most appropriate risk stratification model currently available

TABLE 4-22 continued

is CHADS2 (Cardiac Failure, Hypertension, Age, Diabetes, Stroke and transient ischemic attack [TIA]). The CHADS2 risk index is based on a point system in which two points are assigned for a history of stroke or TIA and 1 point each is assigned for age over 75 years, a history of hypertension, diabetes, or recent heart failure (HF).

3   FMCSA requested clarification of the relative role of aspirin and vitamin K inhibitors in reducing stroke risk in individuals with atrial fibrillation. The MEP referred FMCSA to the current ACC/AHA/European Society of Cardiology (ESC) guidelines for appropriate antithrombotic treatment of individuals with atrial fibrillation. The MEP noted that the current FMCSA guideline for the certification of individuals with atrial fibrillation is applicable to individuals undergoing antithrombotic therapy who have at least one moderate-risk factor for stroke, any high-risk factor for stroke, or more than one moderate-risk factor for stroke.

4   The MEP recommends that individuals with atrial fibrillation at moderate to high risk for a stroke be recertified annually. Furthermore, the members recommend that the guidelines make it clear that in order to be recertified the individual must have his or her anticoagulation monitored by at least monthly International Normalized Ratio (INR) and demonstrate adequate rate/rhythm control.

Section 5: CMV drivers with pacemakers

1   The MEP recommends that the current guideline pertaining to the use of pacemakers in individuals with neurocardiogenic syncope be revised. Current guidelines state that individuals with recurrent neurocardiogenic syncope who have received a pacemaker as a treatment for the condition may be certified three months following implantation. The MEP no longer accepts a pacemaker as definitive treatment for neurocardiogenic syncope.

2   The MEP recommends that text be added to documentation accompanying the cardiovascular disease (CVD) guideline update that describes the appropriate evaluation of an individual who presents with syncope. The purpose of this new text will be to ensure that efforts are made to distinguish individuals with cardiogenic syncope from those with syncope from other causes.

Section 6: CMV drivers and implantable cardioverter defibrillators

The MEP made a single recommendation on the guideline statements in Section 6.

1   The MEP recommends that the current FMCSA CVD guidelines, which preclude any individual with an implanted cardioverter defibrillator (ICD) from being certified to drive a CMV, be upheld.

Section 7: CMV drivers with abdominal or thoracic aortic aneurysms

The MEP made several recommendations for changes to the guideline statements in Section 7.

1   The MEP recommends that the upper limit for the abdominal aortic aneurysm (AAA) diameter below which an asymptomatic individual may be certified to drive a CMV be increased to 5.5 cm for men and that an upper limit of 5.0 cm be set for women.

TABLE 4-22 continued

2 The MEP recommends that FMCSA make changes to some of the wording of the current guidelines on certification of individuals with AAAs. The recommended changes are presented below.

3 a   Individuals with an AAA 4.0 to 5.4 cm in diameter can be certified if they are asymptomatic AND they are cleared by a vascular specialist. (The word AND is not included in the current guidelines.)

   b   Individuals with an AAA 4.0 to 5.4 cm in diameter cannot be certified if they are either symptomatic OR a vascular specialist has recommended that they undergo surgery. (The word OR is not included in the current guidelines.)

4 The MEP recommends that FMCSA add guidance to the current guideline on certification of individuals who have undergone endovascular AAA repair (EVAR). It recommends that text be added to the current guideline that ensures that recertification of individuals who have undergone EVAR comply with the follow-up protocol required following such an intervention. Compliance with the follow-up protocol is necessary following EVAR because the implanted stent may become dislodged. This in turn may result in endovascular leak that, in some cases, can result in aneurysm rupture.

5 The MEP recommends that the upper limit for the thoracic aortic aneurysm (TAA) diameter below which an asymptomatic individual may be certified to drive a CMV be increased from 3.0 cm to 5.0 cm.

Section 8: CMV drivers with peripheral vascular disease

1 The current guidelines for certification of individuals with intermittent claudication state that an individual who is symptomatic should not be certified to drive a CMV. The MEP recommends that this be changed to disqualification from driving a CMV when pain occurs at rest.

Section 9: CMV drivers with venous disease

1 Active DVT should disqualify an individual from driving a CMV.

2 Individuals who have experienced DVT that has resolved should be maintained on anticoagulation with a Vitamin K antagonist for a minimum of three months (preferably 6 months) following resolution.

3 If on a Vitamin K antagonist such as warfarin (Coumadin), drivers need to be regulated for at least 1 month prior to certification (or recertification) and have their INR monitored at least monthly thereafter.

4 INR should be maintained within the target range: 2.0–3.0.

5 Individuals treated with subcutaneous heparin or low molecular weight heparin may be certified (or recertified) to drive a CMV as soon as the DVT has resolved.

Section 10: CMV drivers with cardiomyopathy

1 Since the development of the CVD guidelines published in 2002, changes have occurred in the classification of the cardiomyopathies. Consequently, the MEP recommends that the current guidelines for cardiomyopathies be updated to reflect this.

TABLE 4-22 continued

2 The current guidelines state that an individual with hypertrophic cardiomyopathy should not be certified to drive a CMV. The MEP recommends that the guideline be changed to reflect the fact that not all individuals with hypertrophic cardio-myopathy are at risk for sudden incapacitation or death. Specifically the panel recommends that individuals who meet all the following criteria are at low risk and may be certified to drive:
   - No history of cardiac arrest
   - No spontaneous sustained VT
   - Normal exercise BP (e.g., no decrease at maximal exercise)
   - No non-sustained VT
   - No family history of premature sudden death
   - No syncope
   - Left ventricular (LV) septum thickness <30mm<TBL>

3 The MEP noted that low-risk individuals must be followed closely for changes in risk status.

4 The MEP recommends changes to the text explaining the criteria that defines who should not be certified to drive a CMV, relative to those individuals with idiopathic dilated cardiomyopathy who do not have symptomatic HF. The current guidelines state that individuals with ventricular arrhythmia who present an LVEF<50% be precluded from certification. The MEP recommends that these criteria be changed to the following:
   - Sustained ventricular arrhythmia for 30 seconds or more OR requiring intervention
   - LVEF ≤40%

CHD = coronary heart disease; CMV = commercial motor vehicles; CVD = cardiovascular disease; DVT = deep venous thrombosis; MRB = Medical Review Board.

Presented to the FMCSA and Medical Review Board April 25, 2007 (https://www.fmcsa. dot.gov/regulations/medical/recommended-changes-cardiovascular-disease-guidelines)

Conclusion

It is important not to evaluate the cardiovascular condition in isolation. A driver with multiple medical problems, all with borderline control, may be at greater risk than a driver with only one condition at the same level of stability.

The most important aspect of evaluating a cardiac patient's ability to operate a commercial motor vehicle safely is the individual's underlying cardiac status. Will such a driver's heart allow the individual to perform the required tasks safely without ischemia or arrhythmia? Is the driver likely to have one's level of alertness impaired owing to cardiac conditions or medications? Assessment of most drivers with cardiac disease should include an ECG, echocardiogram, and ETT and, depending on the diagnosis, 24-hour ambulatory monitoring. In select cases, cardiac catheterization or electrophysiologic studies may be indicated.

References

1. National Transportation Safety Board. Fatigue, Alcohol, Other Drugs and Medical Factors in Fatal-to-Driver Heavy Truck Crashes. PB90-917992, NTSB/ SS-90/01. Washington: NTSB, 1990. National Transportation Safety Board. Fatigue, Alcohol, Other Drugs and Medical Factors in Fatal-to-Driver Heavy Truck Crashes

2. Blumenthal RS, Epstein AE, Kerber RE. Expert Panel Recommendations. Cardiovascular disease and commercial motor vehicle driver safety. Presented to FMCSA, April 25, 2007. https://www.fmcsa.dot.gov/sites/fmcsa.dot.gov/files /docs/Cardiovascular_Disease.pdf.

3. *Evidence Report Cardiovascular Disease and Commercial Motor Vehicle Driver Safety.* April 27, 2007. http://ntl.bts.gov/lib/30000/30100/30123/Final_CVD _Evidence_Report_v2.pdf.

4. Ronna BB, Thiese MS, Ott U, et al. The association between cardiovascular disease risk factors and motor vehicle crashes among professional truck drivers. *J Occup Environ Med.* 2016 Jul 12. [Epub ahead of print]

5. Appendix A to Part 391—Medical Advisory Criteria. http://www.ecfr.gov/cgi -bin/text-idx?SID=acae60ac272c7c329e4926be905433c5&mc=true&node=pt49 .5.391&rgn=div5#ap49.5.391_171.a

6. Federal Motor Carrier Safety Administration Medical Frequently Asked Questions. http://www.fmcsa.dot.gov/rules-regulations/topics/medical/faq.asp.

7. Medical Examiner Handbook, currently in the process of revision. https://www .fmcsa.dot.gov/regulations/medical/fmcsa-medical-examiner-handbook.

8. U.S. Department of Transportation, Federal Highway Administration. Conference on Cardiac Disorders and Commercial Drivers. Publication No. FHWA-MC-88-040. Washington: U.S. Department of Transportation, Federal Highway Administration, Office of Motor Carriers, 1987. https://ntrl.ntis.gov /NTRL/dashboard/searchResults/titleDetail/PB88233960.xhtml.

9. Blumenthal R, Braunstein J, Connolly H, et al. Cardiovascular Advisory Panel Guidelines for the Medical Examination of Commercial Motor Vehicle Drivers. FMCSA-MCP-02-002. Washington: U.S. Department of Transportation, Federal Motor Carrier Safety Administration, October 2002. https://www.fmcsa.dot .gov/regulations/medical/cardiovascular-advisory-panel-guidelines-medical -examination-commercial-motor.

10. Federal Motor Carrier Safety Administration Cardiovascular Recommendation Tables – updated 2009. http://nrcme.fmcsa.dot.gov/documents/Cardiovascular %20Recommendation%20Tables.pdf.

11. Summary for the April 25, 2007 Medical Review Board Public Meeting. https://www.fmcsa.dot.gov/regulations/medical/summary-april-25-2007 -medical-review-board-public-meeting

12. Canadian Medical Association. Determining Medical Fitness to Drive, A Guide for Physicians, 8th ed. https://www.cma.ca/En/Pages/drivers-guide.aspx.

13. Driver and Vehicle Licensing Agency—United Kingdom. At a Glance Guide to the Current Standards of Fitness to Drive. Updated August 2016. https://www .gov.uk/government/publications/assessing-fitness-to-drive-a-guide-for -medical-professionals.

14. Assessing Fitness to Drive, for Commercial and Private Vehicle Drivers, Austroads, National Transportation Commission, Melbourne, Australia, 2016. http://www.austroads.com.au/drivers-vehicles/assessing-fitness-to-drive.

15. *Sixth Report of the Joint National Committee on the Prevention, Detection, Evaluation and Treatment of High Blood Pressure. Arch Intern Med.* 1997;157:2413–2446. http://jamanetwork.com/journals/jamainternalmedicine /article-abstract/624075.

16. *Seventh Report of the Joint National Committee on Prevention, Detection, Evaluation, and Treatment of High Blood Pressure.* National Heart, Blood and Lung Institute. http://www.nhlbi.nih.gov/files/docs/guidelines/jnc7full.pdf.

17. James PA, Oparil S, Carter BL et al. 2014 Evidence-Based Guideline for the Management of High Blood Pressure in Adults. *JAMA* 2014;311(5):507–520. http://jama.jamanetwork.com/article.aspx?articleid=1791497.

18. CDME Review. Fall 2009. CDME Review. American College of Occupational and Environmental Medicine.

19. FAQs for National Registry Driver Examination Forms, issued 1/21/2016. https://nationalregistry.fmcsa.dot.gov/ResourceCenter/documents/FAQs %20New%20Driver%20Examination%20Forms%20011216.pdf

20. Hartvig P, Midttun O. Coronary heart disease risk factors in bus and truck drivers. A controlled cohort study. *Int Arch Occup Environ Health.* 1983;52(4):353–360.

21. Sieber WK, Robinson CF, Birdsey J, et al. Obesity and Other Risk Factors: The National Survey of U.S. Long-Haul Truck Driver Health and Injury. *Am J Ind Med.* 2014 Jun; 57(6): 615–626.

22. U.S. Preventive Services Task Force Recommendation Statement in Screening for Coronary Heart Disease July 2012. https://www.uspreventiveservicestaskforce .org/Page/Document/RecommendationStatementFinal/coronary-heart-disease -screening-with-electrocardiography.

23. Smith SC Jr, Feldman TE, Hirshfeld JW Jr, et al. *ACC/AHA/SCAI 2005 Guideline Update for Percutaneous Coronary Intervention: A Report of the American College of Cardiology/American Heart Association Task Force on Practice Guidelines ACC/AHA/SCAI Writing Committee to Update the 2001 Guidelines for Percutaneous Coronary Intervention. Circulation.* 2005;113:156–175. http://circ.ahajournals.org/content/113/1/156.

24. Gibbons RJ, Balady GJ, Bricker JT, et al. *ACC/AHA 2002 Guideline Update for Exercise Testing—Summary Article: A Report of the American College of Cardiology/American Heart Association Task Force on Practice Guidelines (Committee to Update the 1997 Exercise Testing Guidelines). Circulation.* 2002;106:1883–1892. http://circ.ahajournals.org/content/106/14/1883.

25. Maron BJ, Towbin JA, Thiene G, et al. American Heart Association; Council on Clinical Cardiology, Heart Failure and Transplantation Committee; Quality of Care and Outcomes Research and Functional Genomics and Translational Biology Interdisciplinary Working Groups; Council on Epidemiology and Prevention. Contemporary definitions and classification of the cardiomyopathies: An American Heart Association Scientific Statement from the Council on Clinical Cardiology, Heart Failure and Transplantation Committee; Quality of Care and Outcomes Research and Functional Genomics and Translational Biology Interdisciplinary Working Groups; and Council on Epidemiology and Prevention. *Circulation.* 2006;113:1807–1816. http://circ.ahajournals.org/content/113/14/1807.

26. McKenna WJ, Behr ER. Hypertrophic cardiomyopathy: Management, risk stratification and prevention of sudden death. *Heart.* 2002;87:168–176.

27. Epstein AE, Miles WM, Benditt DG, et al. Personal and public safety issues related to arrhythmias that may affect consciousness: Implications for regulation and physician recommendations. *Circulation.* 1996;94:1147–1166. http://circ.ahajournals.org/content/94/5/1147.long.

28. Epstein AE, Baessler CA, Curtis AB, et al. Addendum to "Personal and public safety issues related to arrhythmias that may affect consciousness: Implications for regulation and physician recommendations: A medical/scientific statement from the American Heart Association and the North American Society of Pacing and Electrophysiology": Public safety issues in patients with implantable defibrillators: A scientific statement from the American Heart Association and the Heart Rhythm Society. *Circulation.* 2007;115(9):1170–1176. http://circ.ahajournals.org/content/115/9/1170.

29. van Walraven WC, Hart RG, Wells GA, et al. A clinical prediction rule to identify patients with atrial fibrillation and a low risk for stroke while taking aspirin. *Arch Intern Med.* 2003;163:936–943.

30. Fuster V, Ryden LE, Cannom DS, et al. *ACC/AHA/ESC 2006 Guidelines for the Management of Patients with Atrial Fibrillation—Executive Summary: A Report of the American College of Cardiology/American Heart Association Task Force on Practice Guidelines and the European Society of Cardiology Committee for Practice Guidelines (Writing Committee to Revise the 2001 Guidelines for the Management of Patients with Atrial Fibrillation). Circulation.* 2006;114:700–752. http://circ.ahajournals.org/content/circulationaha/114/7/700.full.pdf.

31. January CT, Wann S, Alpert JS, et al. *2014 AHA/ACC/HRS Guideline for the Management of Patients With Atrial Fibrillation: Executive Summary. A Report of the American College of Cardiology/American Heart Association Task Force on Practice Guidelines and the Heart Rhythm Society. J Am Coll Cardiol.* 2014;64(21):2246–2280. doi:10.1016/j.jacc.2014.03.02. http://content.onlinejacc.org/article.aspx?articleid=1854230.

32. Strickberger SA, Benson DW, Biaggioni I, et al. AHA/ACCF Scientific Statement on the evaluation of syncope: From the American Heart Association Councils on Clinical Cardiology, Cardiovascular Nursing, Cardiovascular Disease in the Young, and Stroke, and the Quality of Care and Outcomes Research Interdisciplinary Working Group; and the American College of Cardiology Foundation: In collaboration with the Heart Rhythm Society: Endorsed by the American Autonomic Society. *Circulation.* 2006;113:316–327. http://circ.ahajournals.org/content/113/2/316.

33. Focused Report. *Cardioverter implantable defibrillators (ICD) and cardiac resynchronization therapy (CRT).* 2009. http://ntl.bts.gov/lib/34000/34000/34007/Focused_report_ICD_03222009_.pdf.

CHAPTER 5
Pulmonary Disorders

NATALIE P. HARTENBAUM, MD, MPH, FACOEM

Since the prior edition of this book, the Commercial Driver Medical Examiner (CDME) processes have undergone significant changes, mostly related to the National Registry of Certified Medical Examiners (NRCME). In 2014, the Federal Motor Carrier Safety Administration Medical Examiner Handbook (ME Handbook) was taken off the Federal Motor Carrier Safety Administration (FMCSA) website for update and revision. As this edition is being prepared, examiners still should consider guidance from the prior handbook, as that is what is being taught in the training programs, but should base their final decision on current best medical practice remembering that our ultimate responsibility is to ensure the safety of the motoring public to the extent reasonably possible. Chapters will include information from the most recent ME Handbook, Medical Expert Panel (MEP) reports, and Medical Review Board (MRB) recommendations as well as other relevant reports and literature.

The FMCSA Medical Review Board (MRB) initially heard recommendations from the MEP on Obstructive Sleep Apnea (OSA) in 2008 and made formalized recommendations to FMCSA. Since then, there have been additional meetings and recommendations, requests for comments, and even congressional action to prevent guidance on OSA without formal rulemaking. However, at this time, there is no official guidance from FMCSA on screening, diagnosing, or treating drivers at risk of OSA.

As significant changes occur, they will be noted at the end of each chapter in the online version of this book at least twice a year.

The respiratory system is responsible for providing adequate oxygen to the tissues and removing carbon dioxide from the bloodstream. The brain and heart are particularly sensitive to oxygen deprivation. Acute or chronic abnormalities in oxygen content or carrying capacity of the blood may result either directly or indirectly in confusion, dizziness, or loss of consciousness.

The standard addressing respiratory function states:

[49 CFR 391.41(b)(5)] *Has no established medical history or clinical diagnosis of a respiratory dysfunction likely to interfere with his/her ability to control and drive a motor vehicle safely.*

The examination form includes two questions on pulmonary conditions: (1) chronic (long-term) cough, shortness of breath, or other breathing problems; and (2) lung disease (e.g., asthma).

Most respiratory problems are not as likely as cardiac or neurologic dysfunction to suddenly incapacitate or impair a driver. As pulmonary function declines, it becomes more difficult for a driver to perform required tasks aside from driving. It is estimated that truck driving itself requires 3.0 metabolic equivalents [METs, defined as the energy demand in liters of oxygen consumption per minute of basal oxygen consumption (3.5 mL/kg per minute)], whereas lifting and carrying 60 to 80 pounds requires 7.5 METs.[1] With mild impairment, pulmonary function test (PFT) abnormalities may not correlate well with complaints of dyspnea. As respiratory function declines, however, there is a direct correlation. The more abnormal the PFT, the less likely it is that the individual will be able to work as a commercial motor vehicle (CMV) operator.

OSA and its resulting daytime somnolence or decreased alertness has been the one medical condition getting the most focus in commercial driver medical fitness over the past decade. It is recognized as a risk for motor vehicle crashes, with the challenge being how to identify those drivers most at risk of sleep apnea and most at risk of being involved in a crash due to that diagnosis. The current Medical Examination Reporting Form[2] asks drivers if they have or ever had the following: sleep disorder, pauses in breathing while sleeping, daytime sleepiness, or loud snoring. There is also a question on whether they ever "had a sleep test (e.g., sleep apnea)?" A proposed form[3] included an option for the examiner to measure and record body mass index (BMI) and a neck circumference, but this was not included on the final form.

The Federal Motor Carrier Safety Administration (FMCSA) advisory criteria[4] explain that impairment in respiratory function, especially when there is greater oxygen demand, as in emergency situations, may be "detrimental to safe driving." The advisory criteria list several conditions that may result in incapacitation, "including emphysema, chronic asthma, carcinoma, tuberculosis, chronic bronchitis and sleep apnea." The medical examiner is advised to refer to a specialist if any abnormality that may interfere with safe operation of the CMV is detected. If the driver is on anticoagulation therapy for deep venous thrombosis (DVT) or pulmonary embolus (PE), the individual can be qualified once the lower extremity vascular studies are normal and the optimal dose of anticoagulation has been reached. Prior to the new examination form, the advisory criteria referred examiners to the Conference on Pulmonary/Respiratory Disorders and Commercial Drivers.[5] Guidance on the driver with DVT or PE was also suggested in the Cardiovascular Panel Guidelines.[6] Much of that material had been included in the ME Handbook, which is now down for revision.

There were several Frequently Asked Questions (FAQs) that addressed pulmonary issues,[7] mostly on OSA, which had been removed. One that remains is on the use of oxygen; it explains that, in most cases, the use of oxygen while driving would be disqualifying. Aside from the risk of explosion and equipment malfunction, the underlying pulmonary condition may also be disqualifying if the driver was unable to meet the PFT criteria. One of the questions that was removed advised examiners that drivers should be disqualified until the diagnosis of sleep apnea has been ruled out or has been treated successfully. In addition, drivers with OSA should be qualified only if they agree to continue uninterrupted therapy, submit to ongoing monitoring, and undergo objective testing as required. While no longer part of the FMCSA FAQs, the content is still consistent with other recommendations and best practice.

There is still an FAQ on narcolepsy, which indicates that "guidelines recommend disqualifying a CMV driver with a diagnosis of Narcolepsy, regardless of treatment because of the likelihood of excessive daytime somnolence." Another FAQ that remains reviews the use of modafinil (Provigil) in obstructive sleep disorder, narcolepsy, or shift work sleep disorder. It noted that modafinil has several concerning side effects, such as chest pain, dizziness, difficulty breathing, heart palpitations, irregular and/or fast heartbeat, increased blood pressure, tremors or shaking movements, anxiety, nervousness, rapidly changing mood, problems with memory, and blurred vision or other vision changes. There was also concern that many medications may interact with modafinil and that its use requires close supervision and may hide signs that an individual is tired.

The original FAQ advised against modafinil in commercial drivers; a subsequent update suggested that drivers being prescribed Provigil should be closely monitored for 6 weeks before they are certified, with both the treating physician and the medical examiner agreeing that Provigil is effective in preventing daytime somnolence and documenting that no untoward side effects are present. Annual certification had been recommended. In the current version on the FMCSA website, the 6-week wait and annual certification is not mentioned, only that "it is recommended that until an individual knows how Provigil affects him/her, they may not drive, use machinery or do any activity that requires mental alertness."

Recommendations

The qualification recommendations in the remainder of this chapter are from the FMCSA ME Handbook,[8] except where indicated.

In screening drivers for pulmonary disease, questions that should be asked include the following:

- Do you smoke? If so, how much? For how many years?
- Do you feel short of breath with activity or while driving?
- Do you cough? If so, is your cough productive of sputum?
- Do you have tightness in your chest during exercise or at rest?
- Do you snore? If so, do you feel sleepy during the day?
- Do you wheeze?

In addition to obvious signs of shortness of breath (e.g., a patient becomes short of breath just getting onto the examining table), other physical signs of pulmonary disease may include clubbing; cyanosis; slowing of expiration; tachypnea at rest; diffuse rhonchi, wheezes, or rales; decreased or absent breath sounds; pleural rubs; significant kyphosis; or use of accessory muscles of ventilation at rest. Any of these findings may lead the examiner to obtain a consultation with a pulmonary specialist.

Any guidance on screening, diagnosing, or treating OSA that had been in the ME Handbook had been removed, prior to the Handbook being taken off the FMCSA website. Examiners should have some criteria they use for evaluation of this condition; additional information is in the section on OSA to follow.

Most of the conditions that were mentioned in the ME Handbook—such as cystic fibrosis, chest wall deformities, interstitial fibrosis, and chronic obstructive pulmonary disease (COPD)—had similar general guidance. This includes to not certify if the driver has the following:

- Hypoxemia at rest

- Chronic respiratory failure
- History of continuing cough with cough syncope
- Extensive pulmonary dysfunction
- Weakness
- Fatigue
- Unstable condition and/or treatment regimen
- Adverse reaction to medical treatment
- Does not meet spirometry parameters

It was advised that the driver could be certified if it was documented that treatment has been shown to be adequate/effective, safe, and stable; that the driver complies with continuing medical surveillance by the appropriate specialist; and that "as the medical examiner, you believe that the nature and severity of the medical condition of the driver does not endanger the health and safety of the driver and the public." Follow-up should be dependent on the clinical course of the condition and the recommendation of the treating provider but should be at least annually.

It was advised that smokers over age 35 years should have spirometry due to the high incidence of COPD even without symptoms. A response from FMCSA[9] reminds examiners that this guidance, along with most other information in the ME Handbook, is simply guidance and at the discretion of the medical examiner.

Many medications used to treat respiratory conditions, such as allergies or cough, have potentially impairing side effects. These side effects must be taken into account during the decision-making process.

The Handbook advised that driving be precluded for 12 hours after taking any sedating medication. The old examination form instructed examiners to warn drivers about the "potential hazards of medications, including over-the-counter medications, while driving".[10] Several studies have demonstrated that antihistamines, especially the first-generation antihistamines, have a significantly impairing cognitive effect and increase the risk of crashes.[11-13] Some states have laws against driving under the influence of any agent that impairs performance, including antihistamines.[14]

Drivers with a history of pneumothorax can be qualified if the pneumothorax has resolved and they meet the general criteria outlined earlier. Those who have a history of two or more spontaneous pneumothoraces on the same side should not be qualified unless there has been a successful procedure to prevent recurrence.

Drivers with cor pulmonale or pulmonary hypertension, defined as pulmonary artery pressure greater than 50% of systemic blood pressure, can be certified if they meet general criteria and do not have dyspnea at rest, dizziness, hypotension, or a partial pressure of arterial oxygen (PaO2) in arterial blood less than 65 millimeters of mercury (mm Hg).

Allergies are very common and, in and of themselves, are unlikely to cause a problem for commercial drivers. Drivers with allergic rhinitis should be advised to use the nonsedating antihistamines or local steroid sprays. Those with severe symptoms—such as uncontrollable sneezing, sinusitis with headaches, or impaired vision due to ophthalmic involvement—should refrain temporarily from driving.

Drivers with a history of allergy to stinging insects not only may be incapacitated from a sting but also may panic at the sight of an insect. Immunotherapy may be indicated depending on the severity of reactions, and injectable epinephrine must be available.

Hereditary or acquired angioedema can be controlled with treatment; if it is controlled, commercial driving is acceptable. Recurrent episodes of idiopathic anaphylaxis may be difficult to control. If such episodes are due to a recognized allergen that can be avoided or if the symptoms can be managed, driver qualification may be acceptable. When such a driver is unable to prevent the sudden onset of dyspnea or loss of consciousness, that driver should be medically disqualified.

Drivers with life-threatening allergies should be considered able to be qualified only if they have undergone successful preventive measures or treatments without adverse effect.

Asthmatics can be certified, but their pulmonary function should meet the recommended criteria. Some tasks associated with commercial driving may exacerbate asthma, such as exposure to nonspecific irritants or cold temperatures. Recurrent hospitalizations or a frequent need for high-dose steroids should prompt further evaluation. If a driver is severely symptomatic, or if there is significant pulmonary impairment [forced expiratory volume 1 (FEV1) < 65% or PaO2 < 65 mm Hg) that cannot be reversed by treatment, the driver should not be medically qualified.

Hypersensitivity pneumonitis can be associated with dyspnea, cough, or fever. However, drivers with hypersensitivity pneumonitis can be qualified, but they should avoid the causative agent, and, if possible, they should take preventive precautions.

Acute respiratory infections—such as influenza, bronchitis, or the common cold—generally will not have long-term safety implications. During an acute infection, the symptoms may interfere with the ability to perform heavy work and with alertness. Regulating these short-term diseases is not practical. Pneumonia should preclude commercial driving until the infection has been adequately treated.

Both tuberculosis and atypical tuberculosis were mentioned in the handbook and, in general, could be certified provided they were not infectious, and that the driver was compliant with therapy and had no side effect from treatment that would interfere with safe driving.

Pulmonary Function Testing

Although few examiners routinely obtain PFTs, the Handbook had recommended PFTs for any driver with a history of lung disease or symptoms of shortness of breath, cough, chest tightness, or wheezing. PFTs were also recommended for all cigarette smokers older than 35 years but, as mentioned earlier, that is at the discretion of the examiner.

For drivers who have normal PFTs, no further evaluation is needed. Pulse oximetry or arterial blood gases (ABGs) were recommended for obstructive disease if the PFT results have an FEV1 less than 65 percent of the predicted value and/or FEV1/FVC ratio less than 65 percent. If there is restrictive disease, additional studies would be indicated if the FVC is less than 60 percent. If oximetry is less than 92 percent (oximetry = 70), ABGs should be obtained and if the driver does not meet the following criteria, the driver should not be qualified.

- Partial pressure of arterial oxygen (PaO2) less than:
  - 65 millimeters of mercury (mm Hg) at altitudes below 5,000 feet
  - 60 mm Hg at altitudes above 5,000 feet
- Partial pressure of arterial carbon dioxide (PaCO2) greater than 45 mm Hg at any altitude

Sleep Disorders—Obstructive Sleep Apnea (OSA) and Narcolepsy

This section will not be an exhaustive review of the condition and its relationship to driving safety. For that, refer to the references and review articles listed. The focus will be on guidance from FMCSA and other groups (including the FMCSA Medical Review Boards and Motor Carrier Safety Advisory Committee), how we got where we are, what examiners can and should do (as well as what they should not). The hope is to provide examiners with reasonable options they can use in reaching their certification determinations based on current literature and best practices.

OSA is probably the one medical condition that has gotten the most attention in commercial drivers over the past 10 years. A lot has changed since it was mentioned in the pulmonary/respiratory report.[5] While not specifically named in the standards, it is mentioned in the advisory criteria as a respiratory condition that may "result in incapacitation."

There is evidence that drivers with sleep disorders have as much as a seven-fold increased risk of accidents[15-20] and that adequate treatment can decrease the risk to those with the condition.[16,21-22]

Although drivers may be aware that they are sleepy, they may not realize that they are impaired and may not take action to stop driving and prevent accidents. The role OSA and its related conditions may play on vehicle crashes, especially CMVs, is gaining increased attention in other countries. While some have criteria for evaluating drivers with or suspected of having OSA, others are introducing or enhancing their screening criteria.[23-26] The Federal Aviation Administration (FAA) also updated its guidance on pilots with or at risk of OSA[27] primarily drawing from guidelines from the American Academy of Sleep Medicine.[28]

The National Transportation Safety Board (NTSB) has included sleep disorders on its Most Wanted List[29] for many years and in 2009 issued specific OSA Safety Recommendations for highway[30] (Table 5-1) as well as other modes.

TABLE 5-1 National Transportation Safety Board Recommendations to the Federal Motor Carrier Safety Administration October 20, 2009

- Implement a program to identify commercial drivers at high risk for obstructive sleep apnea and require that those drivers provide evidence through the medical certification process of having been appropriately evaluated and, if treatment is needed, effectively treated for that disorder before being granted unrestricted medical certification (H-09-15).
- Develop and disseminate guidance for commercial drivers, employers, and physicians regarding the identification and treatment of individuals at high risk of obstructive sleep apnea (OSA), emphasizing that drivers who have OSA that is effectively treated are routinely approved for continued medical certification (H-09-16).

OSA is characterized by episodes of nocturnal apnea or hypopnea, with brief episodes of waking, snoring, and resultant excessive daytime somnolence (EDS). The hypersomnolence that occurs during waking hours is seen most frequently during monotonous activities, such as driving. The use of alcohol or sedatives, shift work, and sleep deprivation can further exacerbate the degree of impairment. Drivers with sleep apnea also tend to underreport or underestimate their level of daytime sleepiness on an Epworth Sleepiness Scale (ESS); thus, reliance on subjective report of somnolence may be unreliable.[31] Without specific criteria, examiners on the National Registry of Certified Examiners are extremely inconsistent in identifying which drivers should be referred for additional evaluation for OSA.[32]

While the most concerning symptom of OSA is EDS, symptoms can include:[33]

- Loud snoring
- Periods of not breathing (apnea)
- Awakening not rested in the morning
- Dry mouth upon awakening
- Morning headaches
- Erectile dysfunction
- Recent weight gain
- Limited attention
- Memory loss
- Poor judgment
- Irritability
- Personality changes
- Depression
- Lethargy

Physical findings to suggest OSA may include obesity (BMI > 28), increased neck circumference (16 inches in women and 17 inches in men), craniosynostosis, mandibular hypoplasia, and retrognathia. Other findings may include elongated soft palate and uvula, high arched palate, and enlarged tonsils. There also is a relationship between hypertension, metabolic syndrome, and other medical conditions and OSA.[20,27,28,34,35]

In a 2002 project[36] sponsored by FMCSA and the American Transportation Research Institute of the American Trucking Association, among their sample of commercial driver's license holders, 17.6 percent had mild sleep apnea, 5.8 percent had moderate sleep apnea, and 4.7

percent had severe sleep apnea, a prevalence similar to the general population. Current estimates are that among an estimated 14 million US commercial drivers, 17 percent to 28 percent, or 2.4 to 3.9 million, are expected to have OSA.[37]

One of the challenges is in identifying those drivers who are at highest risk of OSA and are at highest risk of being involved in a motor vehicle crash.

The polysomnogram is considered the gold standard in the diagnosis of OSA. It simultaneously measures electroencephalography, respiration, electrocardiography, and oxygenation, assessing apneic episodes and sleep stages. The Apnea-Hypopnea Index (AHI) is the measurement generally used to determine the severity of OSA. It is calculated by adding the total number of apneas and the total number of hypopneas and dividing the sum by the total number of sleep hours. The accepted criteria are that an AHI between 5 and 15 constitutes mild disease, between 15 and 30 moderate, and greater than 30 represents severe disease. The American Academy of Sleep Medicine has excellent reviews on the evaluation, management, and long-term treatment of those at risk or diagnosed with OSA.[28,38]

The original guidance from FMCSA on evaluating the commercial driver with OSA was from the 1991 respiratory conference report.[5] That panel recommended that if there is any suspicion that sleep apnea exists, the driver should be evaluated and the condition successfully treated prior to returning to work. They acknowledged that treatment may consist of continuous positive airway pressure (CPAP), uvulopalatopharyngoplasty, weight loss, and/or tracheostomy. They recommended at least a 1-month waiting period after initiating treatment before returning to commercial driving and indicated that compliance was a concern. Effectiveness of treatment was recommended through either multiple sleep-latency testing (MSLT) or polysomnograms. MSLT is able to evaluate the ease with which an individual can fall asleep during normal waking hours. Some examiners used the Maintenance of Wakefulness Test (MWT) because it measures the ability to stay awake rather than how quickly an individual can fall asleep. Neither test, however, has been consistently shown to predict risk of crashes.[18]

A task force composed of members from the American College of Occupational and Environmental Medicine (ACOEM), American College of Chest Physicians (ACCP), and the National Sleep Foundation (NSF) prepared a review of the commercial driver with OSA, including recommendations on screening, diagnosis, treatment, and follow-up.[18] Talmage and colleagues[31] found that these criteria had a high positive predictive value in determining which drivers should undergo evaluation for OSA. Of the 134 drivers who met the screening criteria and had polysomnograms, 98% were diagnosed with OSA. In another study by Parks and colleagues,[39] 20 out of 20 drivers who meet the criteria for further evaluation were diagnosed with OSA. In order for their criteria to be acceptable, the Task Force participants aimed for the "tip of the iceberg," hoping to identify those at highest risk of having OSA and to have them evaluated. They recognized that the screening criteria had a low sensitivity, which means that there are many who also had OSA who would not meet the criteria to undergo additional evaluation.

In 2008, a medical expert panel on OSA made several recommendations.[20] They recommended that drivers who meet any of the following conditions should be disqualified:

- EDS or a crash resulting from falling asleep
- AHI greater than 20 until compliant with PAP
- Surgery for treatment of OSA until a 3-month postsurgical evaluation has demonstrated effectiveness or PAP treatment has been shown to be effective
- Noncompliant with treatment

They further recommended that a driver with a BMI of greater than 33 be conditionally certified for 1 month pending a sleep study. If the driver was diagnosed with OSA, the individual could be certified for 1 month and then, if shown to be compliant, certified for 3 months. If compliance is maintained, the driver could be qualified annually. Compliance was defined as at least 4 hours of use, 70% of evenings, and drivers would be required to use machines that could measure compliance.

While the MEP recognized that polysomnography (PSG) was the ideal method to assess OSA, given the large numbers of drivers that would require screening, they felt that certain portable models would be acceptable. These include objective recording devices validated against PSG that include at least 5 hours of measurement of oxygen saturation, nasal pressure, and sleep/wake time.

CPAP was identified as the best treatment. Dental appliances were not considered an acceptable treatment for commercial drivers, as compliance could not be monitored. Several surgical treatments were thought to be acceptable.

The MRB[40] accepted most of the MEP recommendations; however, they indicated that the criterion for a conditional certification be a BMI of greater than 30, requiring those drivers to undergo evaluation. It was discussed that, based on available data, approximately 24% of drivers would require testing if the cutoff was a BMI of 33 and 42 percent if the cutoff was 30.

The ME Handbook section on OSA was not posted until mid-2010 and contained recommendations derived from the pulmonary respiratory report mentioned earlier. This was removed prior to the other portions of the ME Handbook, along with the OSA FAQs and the section of the FMCSA website ("Spotlight on Sleep Apnea") as a result of Congressional action[41] in 2013.

In 2012, the FMCSA Motor Carrier Safety Advisory Committee (MCSAC), an industry advisory group, and the FMCSA's MRB jointly offered recommendations.[42] A Notice of Proposed Rulemaking, with guidance derived from those recommendations, was published in the Federal Register[43] but withdrawn days later.[44]

As the NRCME was going into effect, several groups objected to training organizations even mentioning OSA. While some training organizations were mentioning the recommendations from either the Tri-Medical Society Task Force,[25] the 2007 MEP[20] or MRB,[40] or the 2012 MRB/MCSAC,[42] some were teaching that these were FMCSA requirements and others were not mentioning sleep apnea at all. The NRCME Sample Training Document[45] had a section on OSA that indicated that training programs could teach material beyond the ME Handbook; it was clearly differentiated what was endorsed by FMCSA and what was not. FMCSA also noted that examiners could use more current guidance than was issued by FMCSA in making certification determinations.

In 2013, with recommendations from the National Transportation Safety Board,[30] multiple sets of expert recommendations, requests from the American College of Occupational Medicine and other organizations, and a withdrawn Advance Notice of Proposed Rulemaking (ANPRM), there was still no current guidance on OSA from FMCSA. As it appeared that FMCSA was preparing to again provide guidance on OSA—acting on requests from several truck, bus, and school bus organizations—a bill was introduced in Congress that would require that "any new or revised requirement providing for the screening, testing, or treatment of individuals operating commercial motor vehicles for sleep disorders is adopted pursuant to a rulemaking proceeding."

This does not require that a regulation or standard be promulgated, nor does it prohibit guidance, only that any *requirement* be adopted through rulemaking. Guidance issued by FMCSA is not a requirement. FMCSA had, however, indicated that it would approach sleep apnea through a rulemaking, rather than a guidance. The House of Representatives unanimously passed the bill on September 26, 2013. The same bill was approved in the Senate on October 4, 2013 and signed by President Obama on January 3, 2013.[41]

Training programs continued to vary in what they were teaching and Congressional representatives sent FMCSA a request[46] to:

1. Instruct training organizations that examiners are not to be instructed to follow any specific steps with respect to sleep apnea testing and treatment;
2. Instruct training programs to remove all references to MRB, MCSAC, and FMCSA recommendations on sleep apnea from their training materials; and
3. Provide specific instructions to examiners who have already been trained to correct the previous training they received.

After the request, FMCSA agreed to issue an advisory, clarifying examiners' and training programs' roles. At the same time, they confirmed that training programs were not prohibited from teaching the additional information and that examiners should refer drivers for evaluation and potential treatment if the examiner suspects a sleep disorder that could affect safe vehicle operation.

On January 20, 2015, FMCSA issued a Bulletin to Medical Examiners[47] (see Table 5-2) which clarified that while FMCSA had no specific criteria for screening, diagnosing, or treating drivers with or at risk of OSA, the agency did consider OSA a condition that could interfere with safe driving. Examiners should consider this as not only permission to screen drivers for OSA but clearly indicates that examiners should not ignore the risk factors for OSA and *should* refer those drivers they determine are at a sufficient risk for additional testing.

TABLE 5-2 Federal Motor Carrier Safety Administration Bulletin to Medical Examiners and Training Organizations Regarding Obstructive Sleep Apnea

The purpose of this bulletin is to remind healthcare professionals on FMCSA's National Registry of Certified Medical Examiners (the National Registry) of the current physical qualifications standard and advisory criteria concerning the respiratory system, specifically how the requirements apply to drivers that may have obstructive sleep apnea (OSA).

TABLE 5-2 continued

Current Physical Qualifications Standard for Respiratory Conditions

FMCSA's physical qualifications standards prohibit individuals from receiving a medical examiner's certificate to operate commercial motor vehicles in interstate commerce if they have an "established medical history or clinical diagnosis of a respiratory dysfunction likely to interfere with his or her ability to control and drive a commercial motor vehicle safely." (49 CFR 391.41(b)(5)). OSA is considered a respiratory dysfunction when there is a determination that it is likely to interfere with the driver's ability to operate safely because of the severity of the case.

OSA is a respiratory disorder characterized by a reduction or cessation of breathing during sleep coupled with symptoms such as excessive daytime sleepiness. Given this, OSA may culminate in unpredictable and sudden incapacitation (e.g., falling asleep at the wheel), thus contributing to the potential for crashes, injuries, and fatalities.

During sleep, OSA blocks the airway and prevents the individual from breathing up to dozens of times per hour, awakening the sleeper. This means that the time in bed does not equal time slept – in fact, eight hours of sleep with OSA can be less refreshing than four hours of ordinary, uninterrupted sleep, posing serious cognitive and neuropsychological risks. Moreover, someone without enough restorative sleep is often unaware of impairments to a range of cognitive abilities such as vigilance, reaction time, attention span, memory, learning, problem-solving, decision making, and multi-tasking. OSA can also lead to mood swings and difficulty controlling inappropriate feelings. In driving simulations, OSA patients were more likely to unintentionally swerve and strike objects – a serious and dangerous outcome for the transportation industry.

OSA raises health and safety concerns beyond those of other sleep disorders. Near-term increases in fatigue and cognitive dysfunction can result. Also, there are long-term adverse health effects such as dramatically increased risk for hypertension, heart disease, stroke, diabetes, and obesity.

FMCSA's Advisory Criteria from 2000

In 2000, FMCSA issued advisory criteria providing interpretive guidance to medical examiners concerning its physical qualifications standards. These advisory criteria are recommendations from FMCSA to assist medical examiners in applying the minimum physical qualification standards. The advisory criteria have been published with the Federal Motor Carrier Safety Regulations as part of the medical examination report form in 49 CFR 391.43 (Physical Qualification of Drivers; Medical Examination; Certificate, 65 FR 59363 (October 5, 2000)).

The advisory criterion for § 391.41(b)(5), which has been unchanged since 2000, provides the following guidance for medical examiners in making the determination whether a driver satisfies the respiratory standard:

> *Since a driver must be alert at all times, any change in his or her mental state is in direct conflict with highway safety. Even the slightest impairment in respiratory function under emergency conditions (when greater oxygen supply is necessary for performance) may be detrimental to safe driving.*

TABLE 5-2 continued

There are many conditions that interfere with oxygen exchange and may result in incapacitation, including emphysema, chronic asthma, carcinoma, tuberculosis, chronic bronchitis and sleep apnea. If the medical examiner detects a respiratory dysfunction, that in any way is likely to interfere with the driver's ability to safely control and drive a commercial motor vehicle, the driver must be referred to a specialist for further evaluation and therapy. Anticoagulation therapy for deep vein thrombosis and/or pulmonary thromboembolism is not unqualifying once optimum dose is achieved, provided lower extremity venous examinations remain normal and the treating physician gives a favorable recommendation.

Based on the above advisory criterion, it is clear that FMCSA has considered OSA a respiratory dysfunction that interferes with oxygen exchange. And the Agency recommends that, if a medical examiner believes the driver's respiratory condition is in any way likely to interfere with the driver's ability to safely control and drive a commercial motor vehicle, the driver should be referred to a specialist for further evaluation and therapy. This advisory criterion is helpful to medical examiners when the examiner has sufficient experience or information to recognize certain risk factors for OSA, or when a driver tells the examiner that he or she has been diagnosed with OSA. Under these circumstances, the medical examiner should consider referring the driver to a specialist for evaluation before issuing a medical examiner's certificate, or request additional information from the driver and his or her treating healthcare professional about the management of the driver's OSA, respectively.

Role of Medical Examiners' Clinical Judgment in the Medical Certification Process
FMCSA's physical qualifications standards and advisory criteria do not provide OSA screening, diagnosis or treatment guidelines for medical examiners to use in determining whether an individual should be issued a medical certificate. Medical examiners may exercise their medical judgment and expertise in determining whether a driver exhibits risk factors for having OSA and in determining whether additional information is needed before making a decision whether to issue the driver a medical certificate and the duration of that medical certification.

FMCSA urges medical examiners to explain clearly to drivers the basis for their decision concerning the issuance of a medical certification for a period of less than two years or the denial of a medical certification. The Agency encourages medical examiners to consider the following in making the medical certification decision:

- The primary safety goal regarding OSA is to identify drivers with moderate-to-severe OSA to ensure these drivers are managing their condition to reduce to the greatest extent practical the risk of drowsy driving. Moderate-to-severe OSA is defined by an apnea-hypopnea index (AHI)[1] of greater than or equal to 15.
- The Agency does not require that these drivers be considered unfit to continue their driving careers; only that the medical examiner make a determination whether they need to be evaluated and, if warranted, demonstrate they are managing their OSA to reduce the risk of drowsy driving.

TABLE 5-2 continued

- **Screening:** With regard to identifying drivers with undiagnosed OSA, FMCSA's regulations and advisory criteria do not include screening guidelines. Medical examiners should consider common OSA symptoms such as loud snoring, witnessed apneas, or sleepiness during the major wake periods, as well as risk factors, and consider multiple risk factors such as body mass index (BMI), neck size, involvement in a single-vehicle crash, etc.
- **Diagnosis:** Methods of diagnosis include in-laboratory polysomnography, at-home polysomnography, or other limited channel ambulatory testing devices which ensure chain of custody.
- **Treatment:** OSA is a treatable condition, and drivers with moderate-to-severe OSA can manage the condition effectively to reduce the risk of drowsy driving. Treatment options range from weight loss to dental appliances to Continuous Positive Airway Pressure (CPAP) therapy, and combinations of these treatments. The Agency's regulations and advisory criteria do not include recommendations for treatments for OSA and FMCSA believes the issue of treatment is best left to the treating healthcare professional and the driver.

Conclusion

FMCSA relies on medical examiners to make driver qualification decisions based on their clinical observations, findings and standards of practice. The current regulations and advisory criteria do not include guidelines concerning OSA screening, diagnosis and treatment. Medical examiners should rely upon their medical training and expertise in determining whether a driver exhibits symptoms and/or multiple risk factors for OSA, and they should explain to the driver the basis for their decision if the examiner decides to issue a medical certificate for a period of less than two years to allow for further evaluation, or to deny a driver the medical certificate.

[1]AHI = (apneas + hypopneas)/hours of sleep. Apnea is a term for the involuntary suspension of breathing during sleep. During an apnea there is no movement of the respiratory muscles and the volume of air in the lungs initially remains unchanged. Hypopnea is a term for a disorder which involves episodes of overly shallow breathing or an abnormally low respiratory rate. This differs from apnea in that there remains some flow of air. Hypopnea events may happen while asleep or while awake.

FMCSA Bulletin to Examiners January 20, 2015.

With several sets of recommendations, the disparity between examiners evaluating drivers potentially at risk for OSA continuing,[32,48] some have recommended that all commercial motor vehicle operators be screened for OSA.[49–51]

A 2016 ANPRM[52] from FMCSA and the Federal Railroad Administration sought comments on CMV operators and OSA as a first part of formal rulemaking. As part of the assessment, FMCSA will consider the impact on stakeholders when it does proceed with rulemaking. The American Transportation Research Institute (ATRI)[53] conducted a survey of truck drivers regarding screening and treatment for OSA, reviewing the costs and experiences of drivers with respect to OSA screening. The MRB and MCSAC met and again issued recommendations,[54] which are for now the most current "nonofficial" recommendations (Table 5-3).

TABLE 5-3 Recommendations from the Medical Review Board on Commercial Motor Vehicle Operators at Risk of Obstructive Sleep Apnea (10/25/2016)

I. General Recommendations Regarding OSA
   A. Certified Medical Examiners (CMEs) must screen drivers presenting for medical certification for OSA diagnostic testing in accordance with Section III.B.
   B. CMEs cannot issue a medical card for more than 1 year to a driver with an established diagnosis of OSA, regardless of severity.
   C. A CME may certify a driver with an OSA diagnosis if the driver is being treated effectively (see Sections V through IX).
   D. For certification purposes, "effective treatment" or "treated effectively" is defined as the resolution of moderate to severe OSA to mild OSA or better, as determined by a board-certified sleep specialist.
II. Immediate Disqualification
   A. Drivers should be disqualified immediately and referred for OSA diagnostic testing if any of the following conditions exist:
      1. Individuals who have admitted fatigue or sleepiness during the wake period.
      2. Individuals who have been involved in a sleep-related motor vehicle crash or accident or near crash.
   B. Drivers found non-compliant with treatment per Sections V through IX should be disqualified immediately until evaluated and treated effectively.
   C. The CME should have the discretion to disqualify any driver who appears to be at extremely high risk.
   D. Drivers disqualified for any of the above reasons must remain disqualified until evaluated and treated effectively.
III. Conditional Certification
   A. Conditional certification should include the following elements:
      1. A driver determined to be at risk for OSA based on Body Mass Index (BMI) (with or without risk factors) may be certified for 90 days pending sleep study and treatment (if the driver is diagnosed with OSA).
      2. Within 90 days, if a driver being treated with OSA is compliant with treatment (per Sections V through IX), the driver may be certified for no more than 1 year. Drivers with a diagnosis of moderate to severe OSA should be re-certified based on documented effective treatment and compliance (see Sections V through IX).
   B. Referral to OSA Diagnostic Testing Based on Screening (i.e., identifying individuals with undiagnosed OSA)
      1. **MRB Recommendation:** Individuals with the following should be referred for diagnostic sleep evaluations:
         a. Individuals with a BMI ≥ 40 mg/kg2.

TABLE 5-3 continued

b. Individuals with a BMI ≥ 33 and < 40 mg/kg2 in addition to and at least 3 or more of the following (For – 3; Against – 1):
   i. Hypertension (treated or untreated);
   ii. Type 2 diabetes (treated or untreated);
   iii. History of stroke, coronary artery disease, or arrhythmias;
   iv. Micrognathia or retrognathia;
   v. Loud snoring;
   vi. Witnessed apneas;
   vii. Small airway (Mallampati Classification of Class III or IV);
   viii. Neck size > 17 inches (male), 15.5 inches (female);
   ix. Hypothyroidism (untreated);
   x. Age 42 and above; or
   xi. Male or post-menopausal female.
c. Note: One MRB member thought that there should be at least 4 of other risk factors in addition to BMI ≥ 33 and < 40 mg/kg2 instead of 3.

2. **Rationale:** Based on public comments that other factors should be considered in addition to BMI, MRB recommends increasing the BMI threshold for recommending a sleep study based on BMI alone to 40, but add factors that in combination (e.g., having 3 or more) could trigger a sleep study recommendation, with a BMI between 33 and 39.
   a. Self-reported sleepiness during major wake periods or history of a fatigue-related crash should also be standalone triggers that require a CME to require a sleep study.
   b. However, the MRB removed the single-vehicle crash from the list of risk factors above because members expressed concern that CMEs would not have access to crash information except for instances of self-reporting or a referral from an employer.
   c. Subjective sleepiness questionnaires would not be helpful because of unlikelihood of truthfulness.
   d. Note, craniofacial abnormalities and Mallampati Classification may be difficult for some CMEs to assess.
   e. The MRB replaced the "small or recessed jaw" risk factor with "micrognathia or retrognathia" because those terms are more clinical and objective.

3. Frequency of OSA Diagnostic Testing
   a. **MRB Recommendation:** If a driver has had a sleep evaluation study in the past that returned a negative diagnosis for sleep apnea or a diagnosis of mild sleep apnea, indications that would warrant a recommendation for a new sleep study would be the appearance of one or more additional risk factors beyond those that required the original sleep study or a 10 percent increase in weight.
      i. Caveat: If age of 42 is the only additional risk factor that has changed, there should be a 3-year period between the prior sleep study and a newly recommended sleep study.

TABLE 5-3 continued

      ii.   B. Morris expressed concerns that not enough evidence exists regarding retesting. For this reason, he would recommend that requirement for retesting should be left at the discretion of the CME.

    b. **Rationale:** Some public comments expressed concern with the situation where a driver was sent for a sleep study due to risk factors in the CME guidelines, the study came back negative for sleep apnea, and the driver gets referred for another sleep study the next time he/she is examined because the same risk factors are still present. It could be an unnecessary cost imposed on these drivers.

IV. Method of Diagnosis and Severity

  A. Methods of diagnosis include in-laboratory polysomnography (which is preferred), as well as at-home sleep apnea testing that ensures chain of custody.

    1. In-laboratory polysomnography should be considered when the clinician suspects:

      a. Another medical disorder occurring during sleep (e.g., a seizure disorder, restless leg syndrome, narcolepsy, central sleep apnea), and/or

      b. The individual has significant co-morbidities (e.g., neuromuscular disorder or chronic obstructive pulmonary disease [COPD]).

    2. All sleep studies must be interpreted by a board-certified sleep specialist.

    3. New OSA screening technologies will likely emerge.

  B. The driver should be tested while on usual chronic medications.

  C. If the CME, in consultation with the sleep specialist, determines that the in-home sleep study is inadequate, then an in-laboratory test must be performed.

V. Treatment: Positive Airway Pressure (PAP)

  A. Based on the available medical literature, PAP therapy is the preferred OSA treatment.

  B. Adequate PAP pressure should be established through one of the following methods:

    1. Titration study with polysomnography.

    2. Auto-titration system.

  C. A driver may be certified initially for up to 1 year (per Section III.A) if the following conditions are met:

    1. The driver must document PAP use for a time period no less than 30 consecutive days (minimum records requirement – initial certification), and

    2. The driver's PAP use records must demonstrate at least 4 hours per night use on 70 percent of nights (minimum compliance standard), and

    3. The driver does not report excessive sleepiness during the major wake period.

  D. A driver may be re-certified for up to 1 year (per Section III.A) if the following conditions are met:

TABLE 5-3 continued

1. The driver must document PAP use for a time period no less than the number of days between the expiration of the driver's previous medical card and the time at which they receive their medical exam (minimum records requirement – re-certification), <u>and</u>
2. The driver's PAP use records must demonstrate at least 4 hours per night use on 70 percent of nights (minimum compliance standard), and
3. The driver does not report excessive sleepiness during the major wake period.

E. If a driver fails to meet compliance standards, the CME may provide a 30-day certification to allow the driver to produce 30 days of consecutive PAP use data that meets the minimum compliance standard.

    1. After the driver demonstrates compliance with 30 days of PAP use data, the CME may issue a 60-day certification to allow the driver to produce 60 days of consecutive PAP use data that meets the minimum compliance standard.

    2. After the driver demonstrates compliance with 60 days of PAP use data, the CME may issue a 90-day certification to allow the driver to produce 90 days of consecutive PAP use data that meets the minimum compliance standard.

    3. After the driver demonstrates compliance with 90 days of PAP use data, the CME may issue a 1-year certification.

    4. If the driver cannot produce 30 days of consecutive PAP use data, the driver must be disqualified and cannot be re-certified until he or she is able to provide 30 days of compliant PAP use data.

VI. Treatment: Oral appliance

A. **MRB Recommendation:** A driver with a diagnosis of moderate to severe OSA should try PAP therapy before oral appliance therapy, unless a board-certified sleep specialist has determined that an alternative therapy such as PAP is intolerable for a driver, in which case the driver should have the option to pursue oral appliance therapy to treat OSA.

    1. **Rationale:** Based on the available medical literature, drivers with a diagnosis of moderate to severe OSA are less likely to achieve resolution of moderate to severe OSA with an oral appliance than with PAP therapy.

    2. There is limited data regarding compliance and long-term efficacy of oral appliances.

B. A driver may be certified or re-certified for up to 1 year (per Section III.A) if the following conditions are met:

    1. A repeat sleep study shows resolution of moderate to severe OSA, <u>and</u>

    2. The driver has been cleared by the treating clinician, <u>and</u>

    3. c, <u>and</u>

    4. The driver does not report excessive sleepiness during the major wake period.

TABLE 5-3 continued

VII. Treatment: Bariatric surgery
   A. Post-op, first 6 months: A driver with an established diagnosis of moderate to severe OSA may be certified if he/she:
      1. Has been cleared by the treating clinician, <u>and</u>
      2. Is able to provide evidence of compliance with PAP or oral device OSA therapy (see Sections V and VI).
   B. Post-op, after 6 months: After 6 months have passed since surgery, a driver may be certified, provided that:
      1. A repeat sleep study shows that the driver no longer has a moderate to severe OSA diagnosis, <u>and</u>
      2. The driver does not report excessive sleepiness during the major wake period.
   C. Annual recertification
      1. If clinically indicated, repeat the sleep study.
VIII. Treatment: Oropharyngeal surgery, Facial bone surgery
   A. Post-op, less than 1 month: A driver with an established diagnosis of moderate to severe OSA may be certified if he/she:
      1. Has been cleared by the treating clinician, <u>and</u>
      2. Is able to provide evidence of compliance with PAP or oral device OSA therapy (see Sections V and VI).
   B. Post-op, after 1 month: After 1 month has passed since surgery, a driver may be certified, provided that:
      1. A repeat sleep study shows that the driver no longer has a moderate to severe OSA diagnosis, <u>and</u>
      2. The driver does not report excessive sleepiness during the major wake period.
   C. Annual recertification
      1. If clinically indicated, repeat the sleep study.
IX. Treatment: Tracheostomy
   A. Post-op, less than 1 month: A driver with an established diagnosis of moderate to severe OSA may be certified if he/she:
      1. Has been cleared by the treating clinician, <u>and</u>
      2. Is able to provide evidence of compliance with PAP or oral device OSA therapy (see Sections V and VI).
   B. Post-op, after 1 month: After 1 month has passed since surgery, a driver may be certified, provided that:
      1. A repeat sleep study shows that the driver no longer has a moderate to severe OSA diagnosis, <u>and</u>
      2. The driver does not report excessive sleepiness during the major wake period.
   C. Annual recertification
      1. If clinically indicated, repeat the sleep study.

Narcolepsy is the one sleep disorder which is still mentioned in FAQ as disqualifying. An evidence-based review[55] was conducted in 2010 and the MRB recommended that the prohibition on certification of drivers with narcolepsy be upheld.[56] Since then, FMCSA has accepted a few applications for exemptions from the prohibition on certifying drivers with narcolepsy, but none have been granted.

Conclusion

The bottom line with pulmonary disorders and medical certification, with the exception of OSA, is that, regardless of the disease, the decision should be based on lung function. Medications and accompanying side effects may be significant and should be evaluated and the driver counseled on the potential safety hazards of certain medications.

OSA is a challenge, and consistent with other medical conditions for which there is no formal direction from FMCSA, examiners should consider all current literature, especially the evidence based reviews and recommendations from experts in reaching certification determination. Examiners should "do the right thing," remembering that these are fitness for duty examinations whose purpose is to protect the motoring public and vehicle passengers. While FMCSA has not yet issued official recommendations on the screening, diagnosis, and treatment of drivers with OSA, given the multiple sets of expert recommendations and the recognition of the role that OSA has in crashes, the only incorrect approach for examiners is to do nothing.

References

1. Harber P, Fedoruk MJ. Work placement and worker fitness: Implications of the Americans with Disabilities Act for pulmonary medicine. *Chest.* 1994;105:1564–1571.
2. Medical Examination Report Form 09/16/16. MCSA 5875. https://www.fmcsa .dot.gov/sites/fmcsa.dot.gov/files/docs/MedicalExaminationReportForm _091616_MCSA_5875.pdf
3. Federal Motor Carrier Safety Administration, U.S. Department of Transportation. Medical Examiner's Certification Integration. Notice of proposed rulemaking. Docket No. FMCSA–2012–0178. *Fed Reg.* May 10, 2013. Vol. 78, No. 91;27343– 27363. https://www.gpo.gov/fdsys/pkg/FR-2013-05-10/pdf/2013-11080.pdf.
4. Appendix A to 49 CFR Part 391—Medical Advisory Criteria. http://www.ecfr .gov/cgi-bin/retrieveECFR?gp=1&ty=HTML&h=L&mc=true&=PART&n=pt49 .5.391#ap49.5.391_171.a
5. U.S. Department of Transportation, Federal Highway Administration. Conference on Respiratory/Pulmonary Disorders and Commercial Drivers. Publication No. FHWA-MC-91-004. Washington: U.S. Department of

Transportation, Federal Highway Administration, Office of Motor Carriers, 1991. https://www.fmcsa.dot.gov/regulations/medical/conference-pulmonaryrespiratory-disorders-and-commercial-drivers

6. Blumenthal R, Braunstein J, Connolly H, et al. Cardiovascular Advisory Panel Guidelines for the Medical Examination of Commercial Motor Vehicle Drivers. FMCSA-MCP-02-002. Washington: U.S. Department of Transportation, Federal Motor Carrier Safety Administration, October 2002. https://www.fmcsa.dot .gov/regulations/medical/cardiovascular-advisory-panel-guidelines-medical -examination-commercial-motor

7. Federal Motor Carrier Safety Administration, U.S. Department of Transportation. Federal Motor Carrier Safety Administration Frequently Asked Questions—Medical. https://www.fmcsa.dot.gov/faq/Medical-Requirements.

8. Federal Motor Carrier Safety Administration, U.S. Department of Transportation. Medical Examiner Handbook, currently in the process of revision. https://www.fmcsa.dot.gov/regulations/medical/fmcsa-medical-examiner -handbook.

9. Hartenbaum NP. Commercial Driver Medical Examiner Review. Winter 2014.

10. Federal Motor Carrier Safety Administration, U.S. Department of Transportation. Physical qualification of drivers; Medical examination; Final rule. *Fed Reg.* 2000;65(Oct. 5):59363–59380. https://www.gpo.gov/fdsys/pkg/FR-2000-10-05 /pdf/00-25337.pdf.

11. O'Hanlon JF, Ramaekers JG. Antihistamine effects on actual driving performance in a standard test: a summary of Dutch experience, 1989–1994. Allergy. 1995;50:234–242.

12. Kay GG. The effects of antihistamines on cognition and performance. *J Allergy Clin Immunol.* 2000;105(6, part 2) (Supplement):S622–S627.

13. Couper FJ, Logan BK. Drugs and human performance fact sheets. NHTSA Revised April 2014. www.nhtsa.dot.gov/people/injury/research/job185drugs.

14. National Highway Traffic Safety Administration. Digest of Impaired Driving and Selected Beverage Control Laws. 29th ed. April 2016. http://www.nhtsa.gov /staticfiles/nti/pdf/812267_2014-ImpairedDrivingDigest.pdf

15. Teran-Santos J, Jimenez-Gomez A, Cordero-Guevara J. The association between sleep apnea and the risk of traffic accidents. *N Engl J Med.* 1999;340:847–851.

16. Tregear SJ et al. *Obstructive Sleep Apnea and Commercial Motor Vehicle Driver Safety – Evidence Report.* Prepared by Manila Consulting Incorporated and the ECRI Institute for the Federal Motor Carrier Safety Administration. 2007.

17. Horstman S, Hess CW, Bassetti C, et al. Sleepiness related accidents in sleep apnea patients. *Sleep.* 2000;23:283–289.

18. Hartenbaum N, Collop N, Rosen IM, et al. Sleep apnea and commercial motor vehicle operators: statement from the Joint Task Force of the American College of Chest Physicians, American College of Occupational and Environmental Medicine, and the National Sleep Foundation. *J Occup Environ Med.* 2006;48(9 Suppl):S4–S37.

19. Burks SV, Anderson JE, Bombyk M, et al. Nonadherence with employer-mandated sleep apnea treatment and increased risk of serious truck crashes. *Sleep.* 2016;39(5)967–975.

20. Ancoli-Israel S, Czeisler CA, George CFP, et al. Expert Panel Recommendations. Obstructive sleep apnea and commercial motor vehicle driver safety. Presented to the Federal Motor Carrier Safety Administration January 14, 2008. www.fmcsa.dot.gov/rules-regulations/TOPICS/mep/report/Sleep-MEP-Panel -Recommendations-508.pdf.

21. Weaver TE, Maislin G, Dinges DF, et al. (2007) Relationship between hours of CPAP use and achieving normal levels of sleepiness and daily functioning. *Sleep*. 30:711–719.

22. George CF. Reduction in motor vehicle collisions following treatment of sleep apnea with nasal CPAP. *Thorax*. 2001;56(7):508–512.

23. Ayas N, Skomro R, Blackman A. Obstructive sleep apnea and driving: A Canadian Thoracic Society and Canadian Sleep Society position paper. *Can Respir J.* 2014;21(2):114–123. http://www.respiratoryguidelines.ca/sites/all/files/CTS _CSS_Position_Paper_OSA_Driving_2014.pdf.

24. Driver and Vehicle Licensing Agency, United Kingdom. At a glance guide to the current standards of fitness to drive. August 2016. https://www.gov.uk /government/publications/assessing-fitness-to-drive-a-guide-for-medical -professionals.

25. de Mello MT, Bittencourt LR, Cunha Rde C, et al. Sleep and transit in Brazil: new legislation. *J Clin Sleep Med.* 2009;5(2):164–166.

26. Sharwood LN, Elkington J, Stevenson M, et al. Assessing sleepiness and sleep disorders in Australian long-distance commercial vehicle drivers: self-report versus an "at home" monitoring device. *Sleep*. 2012;35(4):469–475.

27. Federal Aviation Administration. Guide for Aviation Medical Examiners, Decision Considerations Disease Protocols — Obstructive Sleep Apnea (OSA). OSA Reference Materials. https://www.faa.gov/about/office_org/headquarters _offices/avs/offices/aam/ame/guide/dec_cons/disease_prot/osa/ref_materials/

28. Epstein LJ, Kristo D, Strollo PJ, et al. Clinical Guideline for the Evaluation, Management and Long-term Care of Obstructive Sleep Apnea in Adults. *J Clin Sleep Med*. 2009 Jun 15;5(3):263–276. http://www.aasmnet.org/Resources/ ClinicalGuidelines/OSA_Adults.pdf.

29. National Transportation Safety Board 2016 Most Wanted. http://www.ntsb.gov/ safety/mwl/Pages/default.aspx.

30. National Transportation Safety Board Safety Recommendation. Obstructive Sleep Apnea. H-09-15 and -16. October 20, 2009. http://www.ntsb.gov/safety/ safety-recs/recletters/H09_15_16.pdf.

31. Talmage JB, Hudson TB, Hegmann KT, et al. Consensus criteria for screening commercial drivers for obstructive sleep apnea: evidence of efficacy. *J Occup Environ Med*. 2008;50(3):324–329.

32. Hartenbaum NP. Certified medical examiners and screening for obstructive sleep apnea. *J Occup Environ Med*. 2015;57:e19–e22.

33. Williams A, Amana A, Tregear S. Evidence Report Obstructive Sleep Apnea and Commercial Motor Vehicle Driver Safety: Updated Review. Presented to Federal Motor Carrier Safety Administration 11/30/2011. http://ntl.bts.gov/lib /44000/44400/44452/OSA_Update_11302011.docx.

34. Attarian HP, Sabri AN. When to suspect obstructive sleep apnea syndrome: symptoms may be subtle, but treatment is straightforward. *Postgrad Med.* 2002;111:70–76.
35. Dagan Y, Doljansky JT, Green A, et al. Body mass index (BMI) as a first-line screening criterion for detection of excessive daytime sleepiness among professional drivers. *Traffic Inj Prev.* 2006;7:44–48.
36. Pack AI, Dinges DF, Maislin G. A study of prevalence of sleep apnea among commercial truck drivers. Federal Motor Carrier Safety Administration Publication No. DOT-RT-02-030. Washington, DC: FMCSA, 2002.
37. Kales SN, Straubel MG. Obstructive sleep apnea in North American commercial drivers. *Ind Health.* 2014 Jan; 52(1): 13–24.
38. Ramar K, Dort LC, Katz SG. Clinical Practice Guideline for the Treatment of Obstructive Sleep Apnea and Snoring with Oral Appliance Therapy: An Update for 2015. *J Clin Sleep Med.* 2015;11(7):773–827.
39. Parks PD, Durand G, Tsismenakis AJ, et al. Screening for obstructive sleep apnea during commercial driver medical examinations. *J Occup Environ Med.* 2009;51(3):275–282.
40. Meeting Summary of the FMCSA Medical Review Board. January 28, 2008. Available at www.mrb.fmcsa.dot.gov/documents/Fin_Meet_Min_Jan28 _2008MRB_Meet_Revised11-24-09.pdf.
41. Public Law 113–45— OCT. 15, 2013. Commercial Motor Vehicle Operator Requirements Relating To Sleep Disorders. https://www.congress.gov/113/plaws /publ45/PLAW-113publ45.pdf.
42. Motor Carrier Safety Advisory Committee. February 6, 2012 MCSAC and MRB Task 11-05 Final Report on Obstructive Sleep Apnea (OSA). http://www.mrb.fmcsa.dot.gov/documents/Meetings2012/Task11 -05FinalCoverLetterandReport_2-21-12.docx.
43. Federal Motor Carrier Safety Administration. Proposed recommendations on obstructive sleep apnea. notice; request for comments. *Fed Reg.* 2012;77:23794–23797.
44. Federal Motor Carrier Safety Administration. Proposed Recommendations on Obstructive Sleep Apnea; Withdrawal of Notice. *Fed Reg.* 2012;77:25226–25227. https://www.gpo.gov/fdsys/pkg/FR-2012-04-27/pdf/2012-10176.pdf
45. Federal Motor Carrier Safety Administration. Medical Examiner Sample Training Handbook. https://nationalregistry.fmcsa.dot.gov/NRPublicUI/documents /ME_Training_Document.pdf.
46. Letter to Administrator Darling on Training of Certified Medical Examiners on Obstructive Sleep Apnea. October 2, 2014. http://www.ooida.com/ IssuesActions/Regulatory/docs/Bucshon_Lipinski_Letter_on_Sleep-Apnea _100214.pdf.
47. Federal Motor Carrier Safety Administration Bulletin to Medical Examiners and Training Organizations Regarding Obstructive Sleep Apnea. January 20, 2015. https://nationalregistry.fmcsa.dot.gov/NRPublicUI/documents/OSA %20Bulletin%20to%20MEs%20and%20Training%20Organizations-01122015 .pdf.

48. Durand G1, Kales SN. Obstructive sleep apnea screening during commercial driver medical examinations: a survey of ACOEM members. *J Occup Environ Med.* 2009;51:1220–1226.

49. Platt AB1, Wick LC, Hurley S, et al. Hits and misses: screening commercial drivers for obstructive sleep apnea using guidelines recommended by a joint task force. *J Occup Environ Med.* 2013;55:1035–1040.

50. Hartenbaum NP, Phillips B, Collop N. Response to "Hits and Misses: Screening Commercial Drivers for Obstructive Sleep Apnea Using Guidelines Recommended by a Joint Task Force" by Platt et al. *J Occup Environ Med.* 2014;56:119–121.

51. Platt AB, Gurubhagavatula I. Rationale for broader testing of drivers for obstructive sleep apnea: a response to Hartenbaum and colleagues. *J Occup Environ Med.* 2014;56:121–122.

52. Federal Motor Carrier Safety Administration and Federal Railroad Administration. Evaluation of Safety Sensitive Personnel for Moderate-to-Severe Obstructive Sleep Apnea. Advance Notice of Proposed Rulemaking. *Fed Reg.* 2016;81(47):12642–12647. https://federalregister.gov/a/2016-05396.

53. American Transportation Research Institute White Paper - Commercial Driver Perspectives on Obstructive Sleep Apnea. May 2016. http://atri-online.org/2016/05/26/commercial-driver-perspectives-on-obstructive-sleep-apnea/

54. Federal Motor Carrier Safety Administration Medical Review Board Task 16-01 Letter Report on OSA. https://www.fmcsa.dot.gov/advisory-committees/mcsac/mrb-task-16-01-letter-report.

55. Bieber-Tregear M, Williams JR, Tregear S. Evidence Report Narcolepsy (with and without Cataplexy) and Commercial Motor Vehicle Driver Safety. October 6, 2009. http://ntl.bts.gov/lib/55000/55200/55225/Narcolepsy_and_CMV_drivers_-_FINAL_10302009.pdf

56. Federal Motor Carrier Safety Administration Medical Review Board Summary. January 6, 2010. https://www.fmcsa.dot.gov/sites/fmcsa.dot.gov/files/docs/Final_Jan_6_2010_MRB_Meeting_Summary.pdf

CHAPTER 6

Musculoskeletal Disorders

ERIC WOOD, MD, MPH, FACOEM

Since the prior edition of this book, the Commercial Driver Medical Examiner (CDME) processes have undergone significant changes, mostly related to the National Registry of Certified Medical Examiners (NRCME). In 2014, the Federal Motor Carrier Safety Administration Medical Examiner Handbook (ME Handbook) was taken off the Federal Motor Carrier Safety Administration (FMCSA) website for update and revision. As this edition is being prepared, examiners still should consider guidance from the prior handbook, as that is what is being taught in the training programs, but should base their final decision on current best medical practice remembering that our ultimate responsibility is to ensure the safety of the motoring public to the extent reasonably possible. Chapters will include information from the most recent ME Handbook, Medical Expert Panel (MEP) reports, and Medical Review Board (MRB) recommendations as well as other relevant reports and literature.

The FMCSA Medical Review Board heard recommendations from the MEP on musculoskeletal disorders in 2008 and made formalized recommendations to FMCSA. However, adoption of any of these recommendations by FMCSA has not occurred.

As significant changes occur, they will be noted at the end of each chapter in the online version of this book at least twice a year.

Operation of commercial motor vehicles (CMVs) requires musculoskeletal capabilities that extend well beyond the routine demands of noncommercial driving. Despite advances in electronics and power-assisted devices, the forces and frequencies of manual activities performed by commercial drivers require a high level of both fine and gross motor control and skill. Additionally, the act of driving and maintaining safe function of the vehicle places specific demands on the musculoskeletal system. Mazer et al. looked at the interplay between functional abilities and operation of motor vehicles—including shifting gears, use of the emergency brake, and manipulation of the steering wheel—and found that safe operation was dependent on sufficient range of motion.[1] The medical examiner must be able to address strength, dexterity, endurance, range of motion, and overall musculo-skeletal function of drivers in order to assess their capabilities for safe operation of commercial vehicles.

With respect to motor vehicle crash risk and musculoskeletal disorders (MSDs), little data have been reported, especially for commercial drivers. Despite the paucity of data, there exists some literature to suggest that drivers with MSDs are at increased risk for crashes. In a retrospective study of truck drivers involved in crashes in Australia from 1988 to 2000, MSDs were the most common cause for prior hospitalization, with 27 percent of the cohort ever admitted for MSDs.[2] Data from a population-based, 5-year retrospective study from the general driving population showed that the risk for at-fault motor vehicle crashes among noncommercial drivers with licensing restrictions owing to MSDs was quite elevated (relative risk [RR] = 11.3, 95% confidence interval [CI] = 2.39, 53.3), as was that among drivers without restrictions (RR = 1.84, 95% CI = 1.14, 2.98). The RRs for all motor vehicle crashes for those with MSDs but not restricted were elevated (RR = 1.59, 95% CI = 1.10, 2.29), as were those for restricted drivers (RR = 4.51, 95% CI = 1.01, 20.1).[3]

An additional concern for the medical examiner relates to possible risks associated with self-treatment for pain related to MSDs. Prescription medications to treat musculoskeletal pain may include narcotic analgesics, muscle relaxants, benzodiazepines, and other potentially sedating medications, including "off-label" adjunctive pain medications. Over-the-counter medications such as nonsteroidal anti-inflammatory drugs (NSAIDs), antihistamines, and others are often used by themselves or in combination with other medications to alleviate pain as well.[4,5]

Musculoskeletal Disorders and the Commercial Driver Medical Examiner Certification Process

In addition to the regulations that address musculoskeletal conditions, FMCSA has issued Advisory Criteria,[6] interpretations,[7] and Frequently Asked Questions (FAQs)[8] for musculoskeletal disorders. FMCSA had previously posted the portion of the ME Handbook[9] on musculoskeletal conditions, but this has been taken off the FMCSA website at the time of this edition. There is also a process for those drivers with a loss of limb or fixed defect of an extremity to apply for a variance from the medical standard.[10] Finally, FMCSA commissioned the *Evidence Report: Musculoskeletal Disorders and Commercial Motor Vehicle Driver Safety*[11] and convened an MEP[12] on musculoskeletal disorders. A public meeting with the MRB and MEP was held on April 7, 2008,[13] where the MEP proposed a series of recommendations[12] to address specific health-related safety concerns of commercial drivers based on the evidence report.

Regulations

The Federal Motor Carrier Safety Regulations (FMCSRs) addressing musculoskeletal conditions are as follows:

Loss of Limb §391.41(b)(1) A person is physically qualified to drive a commercial motor vehicle if that person:

Has no loss of a foot, leg, hand, or arm, or has been granted a Skill Performance Evaluation (SPE) Certificate pursuant to Section 391.49.

Limb Impairment §391.41(b)(2) A person is physically qualified to drive a commercial motor vehicle if that person:

Has no impairment of: (i) A hand or finger which interferes with prehension or power grasping; or (ii) An arm, foot, or leg which interferes with the ability to perform normal tasks associated with operating a commercial motor vehicle; or (iii) Any other significant limb defect or limitation which interferes with the ability to perform normal tasks associated with operating a commercial motor vehicle; or (iv) Has been granted a Skill Performance Evaluation (SPE) Certificate pursuant to Section 391.49.

Rheumatic, Arthritic, Orthopedic, Muscular, Neuromuscular, or Vascular Disease: §391.41(b)(7) A person is physically qualified to drive a commercial motor vehicle if that person:

Has no established medical history or clinical diagnosis of rheumatic, arthritic, orthopedic, muscular, neuromuscular, or vascular disease which interferes with his/her ability to control and operate a commercial motor vehicle safely.

Musculoskeletal History and Examination

The musculoskeletal examination of the commercial driver needs to be both focused and comprehensive. The medical examiner must be able to provide an assessment that the individual has adequate function and lack of any significant impairment to allow safe operation of a commercial vehicle.

There are four questions from the Medical Examination Report Form that address musculoskeletal conditions:

1. Missing or limited use of arm, hand, finger, leg, foot, toe
2. Neck or back problems
3. Bone, muscle, joint, or nerve problem
4. Have you ever had a broken bone?

The self-reported medical history provided by the individual on the written medical form may provide assistance in understanding preexisting musculoskeletal problems, but it is not in itself adequate to determine prior or existing musculoskeletal problems. The medical examiner should query the individual directly with a focused musculoskeletal history. This line of inquiry should include questions about prior medical care, surgeries, trauma, or other problems. Specific questions regarding subjective symptoms of pain, paresthesia, weakness, or limitations in range of motion or other limitations in function also should be addressed. If musculoskeletal pain is an issue, the examiner should also attempt to evaluate the severity and frequency of the pain and whether any potentially impairing medications are used, such as narcotics or muscle relaxants.

In addition to direct questions regarding potential musculoskeletal problems, the medical examiner, as well as ancillary office staff, needs to be observant of behavior and activities prior to the formal examination. Gait disturbances, behavior suggestive of pain (e.g., grimaces, guarding, verbalization or vocalization of pain), or other abnormalities should be noted and followed up with appropriate questions and examination.

The examination should be comprehensive to include all aspects of the musculoskeletal system and focused to specific areas intrinsic to the demands of commercial driving. Specifically, the medical examiner must pay attention to the back and extremities. The examination must ensure that the individual has adequate strength, range of motion, and intact sensory and proprioceptive responses to perform the essential job functions and ensure safe operation of the commercial vehicle. The examination should be methodical to ensure that each component is adequately assessed. It also must be focused to more carefully assess specific areas identified in the history or that otherwise might merit more careful attention (e.g., past surgical problems, complaints of pain, noted asymmetries).

The examination should include a thorough evaluation of the back and neck for range of motion, posture, and appropriate neurologic responses of reflexes, sensation, and motor function. Upper and lower extremities should be examined for symmetry, range of motion, strength, sensation, and other neurovascular parameters. Suspected abnormalities may be referenced to accepted normal values such as those published in the *Guides to the Evaluation of Permanent Impairment*[14] or other accepted standard references.[15-17] In some cases, specific tests or examination maneuvers might be warranted. This might include strength testing (e.g., hand-grip dynamometer or other objective measures), range of motion testing (e.g., goniometer or other objective measures), sensory testing (e.g., two-point discrimination, filament sensation, or other objective measures), and/or provocative physical examination tests for ligamentous or joint stability. FMCSA had posted guidance for evaluation of grip strength on the ME Handbook site; examples of recommended tests include use of a dynamometer or repeated squeezing of a sphygmomanometer. While no inclusion or exclusion guidance was described, FMCSA states that "the driver must have sufficient grasp and prehension to control an oversize steering wheel, shift gears using a manual transmission, and maneuver a vehicle in crowded areas".[9] Specific abnormalities found on examination or subjective symptoms may at times require further evaluation, such as laboratory tests, radiologic imaging, nerve conduction testing, or specialty referral. As noted previously, loss of limb or a stationary limb impairment would require appropriate evaluation per the SPE Certification Program.[10]

Ultimately, the medical examiner must be able to provide an assessment that the individual has the functional capability to perform the essential job functions of a commercial driver and to do so in a manner consistent with safe operation of a commercial vehicle. Anything short of this objective requires that the medical examiner fail to qualify the individual on medical grounds.

The FMCSRs and Advisory Criteria provide guidance for evaluation of commercial drivers with respect to loss of limb, limb impairment, and diseases of the musculoskeletal system. The guidance is directed at an assessment of performance in tactile, manipulative, range of motion, and strength capabilities of the upper and lower extremities. Although explicit criteria for evaluating these capabilities have not been described, an examination directed toward these functions can provide a basis for rendering an appropriate recommendation by the medical examiner.

Implicit in determining "the ability to perform normal tasks associated with operating a commercial motor vehicle" or in determining what "interferes with his/her ability to control and operate a commercial motor vehicle safely" is an understanding by the medical examiner of the work environment of the commercial driver and the essential job functions performed by the commercial driver. Although no two drivers may have the same vehicle or duties, certain factors are common to this role.

The primary worksite of commercial drivers is their vehicle and the area immediately surrounding that vehicle. A commercial driver medical certificate allows a driver to operate any commercial vehicle as defined by 49 CFR 390.5. These vehicles may weigh from 10,000 pounds to upwards of 80,000 pounds or more when fully loaded. They may be of a straight (one-piece) vehicle design or a tractor-trailer design. Straight trucks include vans, panel trucks, flatbeds, and dump-bodies. Tractor trailers consist of the tractor power unit, which may include a sleeping compartment, and from one to three trailers.[18,19] In the course of routine operations, drivers are required to climb in and out of their truck cabs, perform safety inspections, and respond to emergency situations in variable weather, lighting, and surface conditions. Drivers also may be required to load and unload material or equipment from their vehicles, couple and uncouple the trailer units, affix tire chains for travel over snow and ice, fix tarps and straps over loads to secure the loads in transit, and climb onto and over the vehicle or trailer units. These activities often are physically demanding, and the driver may be required to perform them in isolated settings without opportunity for assistance.

At a minimum, FMCSA has stated within the Frequently Asked Questions[8] that all drivers must have the capability "to not only drive the vehicle safely, but also to do pre- and post-trip safety inspections, secure the load and make sure it has not shifted." Bus drivers have some different physical requirements.

Advisory Criteria

Loss of Limb

The medical evaluation of an individual with loss of limb is a relatively straightforward exercise for the medical examiner. During the course of the medical examination, should the examiner observe the loss or absence of a foot, leg, hand, or arm, the examiner should determine if the driver is otherwise medically qualified and, if so, issue the medical certificate, noting that it must be accompanied by a Skill Performance Evaluation (SPE) Certificate pursuant to Section §391.49.[10]

The SPE Certification Program (formerly known as the Limb Waiver Program) was designed to allow persons with the loss of a foot or limb or with functional impairment to qualify under the FMCSRs by demonstrating adequate function or by use of prosthetic devices or equipment modifications if they are to safely operate a CMV. Certain risks still may be present; therefore, restrictions may be included on individual SPE certificates when a state director for FMCSA determines they are necessary to be consistent with safety and the public interest.

If the examiner finds the driver otherwise qualified, the examiner may sign the medical certificate and mark on the medical certificate that the driver is qualified only if accompanied by an SPE certificate. The driver or the driver jointly with the motor carrier is then responsible for applying for the SPE, and both are subject to appropriate penalty if the driver operates a CMV in interstate or foreign commerce without a current SPE certificate.

The certification process for an SPE certificate includes completion of a formal application submitted to the regional service center for the state in which the co-applicant motor carrier's principal place of business is located or, if submitted unilaterally by a driver applicant, the application must be addressed to the FMCSA field service center for the state in which the driver has legal residence. The driver is also responsible for submission of appropriate medical documentation.

The medical evaluation and documentation specific to the requirements of the SPE certification process is a formal evaluation that must be completed by either a board-qualified or board-certified physiatrist (doctor of physical medicine) or orthopedic surgeon. In order to successfully complete this evaluation, the physiatrist or orthopedic surgeon must be provided a description of the job-related tasks that the driver applicant will be required to perform by the co-applicant motor carrier or the driver applicant. The medical evaluation summary is required to include the following:

§391.49(d)(3)(i)(A) *An assessment of the functional capabilities of the driver as they relate to the ability of the driver to perform normal tasks associated with operating a commercial motor vehicle; and*

(d)(3)(i)(B) *A statement by the examiner that the applicant is capable of demonstrating precision prehension (e.g., manipulating knobs and switches) and power grasp prehension (e.g., holding and maneuvering the steering wheel) with each upper limb separately. This requirement does not apply to an individual who was granted a waiver, absent a prosthetic device, prior to the publication of this amendment.*

If the letter of application is accepted by the state director, FMCSA, then the state director may require the driver applicant to demonstrate his or her ability to safely operate the commercial motor vehicle(s) the driver intends to drive to the state agency or to an agent authorized by the state agency. Demonstration of these abilities may be accomplished by an evaluation of necessary skill sets, including safety checks, skill-specific driving tasks, and an over-the-road driving test.

Limb Impairment

Evaluating an individual with limb impairment poses additional challenges to the medical examiner. Although in some cases these impairments may be frankly obvious, in other cases, they may be rather subtle and may even escape notice from the less experienced or less observant examiner. Examples of limb impairments may include conditions such as posttraumatic changes resulting in loss of range of motion or strength, neurodegenerative disorders with accompanying decreased sensory or motor function, or other organic impairments that prevent normal functional use of limbs.

As with loss of limb, FMCSA has developed a mechanism for individuals with limb impairment who meet specific criteria to qualify as a commercial driver. For the most part, this process is identical to that for loss of limb. A person whose limb impairment in any way interferes with the safe performance of normal tasks associated with operating a commercial motor vehicle is subject to the SPE Certification Program pursuant to Section 391.49, assuming the person is otherwise qualified. Application to this program is identical to that outlined for loss of limb. Again, similar to requirements in loss of limb, the medical evaluation and documentation for limb impairment includes a formal evaluation that must be completed by either a board-qualified or board-certified physiatrist or orthopedic surgeon. In addition to the requirements of the loss of limb, the physiatrist or orthopedic surgeon must also provide the following:

§391.49(d)(3)(ii)(A) *An explanation as to how and why the impairment interferes with the ability of the applicant to perform normal tasks associated with operating a commercial motor vehicle;*

(d)(3)(ii)(B) *An assessment and medical opinion of whether the condition will likely remain medically stable over the lifetime of the driver applicant; and*

(d)(3)(ii)(C) *A statement by the examiner that the applicant is capable of demonstrating precision prehension (e.g., manipulating knobs and switches) and power grasp prehension (e.g., holding and maneuvering the steering wheel) with each upper limb separately. This requirement does not apply to an individual who was granted an SPE Certificate, absent an orthotic device, prior to the publication of this amendment.*

(d)(4) *A description of the driver applicant's prosthetic or orthotic device worn, if any.*

The FMCSA ME Handbook indicated that the SPE is only for fixed defects of an extremity; it is not applicable for those individuals with impairments of extremities due to progressive disease, such as multiple sclerosis.

Rheumatic, Arthritic, Orthopedic, Muscular, Neuromuscular, or Vascular Disease

Evaluation of the individual with rheumatic, arthritic, orthopedic, muscular, neuromuscular, or vascular disease has the potential to pose even more challenges to the medical examiner. Even subtle manifestations of some of these disorders have the potential to pose significant risk for sudden incapacitation to drivers. Evaluation of some of these conditions warrants careful attention to appropriate screening instruments and use of expert consultation when warranted.

The FMCSR for this section states the following:

§391.41(b)(7) *A person is physically qualified to drive a commercial vehicle if that person:*

Has no established medical history or clinical diagnosis of rheumatic, arthritic, orthopedic, muscular, neuromuscular or vascular disease which interferes with ability to control and operate a commercial motor vehicle safely.

Certain diseases are known to have acute episodes of transient muscle weakness, poor muscular coordination (ataxia), abnormal sensations (paresthesia), decreased muscle tone (hypotonia), and pain that suddenly may be incapacitating. With each recurring episode, these symptoms may become more pronounced and remain for longer periods of time. Other diseases have more insidious onset and display symptoms of muscle wasting (atrophy), swelling, and paresthesia that may not suddenly incapacitate a person but may restrict the individual's movements and eventually interfere with the ability to safely operate a motor vehicle. In many instances, these diseases are degenerative in nature or may result in deterioration of the involved area.

Once the driver has been diagnosed as having a rheumatic, arthritic, orthopedic, muscular, neuromuscular, or vascular disease, then the person has an established history of that disease. The physician, when examining an individual, should consider the following:

1. The nature and severity of the individual's condition (such as sensory loss or loss of strength)
2. The degree of limitation present (such as range of motion)
3. The likelihood of progressive limitation (not always present initially but may manifest itself over time)
4. The likelihood of sudden incapacitation

If severe functional impairment exists, the driver does not qualify. In cases in which more frequent monitoring is required, a certificate for a shorter period of time may be issued.

In general, as §391.41(b)(7) implies, this subpart includes an enormously broad class of diseases and disorders. The various conditions may have temporary, stable, progressive, or relapsing courses over their natural history. Because of this, the medical examiner needs to be aware of the natural history of these conditions in order to make appropriate recommendations regarding the capability of the individual to operate a commercial vehicle safely. When evaluating these drivers, the medical examiner should certify only those drivers whose current status is unlikely to interfere with the safe operation of the commercial vehicle. If there is any question of deterioration that would pose a risk for safe operation of the commercial vehicle, the medical examiner may qualify the driver for a period of less than 2 years.

FMCSA had posted additional guidance and advisory criteria for specific neuromuscular diseases in the ME Handbook. The categories of diseases include autonomic neuropathies, conditions associated with abnormal muscle activities, congenital myopathies, metabolic muscle diseases, motor neuron diseases, muscular dystrophies, neuromuscular junction disorders, and peripheral neuropathies. Table 6-1 summarizes FMCSA guidance and advisory criteria for each of these categories of neuromuscular disease. General guidance in the handbook indicated that a driver with a musculoskeletal condition should not be certified until "etiology is confirmed and treatment has been shown to be adequate/effective, safe and stable." Additional details can be found in Chapter 7, Table 7-1.

TABLE 6-1 Federal Motor Carrier Safety Administration Guidance/Advisory Criteria for Neuromuscular Diseases

Condition	Waiting Period	Decision	Monitoring/ Testing	Follow-Up
Autonomic neuropathies	No time frame Requires a confirmed etiology and adequate treatment	Max. 2 year Do not certify if: Diagnosis of cardiovascular autonomic neuropathy with resting tachycardia, orthostatic BP	Case-by-case basis	Biennial or more frequently as needed
Conditions associated with abnormal muscle activities	No time frame Requires a confirmed etiology and adequate treatment	Max. 2 year Do not certify if diagnoses include: myotonia, Isaac's syndrome, stiff-man syndrome	Case-by-case basis	Biennial or more frequently as needed
Congenital myopathies (central core disease, centronuclear myopathy, congenital muscular dystrophy, rod myopathy)	N/A	Do not certify*	N/A	N/A
Metabolic muscle diseases	N/A	Do not certify*	N/A	N/A
Motor neuron diseases (hereditary spinal muscular atrophy, amyotrophic lateral sclerosis)	N/A	Do not certify*	N/A	N/A

TABLE 6-1 continued

Condition	Waiting Period	Decision	Monitoring/ Testing	Follow-Up
Muscular dystrophies	N/A	Do not certify*	N/A	N/A
Neuromuscular junction disorders	N/A	Do not certify*	N/A	N/A
Peripheral neuropathies	N/A	Do not certify*	N/A	N/A

BP = blood pressure

* As the severity of these conditions may vary on an individual basis, guidelines for reconsideration of decision not to certify include:

1. Evaluation by a neurologist or physiatrist who understands the functions and demands of commercial driving.
2. Specialist may recommend a simulated driving skills test or equivalent functional test (annual re-evaluation as indicated).

Source: Adapted from the FMCSA Medical Examiner Handbook.

Individuals may present for a commercial driver medical examination with a diagnosis of these related musculoskeletal disorders or they may have symptoms and/or findings suggestive of subclinical disease that has yet to be diagnosed. These conditions may cause pain, deformity, and functional limitations of the musculoskeletal system. Many of these disorders, particularly the rheumatic and neuromuscular diseases, can be exacerbated by conditions of commercial driving. These factors include lifestyle limitations of diet, exercise, and sleep; cyclic periods of relative inactivity interspersed with high-exertion activities; mechanical stress and trauma associated with vibration during driving and idling; and mental stressors associated with driving under time pressures or variable weather and traffic conditions.

The natural history of these related musculoskeletal disorders must be considered when making decisions for qualifying drivers or for assigning duration of the medical certificate. In coming to this decision, the examiner will need to consider the individual's report of history, medication usage, the physical examination, and additional ancillary information, including medical records from treating physicians and available laboratory and imaging studies. Often, direct communication with the individual's treating physician will be required to better gauge current limitations, potential complications from medication regimens, and ultimate near and long-term prognosis.

Medical Expert Panel

The evidence report on musculoskeletal disorders[11] evaluated four "key questions" posed by FMCSA:

1. Does amputation of an extremity increase crash risk and/or affect driving ability?
2. Does inflammatory arthritis increase crash risk and/or affect driving ability?
3. Does decreased angle of rotation at the level of the spine and neck increase crash risk and/or affect driving ability?
4. Do vehicle modifications and/or appropriate limb prosthetics decrease crash risk in disabled individuals?

Findings included that there was indirect evidence for potential compromise in driving performance for below-the-knee amputees, various arthritides, and limitations in cervical range of motion, but there was insufficient evidence to link crash risk to any of these conditions. No literature was found that met inclusion criteria to allow for recommendations in response to question four.

The MEP discussed the findings and offered their recommendations in *Expert Panel Recommendations: Musculoskeletal Disorders and Commercial Motor Vehicle Driver Safety*.[12] They recommended that FMCSA should revise the standards to more clearly address musculoskeletal conditions, develop a functional screening protocol to assist examiners in qualifying individual drivers, develop a functional test of capacity for driving examiners who perform the SPE that could potentially allow qualification of individuals who pass the test, and continue research into crash risk among musculoskeletal conditions. The FMCSA MRB met on April 7, 2008, and essentially endorsed these recommendations. The MRB also recommended that when evaluating individual drivers with multiple medical conditions, musculoskeletal conditions should be included in consideration of length of certification.[13]

An MEP on multiple sclerosis had also been convened and recommendations from that group will be reviewed in the neurologic condition chapter, Chapter 7.

References

1. Mazer B, Gelinas I, Benoit D. Evaluating and retraining driving performance in clients with disabilities. *Crit Rev Phys Rehabil Med.* 2004;16(4):291–326.
2. Meuleners LB, Lee AH, Legge M, et al. Health conditions of heavy vehicle drivers involved in a crash in western Australia: A retrospective study using linked data. *Health Promot J Austr.* 2005; Apr:16(1): 37–40.
3. Diller E, Cook L, Leonard D, et al. Evaluating drivers licensed with medical conditions in Utah, 1992–1996. Technical Report No. DOT HS 809 023. Washington: National Highway Traffic Safety Administration, June 1999.
4. Gagnier JJ, vanTulder M, Berman B, et al. Herbal medicine for low back pain. *Cochrane Database Syst Rev.* Art. No.: CD004504. DOI: 10.1002/14651858. CD004504.pub3.
5. McGwin G, Sims RV, Yulley L, et al. Relations among chronic medical conditions, medications, and automobile crashes in the elderly: A population-based case-control study. *Am J Epidemiol.* 2000;152(5):424– 431.
6. Federal Motor Carrier Safety Administration, 49 CFR Part 391.41, Appendix A – Advisory Criteria (includes Physical Qualifications for Drivers). http://www .ecfr.gov/cgi-bin/retrieveECFR?gp=1&ty=HTML&h=L&mc=true&=PART&n =pt49.5.391#ap49.5.391_171.a.
7. Federal Motor Carrier Safety Administration. Interpretation to 49 CFR 391.49. Alternative physical qualification standards for the loss or impairment of limbs. https://www.fmcsa.dot.gov/regulations/title49/section/391.49.
8. Federal Motor Carrier Safety Administration, Frequently Asked Questions. https://www.fmcsa.dot.gov/faq/Medical-Requirements.
9. Federal Motor Carrier Safety Administration. Medical Examiner Handbook, currently in the process of revision. https://www.fmcsa.dot.gov/regulations /medical/fmcsa-medical-examiner-handbook.
10. Federal Motor Carrier Safety Administration, 49 CFR 391.49, Skill Performance Evaluation Application Information. https://www.fmcsa.dot.gov/medical/driver -medical-requirements/skill-performance-evaluation-certificate-program.
11. Evidence Report—Musculoskeletal Disorders and Commercial Motor Vehicle Driver Safety. Presented to the Federal Motor Carrier Safety Administration April 30, 2008. http://ntl.bts.gov/lib/30000/30400/30455/Musculoskeletal _Evidence_Report-Final.pdf.
12. Opinions of Expert Panel - Musculoskeletal Disorders and Commercial Motor Vehicle Driver Safety. March 14, 2008. https://www.fmcsa.dot.gov/regulations /medical/opinions-expert-panel-musculoskeletal-disorders-and-commercial -motor-vehicle
13. Federal Motor Carrier Safety Administration Medical Review Board Meeting Summary April 7, 2008. https://www.fmcsa.dot.gov/sites/fmcsa.dot.gov/files /docs/April_7_MRB_Meeting_Minutes_71708_Final_Updated10108.pdf.
14. American Medical Association. *Guides to the Evaluation of Permanent Impairment,* 6th ed. Chicago, IL: American Medical Association, 2009.
15. Armstrong AD, Hubbard MC. *Essentials of Musculoskeletal Care,* 5th ed. Rosemont, IL: American Academy of Orthopaedic Surgeons, 2015.

16. Hoppenfeld S. *Physical Examination of the Spine and Extremities*. Norwalk, CT: Appleton-Century-Crofts, 1976. http://global-help.org/publications/books/help_physicalexaminationspineextremities.pdf.
17. Hegmann KT, ed. *ACOEM's Occupational Medicine Practice*, 3rd ed., 2011. Elk Grove Village, IL: American College of Occupational and Environmental Medicine, 2011.
18. Federal Highway Administration. Subchapter G Part 658, Truck Size and Weight, Route Destinations. Length, Width, and Weight Limitations. http://www.fhwa.dot.gov/legsregs/directives/fapg/cfr0658b.htm.
19. The Truckers Report—Facts about Trucks—Everything you Want to Know about Eighteen Wheelers. https://www.thetruckersreport.com/facts-about-trucks/.

CHAPTER 7
Neurologic Disorders

NATALIE P. HARTENBAUM, MD, MPH, FACOEM

Since the prior edition of this book, the Commercial Driver Medical Examiner (CDME) processes have undergone significant changes, mostly related to the National Registry of Certified Medical Examiners (NRCME). In 2014, the Federal Motor Carrier Safety Administration Medical Examiner Handbook (ME Handbook) was taken off the Federal Motor Carrier Safety Administration (FMCSA) website for update and revision. As this edition is being prepared, examiners still should consider guidance from the prior handbook, as that is what is being taught in the training programs, but should base their final decision on current best medical practice remembering that our ultimate responsibility is to ensure the safety of the motoring public to the extent reasonably possible. Chapters will include information from the most recent ME Handbook, Medical Expert Panel (MEP) reports, and Medical Review Board (MRB) recommendations as well as other relevant reports and literature.

The FMCSA Medical Review Board (MRB) has heard recommendations from the Medical Expert Panels and the Medical Review Board on seizure disorders, vision, traumatic brain injuries, and other neurologic disorders, including Parkinson's Disease, and multiple sclerosis. FMCSA has accepted and granted exemptions to drivers that did not meet the seizure or hearing standards (had been granting vision exemptions for several years).

As significant changes occur, they will be noted at the end of each chapter in the online version of this book at least twice a year.

There are numerous common disorders affecting the nervous system and the ability to operate the commercial motor vehicle (CMV) safely. In 2014, cerebrovascular disorders were the fifth-leading cause of death in the United States.[1] Headaches, fatigue, vertigo, and dizziness are among common reasons to visit a physician in the United States. Data suggest that some of these disorders present an increased risk for motor vehicle crashes.[2]

Regulations, Medical Advisory Criteria, and Frequently Asked Questions

Several regulations either directly or indirectly address neurologic conditions in the commercial driver. They are:

---

§391.41(b)(7) *Has no established medical history or clinical diagnosis of rheumatic, arthritic, orthopedic, muscular, neuromuscular, or vascular disease which interferes with his/her ability to control and operate a commercial motor vehicle safely;*

§391.41(b)(8) *Has no established medical history or clinical diagnosis of epilepsy or any other condition which is likely to cause loss of consciousness or any loss of ability to control a commercial motor vehicle;*

§391.41(b)(9) *Has no mental, nervous, organic, or functional disease or psychiatric disorder likely to interfere with his/her ability to drive a commercial motor vehicle safely;*

§391.41(b)(10) *Has distant visual acuity of at least 20/40 (Snellen) in each eye without corrective lenses or visual acuity separately corrected to 20/40 (Snellen) or better with corrective lenses, distant binocular acuity of at least 20/40 (Snellen) in both eyes with or without corrective lenses, field of vision of at least 700 in the horizontal meridian in each eye, and the ability to recognize the colors of traffic signals and devices showing standard red, green, and amber;*

§391.41(b)(11) *First perceives a forced whispered voice in the better ear at not less than 5 feet with or without the use of a hearing aid or, if tested by use of an audiometric device, does not have an average hearing loss in the better ear greater than 40 decibels at 500 Hz, 1,000 Hz, and 2,000 Hz with or without a hearing aid when the audiometric device is calibrated to American National Standard (formerly ASA Standard) Z24.5-1951.*

Standards 391.41b(7) and part of 391.41b(9) will be discussed in greater detail in Chapters 6 and 9, respectively.

Medical Advisory Criteria and FAQs: Seizures

Seizures is one area in which there have been significant changes since the prior edition of this book. At that time, current use of medication to prevent seizures was disqualifying. Exemptions are now being granted to drivers that do not meet the following advisory criteria;[3]

1. *A person is physically qualified to drive a commercial motor vehicle if that person: Has no established medical history or clinical diagnosis of epilepsy or any other condition which is likely to cause loss of consciousness or any loss of ability to control a motor vehicle.*

2. *Epilepsy is a chronic functional disease characterized by seizures or episodes that occur without warning, resulting in loss of voluntary control which may lead to loss of consciousness and/or seizures. Therefore, the following drivers cannot be qualified:*

   (i)   *A driver who has a medical history of epilepsy;*

   (ii) *A driver who has a current clinical diagnosis of epilepsy; or*

   (ii) *A driver who is taking anti-seizure medication.*

3. *If an individual has had a sudden episode of a nonepileptic seizure or loss of consciousness of unknown cause which did not require anti-seizure medication, the decision as to whether that person's condition will likely cause loss of consciousness or loss of ability to control a motor vehicle is made on an individual basis by the medical examiner in consultation with the treating physician. Before certification is considered, it is suggested that a 6 month waiting period elapse from the time of the episode. Following the waiting period, it is suggested that the individual have a complete neurological examination. If the results of the examination are negative and anti-seizure medication is not required, then the driver may be qualified.*

4. *In those individual cases where a driver has a seizure or an episode of loss of consciousness that resulted from a known medical condition (e.g., drug reaction, high temperature, acute infectious disease, dehydration or acute metabolic disturbance), certification should be deferred until the driver has fully recovered from that condition and has no existing residual complications, and not taking anti-seizure medication.*

5. *Drivers with a history of epilepsy/seizures off anti-seizure medication and seizure-free for 10 years may be qualified to drive a commercial motor vehicle in interstate commerce. Interstate drivers with a history of a single unprovoked seizure may be qualified to drive a commercial motor vehicle in interstate commerce if seizure-free and off anti-seizure medication for a 5-year period or more.*

There is one FAQ[4] indicating that if a driver with epilepsy is interested in applying for a waiver (although that would now be an exemption, not a waiver) the individual can do so if safety would not be compromised. There have been many applications for exemptions from the epilepsy/loss of consciousness standard;[5] several have now been granted based on the MEP recommendations,[6] the earliest exemptions granted in early 2013.[7] Details of the MEP/MRB recommendations on drivers with seizure disorders will be discussed later. Information for drivers who wish to apply for a seizure exemption can find information at the Driver Exemption Program page.[8]

Medical Advisory Criteria and FAQs: Vision and Hearing

Vision advisory criteria[3] explain that:

1. *A person is physically qualified to drive a commercial motor vehicle if that person: Has distant visual acuity of at least 20/40 (Snellen) in each eye with or without corrective lenses or visual acuity separately corrected to 20/40 (Snellen) or better with corrective lenses, distant binocular acuity of at least 20/40 (Snellen) in both eyes with or without corrective lenses, field of vision of at least 70 degrees in the horizontal meridian in each eye, and the ability to recognize the colors of traffic signals and devices showing standard red, green, and amber.*

2. *The term "ability to recognize the colors of" is interpreted to mean if a person can recognize and distinguish among traffic control signals and devices showing standard red, green and amber, he or she meets the minimum standard, even though he or she may have some type of color perception deficiency. If certain color perception tests are administered, (such as Ishihara, Pseudoisochromatic, Yarn) and doubtful findings are discovered, a controlled test using signal red, green and amber may be employed to determine the driver's ability to recognize these colors.*

3. *Contact lenses are permissible if there is sufficient evidence to indicate that the driver has good tolerance and is well adapted to their use. Use of a contact lens in one eye for distance visual acuity and another lens in the other eye for near vision is not acceptable, nor telescopic lenses acceptable for the driving of commercial motor vehicles.*

4. *If an individual meets the criteria by the use of glasses or contact lenses, the following statement shall appear on the Medical Examiner's Certificate: "Qualified only if wearing corrective lenses." Commercial motor vehicle drivers who do not meet the Federal vision standard may call 202-366-4001 for an application for a vision exemption.*

Information on vision exemptions can be found at the Driver Exemption Program page.[8]

The Medical Advisory Criteria[3] for the hearing standard is:

1. *A person is physically qualified to drive a commercial motor vehicle if that person: First perceives a forced whispered voice in the better ear at not less than 5 feet with or without the use of a hearing aid, or, if tested by use of an audiometric device, does not have an average hearing loss in the better ear greater than 40 decibels at 500 Hz, 1,000 Hz, and 2,000 Hz with or without a hearing aid when the audiometric device is calibrated to American National Standard (formerly ADA Standard) Z24.5-1951.*

2. *Since the prescribed standard under the Federal Motor Carrier Safety Regulations is from the American National Standards Institute, formerly the American Standards Association, it may be necessary to convert the audiometric results from the International Organization for Standardization standard to the American National Standards Institute standard. Instructions are included on the Medical Examination Report Form.*

3. If an individual meets the criteria by using a hearing aid, the driver must wear that hearing aid and have it in operation at all times while driving. Also, the driver must be in possession of a spare power source for the hearing aid.

4. For the whispered voice test, the individual should be stationed at least 5 feet from the medical examiner with the ear being tested turned toward the medical examiner. The other ear is covered. Using the breath which remains after a normal expiration, the medical examiner whispers words or random numbers such as 66, 18, 3, etc. The medical examiner should not use only sibilants (s sounding materials). The opposite ear should be tested in the same manner.

5. If the individual fails the whispered voice test, the audiometric test should be administered. If an individual meets the criteria by the use of a hearing aid, the following statement must appear on the Medical Examiner's Certificate "Qualified only when wearing a hearing aid."

There are two frequently asked questions[4] on Ménière's disease. In one, Ménière's disease is noted to be disqualifying due to severe and unpredictable bouts of vertigo. The other acknowledges that there is now surgery for Ménière's, and the issue is being reviewed.

Exemptions have been granted to drivers who do not meet the hearing standard. Information on hearing exemptions can be found on the Driver Exemption Program page.[8]

Guidance

The remainder of this chapter focuses on recommendations that had been in the Medical Examiner Handbook (now down for review),[9] the evidence reports, MEPs, and MRB recommendations. The neuromuscular conditions are also discussed in the musculoskeletal chapter (Chapter 6).

The Medical Examination Report Form contains the following questions related to neurologic conditions (with numbers from the form).

Do you have or have you ever had:
1. Head/brain injuries or illnesses (e.g., concussion)
2. Seizures, epilepsy
3. Eye problems (except glasses or contacts)
4. Ear and/or hearing problems
15. Fainting or passing out
16. Dizziness, headaches, numbness, tingling, or memory loss
18. Stroke, mini-stroke (TIA), paralysis, or weakness

Of course, the first issue is to secure an accurate diagnosis and then to evaluate the following categories of risk.

1. The prognosis/risk of the disease itself
2. The risk of a complication or recurrence
3. The risk of a therapeutic complication

Building on the questions from the Examination Report form, the examiner should review whether the driver has the following:

- Seizures, epilepsy, and/or use of anticonvulsant medication
- History of head/brain injuries, disorders, or illnesses
- Episodes of loss of or altered consciousness
- Episodes of fainting or dizziness
- History of stroke with residual paralysis
- Spinal injury or disease with residual effects

The general neurologic exam should evaluate whether the driver has the following:

- Compromised equilibrium, coordination, and/or speech pattern
- Asymmetrical deep tendon reflexes
- Abnormal patellar and Babinski reflexes
- Sensory abnormalities
- Positional abnormalities
- Ataxia

For vision, in addition to evaluating visual fields, distance, and color vision, the examiner should also evaluate the following:

- Pupillary equality
- Reaction to light and accommodation
- Ocular motility
- Ocular muscle imbalance
- Extraocular movements
- Nystagmus
- Exophthalmos

The hearing evaluation should not only determine whether the driver meets the hearing requirement but whether there is any ear condition that may interfere with balance or if the individual may be taking any medication that could interfere with safe operation of the CMV.

There was an evidence report on hearing, vestibular function, and commercial vehicle driver safety which found three studies evaluating crash risk among hearing-impaired drivers and found conflicting evidence[10] regarding increased risk of crash. The available evidence suggested that those wearing a hearing aid may still have increased risk of crash, although it was considered insufficient to be conclusive.

FMCSA has a website devoted to hearing impairment resources.[11]

There are many neurologic conditions, primarily neuromuscular, that were recommended to be disqualifying in the ME Handbook,[9] which are listed in Table 7-1.

TABLE 7-1 Neurological Conditions Recommended to be Disqualifying

Conditions with Abnormal Muscle Activity*
   Myotonia
   Isaac's syndrome
   Stiff-man syndrome

Congenital Myopathies*
   Central core disease
   Congenital muscular dystrophy
   Rod (nemaline) myopathy

Inflammatory Myopathies*
   Dermatomyositis
   Inclusion body myositis
   Polymyositis

Metabolic Muscle Diseases*

Motor Neuron Diseases*
   Hereditary spinal muscular atrophy (juvenile and adult forms)
   Acquired amyotrophic lateral sclerosis producing degeneration of the motor nerve
      cells in the spinal cord

Muscular Dystrophies*

Neuromuscular Junction Disorders*
   Myasthenia gravis
   Myasthenic syndrome

Peripheral Neuropathies*

Dementia

* NOTE: Neuromuscular disorders represent a complex group of conditions. The severity can vary with the individual and in certain instances may be treatable or nonprogressive. Guidelines for reconsideration of the decision not to certify include:
   • Evaluation by a neurologist or physiatrist who understands the functions and demands of commercial driving. A specialist may recommend a simulated driving skills test or equivalent functional test.
   • Annual recertification that repeats specialist evaluation and driving test when indicated.
Adapted from the Federal Motor Carrier Safety Administration Medical Examiner Handbook[9]

Seizures

Many of the concerns with neurologic conditions focus on the risk of seizures. A summary of the recommended seizure-free and off-medication wait times can be found in Table 7-2.

TABLE 7-2 Medical Examiner Handbook Seizure Waiting Period

Waiting Period	Diagnosis
10 years	• History of epilepsy • Viral encephalitis with early seizures
5 years	• Single unprovoked seizure, no identified acute change* • Bacterial meningitis and early seizures • Moderate traumatic brain injury (TBI) with early seizures • Stroke with risk for seizures • Intracerebral or subarachnoid hemorrhage with risk for seizures
2 years	• Acute seizure with acute structural central nervous system insult • Moderate TBI without early seizures. Surgically removed supratentorial or spinal tumors
1 year	• Transient ischemic attack, stroke, or intracerebral or subarachnoid hemorrhages with no risk for seizures • Surgically repaired arteriovenous malformations/aneurysm with no risk for seizures
Based on risk of recurrence of primary condition	• Acute seizure with acute systemic/metabolic illness

Federal Motor Carrier Safety Administration Medical Examiner Handbook – Seizure Waiting Period
* May be distant cause (possible earlier return to driving if normal neurologic examination by a specialist in epilepsy who understands the functions and demands of commercial driving, and the driver has a normal electroencephalogram).

FMCSA has been granting exemptions to drivers on anti-seizure medication to prevent seizures based on the recommendations of the MEP as discussed earlier and in Chapter 1.

The following are recommendations from the seizure MEP.[6] Examiners can consider these recommendations in determining whether the driver is otherwise medically qualified *but* should remember and explain to both driver and employer that the driver is *only* qualified to drive once that driver has been granted the exemption.

The Medical Expert Panel on Seizure Disorders and Commercial Motor Vehicle Driver Safety[6] recommended that drivers who were on or off medications and seizure free for 8 years could be permitted to operate a CMV.

If all anti-seizure medications had been discontinued, they recommended that the individual must have been seizure free for a minimum of 8 years from the time of medication cessation. If still using anti-seizure medication, the individual must have been seizure free for a minimum of 8 years and on a stable medication regimen for a minimum of 2 years. Certification should be annual.

Those with a single unprovoked seizure were felt to be able to drive after a minimum of 4 years seizure free on or off medication. If all anti-seizure medications have been stopped, the individual must have been seizure free for a minimum of 4 years from the time of medication cessation. If still on medication, the driver must have been seizure free for 4 years and on a stable medication regimen at least 2 years. With a single unprovoked seizure, certification could be biennial.

Provoked seizures were felt to require stratification based on low versus moderate to high risk of recurrence. Examples of low risk situation were:

- A lidocaine-induced seizure during a dental appointment
- A concussive seizure, loss of consciousness less than or equal to 30 minutes, no penetrating injury
- A seizure due to syncope not likely to recur while driving
- A seizure from an acute metabolic derangement not likely to recur
- Drug withdrawal

The MEP recommended similar criteria for drivers with an established history of seizure for those with conditions considered moderate or high risk. They advised that the driver must have been seizure free for a minimum of 8 years on or off anti-seizure medication. If all anti-seizure medications have been stopped, the individual must have been seizure free for a minimum of 8 years from the time of medication cessation. If still using anti-seizure medication, the individual must have been seizure free for 8 years and on a stable medication regimen for a minimum of 2 years. Those conditions considered high risk requiring more caution would include the following:

Examples of seizure-provoking conditions that are at moderate to high risk for further seizures and therefore would weigh against certification:

- Head injury with loss of consciousness or amnesia greater than or equal to 30 minutes or penetrating head injury
- Intracerebral hemorrhage of any etiology, including stroke and trauma
- Brain infection: encephalitis, meningitis, abscess, cysticercosis
- Stroke
- Intracranial hemorrhage
- Postoperative brain surgery with significant brain hemorrhage
- Brain tumor

The MRB[12] disagreed with the MEP.[6] The MRB explained that the risk of seizure in these populations is unknown as there are no quality data beyond a few years of follow-up. The evidence report[13] noted low confidence in the estimates of risk over time. Also, the MEP had accepted a 2% threshold for risk. Yet, risk of seizure with age is not uniform, and the 2% threshold was developed by taking elderly who have much higher seizure risks and mixing them with other adults who have substantially lower risk. Accepting a 2% threshold thus accepts a potentially markedly increased relative risk of seizure and crash. The evidence report also noted that the risk of seizures in individuals still being treated did not return to that of an age-comparable driver. Similarly, among those with seizure disorder who had undergone surgery and appeared seizure free, it was estimated the risk for recurrence was 2% at 8 years, again with a low stability estimate.

The MRB recommended that FMCSA not change the regulations on seizure disorder.[12]

Remember that these are only recommendations from the MEP but they are the criteria that FMCSA is utilizing to determine if the driver might be granted an exemption.

Some anti-epileptics are utilized for reasons unrelated to epilepsy, such as chronic pain. The MEP on Psychiatric Disorders[14] evaluated these medications and recommended careful evaluation of drivers using these medications, particularly as they may convey either direct risk or signal increased associated risks. The MRB recommended to FMCSA on January 6, 2010 that commercial drivers taking anticonvulsant medications for other than prevention of seizures be evaluated individually by their health care provider prescribing the medication and that a supportive opinion regarding driving safety be obtained prior to consideration of CMV operation.[15] The supportive opinion should also state the purpose of the medication and that the medication is not used for control of a seizure disorder. Those with mild, stable conditions and a lack of adverse effects were recommended to be qualified for up to 1 year. However, the FMCSA Medical Examiner Handbook[9] suggests that 2 years may be permissible.

Headaches

Although headaches are common, only rarely are they considered to be a disqualifying condition. A history of any of the following were believed to warrant a more detailed history, as they may interfere with safe driving: migraines, tension-type headaches, cluster headaches, posttraumatic head injury syndrome, headaches associated with substances or withdrawal, cranial neuralgias, or atypical facial pain. Examiners should consider the frequency and severity of headache as well as any associated symptom (visual loss, dizziness, nausea). They should also consider any effect the treatment may have on cognition. If headaches are severe, incapacitating, and unpredictable, or if medications being used to treat the headache can impair the ability to drive, then the condition may be disqualifying.

Examiners should keep in mind the standard recommendations: The driver should not be certified "until etiology is confirmed and treatment has been shown to be adequate/effective, safe, and stable." Once that has occurred, the driver with headaches can be certified if the medical examiner believes that the nature and severity of the medical condition of the driver does not endanger the health and safety of the driver and the public.[9]

Vertigo and Dizziness

The ME Handbook and other FMCSA resources mention three specific conditions for which vertigo and/or dizziness are the main manifestations. It was recommended that for drivers with Benign Positional Vertigo (BPV) or acute or chronic vestibulopathy, there should be at least a two-month asymptomatic period prior to certification. Examiners should carefully evaluate potential side effects of the medications that may be used, such as antihistamines, which are associated with sedation.

It was noted that drivers with BPV or acute or chronic peripheral vestibulopathy who have been symptomatic within the past two months, Ménière's disease, or a labyrinthine fistula or a nonfunctioning labyrinth should be disqualified. Ménière's disease is also noted to be disqualifying in the otic condition section of the handbook, and there are two FAQs as mentioned earlier.

While a driver who meets certification criteria could be certified for 2 years, it is noted that if there is any deficit that requires special evaluation, the driver should be certified annually.

The evidence report on Hearing, Vestibular Function and Commercial Motor Vehicle Safety (August 26, 2008) found no quality studies evaluating the risk of crash among those with vestibulopathies.[10] There also was no quality evidence to allow for a conclusion for an adequate period of time after vertigo prior to resuming driving. There was no evidence that endolymphatic sac shunt surgery is effective. FMCSA has not convened an MEP on this topic. The MRB addressed vestibular function[16] and made no motions, thus retaining existing guidance.

Infections of the Central Nervous System

The major concern with central nervous system (CNS) infections is whether the individual has had an early seizure and whether there is a risk of future seizures. The ME Handbook indicated that aseptic meningitis is generally not associated with seizures and once the condition has cleared, no limitations would be needed. Recommendations for waiting periods for other infections of the CNS can be found in Table 7-3. Once the infection has cleared and the appropriate waiting period has been met, maximal certification could be 2 years.

TABLE 7-3 Medical Examiner Handbook Recommended Waiting Period after Resolution of Central Nervous System Infection

CNS Infection	Minimum Waiting Period
Bacterial meningitis without early seizures	1 year seizure free and off anticonvulsant medication
Viral encephalitis without early seizures	1 year seizure free and off anticonvulsant medication
Bacterial meningitis with early seizures	5 years seizure free and off anticonvulsant medication
Viral encephalitis with early seizures	10 years seizure free and off anticonvulsant medication

CNS = central nervous system.

Adapted from the Federal Motor Carrier Safety Administration Medical Examiner Handbook.[9]

Tumors

There is a wide range in potential impairments from tumors, ranging from no impairment to permanent total disability. Treated benign CNS tumors may lead to no long-term certification limitations, provided there is no neurologic deficit or seizure disorder and the individual is off anti-seizure medication.

Malignant CNS tumors, however, do present significant problems that generally necessitate disqualification. It was recommended that drivers should not be certified if they have primary or metastatic tumors of the CNS. Other ME Handbook recommendations on tumors[9] are in Table 7-4. If the driver is able to be qualified, has completed the recommended waiting period, and has either a stable nonprogressive deficit (that does not interfere with safe driving) or no neurologic deficit and imaging that shows no tumor, annual certification is recommended.

TABLE 7-4 Medical Examiner Handbook Recommendations for Central Nervous System Tumors

CNS Tumor	Minimum Waiting Period
• Infratentorial meningiomas • Acoustic neuromas • Pituitary adenomas • Benign spinal tumors • Benign extra-axial tumors	1 year postsurgical removal and seizure free and off anticonvulsant medication
• Benign supratentorial tumors • Spinal tumor	2 years postsurgical removal and seizure free and off anticonvulsant medication

CNS = central nervous system.

Adapted from the Federal Motor Carrier Safety Administration Medical Examiner Handbook.[9]

Cerebrovascular Disease, Strokes, and Transient Ischemic Attacks

Transient ischemic attacks (TIAs) are often one of the first manifestations of cerebrovascular disease. The ME Handbook[9] recommended that a person with a history of TIAs be disqualified from driving a CMV interstate for 1 year because of the high rate of recurrence and/or stroke within the first year. Subsequent clearance by a neurologist was recommended.

Drivers with thromboembolic strokes involving the brainstem or cerebellum were recommended to be handled the same as those with TIAs. However, strokes more commonly involve the middle/anterior cerebral distributions and have a worse prognosis. For such drivers, it was recommended that 5 years elapse prior to a neurology clearance examination to consider up to a 1-year certification, particularly if there is evidence of neurologic deficit. Drivers with deficits and stability such that a license can be granted should be recertified for no more than 1 year. Similar recommendations were made for drivers with intracerebral or subarachnoid hemorrhage (see Table 7-2).

The *Evidence Report: Stroke and Commercial Motor Vehicle Driver Safety* identified four studies and concluded that drivers who have suffered a stroke are at increased risk of crash.[17] The MEP on stroke and commercial motor vehicle driver safety recommended the following for CMV operators who have had a TIA or cerebrovascular accident (CVA):[18]

TIA

1. All drivers experiencing a TIA should be immediately excluded from driving.
2. Individuals free of recurrence of TIA or stroke for at least 1 year who are otherwise medically qualified may be considered for certification.
3. While preventive treatment may substantially reduce risk of TIA recurrence or CVA, there is insufficient evidence to recommend a different evaluation for those who received treatment.
4. To clear a driver requires a thorough evaluation of physical and mental function by a qualified neurologist.
5. The certification process should include an on-road driving evaluation comparable to that done for new drivers.
6. Certifications should be performed on at least an annual basis. The annual recertification process should include an evaluation by a qualified neurologist and an on-road driving test. Driving history was recommended to be considered, including miles driven, traffic violations, and crashes (the means to accomplish these three items were not specified). They also recommended that any at-fault accident should result in permanent disqualification.

CVA

1. All drivers experiencing a CVA should be immediately excluded from driving.
2. Individuals free of recurrence of CVA for at least 1 year who are otherwise medically qualified may be considered for certification.

3. Those with severe disabling stroke are to be "disqualified from driving due to the severity of their impairments."
4. Those experiencing a stroke should not be certified as physically qualified to drive a commercial vehicle.
5. To clear a driver requires a thorough evaluation of physical and mental function by a qualified neurologist.
6. The certification process should include an on-road driving evaluation comparable to that done for new drivers.
7. Certifications should be performed on at least an annual basis. The annual recertification process should include an evaluation by a qualified neurologist and an on-road driving test. Driving history was recommended to be considered, including miles driven, traffic violations, and crashes (the means to accomplish these three items were not specified).

They also recommended that any at-fault accident should result in permanent disqualification.

The MRB agreed with most of the MEP recommendations but they added that after a TIA or CVA, an examination by a neurologist who is an MD or DO in addition to a CDME examination by an MD or DO would be required.[19] The annual examination should also include an evaluation by a neurologist and a CDME examination by an MD or DO. They also recommended that the current guidance on middle/anterior cerebral distributions CVA be maintained for a 5-year wait.

Narcolepsy

Narcolepsy is considered disqualifying in the United States. A recent evidence report on narcolepsy found nine studies of risks of crash[20] and found an increased risk of crash. Additionally, the evidence report of available studies found evidence that treatment did not return a driver to the risk level of someone without narcolepsy.

FMCSA did not convene an MEP. The MRB reviewed the evidence report and recommended no changes in guidance for this disorder to FMCSA.[15] They recommended that the agency continue to prohibit drivers with treated or untreated narcolepsy from operating CMVs, regardless of treatment. Since then, FMCSA has accepted applications for exemptions from the narcolepsy criteria, but none have been granted.

Dementias

The ME Handbook[9] recommended that dementias be considered disqualifying conditions. Dementias are likely to preclude CMV operation in nearly all circumstances other than potentially the mildest forms. Although not addressed by the MEP and MRB processes recently, it seems highly unlikely that revised guidance would differ substantially from that in the conference report. The ME Handbook has recommended preclusion of driving.

Traumatic Brain Injury

The ME Handbook classified traumatic brain injuries (TBIs) based on dural penetration and duration of loss of consciousness.

- Severe head injury penetrates the dura and causes a loss of consciousness lasting longer than 24 hours. There is a high risk for unprovoked seizures, and the risk does not diminish over time.
- Moderate head injury does not penetrate the dura but causes a loss of consciousness lasting longer than 30 minutes, but less than 24 hours.
- Mild head injury has no dural penetration or loss of consciousness and lasts for fewer than 30 minutes. It was advised to be certain to distinguish between mild TBI with or without early seizures.

There are other and more recent criteria to define the severity of TBI.

It was recommended that those with a severe TBI not be certified. The ME Handbook noted that those who had surgical procedures that penetrated the dura, including surgery for seizures, had a similar risk to those with a severe TBI and should not be certified. If the driver has completed the recommended waiting period (see Table 7-2); is seizure free and off anticonvulsant medication; has a normal physical examination; has a neurologic examination, including a neuro-ophthalmologic evaluation and neuropsychological test, along with a clearance from a neurologist who understands the functions and demands of commercial driving, the ME Handbook indicated that the driver could be qualified for up to 1 year.

There was an evidence-based review[21] and an MEP presented recommendations[22] to the FMCSA MRB in January 2010, which recommended these be adopted by FMCSA. The MRB agreed with these recommendations and recommended that FMCSA adopt them.[15]

The MEP and MRB Recommendations on traumatic brain injury include the following:[15,22]

1. Drivers with sustained penetrating injuries to the brain or severe TBI (loss of consciousness for at least 24 hours) should be permanently precluded from operating a CMV.

2. Those with moderately severe TBI (i.e., loss or altered consciousness for over 1 hour but less than 24 hours) should be precluded from operating a CMV for 3 years. Subsequent clearances should be based on a detailed assessment by an MD/DO, including consideration of symptoms such as headaches, irritability, dizziness, imbalance, fatigue, sleep disorders, inattention, decreased concentration and memory, noise and light sensitivity, slowed thinking, difficulty recalling new material, personality change, difficulty starting or initiating things, difficulty sequencing information, impaired attention to details, impaired ability to benefit from experience, deficits in planning and carrying out activities, seizures (see seizure guidance), and cognitive domains. Evaluation by a neurologist was felt to be required as part of this assessment. If the driver is able to be cleared, recertification every 6 months while under treatment was recommended.

3. Those with mild TBI (<1 hour of loss or altered consciousness) were felt to be medically qualified if the treating MD/DO provider felt they were symptom-free (see domains for assessment of moderately severe TBI in #2).

4. Those treated with seizure medication were recommended to be unqualified until fulfilling seizure criteria (see earlier in this chapter).

5. Skill performance evaluations are necessary for those with impaired extremities.

6. Both the neurologist and commercial driver medical examiner were recommended to be limited to MD/DOs.

Supporting evidence includes elevated risks of epilepsy, including many years after the injury, that are approximately 7.4-fold.

Neuromuscular Disorders

This group of disorders includes hereditary degenerative disorders, alcoholism, hypothyroidism, multiple sclerosis, infections, and consequences of tumors. Individuals with cerebellar ataxia were recommended to be disqualified from CMV operation by the conference report. Generally, the same is true for the other disorders. However, it was believed that if the symptoms were mild or due to a treatable problem, then a second opinion from a neurologist might be reasonable. Many of these are recommended to be disqualifying (Table 7-1) and other recommendations for these conditions from the ME Handbook are summarized in Table 6-1.

Most of these have not been addressed by an evidence report or MEP, nor have they been evaluated by the MEP. There is an evidence review[23] and MEP[24]/MRB[15] recommendations for Parkinson's disease and multiple sclerosis discussed in the next section that may potentially be helpful for an approach that could be applied to these disorders.

Multiple Sclerosis

Multiple sclerosis is one of the more common and complex disorders encountered in the commercial driver certification process. The wide divergence in clinical course, treatment, impairment, cognitive involvement, and prognoses makes this disorder among the most challenging.

Based on an evidence review,[23] the MEP on multiple sclerosis and Parkinson's disease formulated recommendations that included an evaluation of the individual's diagnosis, clinical course, and complications.[24] They opined that some drivers with multiple sclerosis may be potentially able to be qualified to drive vehicles. Significant judgment and the opinions of the treating neurologist are felt to be required in these circumstances. The MRB concurred with the recommendations, which were forwarded to FMCSA on January 6, 2010,[15] and include the following:

1. Multiple sclerosis precludes unconditional certification.
2. There should be an evaluation by a qualified specialist, nearly always a neurologist. It may also include a multiple sclerosis specialist, neuropsychologist, ophthalmologist, occupational therapist, or other appropriate professional.
3. There should be no signs of relapse or progression.
4. Medications should be well tolerated, including no cognitive, motor, or other adverse effects that may affect driving.
5. Satisfactory vision—including acuity, fields, and ocular alignment—must be present (see Vision MEP Report).[25]
6. Satisfactory cognitive functioning based on standardized neuropsychological test battery(ies) should be demonstrated (e.g., processing speed, executive functioning, attention, perception, memory, and emotion). Satisfactory functioning should be defined as performing within or above the normal range using test norms adjusted for age and education.
7. Drivers should show no evidence of mood disorders or have satisfactory control of a mood disorder.

8. There should be satisfactory motor function and mobility (referencing the Musculoskeletal Disorders MEP Report).[26]
9. There should be no history of excessive fatigability or periodic fluctuations of motor performance, for example, related to heat, physical and emotional stress, and infections.
10. A written report from the specialist is required. It was recommended that the examiner form be modified to provide a location to designate referral to a specialist.
11. Reevaluations should be every 6 months by the neurologist or other qualified specialist and include an annual neuropsychological evaluation.

The MRB also noted that a function-based examination protocol would assist in the evaluation of these drivers.[15]

Parkinson's Disease

The evidence report on multiple sclerosis and Parkinson's disease found evidence of approximately 3-fold increased risk of crash among those with Parkinson's disease Hoehn and Yahr Stage 2 or higher as assessed in 3 studies.[23] (This scale is widely used and Stage 2 or higher involves affected posture and gait.) Many medications used for the condition also have adverse effects, which includes somnolence. Additionally, this disorder typically occurs in older individuals; thus, concomitant diseases that may be disqualifying in and of themselves are possible and should be evaluated. Those with Parkinson's disease have been reported to have significant daytime somnolence (51%).

The MEP[24] on multiple sclerosis and Parkinson's disease recommended assessment of drivers, particularly with mild symptoms who are well controlled. They recommended that these drivers could be qualified after careful evaluation by a treating neurologist. The MRB reviewed this report and recommended that the agency adopt the MEP recommendations. The MRB also reiterated the need for a function-based examination.[15]

The MEP/MRB recommendations on CMV operators with Parkinson's disease are as follows:[15,24]

1. Parkinson's disease precludes unconditional certification.
2. There should be an evaluation by a qualified specialist—generally, a neurologist. It may also include a movement disorders specialist, neuropsychologist, or other appropriate professional.
3. Only patients with mild symptoms may be qualified. These include Hoehn and Yahr Stage 1 or less and a high score (at least

90%) on the Schwab and England Activities of Daily Living Scale.

4. Patients should tolerate medications well; not have cognitive motor or other adverse effects that may affect driving; not have significant fluctuations in motor response or on-off effects; and demonstrate satisfactory functioning on a battery of tests assessing key cognitive functions (e.g., processing speed, attention, perception, memory, executive functions, and emotion). Satisfactory functioning should be defined as performing within or above the normal range using test norms adjusted for age and education. Subjects should show no evidence of mood disorders or have satisfactory control of a mood disorder.

5. A written report from the specialist is required.

6. Reevaluations should be every 6 months by the neurologist or other qualified specialist and include an annual neuropsychological evaluation.

Visual Impairment

The current standard requires that drivers have a visual acuity of at least 20/40 in both eyes and each eye separately, although drivers who have at least 20/40 corrected visual acuity in the better eye may be eligible for a vision exemption. A provisional waiver program for monocular drivers was begun in 1992.[27] A total of 2,686 drivers were enrolled in the waiver program prior to a court injunction that stopped further enrollments in the mid-1990s. Nevertheless, these drivers were allowed to continue to operate CMVs but were followed as part of an uncontrolled study. To be eligible for enrollment in the original program, drivers were required to have operated a CMV safely for 3 years prior to enrollment, to have no licensure suspensions/restrictions, and to have a doctor's approval that they could operate such a vehicle safely. There were 2,234 drivers participating as of November 1995, with a total dropout rate of approximately 16.8 percent.[28] All measures of accident rates were lower for the waived drivers compared with the national accident rate.

Nevertheless, based in part on the preceding findings, drivers who were in the program after its termination were permitted to continue operating in interstate commerce provided that the following conditions are met:

1. Drivers receive an annual ophthalmologic/optometric examination.

2. The vision in the better eye is documented to be 20/40 or better.
3. Annual certification by a medical examiner indicates that the driver is otherwise physically qualified to drive a commercial vehicle for interstate commerce.
4. The driver provides a copy of the ophthalmologic/optometric evaluation to the medical examiner at the time of examination.
5. The driver provides a copy of the annual medical certification to his or her employer or retains it in his or her driver qualification file if self-employed.

Vision exemptions now are being issued provided that the individual is able to demonstrate to FMCSA that the degree of safety is at least equal to what would be present were the exemption not needed.[8]

The evidence report[29] on visual impairments looked at crash risk in monocular drivers, those with cataracts, and red-green color-deficient drivers. Inconsistent findings of the studies led the investigators to conclude that the risks were indeterminate for most conditions but that there was an increased risk of crash found among those with visual field loss.

The MEP[25] included a review of the finding from the earlier waiver program and concluded that the comparison group was suboptimal and precluded use of these findings for evidence-based guidance. Based on the evidence report, they recommended that all the standards be maintained. They recommended that the prohibition against monocular drivers as well as the red-green and field of vision standards not be changed. They also recommended continuation of the exemption program. Cataracts were felt to be addressed through the existing criteria, and evidence was lacking for further clarifications. There was no additional guidance regarding diplopia. They also recommended that the testing for color deficiencies be standardized. The MRB[30] concurred with the MEP's recommendations and recommended that FMCSA adopt these recommendations.

References

1. National Center for Health Statistics. Health, United States, 2015. Number of deaths for leading causes of death https://www.cdc.gov/nchs/fastats/leading-causes-of-death.htm.

2. Diller E, Cook L, Leonard D, Reading J, Dean JM, Vernon D. Evaluating drivers licensed with medical conditions in Utah, 1992–1996. Technical Report DOT HS 809 023. Washington: National Highway Traffic Safety Administration, June 1999. https://www.nhtsa.gov/people/injury/research/Utahdrivers/Utahmedconditions.html.

3. Advisory Criteria. Appendix A to Part 391—Medical Advisory Criteria. http://www.ecfr.gov/cgi-bin/text-idx?SID=0372f3529f864324d0bb810fcb04fe0b&mc=true&node=pt49.5.391&rgn=div5#ap49.5.391_171.a.

4. Federal Motor Carrier Safety Administration, U.S. Department of Transportation. Frequently Asked Questions. https://www.fmcsa.dot.gov/faq/Medical-Requirements.

5. Federal Motor Carrier Safety Administration, U.S. Department of Transportation. Qualification of Drivers; Exemption Requests; Epilepsy and Seizure Disorders, Notice of applications for exemptions, request for comments. *Fed Reg* 2006;71(Oct. 13):60606–60607. https://www.gpo.gov/fdsys/pkg/FR-2006-10-13/pdf/E6-17032.pdf.

6. Expert Panel Recommendations: Seizure Disorders and Commercial Motor Vehicle Driver Safety. Presented October 15, 2007. https://www.fmcsa.dot.gov/sites/fmcsa.dot.gov/files/docs/Seizure-Disorders-MEP-Recommendations-v2-prot.pdf

7. Federal Motor Carrier Safety Administration, U.S. Department of Transportation. Qualification of Drivers; Exemption Applications; Epilepsy and Seizure Disorders, Notice. *Fed Reg.* January 15, 2013; 78(10):3069–3077. https://www.gpo.gov/fdsys/pkg/FR-2006-10-13/pdf/E6-17032.pdf.

8. Federal Motor Carrier Safety Administration, U.S. Department of Transportation. Driver Exemption Programs. https://www.fmcsa.dot.gov/medical/driver-medical-requirements/driver-exemption-programs.

9. Federal Motor Carrier Safety Administration, U.S. Department of Transportation. Medical Examiner Handbook, currently in the process of revision. https://www.fmcsa.dot.gov/regulations/medical/fmcsa-medical-examiner-handbook

10. Federal Motor Carrier Safety Administration, U.S. Department of Transportation. Hearing, Vestibular Function and Commercial Motor Vehicle Driver Safety. Executive Summary. August 26, 2008. https://www.fmcsa.dot.gov/regulations/medical/hearing-vestibular-function-and-commercial-motor-vehicle-driver-safety-executive.

11. Federal Motor Carrier Safety Administration, U.S. Department of Transportation. Hearing impairment resources. 2016. https://www.fmcsa.dot.gov/registration/commercial-drivers-license/hearing-impairment-resources

12. Federal Motor Carrier Safety Administration, U.S. Department of Transportation. Summary for the January 28, 2008 Medical Review Board Public Meeting.

https://www.fmcsa.dot.gov/summary-january-28-2008-medical-review-board-public-meeting.

13. Federal Motor Carrier Safety Administration, U.S. Department of Transportation. Evidence Report: Seizures and Commercial Motor Vehicle Driver Safety (Comprehensive Review). November 30, 2007. https://ntl.bts.gov/lib/30000/30100/30118/Final-Seizure_Disorders_and_CMV_Driver_Safety.pdf.

14. Federal Motor Carrier Safety Administration, U.S. Department of Transportation. Evidence Report: Psychiatric Disorders and Commercial Motor Vehicle Driver Safety. August 29, 2008. https://ntl.bts.gov/lib/30000/30400/30452/Psychiatric_Disorders_-_FINAL_8-29-08.pdf.

15. Federal Motor Carrier Safety Administration, U.S. Department of Transportation. Summary for the January 6, 2010 Medical Review Board Public Meeting. https://www.fmcsa.dot.gov/summary-january-6-2010-medical-review-board-public-meeting.

16. Federal Motor Carrier Safety Administration, U.S. Department of Transportation. Summary for the October 6, 2008 Medical Review Board Public Meeting. https://www.fmcsa.dot.gov/summary-october-6-2008-medical-review-board-public-meeting.

17. Federal Motor Carrier Safety Administration, U.S. Department of Transportation. Evidence Report: Stroke and Commercial Motor Vehicle Driver Safety Executive Summary. September 2008. https://www.fmcsa.dot.gov/regulations/medical/stroke-and-commercial-motor-vehicle-driver-safety-executive-summary.

18. Expert Panel Recommendations Stroke and Commercial Motor Vehicle Driver Safety. January 2009. https://www.fmcsa.dot.gov/regulations/medical/expert-panel-recommendations-stroke-and-commercial-motor-vehicle-driver-safety

19. Federal Motor Carrier Safety Administration, U.S. Department of Transportation. Medical Review Board Meeting Summary. January 2009. https://www.fmcsa.dot.gov/january-12-2009-meeting-summary.

20. Federal Motor Carrier Safety Administration, U.S. Department of Transportation. Evidence Report. Narcolepsy (with and without Cataplexy) and Commercial Motor Vehicle Driver Safety. October 6, 2009. https://ntl.bts.gov/lib/55000/55200/55225/Narcolepsy_and_CMV_drivers_-_FINAL_10302009.pdf.

21. Evidence Report. Traumatic Brain Injury and Commercial Motor Vehicle Driver Safety. March 30, 2009. https://ntl.bts.gov/lib/31000/31000/31062/TBI_and_CMV_Driver_Safety_Report_-_Final.pdf

22. Federal Motor Carrier Safety Administration, U.S. Department of Transportation. Opinions of Expert Panel: Traumatic Brain Injury and Commercial Motor Driver Safety. https://www.fmcsa.dot.gov/regulations/medical/opinions-expert-panel-traumatic-brain-injury-and-commercial-motor-vehicle-driver.

23. Federal Motor Carrier Safety Administration, U.S. Department of Transportation. Evidence Report: Parkinson's Disease, Multiple Sclerosis, and Commercial Motor Vehicle Driver Safety. June 3, 2009. https://ntl.bts.gov/lib/31000/31000/31002/PD_Final.pdf.

24. Federal Motor Carrier Safety Administration, U.S. Department of Transportation. Opinions of Expert Panel. Parkinson's Disease, Multiple Sclerosis, and

Commercial Motor Vehicle Driver Safety. September 2009. https://www.fmcsa
.dot.gov/sites/fmcsa.dot.gov/files/docs/PD_MS_MEP_Opinions_09212009.pdf

25. Federal Motor Carrier Safety Administration, U.S. Department of Transportation. Expert Panel Recommendations: Vision and Commercial Motor Vehicle
Driver Safety. March 14, 2008. https://www.fmcsa.dot.gov/sites/fmcsa.dot.gov
/files/docs/MEP-Recommendations-Vision-v2-prot.pdf.

26. Federal Motor Carrier Safety Administration, U.S. Department of Transportation. Expert Panel Recommendations: Musculoskeletal Disorders and
Commercial Motor Vehicle Drive Safety. March 14, 2008. https://www.fmcsa
.dot.gov/regulations/medical/opinions-expert-panel-musculoskeletal-disorders
-and-commercial-motor-vehicle.

27. Qualification of drivers: Waiver applications—vision. *Fed Reg* 1992;57(March
25):10295–10297.

28. Office of Motor Carrier Research and Standards. Qualification of Drivers:
Vision and Diabetes. Technical Brief. Publication No. FHWA-MCRT-99-017.
Washington: U.S. DOT, Federal Highway Administration, September 1999.
https://ntl.bts.gov/lib/10000/10100/10100/tb99-017.pdf.

29. Findings of Evidence Report: Vision Deficiency and Commercial Motor Vehicle
Driver Safety. Presented April 7, 2007. https://cms.fmcsa.dot.gov/regulations
/medical/findings-evidence-report-vision-deficiency-and-commercial-motor
-vehicle-driver.

30. Federal Motor Carrier Safety Administration, U.S. Department of Transportation. Medical Review Board Meeting Summary. April 7, 2008. https://www
.fmcsa.dot.gov/april-7-2008-mrb-meeting-summary.

CHAPTER 8
Endocrine Disorders— Diabetes Mellitus

NATALIE P. HARTENBAUM, MD, MPH, FACOEM

Since the prior edition of this book, the Commercial Driver Medical Examiner (CDME) processes have undergone significant changes, mostly related to the National Registry of Certified Medical Examiners (NRCME). In 2014, the Federal Motor Carrier Safety Administration Medical Examiner Handbook (ME Handbook) was taken off the Federal Motor Carrier Safety Administration (FMCSA) website for update and revision. As this edition is being prepared, examiners still should consider guidance from the prior handbook, as that is what is being taught in the training programs, but should base their final decision on current best medical practice remembering that our ultimate responsibility is to ensure the safety of the motoring public to the extent reasonably possible. Chapters will include information from the most recent ME Handbook, Medical Expert Panel (MEP) reports, and Medical Review Board (MRB) recommendations as well as other relevant reports and literature.

While insulin-taking diabetes is considered disqualifying, FMCSA has been granting exemptions to drivers who do not meet this medical standard. There have been several proposed rules which would eliminate the insulin exemption and move the decision to the examiner of whether a driver taking insulin to control their diabetes is safe to drive. These are currently still in the proposed rule stage and exact time for implementation is unknown.

As significant changes occur, they will be noted at the end of each chapter in the online version of this book at least twice a year.

Regulations, Advisory Criteria, and Frequently Asked Questions

Diabetes mellitus is the most common endocrine disorder examiners will encounter. Over the years, there have been many changes to requirements and recommendations for diabetic drivers, which are discussed in Chapter 1. While most of the changes have involved drivers who require insulin to control their diabetes, it is still important for the examiner to carefully evaluate the driver on oral hypoglycemic agents.

The regulation that directly addresses endocrine conditions in the commercial driver is:

49CFR 391.41(b)(3) *Has no established medical history or clinical diagnosis of diabetes mellitus currently requiring insulin for control.*

The advisory criteria explain that a diabetic who uses insulin for control does not meet the minimum physical requirements of the Federal Motor Carrier Safety Regulations (FMCSRs). Hypoglycemic agents are not disqualifying if the diabetes can be controlled. Drivers who do not meet the federal diabetes standard are advised to call 202-366-4001 for information on the diabetes exemption.[1] Information on the diabetes exemption can be found at https://www.fmcsa.dot.gov/medical/driver-medical-requirements/driver-exemption-program.

While the diabetes standard does indicate that the driver should "not require insulin for control" it does not specify how tight that control should be. The Medical Examiner Handbook (ME Handbook) had noted that a hemoglobin A1c (HbA1c) of greater than 10% indicates poor control. The requirement for the drivers who have an insulin exemption is that the HbA1c should be between 7 and 10. Examiners should keep in mind that very tight control has an increased risk of hypoglycemia. Examiners should also evaluate whether complications of diabetes — such as peripheral neuropathy, nephropathy, retinopathy, or heart disease — may be the basis for disqualification.

The examination form only asks if the driver has "Diabetes or blood sugar problems" and whether insulin is used. A urinalysis is required to check for sugar (as well as protein, which could represent diabetic nephropathy), but the only guidance provided is that if blood, sugar, or protein is found in the urine, it may be an indication for further testing.

There are three FAQs[2] that address diabetes, two on the exemption/waiver program. There is also one on whether the driver with noninsulin-treated diabetes mellitus can be certified for 2 years. The response is that the medical examiner makes the determination based on clinical judgment but that the FMCSA guidelines would recommend an annual examination for vision, neurologic function, and cardiovascular disease, including hypertension. They note that, in general, the diabetic driver should have annual recertification examinations.

Recommendations

There have been several conference reports or reports of expert panels presented to the U.S. Department of Transportation for dealing with diabetic drivers, with much of the attention on insulin-using diabetics.[3-6] The Conference on Diabetic Disorders and Commercial Drivers[3] was the basis for much of what was in the ME Handbook while the Expert Panel Commentary and Recommendations — Diabetes and Commercial Motor Vehicle Driver Safety[6] was the basis for the current exemption program. The history of the diabetes waiver and later exemption programs, as well as information on the current Notice of Proposed Rulemaking (NPRM),[7] can be found in Chapter 1.

When evaluating the driver with diabetes mellitus, the examiner should ask about hypoglycemic episodes, especially those that have required the assistance of another person, resulted in loss of consciousness, or if there was a seizure or period of impaired cognitive function without warning. If the driver had one or more of these in the past 12 months or two or more in the past 5 years, the driver should not be qualified.

Several factors are likely to increase the risk of hypoglycemia. A number of these factors are of special concern to the diabetic commercial motor vehicle (CMV) operator — particularly, age, erratic oral intake, variability in medication schedules, and irregular sleep schedules. There also are a number of medications that place the diabetic driver at greater risk for hypoglycemic events. It is recommended that these factors and agents be evaluated carefully when examining a diabetic truck driver who is undergoing a recertification examination.

Other recommendations that had been in the ME Handbook for not certifying the diabetic driver include:

- Loss of position sensation
- Loss of pedal sensation
- Resting tachycardia
- Orthostatic hypotension
- Peripheral neuropathy
- Proliferative retinopathy (e.g., unstable proliferative or nonproliferative)

A driver on any form of insulin is not considered medically qualified unless the driver has been granted an exemption. The examiner should determine if the driver is "otherwise medically qualified." This includes whether the diabetes is adequately controlled and whether there are any other disqualifying conditions associated with the diabetes. If the driver is stable on insulin with no disqualifying complications or end organ damage, the examiner can indicate on the form and medical certificate that the certification *must* be "accompanied by a waiver/exemption for diabetes." The examiner does not grant the exemption; rather, the examiner determines only if the driver is "otherwise medically qualified." The driver must then apply for the exemption and is not permitted to operate a CMV unless and until the exemption is granted. There is currently an NPRM and a request for comment[7,8] that would eliminate the diabetes exemption program and allow the medical examiner to make the determination. All forms of insulin are included in this category. Incretin mimetics were mentioned in the ME Handbook, which pointed out that they are not insulin and do not require an exemption. However, it was also noted that, when used in conjunction with a sulfonylurea, there is an increased risk of hypoglycemia.

The exemption program for drivers on insulin was announced in 2003. Initially, the drivers had to demonstrate a 3-year safe driving record while on insulin, but under current requirements as a result of the Safe, Accountable, Flexible, Efficient Transportation Equity Act — A Legacy for Users (SAFETEA-LU), that requirement has been shortened to 1 month if changing to insulin from oral agents or 2 months if newly diagnosed, unless a longer period is recommended by the treating provider.[9]

The current requirement for a driver needing an exemption from the exclusion for insulin-treated diabetes is to complete a detailed application.[1] Parts of the application must also be completed by an endocrinologist and optometrist or ophthalmologist. The driver must undergo an examination by a board-certified or board-eligible endocrinologist, including an examination specific for diabetes as well as a vision examination by an ophthalmologist or optometrist. In addition, the driver must have the following:

1. A current or past license that was not renewable due to the diabetes mellitus.
2. A safe driving record (e.g., no suspensions/revocations, no moving traffic violations while operating a CMV).
3. "No other disqualifying conditions," including those that are diabetic-related.
4. No recurrent (=2) severe hypoglycemic events (loss of consciousness, seizures, or hypoglycemic reactions requiring the

help of another, or hypoglycemic unawareness) from diabetes in the prior 5 years. One year of stability is needed after the first episode of each of these.

5. No recurrent hypoglycemic reactions with impaired cognitive function occurring without warning in the past 5 years. One year of stability is needed after the first of these events.

Once a driver obtains the exemption and is driving, the individual must:

1. Carry a glucose meter with memory and have available insulin and a rapidly absorbable glucose source.
2. Maintain a daily log of driving time to correlate with daily glucose measurements.
3. Perform frequent glucose checks (before driving and every 2–4 hours while driving).
4. Drive only when the glucose is between 100 and 400 mg/dL.

The monitoring of insulin-using drivers includes these steps:

1. Provision of written confirmation from the endocrinologist quarterly.
2. Include the make/model of the glucometer.
3. Review to make sure that the glucose measurements and glycosylated hemoglobin measures are in the "adequate" range (based on measures).
4. Have the driver undergo an annual comprehensive medical evaluation by an endocrinologist (similar to baseline).
5. If severe hypoglycemia has occurred, then the driver cannot drive until 1 year of stability has been achieved and the severe hypoglycemia cannot be a recurrent problem.

In addition, the driver must report "all episodes of severe hypoglycemia, significant complications, or inability to manage diabetes" and all accidents/adverse events, regardless of whether they are hypoglycemia related.

Drivers who have been granted an exemption should be providing the examiner with a copy of the annual Diabetes Assessment Package, which includes both the endocrinologist and vision checklists.

Medical Expert Panels, Medical Review Board, and Motor Carrier Safety Advisory Committee Recommendations

The MRB has heard evidence-based reviews, MEP recommendations, and comments from the public in response to an NPRM. In the first MEP report, it was found that there was no evidence that drivers on insulin had higher risk than those treated with other therapies. It also concluded that there was inconclusive evidence that drivers treated with insulin were overrepresented among drivers who crashed.[6] It was felt that the 19% increased risk for crash among all diabetics was insufficiently strong to warrant prohibiting all diabetic drivers from obtaining CMV licenses. The MEP explained that "whether hypoglycemia causes an increase in crash risk in individuals with diabetes could not be answered." They felt that the requirement to maintain glucose levels between 100 and 400 mg/dL should be reexamined, as it could encourage hyperglycemia and suggested that hypoglycemia of under 60 mg/dL should generally be avoided. It was recommended that FMCSA convene a panel of endocrinologists to serve as a consultant resource, including for disputes. A skill performance evaluation was recommended for drivers with an absent vibration sense.

The MRB at that time agreed with some conclusions of the MEP and differed with others and produced recommendations on the management of commercial drivers with diabetes mellitus to FMCSA.[10] The MRB felt that the evidence indicated that drivers using insulin likely had elevated crash risks. They also felt that those risks were likely greater compared with those of diabetics treated with either oral agent or dietary modifications. Still, the MRB recommended that those with insulin use be allowed to operate commercial vehicles with close medical supervision, including many of the elements in the exemption program. Additionally, the MRB recommended that those using insulin be restricted from operating commercial passenger vehicles and transporting hazardous materials. All diabetics, with or without use of insulin, were recommended to be limited to 1 year of medical clearance for certification.

The FMCSA has long planned to pursue rulemaking that would permit the medical examiner to make the determination of whether a driver whose diabetes is being treated with insulin is safe to operate a CMV. Comments were initially sought on this in 2006,[11] and it is recommended that the examiner anticipate changes in the medical certification of commercial drivers on insulin and possibly other aspects of certification of drivers with diabetes mellitus.

The current pending rulemaking is based on recommendations of the MRB after hearing new reports and public comments.[12,13] Their recommendations are in Figure 8-1.

FIGURE 8-1

MRB Recommendations on the Disposition of Public Comments from Medical Professionals and Associations to the FMCSA's Notice of Proposed Rulemaking (NPRM) on Insulin-Dependent Drivers of Commercial Motor Vehicles (CMVs) with Diabetes Mellitus.[10]

I. **The baseline for acceptable risk should be the current Diabetes Exemption program.**

  A. If FMCSA removes the prohibition on insulin-dependent individuals from being medically qualified, the Agency should replace it with a requirement that insulin-dependent drivers or commercial driver's license (CDL) applicants are medically qualified to drive only if the individual complies with the ITDM program, as outlined in the regulation (49 CFR 391.46 lays out the proposed requirements in the NPRM).

II. **Recommendations:**

  A. In lieu of the current Diabetes Exemption program, the MRB recommends that ITDM drivers are medically disqualified unless they meet the following requirements demonstrating their stable, well-controlled ITDM:

  1. Driver must provide to the CME the FMCSA Drivers With Insulin Treated Diabetes Mellitus Assessment Form (see section II.E below) that has been completed and signed by the treating clinician, as defined by section II.D below.

  2. Driver must receive a complete ophthalmology or optometry exam, including dilated retinal exam, at least every 2 years documenting the presence or absence of retinopathy/macular edema and the degree of retinopathy and/or macular edema if present (using the International Classification of Diabetic Retinopathy and Diabetic Macular Edema). Increased frequency of exams should be advised based on a finding by the ophthalmological exam.

  B. Disqualifying Factors: CMEs may certify an ITDM driver as medically qualified for a time period of no longer than 1 year only if there are no disqualifying factors (which should be listed in 49 CFR 391.46):

FIGURE 8-1 continued

1. Any episode of severe hypoglycemia within the previous 6 months. For purposes of disqualification, severe hypoglycemia is defined as loss of consciousness, seizures or coma, requiring the assistance of others or needing urgent treatment (glucagon injection or IV glucose).
2. Blood sugar < 60 milligrams per deciliter (mg/dL) demonstrated in current glucose logs.
3. Hypoglycemia appearing in the absence of warning symptoms (i.e., hypoglycemic unawareness).
4. If a driver has had an episode of severe hypoglycemia, blood sugar < 60 mg/dl, or hypoglycemic unawareness within the previous 6 months, the driver is medically disqualified and must remain disqualified for at least 6 months.
5. Uncontrolled diabetes, as evidenced by Hemoglobin A1c (HbA1c) level > 10 percent.
   a. A driver can be reinstated when HbA1c level is ≤ 10 percent.
6. Stage 3 or 4 diabetic retinopathy.
   a. Permanent disqualification.
7. Signs of target organ damage, as evidenced by peripheral neuropathy, diabetic nephropathy, or cardiovascular disease with the risk of impairing the ability to operate a CMV safely.
   a. Disqualification until resolved by treatment, if possible.
8. Inadequate record of self-monitoring of blood glucose (i.e., unreliable or absent capillary blood glucose measurements).
   a. Disqualification for inadequate records is until the driver can demonstrate adequate evidence of glucose records (minimum 1 month).

C. If a driver is medically disqualified due to not meeting the ITDM program criteria above, the driver should remain disqualified for at least 6 months.

D. Definition of Treating Clinician (that would work with the CME to certify that ITDM driver can operate a CMV safely): The treating clinician is the Doctor of Medicine (MD), Doctor of Osteopathy (DO), Nurse Practitioner (NP), or Physician's Assistant (PA) who prescribed insulin to the driver and is knowledgeable regarding the treatment of diabetes.

E. FMCSA Drivers With Insulin Treated Diabetes Mellitus Assessment Form: FMCSA should develop a questionnaire for the treating clinician to send to the CME, which should include the following information, questions, and requests for information:

1. Introduction to the Form:
   a. The above patient/driver is being evaluated to determine whether he/she meets the medical standards of the Federal Motor Carrier Safety Administration (FMCSA) to operate a commercial motor vehicle (CMV). During the medical evaluation, it was determined this

FIGURE 8-1 continued

individual is taking insulin to treat diabetes. As the Certified Medical Examiner (CME), I am requesting that you review the Regulations as noted below *[provide treating clinician with list of diabetes-related disqualifications—See Item 16 below]*, complete this questionnaire, and return it to me at the address specified below. By regulation, the treating clinician must monitor the individual's diabetes and determine if within the previous 12 months the driver has:

    i. Had no severe hypoglycemic reaction resulting in a loss of consciousness or seizure, or requiring the assistance of another person, or resulting in impaired cognitive function and

    ii. Properly managed his or her diabetes.

  b. The final determination as to whether the individual listed in this form is physically qualified to drive a CMV will be made by the CME.

2. Insulin Regimen:

  a. If the patient has type 2 diabetes on insulin, has the patient been on a stable medication regimen for the three (3) months prior to evaluation? Check Yes or No.

  b. New insulin users:

    i. For individuals who have been newly diagnosed with type 1 diabetes, the minimum period of insulin use may not be less than 2 months.

    ii. For individuals who have type 2 diabetes and are converting to insulin use, the minimum period of insulin use may not be less than 1 month.

    iii. Such new insulin users must have documentation of ongoing self-monitoring of blood glucose with a finger stick glucose reader (hand-written glucose logs are not acceptable). This must be done with a glucose meter that stores every reading, records date and time of readings, and from which data can be downloaded.

  c. Established insulin users: Patient must have documentation of ongoing self-monitoring of blood glucose with a finger stick glucose reader (hand-written glucose logs are not acceptable). This must be done with a glucose meter that stores every reading, records date and time of readings, and from which data can be downloaded. Monitoring records must be available covering a minimum period of the most recent 3 months.

3. Blood Glucose Testing—Frequency:

  a. How many times per day is the individual testing blood glucose? ___ times per day.

  b. CMV drivers should test glucose each time before driving and every 4 hours while driving.

4. Has the patient been educated in diabetes and its management? Check Yes or No.

FIGURE 8-1 continued

5. Does the patient understand the procedures that must be followed to monitor and manage his/her diabetes and what procedures should be followed if complications arise? Check Yes or No.

6. Has the patient had Hemoglobin A1c (HbA1c) measured intermittently over the last 12 months, with the most recent HbA1c measured in the last 3 months? Check Yes or No.

   a. Require documentation of these dates and HbA1C values.

7. Impairing Events: Has the individual had any episodes of hypoglycemia within the past one (1) year as follows:

   a. Severe hypoglycemia (loss of consciousness, seizures or coma, requiring the assistance of others or needing urgent treatment [glucagon injection or IV glucose]); or

   b. Blood sugar < 60 mg/dl demonstrated in current glucose logs.

   c. Treating clinician must advise a driver that he/she must report any such impairing events to the treating clinician.

8. Complete Eye Exam:

   a. FMCSA requires a complete eye exam by a qualified ophthalmologist or optometrist, including dilated retinal exam, at least every 2 years documenting the presence or absence of retinopathy/macular edema and the degree of retinopathy and/or macular edema if present (using the International Classification of Diabetic Retinopathy and Diabetic Macular Edema). Increased frequency of exams is advised based on a finding by the ophthalmological exam.

   b. The FMCSA Drivers With Insulin Treated Diabetes Mellitus Assessment Form should require certification that the treating clinician has reviewed the results from the ophthalmology or optometry report.

   c. The patient's most recent ophthalmology or optometry report must be made available to the treating clinician upon request (use current Diabetes Exemption visual evaluation form: "Vision Evaluation Checklist, Federal Diabetes Exemption Program").

9. Does the patient exhibit evidence of diabetic neuropathy? Check Yes or No.

   a. If yes, describe.

10. Does the patient exhibit evidence of diabetic cardiovascular disease? Check Yes or No.

    a. If yes, describe.

11. Does the patient exhibit evidence of diabetic nephropathy? Check Yes or No.

    a. If yes, describe.

12. Section for comments.

FIGURE 8-1 continued

13. Signature area that requires certification that the treating clinician has reviewed the Driver's Role.
    a. Signature should be required by both the driver/patient and the treating clinician.
    b. Add to certification a commitment of the treating clinician to report any severe hypoglycemic episodes to the CME.
    c. "It is my medical opinion that, with awareness of a CMV driver's role (consistent with "The Driver's Role" statement), my patient:
        i. Has stable, well-controlled diabetes; and
        ii. Has had no severe hypoglycemic episodes over the past year; and
        iii. That neither the patient's diabetes nor diabetes-related medical conditions that would impair the ability to operate a CMV safely.
        iv. Check response: Yes ___ No ___"
14. Driver may not be certified for more than one year.
15. Statement of the Drivers Role.
16. Statement of diabetes-related medical disqualifications.

Conclusion

There are several other endocrine disorders that, if not adequately treated, could place the driver at risk of sudden or gradual impairment or incapacitation. As with any condition, including diabetes, the examiner must understand the disease process, its treatment (including side effects), and interaction with other medical conditions and their treatment and complications or end-organ damage. Drivers who are not compliant with treatment or whose conditions are not adequately controlled should not be qualified or should be issued shortened certificates.

References

1. Federal Motor Carrier Safety Administration, U.S. Department of Transportation. Driver Exemption Programs. https://www.fmcsa.dot.gov/medical/driver-medical-requirements/driver-exemption-programs.
2. Federal Motor Carrier Safety Administration, U.S. Department of Transportation. Frequently Asked Questions. http://www.fmcsa.dot.gov/rules-regulations/topics/medical/faqs.aspx.
3. U.S. Department of Transportation, Federal Highway Administration. Conference on Diabetic Disorders and Commercial Drivers. Publication No. FHWA-MC-88-041. Washington: Office of Motor Carriers, 1988. https://www.fmcsa.dot.gov/regulations/medical/conference-diabetic-disorders-and-commercial-drivers.

4. U.S. Department of Transportation, Federal Highway Administration. Insulin-using commercial motor vehicle drivers. Publication No. FHWA-MC-92-012. Washington: Office of Motor Carriers, 1992. Available in four parts at https://www.fmcsa.dot.gov/regulations/medical/medical-reports-archive.
5. Federal Motor Carrier Safety Administration, U.S. Department of Transportation. Executive Summary: Diabetes and Commercial Motor Vehicle Driver Safety. September 8, 2006. https://www.fmcsa.dot.gov/regulations/medical/diabetes-and-commercial-motor-vehicle-driver-safety-executive-summary.
6. Federal Motor Carrier Safety Administration, U.S. Department of Transportation. Expert Panel Commentary and Recommendations — Diabetes and commercial motor vehicle driver safety. September 8, 2006. https://www.fmcsa.dot.gov/regulations/medical/opinions-expert-panel-diabetes-and-commercial-motor-vehicle-driver-safety.
7. Federal Motor Carrier Safety Administration, U.S. Department of Transportation. Qualifications of Drivers; Diabetes Standard. Notice of proposed rulemaking. *Fed Reg* May 4, 2015;80(85):25260–25272. https://www.gpo.gov/fdsys/pkg/FR-2015-05-04/pdf/2015-09993.pdf.
8. Federal Motor Carrier Safety Administration, U.S. Department of Transportation. Medical Review Board Task Report on Insulin Treated Diabetes Mellitus and Commercial Motor Vehicle Drivers. Request for Comments. *Fed Reg* September 9, 2016; 62448–62450. https://www.gpo.gov/fdsys/pkg/FR-2016-09-09/pdf/2016-21724.pdf.
9. Federal Motor Carrier Safety Administration, U.S. Department of Transportation. Notice of revised final disposition. Qualification of drivers; Eligibility criteria and applications; Diabetes exemption. *Fed Reg* 2005;70 (Nov. 8):67777–67781.
10. Federal Motor Carrier Safety Administration, U.S. Department of Transportation. Summary for the July 26, 2007, Medical Review Board Public Meeting, https://www.fmcsa.dot.gov/summary-july-26-2007-medical-review-board-public-meeting.
11. Federal Motor Carrier Safety Administration, U.S. Department of Transportation. Advance notice of proposed rulemaking request for comments. Qualifications of drivers; Diabetes standard. *Fed Reg* 2006;71(March 17):13801–13805. https://www.fmcsa.dot.gov/regulations/rulemaking/06-2417.
12. Federal Motor Carrier Safety Administration, U.S. Department of Transportation. July 21-22, 2015 MRB Meeting — Presenter Handouts. https://www.fmcsa.dot.gov/july-21-22-2015-mrb-meeting-presenter-handouts.
13. Federal Motor Carrier Safety Administration, U.S. Department of Transportation. Final Report MRB Task 15-01: Recommendations on the Disposition of Public Comments from Medical Professionals and Associations to the FMCSA's Notice of Proposed Rulemaking (NPRM) on Insulin-Dependent Drivers of Commercial Motor Vehicles (CMVs) with Diabetes Mellitus. https://www.fmcsa.dot.gov/final-mrb-task-15-01-report.

CHAPTER 9

Psychiatric Disorders

NATALIE P. HARTENBAUM, MD, MPH, FACOEM

Since the prior edition of this book, the Commercial Driver Medical Examiner (CDME) processes have undergone significant changes, mostly related to the National Registry of Certified Medical Examiners (NRCME). In 2014, the Federal Motor Carrier Safety Administration Medical Examiner Handbook (ME Handbook) was taken off the Federal Motor Carrier Safety Administration (FMCSA) website for update and revision. As this edition is being prepared, examiners still should consider guidance from the prior handbook, as that is what is being taught in the training programs, but should base their final decision on current best medical practice remembering that our ultimate responsibility is to ensure the safety of the motoring public to the extent reasonably possible. Chapters will include information from the most recent ME Handbook, Medical Expert Panel (MEP) reports, and Medical Review Board (MRB) recommendations as well as other relevant reports and literature.

The FMCSA MRB has heard recommendations from the MEPs on psychiatric disorders and forwarded recommendations to FMCSA. To date, FMCSA has not adopted any of these recommendations, but changes in the CDME processes for psychiatric disorders may be pending.

As significant changes occur, they will be noted at the end of each chapter in the online version of this book at least twice a year.

Psychiatric conditions present a significant challenge for the commercial driver medical examiner given that both the condition and the treatment may place the driver at risk of sudden or gradual impairment or incapacitation. This chapter reviews the regulations and other supporting material from FMCSA, such as what had been in the ME Handbook[1] (much of which was derived from the 1991 conference report on psychiatric disorders).[2] Recommendations of the MEP[3] and MRB[4] based on an evidence-based review[5] will be discussed.

In evaluating the driver with a psychiatric disorder, examiners need to keep in mind not only the diagnosis but also whether residual symptoms remain after resolution of an acute episode and the impact of any pharmacotherapy. In most cases, the diagnosis will not absolutely disqualify but the more frequent or severe the symptoms, the more likely the driver should be disqualified.

Regulations, Medical Advisory Criteria, and Frequently Asked Questions

The regulation that addresses psychiatric issues is:

391.41 (b)(9) *Has no mental, nervous, organic, or functional disease or psychiatric disorder likely to interfere with his/her ability to drive a commercial motor vehicle safely;*

With the advisory criteria[6] as follows:

Emotional or adjustment problems contribute directly to an individual's level of memory, reasoning, attention, and judgment. These problems often underlie physical disorders. A variety of functional disorders can cause drowsiness, dizziness, confusion, weakness or paralysis that may lead to incoordination, inattention, loss of functional control and susceptibility to accidents while driving. Physical fatigue, headache, impaired coordination, recurring physical ailments and chronic "nagging" pain may be present to such a degree that certification for commercial driving is inadvisable. Somatic and psychosomatic complaints should be thoroughly examined when determining an individual's overall fitness to drive. Disorders of a periodically incapacitating nature, even in the early stages of development, may warrant disqualification.

Many bus and truck drivers have documented that "nervous trouble" related to neurotic, personality, or emotional or adjustment problems is responsible for a significant fraction of their preventable accidents. The degree to which an individual is able to appreciate, evaluate and adequately respond to environmental strain and emotional stress is critical when assessing an individual's mental alertness and flexibility to cope with the stresses of commercial motor vehicle driving.

When examining the driver, it should be kept in mind that individuals who live under chronic emotional upsets may have deeply ingrained maladaptive or erratic behavior patterns. Excessively antagonistic, instinctive, impulsive, openly aggressive, paranoid or severely depressed behavior greatly interferes with the driver's ability to drive safely. Those individuals who are highly susceptible to frequent states of emotional instability (schizophrenia, affective psychoses, paranoia, anxiety or depressive neuroses) may warrant disqualification. Careful consideration should be given to the side effects and interactions of medications in the overall qualification determination.

Aside from the general question on medications, the questions on the Medical Examination Report Form that address psychiatric disorders are:

14. Anxiety, depression, nervousness, other mental health problems
16. Dizziness, headaches, numbness, tingling, or memory loss

There are also questions on drug and alcohol use and these conditions are addressed in Chapter 11.

There are no specific examination components noted, although the examiner should assess the driver's mental status. Some findings that may suggest a mental health issue include:

- Inappropriate dress
- Suspiciousness
- Evasiveness
- Threatening behavior
- Hostility
- Distractibility
- Flat affect or no emotional expression
- Unusual or bizarre ideas
- Auditory or visual hallucinations
- Dishonesty
- Omission of important information

The ME Handbook[1] had pointed out that examiners should consider whether the driver has impairment of any of the following due to a mental health condition or its treatment and, if so, should evaluate whether the impairment is at a level that should lead to disqualification:

- Attention, concentration, or memory affecting information processing and the ability to remain vigilant to the surrounding traffic and environment
- Visual-spatial function (e.g., motor response latency)
- Impulse control, including the degree of risk taking
- Judgment, including the ability to predict and anticipate
- Ability to problem solve (i.e., executive functioning), including the ability to respond to simultaneous stimuli in a changing environment when potentially dangerous situations could exist

Some additional questions the examiner may ask include:
- Have you ever thought of hurting yourself?
- Have you ever thought of suicide?
- Have you ever attempted suicide, including using a vehicle like a car or truck?
- Do you ever get into fights?
- Have you ever thought of hurting or killing other people?
- Do you ever have problems with your concentration or memory?
- Have you ever heard voices that other people don't seem to hear or that weren't really there?

- Have you ever seen things that weren't really there?
- Have you ever been hospitalized for psychiatric problems?
- Are you taking any medication for nerves?
- Have you ever used medicines for a purpose other than what was prescribed?

General Recommendations for Commercial Drivers with Psychiatric Conditions

Only a few diagnoses or treatments were addressed in the ME Handbook.[1] The general recommendation for certification included that the examiner could, on a case-by-case basis, obtain additional tests and/or consult with a mental health specialist, such as a psychiatrist or psychologist, to adequately assess driver medical fitness for duty. The driver should only be certified if "the nature and severity of the underlying condition does not interfere with safe driving" and if the "effects or side effects of medication use while operating a commercial motor vehicle (CMV) do not endanger the safety of the driver and the public." Other general recommendations for determining certification status of drivers with a psychiatric diagnosis are that the driver:

- Completes an appropriate symptom-free waiting period;
- Complies with the treatment program;
- Tolerates the treatment without disqualifying side effects (e.g., sedation or impaired coordination); and
- Has a comprehensive evaluation from an appropriate mental health professional who understands the functions and demands of commercial driving.

It was recommended that drivers not be certified if they have:

- Active psychosis
- Prominent negative symptoms, including:
  - Substantially compromised judgment
  - Attentional difficulties
  - Suicidal behavior or ideation
  - Personality disorder that is repeatedly manifested by overt inappropriate acts
- Treatment side effects that interfere with safe driving

It is important to remember that many psychiatric conditions may also be accompanied by substance abuse.

Psychotherapeutic Medications

Many patients with mental health disorders take multiple medications simultaneously (*polypharmacy*). While this may complicate evaluating fitness for driving, it may indicate the severity of the condition and need for additional evaluation or possible disqualification.

The MEP[3] had significant recommendations, which will be discussed later. The ME Handbook[1] had recommendations on several classes of psychiatric medication (Table 9-1). The general guidance was to evaluate the driver on a case-by-case basis and remember that with long-term use, some drivers may develop tolerance to medication side effects. Examiners should "not certify the driver until the medication has been shown to be adequate/effective, safe, and stable" and to certify the driver only if "the nature and severity of the underlying condition does not interfere with safe driving."

TABLE 9-1 Recommendations from the Medical Examiner Handbook[1] on Psychiatric Medication or Treatment

Medication	Recommended Waiting Period/Maximum Certification	Comment/Recommendation
Antidepressant	None/1 year	Recommends not certifying if using a first-generation tricyclic antidepressant. Noted that "only under exceptional circumstances would continuous use of amitriptyline be acceptable for a commercial driver."
Antipsychotic	None/1 year	Should not qualify if used for a disqualifying condition.
Anxiolytic	None/2 years	Should only certify using a nonsedating anxiolytic.
Sedative hypnotic	None/2 years	Should only certify if the hypnotic is short-acting (half-life of less than 5 hours), used at the lowest effective dose for a short period of time (less than 2 weeks).

TABLE 9-1 continued

Medication	Recommended Waiting Period/Maximum Certification	Comment/Recommendation
Central nervous system (CNS) stimulant therapy	None/1 year	Reminded examiners that CNS stimulants improve performance on simple tasks, but not on tasks requiring complex intellectual functions. Advised that before qualifying a driver with attention deficit hyperactivity disorder (ADHD) who is using a CNS stimulant, the examiner should request evaluation from the treating provider, verify the diagnosis of adult ADHD, and use caution when determining the side effects of medication. Do not qualify if the driver has a disqualifying underlying condition (e.g., narcolepsy) or has a tendency to increase the dose.
Lithium therapy	None/1 year	Lithium levels must be in the therapeutic range.
Electroconvulsive Therapy (ECT)	Six months symptom free following a course of ECT	Consider qualification only if the driver has had a comprehensive evaluation from an appropriate mental health professional who understands the functions and demands of commercial driving and is not undergoing maintenance ECT.

Attention Deficit Hyperactivity Disorder

The ME Handbook points out that features of adult attention deficit hyperactivity disorder (ADHD) include age-inappropriate levels of inattention, impulsiveness, and hyperactivity. Symptoms include mood lability, low frustration tolerance, and explosiveness. It is recommended that while there is no recommended wait period, the driver should have a comprehensive evaluation from an appropriate mental health professional who understands the functions and demands of commercial driving. The driver should be able to tolerate treatment without disqualifying side effects and comply with the recommended treatment program. Certification could be for up to 1 year.

Mood Disorders: Bipolar Mood Disorder, Major Depression

Bipolar mood disorders are characterized by one or more manic episodes, usually accompanied by one or more depressive episodes. Onset of these episodes may be sudden or gradual. Judgment may be diminished during a manic episode and some individuals may have delusions or hallucinations. Symptoms during a depressive episode may include loss of interest and motivation, poor sleep, appetite disturbance, fatigue, poor concentration, and indecisiveness. Symptoms during a severe depressive episode may include psychosis, significant cognitive impairment, or suicidal thoughts or behavior.

Symptoms of a major depression may include a depressed or irritable mood, loss of interest or pleasure, social withdrawal, appetite and sleep disturbance that lead to weight change and fatigue, restlessness and agitation or malaise, impaired concentration and memory functioning, poor judgment, and suicidal thoughts or attempts. Hallucinations and delusions may also develop, but they are less common in depression than in manic episodes.

A waiting period of 6 months symptom free following a nonpsychotic major depression unaccompanied by suicidal behavior or 1-year symptom free following a severe depressive episode, suicide attempt, or manic episode was recommended by the ME Handbook. Drivers diagnosed with bipolar disorder or major depression who meet the waiting period and the general recommendations in Table 9-1 could be certified for up to 1 year.

It was recommended that drivers with a history of a major mood disorder should have an evaluation at least every 2 years by a mental health professional who understands the functions and demands of commercial driving. The ME Handbook indicated that drivers should be advised to report any manic or severe depressive disorder within 30 days to their employer or medical examiner and to seek medical treatment. I would think that drivers should be advised to immediately seek treatment and discuss with their provider whether it is safe to continue to work and, if not, notify their employer as soon as that evaluation is made.

Personality Disorders
Note that those with personality disorders can be qualified if they meet the general conditions for drivers with psychiatric disorders. The concern would be those drivers with repeated severe excessive, aggressive, or impulsive behaviors that would interfere with safe operation of a commercial vehicle.

Schizophrenia and Related Psychotic Disorders
It was advised that individuals with chronic schizophrenia should not be considered qualified for commercial driving. Concerns include psychosis

(e.g., hearing voices or experiencing delusional thoughts); negative or deficit symptoms (e.g., loss of motivation, apathy, or reduced emotional expression); and compromised cognition, judgment, and/or attention.

If the individual has a related condition—such as a schizophreniform disorder, brief reactive psychosis, schizoaffective disorder, or a delusional disorder—the determination should not be based on the diagnosis alone but on an evaluation analyzing the severity and frequency of symptoms and risk of interfering with safe operation of the CMV. A driver whose evaluation indicates a low risk, including consideration of the general psychiatric recommendations, could be certified for up to 1 year after the following recommended wait.

- Minimum: 6 months symptom free if a brief reactive psychosis or schizophreniform disorder
- Minimum: 1 year symptom free if any other psychotic disorder

It was recommended that drivers with a history of a mental health disorder with psychotic features should have an evaluation at least every 2 years by a mental health professional who understands the functions and demands of commercial driving.

Evidence Review/Medical Expert Panel/Medical Review Board

The conclusions from the evidence-based review[5] were as follows:

Key Question 1: Are individuals with a psychiatric disorder at an increased risk for motor vehicle crash? If so, are there specific psychiatric disorders that present a particularly high risk?

The evidence concerning crash risk for drivers with psychiatric disorders is inconclusive. The possibility of an increased risk of crash for some drivers with psychiatric disorders cannot be ruled out. (Strength of Evidence: Minimally Acceptable)

Subgroup Analyses: Specific Psychiatric Disorders and Crash Risk

- Psychotic Disorders. Currently available evidence does not suggest an increased crash risk for individuals with psychotic disorders when compared to individuals without these disorders, but an increased crash risk cannot be ruled out. (Strength of Evidence: Minimally Acceptable)
- Mood Disorders. Although evidence suggests the possibility that individuals with mood disorders are at an increased risk for a motor vehicle crash when compared with drivers who do not have mood disorders, more evidence is needed to reach a firm conclusion.
- Anxiety Disorders. A paucity of evidence prevents us from being able to draw an evidence-based conclusion about the effects of anxiety disorders on the risk of motor vehicle crash.

- Personality Disorders. Due to inconsistencies in the available evidence, we are precluded from drawing an evidence-based conclusion pertaining to the strength of the relationship between personality disorders and crash risk at this time.

Key Question 2: Are individuals using psychotherapeutics for a psychiatric disorder at an increased risk for crash when compared to comparable individuals who are not using psychotherapeutics?

Analysis 1: Benzodiazepine Use and Crash Risk
- Benzodiazepine use is associated with an increased risk for a motor vehicle crash. (Strength of Evidence: Moderate)
- Benzodiazepine anxiolytic use is associated with an increased risk for a motor vehicle crash. (Strength of Evidence: Minimally Acceptable)
- Crash risk may be greater during the first week of an index prescription of benzodiazepines. (Strength of Evidence: Minimally Acceptable)
- Crash risk may be greater among benzodiazepine users ≤40 years of age. (Strength of Evidence: Minimally Acceptable)

Analysis 2: Antipsychotic Use and Crash Risk
- The evidence concerning crash risk associated with antipsychotic use is inconclusive. The possibility of an increased crash risk associated with antipsychotic use cannot be ruled out.

Analysis 3: Antidepressant Use and Crash Risk
- The evidence concerning crash risk associated with antidepressant use is inconclusive. The possibility of an increased crash risk associated with antidepressant use (particularly tricyclic antidepressant [TCA] use) cannot be ruled out. (Strength of Evidence: Minimally Acceptable)

Key Question 3: What traits associated with personality disorders are associated with reductions in motor vehicle driver safety?
- The evidence suggests that individuals with traits associated with personality disorders are at an increased risk for a motor vehicle crash when compared with comparable drivers who do not have a trait associated with a personality disorder. These traits include aggression, hostility, impulsivity, disregard for law (i.e., attitude toward traffic law violations), and various psychological symptoms. However, inconsistencies in the methodologies of the included studies preclude us from drawing an evidence-based conclusion pertaining to the strength of the relationship between traits associated with personality disorders and crash risk at this time.

General Recommendation by Medical Expert Panel

The MEP on Psychiatric Disorders and Commercial Motor Vehicle Driver Safety[3] reviewed the evidence report[5] and made a number of recommendations that—while not adopted by FMCSA—should at least be considered by examiners, as they are based on current medical evidence. They advised that drivers with any of the following conditions be required to undergo additional psychiatric evaluation prior to being qualified for commercial driving:

- Psychotic disorders
- Bipolar disorders
- Major depressive disorder with a history of psychosis, suicidal ideation, homicidal ideation, or a suicide attempt
- Obsessive compulsive disorder
- Antisocial personality disorder

Individuals with any of these conditions who were medically qualified should be reevaluated intermittently by a qualified psychologist or psychiatrist if they had symptoms within the prior 3 years or a history of a recurrence of the disorder of concern.

Medication

Based on the evidence report, the MEP recommended that drivers on lithium not be qualified to operate a CMV at night (or should be required to undergo assessment of their night vision) and those on benzodiazepine or similar drugs that act on benzodiazepine receptors should be immediately prohibited from driving a CMV. Drivers on a benzodiazepine for any duration could be permitted to drive once the drug has cleared their system (seven half-lives of the drug and any active metabolites). It was advised that those who have been on chronic benzodiazepine should be required to wait an additional week.

For those on an antipsychotic, the MEP recommended that they be required to have additional evaluations, including a neuropsychological battery to screen for psychomotor impairments, and if any impairment is suggested, they should have a road test. If a new antipsychotic was started, there should be an evaluation within 1 month.

A concern regarding the risk of sedation was raised for those on antidepressants and anticonvulsants (not for control of seizures) and it was recommended that they also be required to have additional evaluation. In addition to the risk of sedation, other considerations should include:

- Acute effects of the specific antidepressant(s) or anticonvulsant;
- Additive effects of other medications the examinee is currently taking; and
- Additive and cumulative effects of job demands, such as long hours of driving, often over extended periods of many days.

Psychomotor function, including balance and coordination, should be assessed in those on selective serotonin reuptake inhibitors (SSRIs) and anticonvulsants, and a neuropsychological battery of testing was recommended if any impairment was noted.

The MEP also commented on the difference between acute and chronic psychiatric disorders, with those lasting less than six months being considered acute and longer than six months being considered chronic. They defined remission as having no or minimal symptoms and no longer meeting the diagnostic criteria for the disorder.

Medical Review Board

While the Evidence Review was presented to the MRB and FMCSA in October 2008 and the MEP recommendations on July 1, 2009, recommendations were not offered by the MRB until January 2010[4] after a subcommittee was formed to consider the information provided. The MRB agreed with many of the MEP's recommendations but clarified or expanded on many. The MRB recommendations are summarized in Table 9-2.

TABLE 9-2 Medical Review Board Recommendations on Psychiatric Disorders and Commercial Motor Vehicle Driver Safety

Disorder	Comment	Severity[a]	Examiner	Guidance
Psychotic Disorders	Individuals with active psychosis are not qualified. Individuals must be without symptoms at least 1 year prior to consideration of commercial driving. Those with a brief, reactive psychosis may be reevaluated earlier, at 6 months, if the clinical condition has resolved.	Mild[b]	Psychiatrist or advanced-degree mental health professional	May be qualified: Supportive letter from the treating health care professional is required.
		Moderate[c]	Psychiatrist or advanced-degree mental health professional	May be qualified: Supportive letter from a psychiatrist is required.
		Severe[d]	Psychiatrist	Unqualified: These individuals are believed to nearly always be unable to be qualified. There may be limited, highly select exceptions. Careful evaluation of those cases is recommended prior to consideration of potential ability to operate commercial vehicles.

TABLE 9-2 continued

Mood Disorders	This category includes anxiety, depressive, and bipolar disorders. Drivers with mania, severe major depression, or suicidal behavior or ideation are not qualified. Individuals must be without symptoms at least 1 year prior to consideration of commercial driving. Those with a nonpsychotic major depressive disorder without suicidal behavior and symptom free may be reevaluated at 6 months.	Mild[b]	Treating health care and/or mental health professional	May be qualified: Supportive letter from the treating health care professional is required.
		Moderate[c]	Psychiatrist or advanced-degree mental health professional	May be qualified: Supportive letter from a psychiatrist is required.
		Severe[d]	Psychiatrist	Unqualified: These individuals are believed to nearly always be unable to be qualified. There may be limited, highly select exceptions. Careful evaluation of those cases is recommended prior to consideration of potential ability to operate commercial vehicles.
Personality Disorders	This category includes obsessive compulsive and antisocial personality disorders. Individual clinical assessment is recommended with determination of suitability for commercial driving based on whether the disorder and behavior pose a driving risk to the public. These traits include aggression, hostility, impulsivity, disregard for the law, and other psychological symptoms.	Mild[b]	Treating health care and/or mental health professional	May be qualified: Supportive letter from the treating health care professional is required.
		Moderate[c]	Psychiatrist or advanced-degree mental health professional	May be qualified: Supportive letter from a psychiatrist is required.
		Severe[d]	Psychiatrist	Unqualified: These individuals are believed to nearly always be unable to be qualified. There may be limited, highly select exceptions. Careful evaluation of those cases is recommended prior to consideration of potential ability to operate commercial vehicles.

The basis of this matrix was recommended by the MRB subcommittee on January 6, 2010. Slight changes from what had been presented by the subcommittee but approved by the full MRB are presented here.

[a] Severity is suggested to be inferred based on prior history.

The committee also recommends that the duration of certification be a maximum of 1 year for mild conditions and 6 months for moderate conditions.

Conclusion

Psychiatric disorders continue to be challenging for initial evaluations of commercial drivers as well as recertification. The evidence report on psychiatric disorders, MEP recommendations, and MRB findings should assist examiners in better understanding the risks of these conditions. Examiners should obtain past records for review and consider a psychiatrist evaluation if there is any question of the individual's fitness.

References

1. Federal Motor Carrier Safety Administration, U.S. Department of Transportation. Medical Examiner Handbook, currently in the process of revision. https://www.fmcsa.dot.gov/regulations/medical/fmcsa-medical-examiner-handbook.

2. Federal Highway Administration. U.S. Department of Transportation. *Conference on Psychiatric Disorders and Commercial Drivers.* Publication No. FHWA-MC-91-006. Washington: U.S. Department of Transportation, Federal Highway Administration, Office of Motor Carriers, 1991. https://www.fmcsa.dot.gov/regulations/medical/medical-reports-archive.

3. Federal Motor Carrier Safety Administration, U.S. Department of Transportation. Opinions of Medical Expert Panel. Psychiatric Disorders and Commercial Motor Vehicle Driver Safety. July 1, 2009. https://www.fmcsa.dot.gov/regulations/medical/opinions-expert-panel-psychiatric-disorders-and-commercial-motor-vehicle-driver.

4. Medical Review Board, Federal Motor Carrier Safety Administration, U.S. Department of Transportation. Summary for the January 6, 2010, Medical Review Board Public Meeting. https://www.fmcsa.dot.gov/meeting-summaries-2010.

5. Federal Motor Carrier Safety Administration, U.S. Department of Transportation. Evidence Report: Psychiatric Disorders and Commercial Motor Vehicle Driver Safety. October 6, 2008. https://ntl.bts.gov/lib/30000/30400/30452/Psychiatric_Disorders_-_FINAL_8-29-08.pdf.

6. Advisory Criteria. Appendix A to Part 391—Medical Advisory Criteria. March 30, 2017. http://www.ecfr.gov/cgi-bin/text-idx?SID=0372f3529f864324d0bb810fcb04fe0b&mc=true&node=pt49.5.391&rgn=div5#ap49.5.391_171.a

CHAPTER 10

Renal Disease

NATALIE P. HARTENBAUM, MD, MPH, FACOEM

Since the prior edition of this book, the Commercial Driver Medical Examiner (CDME) processes have undergone significant changes, mostly related to the National Registry of Certified Medical Examiners (NRCME). In 2014, the Federal Motor Carrier Safety Administration Medical Examiner Handbook (ME Handbook) was taken off the Federal Motor Carrier Safety Administration (FMCSA) website for update and revision. As this edition is being prepared, examiners still should consider guidance from the prior handbook, as that is what is being taught in the training programs, but should base their final decision on current best medical practice remembering that our ultimate responsibility is to ensure the safety of the motoring public to the extent reasonably possible. Chapters will include information from the most recent ME Handbook, Medical Expert Panel (MEP) reports, and Medical Review Board (MRB) recommendations as well as other relevant reports and literature.

While there have been recommendations regarding chronic kidney disease (CDK) presented to FMCSA in 2008, none have been adopted as formal guidance by FMCSA.

As significant changes occur, they will be noted at the end of each chapter in the online version of this book at least twice a year.

There is currently no specific regulation that directly addresses drivers with renal disease. The question on the history portion of the examination form asks drivers whether they "have or have ever had—Kidney problems, kidney stones, or pain/problems with urination." Renal disease had been previously discussed in two frequently asked questions,[1] only one of which is still posted. In the one that remains, FMCSA indicated that finding proteinuria might indicate renal disease and the examiner may disqualify, issue a time-limited certification, or certify depending on whether the examiner believed the proteinuria could affect safe driving. They also recommended that the driver should be referred for follow-up regardless of the certification decision. In the FAQ that had been removed, FMCSA indicated that, although there is no guidance on patients regarding kidney dialysis, the examiner should require a letter from the treating doctor (nephrologist) outlining the condition, medications, and recommendation regarding certification. As with any opinion from a treating provider, the examiner may or may not accept this recommendation. Examiners are reminded that restrictions other than those on the preprinted form are disqualifying.

While the ME Handbook[2] is no longer on the FMCSA website, there was a statement in the Part III—Medical Examination Guidelines section of the handbook under health history—kidney disease/dialysis that states "REMEMBER: If the driver is on dialysis, he/she cannot drive." The ME Handbook section on specific conditions was very vague and included a section on nephropathy but has only this general statement: "You should not certify the driver until the etiology is confirmed, and treatment has been shown to be adequate/effective, safe, and stable," and that the examiner should only certify the driver if the driver "[m]eets all the physical qualification standards and has a treatment plan that manages the disease and does not interfere with safe driving." There is nothing specific regarding the driver with end-stage renal disease or post renal transplant.

Current information that an examiner may consider can be found in the evidence review on chronic kidney disease (CKD) and commercial drivers[3] and recommendations from the MEP on that topic[4] (both discussed here). The MEP identified fatigue, daytime sleepiness, neurocognitive symptoms, and hypoglycemia (in those with diabetes) as key potential threats to safety in drivers with CKD.

The evidence report and others[5] suggested that individuals with CKD and on dialysis are at an increased crash risk, probably due to cognitive deficits. Neurocognitive deficits appeared to be greater on the day before dialysis than the day after dialysis.[4] Neurologic complications associated with dialysis include dialysis dementia, disequilibrium syndrome, cerebrovascular events, intracranial hypertension, hypertensive encephalopathy, Wernicke's encephalopathy, and others. The type of dialysis may play a role in the maintenance of cognitive function. Memory and cognitive function appears to improve after transplant. Other concerns about drivers on dialysis were related to maintaining compliance with the treatment regimen with long-distance driving and other aspects of the commercial motor vehicle (CMV) operator's work. Hemodialysis patients may have muscle atrophy and weakness that could also be a concern.

In evaluating the fitness of a CMV driver with renal disease, it is important not only to consider the renal disease itself but also to assess coexisting medical conditions. Drivers who also have diabetes, hypertension, or heart disease may be at higher risk of complications or sudden impairment than drivers with renal disease alone. In addition, the fluid shifts and electrolyte disturbances before or after dialysis may impact driver safety.

Renal failure can result in a number of physiologic and clinical abnormalities, including anemia; hypertension (which can lead to or be exacerbated by CKD); cerebrovascular disease; neuropathy; dementia; cardiovascular disease, including hypotension, left ventricular hypertrophy, and potential for arrhythmias; and sleep disorders (4 times more prevalent than in the general population).[3]

The first step in the evaluation must be to assess the degree of renal impairment. Results from laboratory studies—including electrolyte levels, blood urea nitrogen level, creatinine level, and creatinine clearance—should be reviewed, as should the degree of proteinuria, if present.

Two types of dialysis are used: hemodialysis or peritoneal dialysis. Hemodialysis is more common and usually requires 9 to 12 hours of treatment per week, often divided into three sessions per week. Frequently, an artificial shunt is used, which can increase the risk of infection. The significant interruption in normal activities of daily living and altered body image may lead to depression. During dialysis, fluxes in osmolality and electrolytes may lead to a dialysis disequilibrium syndrome or arrhythmias. Hypotension is common. Electrolyte disturbances also may result in muscle cramps. The development of dialysis dementia is another concern.

Dialysis is best performed in a consistent setting, difficult for many long-haul truckers. Arranging dialysis in different locations over the course of several weeks may be a logistical impossibility. A reliable schedule also is required and may present difficulty. Commercial drivers whose routes are solely local, short haul, or intermittent may be able to coordinate their work schedule around their dialysis schedule. Medical examiners, however, are unable to restrict drivers to operating only under these conditions.

The other main method of dialysis is peritoneal dialysis (PD). This could be either continuous or nocturnal. For this method, patients instill dialysate fluid into the peritoneal cavity, seal the catheter, and continue with normal activities. Advantages over hemodialysis include the more gradual shifts in fluid and electrolyte levels and the avoidance of heparinization. Longer treatment times may be a disadvantage to some patients. Complications include catheter infection, peritonitis, and moderate protein loss.

The 5-year survival rate for patients on dialysis in the United States is 35 percent, with the most common cause of mortality being cardiovascular disease.[3] Even with treatment, only about 10 percent to 20 percent of chronic renal failure patients are totally rehabilitated by dialysis, and another 30 percent to 40 percent of nondiabetic patients are returned to a functional level. Mean mortality for all end-stage renal disease patients is approximately 18 percent per year. In those younger than age 45 years with no complicating medical problems, mortality with treatment falls below 5 percent per year.

Patients who undergo renal transplantation often will return to a near-normal lifestyle. One of the greatest risks for these individuals is transplant rejection. Such patients should be able to obtain care in the event of infection or rejection in a reasonable period of time. The risk of rejection is highest in the first year after transplantation. For a CMV driver, one concern should be the potential side effects of the medication in addition to its immunosuppressive effects. Steroids at higher doses can cause confusion, and cyclosporine can lead to tremor. As with all medication use in CMV drivers, it is important for examiners to be in contact with the treating physician to obtain an understanding of the medication and any potential interference with the safe operation of a vehicle.

It is important to remember that as examiners under the FMCSA program, we are unable to limit geographic range or duration of driving or other restrictions aside from requiring hearing aids, corrective lenses, limiting driving within an exempt intracity zone or a variance [Skill Performance Evaluation Certificate (SPE)], or an exemption such as for diabetes or vision.

Medical Expert Panel and Medical Review Board

Although it has been many years since FMCSA has heard the recommendations of the MEP and MRB on CKD, there have been no recent updates in guidance. The MEP[4] recommended that, ideally, medical examiners should determine the kidney function status of all potential CMV drivers and, if this was not feasible, at least for those with risk factors of CKD. The MRB agreed that serologic assessment of serum creatinine and calculation of the glomerular filtration rate (GFR) should be performed but only for those with any of the following risk factors:

- Personal history of potentially chronic renal disease
- Age over 65 years
- Diabetes mellitus
- Hypertension (as specified on the CDME examination form)
- Proteinuria

The calculation of the GFR could be done through the Modification of Diet in Renal Disease calculator that can be found at http://mdrd.com/.[6]

The MEP[4] recommended and the MRB[7,8] concurred that drivers with CKD in Stages 1, 2, or 3 (see Table 10-1) may be considered as physically qualified to drive a CMV. Those in Stages 1 and 2 should be evaluated and recertified at least every 2 years, and those with Stage 3 should be evaluated and recertified at least annually. The MRB added that those in Stages 1, 2, or 3 should have screening with repeat creatinine measurement and GFR performed with each CDME examination.

TABLE 10-1 Stages of Chronic Kidney Disease

Stage 1	Renal damage (protein, normal GFR)	≥90 mL/min/1.73 m²
Stage 2	Mild decrease in GFR	60–89
Stage 3	Moderate decrease in GFR	30–59
Stage 4	Severe decrease in GFR	15–29
Stage 5	Renal failure	≤15

GFR = glomerular filtration rate.

Recommendations from the MEP on drivers with Stage 4 CKD included that those drivers with a normal EKG and a blood pressure less than 140/90 mm Hg could be certified for a period not to exceed 6 months. If the driver has a normal EKG and blood pressure 140–180 mm Hg (systolic) or 90–110 (diastolic), the driver may be certified up to 3 months. If the EKG or echocardiogram reveals left ventricular hypertrophy or if the individual has a blood pressure greater than 180 mm Hg systolic or greater than or equal to 110 mm Hg diastolic, the driver should be disqualified from driving a CMV. As there were panels on cardiovascular disease, the MRB indicated that blood pressure and cardiomyopathy issues should be handled by those panels and that those drivers in Stage 4 CKD be recertified at least every 6 months, including a GFR measurement and a supportive letter from their treating nephrologist. They should also receive a cardiovascular evaluation at least annually. Both the MEP and the MRB recommended that drivers in Stage 5 CKD and/or on hemodialysis or peritoneal dialysis should be precluded from driving CMVs.

Regarding renal transplantation, the MEP[4] and MRB[7,8] both recommended that individuals who have undergone successful renal transplantation could operate a CMV 90 days postoperatively provided they have been cleared as fit for duty by their transplant physician. All individuals who have undergone successful renal transplantation should be recertified at 3 months, 6 months, and 12 months postoperatively and after that as per the other CKD recommendations.

Other Standards and Guidelines

Examiners may want to review criteria from other countries for comparison[9-11] or the Federal Aviation Administration[12] or Coast Guard[13] guidance on renal disease.

Conclusion

End-stage renal disease has the potential to cause impairment in a CMV driver by a number of mechanisms. It is important to evaluate not only the degree and stability of renal impairment but also the presence and status of any coexisting diseases. Information from all treating physicians should be reviewed and arrangements should be made with the primary treating physician that commercial driving status be reviewed with significant changes in medical stability. The 1998 New Orleans bus accident with multiple fatalities involved a driver who was medically qualified and 2 months later began renal dialysis. No evaluation of the individual's ability to perform CMV driver functions occurred once dialysis began or until the time of the accident. The driver's medical conditions, which were found to contribute to that accident, was the impetus for many of the changes that we are now seeing in the medical certification of CMV drivers.

References

1. Federal Motor Carrier Safety Administration, U.S. Department of Transportation. Frequently Asked Question. http://www.fmcsa.dot.gov/rules-regulations /topics/medical/faqs.aspx.
2. Federal Motor Carrier Safety Administration, U.S. Department of Transportation. Medical Examiner Handbook, currently in the process of revision. https://www.fmcsa.dot.gov/regulations/medical/fmcsa-medical-examiner -handbook.
3. Noble M, Reston J, Treager S. Evidence Report: Chronic Kidney Disease and Commercial Vehicle Driver Safety—. Presented to FMCSA November 5, 2007. http://ntl.bts.gov/lib/30000/30300/30316/Chronic_Kidney_Disease_Evidence _Report_-_FINAL.pdf.
4. Fadem S, Szczech L, Unruh M. Expert Panel Recommendations. Chronic Kidney Failure and Commercial Motor Vehicle Driver Safety. Presented to FMCSA March 14, 2008. https://www.fmcsa.dot.gov/regulations/medical/ opinions-expert-panel-chronic-kidney-failure-and-commercial-motor-vehicle -driver.
5. Dobbs BM. Medical conditions and driving: a review of the scientific literature (1960–2000). Report DOT HS 809 690. National Highway Traffic Safety Administration. September 2005. http://www.nhtsa.gov/people/injury/research /medical_condition_driving/pages/Sec1-Intro.htm.
6. The MDRD (Modification of Diet in Renal Disease) GFR—calculates an estimated GFR based on serum creatinine, age, gender and race. In: A.S. Levey, T. Greene, J.W. Kusek, G.L. Beck, MDRD Study Group. A simplified equation to predict glomerular filtration rate from serum creatinine. *J Am Soc Nephrol.* 2000;11(Sept):155A. Calculator can be accessed at http://mdrd.com.
7. Meeting Summary of the Federal Motor Carrier Safety Administration Medical Review Board July 18, 2008. https://www.fmcsa.dot.gov/summary-july-18-2008 -medical-review-board-public-meeting.
8. Meeting Summary of the Federal Motor Carrier Safety Administration Medical Review Board April 7, 2008. https://www.fmcsa.dot.gov/summary-april-7-2008 -medical-review-board-public-meeting.
9. Canadian Medical Association. CMA Driver's Guide. Determining Medical Fitness to Operate Motor Vehicles, 8th ed. http://https://www.cma.ca/En/Pages /drivers-guide.aspx.
10. Driver and Vehicle Licensing Agency—United Kingdom. Assessing fitness to drive: a guide for medical professionals. Updated August 2016. https://www.gov .uk/government/publications/assessing-fitness-to-drive-a-guide-for-medical -professionals.
11. Austroads, National Transport Commission. Assessing Fitness to Drive for Commercial and Private Vehicle Drivers, Austroads, National Transportation Commission, Melbourne, Australia, 2016. http://www.austroads.com.au/drivers -vehicles/assessing-fitness-to-drive.

12. United States Coast Guard, Department of Homeland Security. Coast Guard Medical Manual. 2014. https://www.uscg.mil/directives/cim/6000-6999/CIM _6000_1F.pdf.
13. Federal Aviation Administration. Guide for Aviation Medical Examiners. 2017. https://www.faa.gov/about/office_org/headquarters_offices/avs/offices /aam/ame/guide/.

CHAPTER 11

Substance Abuse and Medication Use

NATALIE P. HARTENBAUM, MD, MPH, FACOEM

Since the prior edition of this book, the Commercial Driver Medical Examiner (CDME) processes have undergone significant changes, mostly related to the National Registry of Certified Medical Examiners (NRCME). In 2014, the Federal Motor Carrier Safety Administration Medical Examiner Handbook (ME Handbook) was taken off the Federal Motor Carrier Safety Administration (FMCSA) website for update and revision. As this edition is being prepared, examiners still should consider guidance from the prior handbook, as that is what is being taught in the training programs, but should base their final decision on current best medical practice remembering that our ultimate responsibility is to ensure the safety of the motoring public to the extent reasonably possible. Chapters will include information from the most recent ME Handbook, Medical Expert Panel (MEP) reports, and Medical Review Board (MRB) recommendations as well as other relevant reports and literature.

The FMCSA MRB heard recommendations from the MEP on Schedule II Medications in 2007, Psychiatric Conditions including Medications in 2009, and an MEP on Schedule II Opioids and Stimulants in 2014, making recommendations to FMCSA. In 2015 and again in 2016, the MRB and Motor Carrier Safety Advisory Committee (MCSAC) also made recommendations based on expert panel reports and submitted comments. However, FMCSA has not made any changes to its guidance at this time.

As significant changes occur, they will be noted at the end of each chapter in the online version of this book at least twice a year.

Few areas cause as much concern and confusion in the commercial driver medical certification arena as medication use and abuse, and substance abuse. Two of the 13 medical standards specifically address substance abuse; the guidance for the others include consideration as to whether the treatment may interfere with safe operation of the commercial motor vehicle (CMV). For a period of time, drug and alcohol testing were a part of the periodic examination process. The prior examination form emphasized the importance of reviewing the use of both prescription and nonprescription medications and the potential impact on safety that these medications may have. Included on that form was a statement that the medical examiner must review and discuss with the driver the "potential hazards including over-the-counter medications, while driving." The current form does not have that same statement.

The Federal Motor Safety Regulations that address substance abuse and alcohol misuse state that a person is physically qualified to drive a CMV if that person:

[49 CFR 391.41(b)]

---

(12) (i)   *Does not use any drug or substance identified in 21 CFR 1308.11 Schedule I, an amphetamine, a narcotic, or other habit-forming drug.*

(ii)   *Does not use any non-Schedule I drug or substance that is identified in the other Schedules in 21 CFR part 1308 except when the use is prescribed by a licensed medical practitioner, as defined in §382.107, who is familiar with the driver's medical history and has advised the driver that the substance will not adversely affect the driver's ability to safely operate a commercial motor vehicle.*

(13) *Has no current clinical diagnosis of alcoholism.*

The advisory criteria[1] explain that the exception permitting drivers who are using a "non-Schedule I drug or substance" does not apply to methadone and that the driver who uses an amphetamine, narcotic, or any other habit-forming drug may be found medically unqualified. Use of any Schedule 1 drug or substance will cause the driver to be medically unqualified. Examiners must determine whether the medication or the medical condition that it is treating may impair the driver's safe operation of the CMV. Motor carriers are encouraged to obtain a written statement from the prescribing provider. In addition to the advisory criteria, methadone is also mentioned in the interpretations[2] and FMCSA's Frequently Asked Questions[3] as not being subject to this exception and that commercial drivers on methadone should be found medically unqualified.

An examiner may determine drug use through interview, available history, or body fluid testing. If testing is done, it is not performed under U.S. Department of Transportation (DOT) authority (do not use a federal form), but any positive screening test should be confirmed. The advisory criteria indicate that if the driver is found to be medically unqualified owing to prohibited drug use, the individual can only return once a second examination finds that the driver is no longer using that substance. An evaluation by a substance abuse professional, completion of a drug rehabilitation program, and a negative drug test result may be required of a driver who was not qualified because of substance use. If a driver is not medically qualified because of a Medical Review Officer (MRO)–verified positive regulated test, a return to duty would have to include all of the components required by the DOT and FMCSA drug testing regulations. The examiner also may certify the driver for less than 2 years if there is a concern that there may be a recurrence of impairing or illegal substance use.

For drivers found not to be medically qualified because of alcohol use, it is explained that "current clinical diagnosis" refers to a "current alcoholic illness or those instances where the individual's physical condition has not fully stabilized." This would seem not to include individuals who are abstinent and have no other alcohol-related medical conditions but who may be considered recovering alcoholics. Individuals who have physical signs of or provide a history consistent with alcohol problems should be referred to a specialist and, after evaluation and/or treatment,[3] if indicated, should then be medically certified.

When state laws were passed legalizing medical marijuana, there were questions on how this would affect federal drug testing policies. Federico Peña, then secretary of the DOT, stated on December 12, 1996 that "any safety-sensitive transportation worker—such as a pilot, railroad engineer, or bus driver—who tests positive under our program may not use Proposition 215 or Proposition 200 as an excuse or defense".[4] He also explained that the MRO should not find that the presence of these substances, even *with* the report of a recommendation of a physician, is due to a legitimate medical use. Use of these substances is not consistent with federal approved use. With more states approving medical marijuana and some permitting or decriminalizing recreational marijuana, the DOT has repeatedly stated that use of marijuana is prohibited in workers covered under DOT testing procedures. The standard addressing medication use was changed in 2012 to specifically indicate that any Schedule 1 substance is prohibited, even if used under the recommendation of a health care provider.[5]

Probably one of the most challenging areas for the medical examiner is determining whether a medication might impair to a degree that would make the driver not qualified. This includes both those substances prescribed by a health care professional and those purchased over the counter. The examiner should review with the driver any medications the driver may be taking and discuss potential hazards. This should include advising drivers to read all package inserts, with special attention to precautions on driving or operating heavy machinery. A search of an electronic version of the Physician's Desk Reference found hundreds of medications with warnings similar to "Use caution when driving a motor vehicle or operating machinery." FMCSA provides a page that includes information on reading medication labels, medication interactions, and questions to ask a health care provider.[6] Drivers also should be made aware that medications that list fatigue or sedation as side effects may not be safe to use while operating a CMV. Medications in several classes, including the first-generation antihistamines, benzodiazepines, antidepressants, anxiolytics, narcotics, and some of the nonnarcotic analgesics, have a high incidence of sedation as a side effect. Studies over the years have shown potential driving impairment with many of these medications.[7-18] The American College of Occupational and Environmental Medicine (ACOEM) practice guidelines[19] state the following:

> Acute or chronic opioid use is not recommended for patients who perform safety-sensitive jobs. These jobs include operating motor vehicles, other modes of transportation, forklift driving, overhead crane operation, heavy equipment operation, sharps work (eg, knives, box cutters, needles), work with injury risks (eg, heights) and tasks involving high levels of cognitive function and judgment.

They did acknowledge that the guideline included the possibility that there are some individuals without increased risk, possibly those on lower-dose or weaker opioids, although they did not find evidence to support this. They also felt that there should be sufficient time after the last dose to have cleared about 90% of the drug or active metabolite from the body prior to performing safety-sensitive duties.

Sleep aids clearly should not be used if the individual may need to drive during the time that the medication is intended to assist the individual in sleeping. A letter from the U.S. Food and Drug Administration (FDA) warned health care providers that 13 sleep medications could result in complex behaviors, such as sleep driving, driving while not fully awake, and with no memory of driving.[20] Menzin and colleagues[21] estimated that the use of a driving-impairing sleep medication would result in about 503 excess accidents per 100,000 drivers during a 14-day period. Recent FDA label changes or advisory indicated that certain sleep aids could cause next-morning impairment.[22,23]

Some of the medications used to treat Parkinson's disease, such as pramipexole and ropinirole (also used in restless leg syndrome), have been associated with sleep attacks. These are unpredictable and have occurred up to 1 year after beginning the medication.[24,25]

Other side effects examiners must consider include dizziness, confusion, fatigue, seizures, headaches, and hypotension. Potential interactions among medications that the driver might be using also should be evaluated. Drivers and health care providers should be encouraged to avoid use of potentially impairing medications whenever possible by utilizing alternatives that do not have an undesirable side effect profile.

In addition, it must be remembered, and the driver must be advised, that many over-the-counter medications contain alcohol and that side effects can be increased when certain medications are used with even small amounts of alcohol or other medications. These medications should not be used while driving until the driver and the driver's health care provider are certain that there are no impairing side effects.

Examiners should discuss the effect that a medication may have with the treating provider; however, the provider may not be aware of or may be unable to assess the risk that a specific medication may have on safety. Similar to alcohol, individuals often are unable to determine whether they are impaired or the degree of impairment with a particular medication. By relying on subjective observations and whether drivers report them to a prescribing provider or the medical examiner is much like permitting individuals who have had several drinks to get behind the wheel because they do not believe that they are impaired.

Drivers should be instructed to always use medications as prescribed, not to increase the dose except under supervision, and to avoid driving until they know how the medication may affect them. They also should inform their health care provider of any and all medications, including herbal or alternative treatments, because side effects may be additive.

It is important that the examiner focus not only on the medication but also on the underlying condition. Although the driver may be on a medication that has the potential to impair performance and the prescribing provider insists that the individual is not impaired, the underlying medical condition itself may interfere with safe operation of a CMV.

Over the years, the DOT repeatedly has reminded those in the transportation industries "of potential threat to public safety caused by the on-duty use of some over-the-counter and prescription medication by persons performing some safety sensitive duties." Employee training was recommended. As a result of studying more than 100 accidents in all modes of transportation that involved prescription or over-the-counter medications that could potentially impair the operator, the National Transportation Safety Board (NTSB) recommended that the DOT develop a list of approved medications/classes of medications and forbid the use of medications not on the list for twice the dosage interval, except when individually assessed.[26] The NTSB recommends against relying on the individual's subjective assessment and reports of this assessment to the treating provider. The NTSB stated in the 2000 safety recommendation that "vehicle operators using such medications might not always be in a position to judge the extent and effect of such impairment; a vehicle operator whose judgment is adversely affected by a medication may decide, inappropriately, that he or she is not impaired."[26]

The current regulation permits a driver to use most medications when prescribed by a licensed health care professional who states that they will not affect the ability to drive safely. Two FAQs[3] address the use of legally prescribed medications. One advises that, although a medication may be legally prescribed, the driver could be disqualified if the medication could impair. The second indicates that an examiner can determine if a medication will adversely affect safe operation of a CMV by reviewing each medication—prescription, nonprescription, or supplement—or by requesting a letter from the prescribing doctor. Even with a statement from the treating health care provider, the examiner may decide not to certify the driver.

Only a few medications are mentioned by name in the regulation or advisory criteria. Schedule 1 medications and methadone, as discussed earlier, and insulin are indicated to be disqualifying although drivers may apply for an exemption from the insulin criteria. Also noted to be disqualifying in the advisory criteria are antiseizure medications. This has caused some confusion, as many antiseizure medications may be prescribed for conditions other than seizure control. The FAQs[3] clarify this by explaining that antiseizure medication used for the prevention of *seizures* is disqualifying. There also is a question that notes that a driver taking medical marijuana cannot be certified.

Another medication addressed in the FAQs is modafinil (Provigil). The original recommendation from FMCSA was that CMV operators on this medication should not be qualified. The current guidance in the FAQs[3] states the following:

> Provigil (Modafinil) is a medication used to treat excessive sleepiness caused by certain sleep disorders. These sleep disorders are narcolepsy, obstructive sleep apnea/hypopnea syndrome and shift work sleep disorders. Provigil has several concerning side effects such as chest pain, dizziness, difficulty breathing, heart palpitations, irregular and/or fast heartbeat, increased blood pressure, tremors or shaking movements, anxiety, nervousness, rapidly changing mood, problems with memory, blurred vision or other vision changes to name a few. Many drugs interact with Provigil which include over-the-counter medications, prescription medications, nutritional supplements, herbal products, alcohol containing beverages and caffeine. The use of Provigil needs careful supervision. Provigil may affect concentration, function or may hide signs that an individual is tired. It is recommended that until an individual knows how Provigil affects him/her, they may not drive, use machinery or do any activity that requires mental alertness.

The FAQ had indicated "that drivers should not be qualified until they have been monitored closely for at least 6 weeks while taking modafinil. Both the treating physician and the medical examiner should agree that modafinil is effective in preventing daytime somnolence and that there are no significant side effects. Commercial motor vehicle drivers on modafinil should be recertified annually." This is no longer included in the FAQ on modafinil.

In 2008, a statement had been issued on the use of varenicline (Chantix) suggesting that examiners should not certify drivers on this medication. This resulted from a report of the Institute for Safe Medication Practices (ISMP)[27] and a Public Health Advisory from the FDA after the Federal Aviation Administration (FAA) prohibited its use by pilots and air traffic controllers. Varenicline is now listed on the FAA "Do Not Fly" list.[28] Since the FMCSA statement, the FDA has issued an updated advisory on varenicline that also included buprorion (Zyban), also used for smoking cessation, with comments on concerns of neuropsychiatric side effects.[29] There have been several other advisories on varenicline and, in December 2016, the FDA removed the Black Box warnings on varenicline and buprorion based on studies that the risk of mental health side effects was lower than expected.[30] FMCSA currently has no statement on varenicline.

There had been guidance on Suboxone which recommended that drivers on Suboxone not be qualified. A more recent statement (no longer posted) is applicable to almost all potentially impairing medications.[31]

Methadone is specifically named as not being permitted for use by CMV drivers in the physical qualification's Advisory Criteria. Suboxone use however, is not discussed in the regulations or the Advisory Criteria concerning physical qualifications for CMV drivers. Therefore, the Agency relies on the certifying medical examiner to evaluate and determine whether Suboxone use by an individual driver will impair his or her ability to safely operate a CMV.

While most medications are not specified in FMCSA regulations, medical examiners may disqualify drivers who take any medications or combination of medications and substances that may impair or interfere with safe driving practices. All medications must be assessed to determine the potential risk of adverse side effects which include but are not limited to; dizziness, drowsiness, and sleepiness and the direct impact that these potential side effects have on commercial motor vehicle driving and operation safety.

In addition, FMCSA regulation 392.3 does not permit a driver to operate a commercial vehicle "while the driver's ability or alertness is so impaired, or so likely to become impaired, through fatigue, illness, or any other cause, as to make it unsafe for him/her to begin or continue to operate the commercial motor vehicle"

In making the medical determination regarding Suboxone, the medical examiner should confer with the treating medical specialist(s) who is(are) familiar with the driver's health history regarding the specialist's opinion whether a certain medication or underlying medical condition may adversely impact the individual driver's ability to safely operate a CMV.

Several medications were mentioned in the ME Handbook, now down for update;[32] these will be discussed with the chapter on those medical conditions. In general, examiners were advised that:

- *As the medical examiner, your fundamental obligation is to establish whether a driver uses one or more medications and supplements that have cognitive or physical effects or side effects that interfere with safe driving, thus endangering public safety.*

- *You should not certify the driver until the medication has been shown to be adequate/effective, safe, and stable.*

- *Effects or side effects of medication use while operating a commercial motor vehicle do not endanger the safety of the driver and the public.*

- *The medical examiner has the authority to disqualify a driver if he/she believes that the medication the driver is taking adversely impacts the ability to safely operate a CMV.*

One of the most challenging areas for the medical examiner is narcotics. FMCSA convened a medical expert panel to review the literature for Schedule II medications.[33] For many of the key questions, the panel had a difficult time reaching an evidence-based conclusion due to the paucity of evidence that met the inclusion criteria. There was evidence that first-time doses of Schedule II opioids had deleterious effects on driving performance as well as cognitive and psychomotor function. The panel recommended that until the NRCME was fully implemented, the exception for drivers on Schedule II opioids should be eliminated. Once the NRCME had been formed, examiners should be provided with standardized forms and specific guidance to aid in determining whether an individual would be able to safely operate a CMV on specific medications. Additional recommendations included expanding the drug testing panel to include synthetic opioids and to conduct additional reviews on the benzodiazepines.

The MRB[34] considered the panel's recommendations but made different suggestions to FMCSA (see Table 11-1). They suggested modifying the standard to specifically include Schedule II medications and benzodiazepines as prohibited. They also recommended limiting the exception to those situations in which the medication is prescribed by a licensed physician (MD, DO) and the medical examiner also would be a physician. The examiner would be required to review a specific form developed by FMCSA and to inform drivers that if they do not take the substance or drug as prescribed, they are using the substance or drug improperly and are not covered by this exception. Specifically excluded from the exception would be drivers who use substances or drugs administered parenterally (e.g., intravenously, transdermally, subcutaneously, intrathecally, or intramuscularly). Driving also would not be permitted when the medication of concern is initiated or dosage increased within the past 2 weeks; if the driver has a history of substance, drug, or alcohol abuse or addiction; or if the medication would be ingested while driving.

Another evidence review[35] was conducted and focused on Schedule II opioids and stimulants. Since the prior reports, a new MRB and the MCSAC have had several meetings on medications. Final recommendations were presented to FMCSA on October 27–28, 2014, with background material discussed at a number of earlier meetings. This material is available through the Medical Review Board meeting webpage.[36] Recommendations from the MRB and MCSAC[37] can be found in Table 11-1.

TABLE 11-1 The Medical Review Board (MRB) and the Motor Carrier Safety Advisory Committee (MCSAC) Joint Recommendations on the Use of Schedule II Medications by Commercial Motor Vehicle (CMV) Drivers

I. **Guidance Regarding CMV Driver Use of Narcotics**
  A. Recommendations: The MRB and MCSAC believe that a driver should not be qualified medically to operate a CMV while he/she is under treatment with narcotics or any narcotic derivative without exception.
    1. However, while the current exception remains in the Federal Motor Carrier Safety Regulations (FMCSRs) (see 49 CFR 391.41(b)(12)(ii)), the MRB and MCSAC recommend that FMCSA provide the following guidelines regarding use of narcotics to CMEs:
      a. A CME should consider whether the underlying medical condition requiring the use of the narcotic(s) is sufficiently impairing to affect whether a driver is qualified medically to perform safety-sensitive duties, including driving a CMV.
      b. A driver should not be under the influence of narcotics while performing safety-sensitive duties, including driving a CMV.
      c. If a driver uses narcotics while off duty, he/she must not use the narcotic for a minimum of 8 hours (if using short-acting narcotics) or 12 hours (if using long-acting narcotics) before resuming safety-sensitive duties, including driving a CMV.
      d. The CME should consider using the CMV Driver Medication Questionnaire or similar document to aid in determining the qualification of the driver. The CME should consider obtaining medical records to ensure that the use of the narcotic medication(s) or narcotic derivative is consistent with current best practices for chronic pain and disease management.
        i. If it is determined that the driver can be qualified medically, certification should be for no more than 1 year.
      e. The CME should consider disqualifying a driver for the usage of other impairing or habit-forming drugs when used in combination with a narcotic or narcotic derivative.
    2. FMCSA should consider issuing guidelines to CMEs relating to other impairing or habit-forming drugs, including benzodiazepines, amphetamines, etc.
  B. Rationale: The MRB and MCSAC based this recommendation on its review of the updated evidence report, *Schedule II Opioids and Stimulants & CMV Crash Risk and Driver Performance: Evidence Report and Systematic Review (C)*. Specifically, this recommendation is based on the following conclusions from the post-2006 evidence report:
    1. There is moderate evidence to support the contention that the licit use of opioids increases the risk of a motor vehicle crash and impacts indirect measures of driver performance negatively.
      a. Several large and recent studies link opioid use to increased risk of driver fatalities, driver injury, crash risk, and unsafe driver actions.

TABLE 11-1 continued

2. There is moderate evidence that licit use of opioids impacts indirect measures of driver performance negatively.

    a. Generally, studies found indicators of impairment, especially for drug-naïve individuals (i.e., for those not having previously used a particular drug). Impairment was most pronounced on psychomotor vigilance tasks related to pertinent driving skill such as attention, vision, auditory perception, and reaction time.

II. **Standardized CMV Driver Medication Questionnaire for Commercial Driver Medical Examiners**

    A. Recommendation: FMCSA should develop a standardized Medication Questionnaire to assist the Certified Medical Examiner (CME) when reviewing prescription medications that have been disclosed during the history and physical examination for certification.

III. **Format of the Standardized CMV Driver Medication Questionnaire**

    A. Recommendations: The MRB and MCSAC recommend that the standardized CMV Driver Medication Questionnaire referenced in Recommendation I.A include the following information and questions (see attached "391.41 CMV Driver Medication Questionnaire"):

        1. Questionnaire should be titled *391.41 CMV Driver Medication Questionnaire.*

        2. Questionnaire should request the following information:

            a. Identifying name and date of birth (DOB) of the CMV driver.

            b. Introductory paragraph stating purpose of the CMV Driver Medication Questionnaire.

            c. Statements of *391.41(b)(12)* (Physical Qualifications of Drivers relating to driver use of scheduled substances) and *The Driver's Role,* as found in the Medical Examination Report form found at the end of *49 CFR 391.43 (Medical Examination; Certificate of Physical Examination).*

            d. Name, state of licensure, signature, address and contact information of the prescribing health care provider, as well as the date the form was completed.

            e. Name, signature, date, address and contact information of the CME.

        3. Questionnaire should include the following questions:

            a. Question 1 – List all medications and dosages that you have prescribed to the above named individual.

            b. Question 2 – List any other medications and dosages that you are aware have been prescribed to the above named individual by another treating health care provider.

            c. Question 3 – What medical conditions are being treated with these medications?

            d. Question 4 – It is my medical opinion that, considering the mental and physical requirements of operating a CMV and with awareness of a CMV driver's role (consistent with *The Driver's Role* statement

TABLE 11-1 continued

on page 2 of the form), I believe my patient: (a) has no medication side effects from medication(s) that I prescribe that would adversely affect the ability to operate a CMV safely; and (2) has no medical condition(s) that I am treating with the above medication(s) that would adversely affect the ability to operate a CMV safely.

IV. **Education for CMEs Regarding Medications that May Impair Driver's Ability to Operate a CMV Safely**
   A. Several classes of medications have the potential to affect adversely the driver's ability to operate a CMV safely.
   B. Recommendations:
      1. Therefore, FMCSA should educate the CME regarding safety concerns related to such medications and advise the CME that during the certification process particular attention should be given to the following classes of medications: Anticoagulants, Antivirals, Anxiolytics, Barbiturates, Chemotherapeutic Agents, Experimental, Hypoglycemic, Investigational, Mood-ameliorating, Motion Sickness, Narcotic, Sedating Antihistaminic, Sedative, Steroid drugs, and Tranquilizers; as well as medications with a U.S. Food and Drug Administration (FDA) Black Box warning of side effects that include syncope, loss of consciousness, seizure provoking, arrhythmia, hypoglycemia, and psychosis.
      2. FMCSA should provide the following guidance/educational statement to CMEs regarding over-the-counter medications: CMEs should discuss with a driver relevant over-the-counter medications that may have side effects that could affect adversely a driver's ability to operate a CMV safely.
      3. FMCSA should develop an educational brochure that CMEs or employers could provide to drivers to educate them regarding over-the-counter medications that may have side effects that could affect adversely a driver's ability to operate a CMV safely.

V. **Expert Panel Review of Potentially Impairing Medications**
   A. Recommendation: The FMCSA should develop a panel of experts to review medications as well as categories of medications in order to develop lists of both medications that are permitted and potentially disqualifying medications, based on potential adverse side effects.

The MRB and MCSAC recommended use of the form provided in Table 11-2.

TABLE 11-2 Proposed Form 391.41 CMV Driver Medication Questionnaire (Page 1 of 2)

Driver Name_____ DOB_____

The above patient/driver is being evaluated to determine whether he/she meets the medical standards of the Federal Motor Carrier Safety Administration (FMCSA) to operate a commercial motor vehicle (CMV). During the medical evaluation, it was determined this individual is taking medication(s) that may impair his/her ability to operate a CMV safely. As the Certified Medical Examiner (CME), I request that you review the Regulations as noted below, complete this questionnaire, and return it to me at the address specified below. The final determination as to whether the individual listed in this form is physically qualified to drive a CMV will be made by the CME.

49 CFR 391.41, *Physical Qualifications for Drivers:* **A person is physically qualified to drive a CMV if that person... (12)(i) Does not use any drug or substance identified in 21 CFR 1308.11 Schedule I, an amphetamine, a narcotic, or other habit-forming drug. (ii) Does not use any non-Schedule I drug or substance that is identified in the other Schedules in 21 part 1308 except when the use is prescribed by a licensed medical practitioner, as defined in §382.107, who is familiar with the driver's medical history and has advised the driver that the substance will not adversely affect the driver's ability to safely operate a CMV.**

1. List all medications and dosages that you have prescribed to the above named individual.

   _____

   _____

2. List any other medications and dosages that you are aware have been prescribed to the above named individual by another treating health care provider.

   _____

   _____

3. What medical conditions are being treated with these medications?

   _____

   _____

4. It is my medical opinion that, considering the mental and physical requirements of operating a CMV and with awareness of a CMV driver's role (consistent with "The Driver's Role" statement on page 2), my patient:
   (a) has no medication side effects from medication(s) that I prescribe that would affect adversely the ability to operate a CMV safely; and
   (b) has no medical condition(s) that I am treating with the above medication(s) that would affect adversely the ability to operate a CMV safely.
      ____Yes ____No (check response)

Signature of Prescribing Health Care Provider   Date

Printed Name of Prescribing Health Care Provider   State of Licensure

---

Street Address   City, State, Zip Code

Phone/Fax   Email

THE DRIVER'S ROLE
49 CFR 391.43

Responsibilities, work schedules, physical and emotional demands, and lifestyles among commercial drivers vary by the type of driving that they do. Some of the main types of drivers include the following: turn around or short relay (drivers return to their home base each evening); long relay (drivers drive 9-11 hours and then have at least a 10-hour off-duty period), straight through haul (cross country drivers); and team drivers (drivers share the driving by alternating their 5- hour driving periods and 5-hour rest periods.) The following factors may be involved in a driver's performance of duties: abrupt schedule changes and rotating work schedules, which may result in irregular sleep patterns and a driver beginning a trip in a fatigued condition; long hours; extended time away from family and friends, which may result in lack of social support; tight pickup and delivery schedules, with irregularity in work, rest, and eating patterns, adverse road, weather and traffic conditions, which may cause delays and lead to hurriedly loading or unloading cargo in order to compensate for the lost time; and environmental conditions such as excessive vibration, noise, and extremes in temperature. Transporting passengers or hazardous materials may add to the demands on the commercial driver. There may be duties in addition to the driving task for which a driver is responsible and needs to be fit. Some of these responsibilities are: coupling and uncoupling trailer(s) from the tractor, loading and unloading trailer(s) (sometimes a driver may lift a heavy load or unload as much as 50,000 lbs. of freight after sitting for a long period of time without any stretching period); inspecting the operating condition of tractor and/or trailer(s) before, during and after delivery of cargo; lifting, installing, and removing heavy tire chains; and, lifting heavy tarpaulins to cover open top trailers. The above tasks demand agility, the ability to bend and stoop, the ability to maintain a crouching position to inspect the underside of the vehicle, frequent entering and exiting of the cab, and the ability to climb ladders on the tractor and/or trailer(s). In addition, a driver must have the perceptual skills to monitor a sometimes complex driving situation, the judgment skills to make quick decisions, when necessary, and the manipulative skills to control an oversize steering wheel, shift gears using a manual transmission, and maneuver a vehicle in crowded areas.

Signature of Certified Medical Examiner	Date
Printed Name of Certified Medical Examiner	Email
Street Address	City, State, Zip Code
Phone/Fax	

FMCSA has since published a request for comment on a voluntary medication form[38] similar to the content recommended by the MRB. ACOEM submitted a comment requesting that this be withdrawn as the form was insufficient for examiners to adequately evaluate safety, especially those not familiar with the medications being used.

After CDC[39] advice to medical personnel that morphine milligram equivalents above 50 mg per day of medications such as methadone and morphine doubles the risk of overdose and death, the MRB advised caution in drivers who use above 50 morphine milligram equivalents (MME) per day.[40] They also agreed that treating providers and examiners should consider whether drivers on opioids and benzodiazepines should be found unqualified after FDA warnings on combined use of opioids and benzodiazepines[41]—noting that the combination can result in extreme sleepiness, slowed or difficult breathing, coma, or death.

While FMCSA does not have a definitive list of approved/not approved medications, the FAA recently posted a Do Not Issue/Do Not Fly list (Table 11-3).[28] This list could be used by the examiner as a starting point to determine which medications may present a concern.

TABLE 11-3 FAA Pharmaceuticals (Therapeutic Medications)—Do Not Issue—Do Not Fly

The information in this section is to advise Aviation Medical Examiners (AMEs) about two medication issues:

- Medications for which they should not issue applicants without clearance from the Federal Aviation Administration (FAA), *and*
- Medications for which for which they should advise airmen to not fly and provide additional safety information to the applicant.

The lists of medications in this section are not meant to be all-inclusive or comprehensive, but rather address the most common concerns.

Do Not Issue. AMEs should not issue airmen medical certificates to applicants who are using these medications. If there are any questions, please call the Regional Flight Surgeon's office or the Aerospace Medicine Certification Division.

- Anticholinergics (oral)
- Antiseizure medications, even if used for non-seizure conditions
- Centrally acting antihypertensives, including but not limited to clonidine, reserpine, guanethidine, guanadrel, guanabenz, and methyldopa
- Bromocriptine
- Dopamine agonists used for Parkinson's disease or other medical indications: Pramipexole (Mirapex), ropinirole (Requip) and rotigotine (NeuPro). All carry warnings for suddenly falling asleep during activities of daily living
- Mefloquine (Lariam)

TABLE 11-3 continued

- Over-active bladder medications. Almost all of these medications are antimuscarinic. Antimuscarinic medications carry strong warnings about potential for sedation and impaired cognition
- Varenicline (Chantix)
- An open prescription for regular or intermittent use of any drug or substance classified under the Controlled Substances Act (Schedules I - V).
  — This includes medical marijuana, even if legally allowed or prescribed under state law.
  — Note: exceptions would be for documented temporary use of the drug solely for a medical procedure or for a medical condition, and the medication has been discontinued.
- Most psychiatric or psychotropic medications, including but not limited to antipsychotics, most antidepressants (see SSRI policy), antianxiety drugs, mood stabilizers, attention deficit disorder (ADD) or attention deficit hyperactivity disorder (ADHD) medications, sedative-hypnotics and tranquilizers
- High doses of oral steroids (greater than 20 mg prednisone or prednisone-equivalent per day)
- Agents for treating cancer, including chemotherapeutics, biologics, etc., whether used for induction, "maintenance", or suppressive therapy
- Antiangina medications
- Any medication newly approved by the Food and Drug Administration (FDA) (those drugs issued initial FDA marketing approval within the past 12 months). We require at least one-year of post-marketing experience with a new drug before we will consider whether we can safely certificate an applicant using the drug. New antibiotics, lipid-lowering drugs, and antihypertensive medications can be considered earlier than one year. Please contact the RFS or AMCD for guidance on specific applicants.</TBL>

Do Not Fly. Airmen should not fly while using any of the medications in the Do Not Issue section above or using any of the medications or classes/groups of medications listed below. All of these medications below may cause sedation (drowsiness) or impair cognitive function, seriously degrading pilot performance. This impairment can occur even when the individual feels alert and is apparently functioning normally - in other words, the airman can be "unaware of impair."

For aviation safety, airmen should not fly following the last dose of any of the medications below until a period of time has elapsed equal to:

- 5-times the maximum pharmacologic half-life of the medication; or
- 5-times the maximum hour dose interval if pharmacologic half-life information is not available. For example, there is a 30-hour wait time for a medication that is taken every 4 to 6 hours (5 times 6). </TBL>

Sleep aids. All the currently available sleep aids, both prescription and over-the-counter (OTC), can cause impairment of mental processes and reaction times, even when the individual feels fully awake.

TABLE 11-3 continued

- Wait times for currently available prescription sleep aids
- Diphenhydramine (e.g., Benadryl). Many OTC sleep aids contain diphenhydramine as the active ingredient. The wait time after diphenhydramine is 60 hours (based on maximum pharmacologic half-life).</TBL>

Allergy medications. Antihistamines found in many allergy and other types of medications can cause sedation and may not be used for flight. This applies to nasal formulations as well as oral.

Exception: Nonsedating antihistamines (loratadine, desloratadine, and fexofenadine) may be used while flying, if symptoms are controlled without adverse side effects after an adequate initial trial period.

Label warnings. Airmen should not fly while using any medication, prescription or OTC, that carries a label precaution or warning that **it may cause drowsiness or advises the user "be careful when driving a motor vehicle or operating machinery."** This applies even if label states "until you know how the medication affects you" and even if the airman has used the medication before with no apparent adverse effect. Such medications can cause impairment even when the airman feels alert and unimpaired (see "unaware of impair" above).

"Pre-medication" or "pre-procedure" drugs. This includes all drugs used as an aid to outpatient surgical or dental procedures.

Narcotic pain relievers. This includes but is not limited to morphine, codeine, oxycodone (Percodan; Oxycontin), and hydrocodone (Vicodin, etc.).

Muscle relaxants. This includes but is not limited to carisoprodol (Soma) and cyclobenzaprine (Flexeril).

Over-the-counter active dietary supplements such as Kava-Kava and Valerian

From FAA Guide for Aviation Medical Examiners.[28]

The U.S. Coast Guard's Navigation and Vessel Inspection Circular (NVIC)[42] contains information on medication and medical conditions. They recently updated some sections of NVIC 04-08,[1] including a revised section on medication.

In the update, it is noted that several classes of medications may impair a mariner by causing drowsiness and/or altered cognitive ability, judgment, or reaction time. Mariners who use these medications are subject to further medical review to determine whether their use of the medication is likely to impair their ability to operate safely. If the mariner's medication use is deemed disqualifying by the Coast Guard, then the Coast Guard will determine whether the mariner qualifies for a waiver under 46 CFR 10.303.

A nonexhaustive list of disqualifying or waiverable medications for the Coast Guard can be found in Table 11-4. Intermittent use of these medications generally do not require a waiver; however, mariners are cautioned against acting performing duties while under the influence of medications that can cause drowsiness or impairment or that carry warnings that caution against driving or operating heavy machinery.

TABLE 11-4 Coast Guard's List of Medications Subject to Further Review Due to Risk of Impaired Cognitive Ability, Judgment, or Reaction Time (Adapted from NVIC -4-08)

1. Antidepressants
2. Anti-motion sickness agents
3. Antipsychotics
4. Anticonvulsives, Antiepileptic drugs (medications for treatment of seizures)
5. Antihistamines, allergy medications (nonsedating antihistamines do not require a waiver)
6. Barbiturate medications
7. Benzodiazepine medications
8. Cough and cold medicines (those containing sedating antihistamines or other medicines that can cause drowsiness)
9. Stimulant medications (includes modafinil)
10. Sleep aids
11. Legally prescribed controlled substances
12. Medical use of hallucinogens (examples include, but are not limited to, medical marijuana, nabinol, nabiximols (Sativex), tetrahydrocannabinol, dronabinol (Marinol), Epidiolex, peyote, or Ecstasy. Even if legalized by a state, use of these substances is disqualifying and will **not** be waived under any circumstances.
13. Muscle relaxants

There are several others mentioned that need further review and it is noted that methadone is not waiverable.

After two accidents at Baltimore-Washington International train station, the Federal Transit Administration (FTA) commissioned the creation of a Prescription and Over-the-Counter Tool Kit,[43] which has since been updated. Although intended for the transit industry, the information is relevant to any transportation mode. This kit includes sample policies on the use of medications, training aids, several lists of medications that are permitted (or not permitted) by various federal and private agencies, and an extensive reference list.

This chapter does not discuss the MRO process except where it overlaps with a fitness-for-duty determination. Drug and alcohol testing by the DOT was begun in 1989 and 1994, respectively, after several high-profile accidents in which these substances were implicated as the probable cause. Although the MRO is responsible for determining whether there is a legitimate medical explanation for a laboratory non-negative test result, they currently do not have primary fitness-for-duty responsibility in highway operations. There are several situations in which the MRO's and the examiner's paths may cross, and it is recognized that at times physicians may seem to serve as both MRO and examiner simultaneously or have previously provided MRO services on the same driver for another company. In practice, the two roles should be separate and the physician should "take off one hat and put on the other" when acting as either examiner or MRO.[44] In addition to having knowledge of prior drug test results, an examiner may be aware of medications that could impact a fitness determination. 49 CFR Part 40 (49 CFR Part 40.327)[45] directs the MRO to report information obtained in the verification process to an employer, physician, or other health care provider "responsible for determining the medical qualification of the employee under an applicable DOT agency safety regulation." The September 2001 Q & A issued by the Office of Drug and Alcohol Policy Compliance[46] explains that if the MRO knew the identity of the physician responsible for determining whether the driver was physically qualified under FMCSA regulations for another employer, the MRO could provide the information to that examiner.

The drug testing and examination are totally separate procedures; the only time they might ordinarily be performed at the same office visit would be in the preplacement setting.[47] The employer is responsible for ensuring that a negative drug test result is obtained when required prior to permitting the individual to operate a CMV. Drivers who test positive under the DOT controlled-substance testing regulations[45] must be removed from service until they have completed evaluation, treatment, and return-to-duty testing. Upon returning to service, employers may have them also complete a physical examination.[2]

Additional information on 49 CFR Part 40[45] or 49 CFR Part 382 (the DOT or FMCSA[48] regulations on controlled-substance and alcohol testing, respectively) can be found through the DOT or FMCSA websites.

There are a tremendous number of medications, and more approved regularly, that may cause sedation or other cognitive impairment. For the majority of these, there have not been studies that specifically look at driving risk; therefore, the examiner and treating health care professionals are left to rely on surrogate measures, such as cognitive and psychomotor function. Where both driving and surrogate measures have been assessed, there is not always a consistent relationship between psychomotor impairment and driving impairment. Unlike alcohol, for which there is a direct relationship between blood levels and performance, this has not been clearly demonstrated with medications. With some medication, an individual may develop tolerance, and the greater concern with driving is intermittent use, especially of medications with longer half-lives. Although some medications might not cause impairment as prescribed, an individual frequently will not use a medication as directed—skipping doses, increasing the frequency or dosage, or (as frequently frustrates MROs) using the medication for different reasons than for what the medication was initially intended (e.g., hydrocodone prescribed 6 months earlier for back pain, more recently used for a different musculoskeletal injury without consulting a health care provider). Patients frequently will use multiple potentially impairing medications together, such as pain medications and muscle relaxants, increasing the risk of impairment.

The examiner is in the difficult position of trying to determine whether a particular medication or medications will interfere with a particular driver's performance. Many have utilized questionnaires such as the one proposed by the MRB or have a discussion with the prescribing physician. Whenever possible, the driver should be on medications that do not impair. When new long-term medications are started that carry the warning or precaution against driving or operating heavy machinery, the commercial driver should refrain from driving until aware of how the medication might affect one's abilities to operate their vehicle safely. For acute or intermittent use of medications that might impair, the driver should use only those with shorter half-lives and not while he or she would be pharmacologically active or might be driving.

Examiners and employers should not have blanket exclusions but should review each case on an individual basis, looking at the medications the person might be using, the doses, the frequency, whether chronic or intermittent use (intermittent use has a higher risk of impairment than chronic, stable use, which may still be impairing). Considerations should include both prescription as well as over-the-counter medications and supplements. While medications do contain warning labels, most simply indicate "do not drive or operate heavy machinery until you know how the medication will affect you." In addition, patients often do not read labels or package inserts. Even if it were possible to get drivers and health care providers to read the labels and consider the potential impairment, subjective reports of side effects do not correlate with actual performance decrements.[49]

References

1. Appendix A to Part 391—Medical Advisory Criteria. http://www.ecfr.gov/ cgi-bin/retrieveECFR?gp=1&ty=HTML&h=L&mc=true&=PART&n=pt49.5 .391#ap49.5.391_171.a.

2. Federal Motor Carrier Safety Administration, U.S. Department of Transportation. Guidance for § 391.41: Physical qualifications for drivers. https://www .fmcsa.dot.gov/regulations/title49/section/391.41.

3. Federal Motor Carrier Safety Administration, U.S. Department of Transportation. Frequently Asked Questions—Medical Requirements. https://www.fmcsa .dot.gov/faq/Medical-Requirements.

4. Peña F. Statement on the Use of Proposition 200 and 215, December 12, 1996. Washington, D.C.: U.S. Department of Transportation, Office of the Assistant Secretary of Public Affairs.

5. Federal Motor Carrier Safety Administration, U.S. Department of Transportation. Harmonizing Schedule I Drug Requirements. *Fed Reg.* 77(19);4478–4491. January 30, 2012. https://www.gpo.gov/fdsys/pkg/FR-2012-01-30/pdf/2012 -1905.pdf.

6. Federal Motor Carrier Safety Administration, U.S. Department of Transportation. Driver Medical Requirements, Medication Issues. https://www.fmcsa.dot .gov/medical/driver-medical-requirements/medication-issues.

7. Weiler JM, Bloomfield JR, Woodworth GG, et al. Effects of fexofenadine, diphenhydramine, and alcohol on driving performance: A randomized, placebo-controlled trial in the Iowa Driving Simulator. *Ann Intern Med.* 2000;132:354–363.

8. Moskowitz H, Wilkinson CJ. Antihistamines and driving-related behavior: A review of the evidence for impairment. U.S. Department of Transportation, National Highway Traffic Safety Administration. May 2004. Report No. DOT HS 809 714. http://www.nhtsa.gov/people/injury/research /StateofKnwlegeDrugs/StateofKnwlegeDrugs/index.html.

9. Barbone F, McMahon AD, Davey PG, et al. Association of road-traffic accidents with benzodiazepine use. Lancet. 1998;352:1331–1336.

10. Hemmelgarn B, Suissa S, Huang A, Boivin JF, Pinard G. Benzodiazepine use and the risk of motor vehicle crash in the elderly. *JAMA.* 1997;278:27–31.

11. Verster JC, Volkerts ER, Verbaten MN. Effects of alprazolam on driving ability, memory functioning and psychomotor performance: A randomized, placebo-controlled study. *Neuropsychopharmacology.* 2002;27(2):260–269.

12. Neutel IC. Benzodiazepine-related traffic accidents in young and elderly patients. *Human Psychopharmacology.* 1998;13:S115–S124.

13. Dobbs BM. Medical Conditions and Driving: A Review of the Literature (1960–2000). U.S. Department of Transportation, National Highway Traffic Safety Administration. September 2005. http://icsw.nhtsa.gov/people/injury /research/Medical_Condition_Driving/.

14. LeRoy AA, Lee M, Morse ML. Multiple Medications and Vehicle Crashes: Analysis of Databases. May 2008. U.S. Department of Transportation, National Highway Traffic Safety Administration. www.nhtsa.gov/DOT/NHTSA/Traffic%20Injury%20Control/Articles/Associated%20Files/810858.pdf

15. Leung SY. Benzodiazepines, opioids and driving: an overview of the experimental research. *Drug Alcohol Rev.* 2011 May;30(3):281-6

16. Mailis-Gagnon A, Lakha SF, Furlan A, et al. Systematic review of the quality and generalizability of studies on the effects of opioids on driving and cognitive/psychomotor performance. *Clinical Journal of Pain.* 2012;28(6):542–555.

17. Rudisill TM, Zhu M, Kelley GA, et al. Medication use and the risk of motor vehicle collisions among licensed drivers: A systematic review. *Accid Anal Prev.* 2016;96:255–70.

18. Hels T, Lyckegaard A, Simonsen KW, Steentoft A, Bernhoft IM. Risk of severe driver injury by driving with psychoactive substances. *Accid Anal Prev.* 2013;59:346–356.

19. Hegmann KT, Weiss MS, Bowden K, et al. ACOEM Practice Guidelines: Opioids and Safety-Sensitive Work. *JOEM.* 2014;56(7): e46–53.

20. U.S. Food and Drug Administration. FDA Requests Label Change for All Sleep Disorder Drug Products. March 14, 2007. http://www.fda.gov/NewsEvents/Newsroom/PressAnnouncements/2007/ucm108868.htm.

21. Menzin J, Lang K, Levy P, Levy E. A general model of the effects of sleep medications on the risk and cost of motor vehicle accidents and its application to France. *Pharmacoeconomics.* 2001;19:69–78.

22. U.S. Food and Drug Administration. Drug Safety Communication: FDA approves new label changes and dosing for zolpidem products and a recommendation to avoid driving the day after using Ambien CR. 5/14/13. http://www.fda.gov/drugs/drugsafety/ucm352085.htm

23. U.S. Food and Drug Administration. Drug Safety Communication: FDA warns of next-day impairment with sleep aid Lunesta (eszopiclone) and lowers recommended dose. 5/15/14. http://www.fda.gov/Drugs/DrugSafety/ucm397260.htm.

24. Frucht S, Rogers JD, Greene PE, Gordon MF, Fahn S. Falling asleep at the wheel: Motor vehicle mishaps in persons taking pramipexole and ropinirole. *Neurology.* 1999;52:1908–1910.

25. Requip (ropinirole hydrochloride) Tablets Prescribing Information. http://www.accessdata.fda.gov/drugsatfda_docs/label/2008/020658s018s020s021lbl.pdf.

26. National Transportation Safety Board. Safety Recommendation. Public Meeting: Safety Recommendations to be Issued to the DOT and Other Agencies Concerning the Use of Medications by Vehicle Operators, January 5, 2000. http://www.ntsb.gov/safety/safety-recs/recletters/I00_1_4.pdf.

27. Institute for Safe Medication Practices. Strong Safety Signal Seen for New Varenicline Risks. http://www.ismp.org/quarterwatch/chantixReport.asp.

28. Federal Aviation Administration, U.S. Department of Transportation. FAA Guide for Aviation Medical Examiners. Pharmaceuticals (Therapeutic Medications). FAA Do Not Issue, Do Not Fly. http://www.faa.gov/about/office_org/headquarters_offices/avs/offices/aam/ame/guide/pharm/dni_dnf/.

29. U.S. Food and Drug Administration. Chantix and Zyban to Get Boxed Warning on Serious Mental Health Events. www.fda.gov/ForConsumers/ ConsumerUpdates/ucm170356.htm.

30. U.S. Food and Drug Administration. Drug Safety Communication: FDA revises description of mental health side effects of the stop-smoking medicines Chantix (varenicline) and Zyban (bupropion) to reflect clinical trial findings. http://www.fda.gov/Drugs/DrugSafety/ucm532221.htm.

31. CDME Review – Suboxone – Current Guidance from FMCSA Spring 2013.

32. Federal Motor Carrier Safety Administration, U.S. Department of Transportation. Medical Examiner Handbook, currently in the process of revision. https://www.fmcsa.dot.gov/regulations/medical/fmcsa-medical-examiner -handbook.

33. Hartenbaum NP, Holland M, Osbahr A, Riba M, Swotinsky R. Expert Panel Commentary and Recommendations: Licit Schedule II Drug Use and Commercial Motor Vehicle Driver Safety. www.mrb.fmcsa.dot.gov/documents/Schedule _II_Commentary.pdf.

34. Federal Motor Carrier Safety Administration, U.S. Department of Transportation. Summary for the April 25, 2007 Medical Review Board Public Meeting. https://www.fmcsa.dot.gov/regulations/medical/summary-april-25-2007 -medical-review-board-public-meeting.

35. Federal Motor Carrier Safety Administration, U.S. Department of Transportation. Schedule II Opioids and Stimulants & CMV Crash Risk and Driver Performance: Evidence Report and Systematic Review. Final Report March 21, 2014. https://www.fmcsa.dot.gov/schedule-ii-evidence.

36. Federal Motor Carrier Safety Administration, U.S. Department of Transportation. Medical Review Board (MRB) Meeting Topics. https://www.fmcsa.dot.gov /medical-review-board-mrb-meeting-topics.

37. Federal Motor Carrier Safety Administration, U.S. Department of Transportation. Final MRB-MCSAC Task 14-3 Report: Schedule II Medications. https://www.fmcsa.dot.gov/advisory-committees/mcsac/final-mrb-mcsac-task -14-3-report-schedule-ii-medications.

38. Federal Motor Carrier Safety Administration, U.S. Department of Transportation. 391.41 CMV Driver Medication Form. Notice and request for comments. *Fed Reg.* 2015;80(227): 73871–73874. http://www.gpo.gov/fdsys/pkg/FR-2015 -11-25/pdf/2015-30134.pdf.

39. Centers for Disease Control and Prevention. CDC Guideline for Prescribing Opioids for Chronic Pain — United States, 2016. *MMWR.* 2016; 65(1);1–49. http://www.cdc.gov/mmwr/volumes/65/rr/rr6501e1.htm.

40. Centers for Disease Control and Prevention. Calculating Total Daily Dose of Opioids for Safer Dosage. https://www.cdc.gov/drugoverdose/pdf/calculating _total_daily_dose-a.pdf

41. U.S. Food and Drug Administration. FDA requires strong warnings for opioid analgesics, prescription opioid cough products, and benzodiazepine labeling related to serious risks and death from combined use. August 31, 2016. http://www.fda.gov/NewsEvents/Newsroom/PressAnnouncements/ucm518697 .htm.

42. U.S. Department of Homeland Security, U.S. Coast Guard. Navigation And Vessel Inspection NVIC NO. 04-08, Medical and Physical Evaluation Guidelines For Merchant Mariner Credentials. https://www.uscg.mil/hq/cg5/nvic/pdf/2008/NVIC_04-08.pdf.

43. Federal Transit Administration, U.S. Department of Transportation. Prescription and Over the Counter Medications Tool Kit Updated February 2012. https://transit-safety.fta.dot.gov/DrugAndAlcohol/Publications/Documents/substance/RxOTC/RxOTC_April2011_Feb2012_Update.pdf

44. Hartenbaum NP. MROs, medical examiner and positive drug tests. *CDME Rev.* 2005.

45. U.S. Department of Transportation, Office of the Secretary. Procedures for Transportation Workplace Drug and Alcohol Testing Programs. Overview of 49CFR Part 40. https://www.transportation.gov/odapc/part40

46. Office of Drug and Alcohol Policy Compliance. Part 40 Questions and Answers, September 2001. https://www.transportation.gov/sites/dot.dev/files/docs/01_Part_40_QA.pdf.

47. Commercial driver's license program and controlled substances and alcohol use and testing—Conforming and technical amendments. *Fed Reg* 1997;62(July 11):37150–37153.

48. Controlled substances and alcohol use and testing. 49 CFR Part 382. Federal Motor Carrier Safety Administration, http://www.ecfr.gov/cgi-bin/retrieveECFR?gp=1&ty=HTML&h=L&mc=true&=PART&n=pt49.5.382

49. U.S. Food and Drug Administration. 01N-0397: Transportation Safety and Potentially Sedating or Impairing Medications [Transcripts Only]. https://www.fda.gov/ohrms/dockets/dockets/01n0397/01N-0397_tr00002_111501.htm and https://www.fda.gov/ohrms/dockets/dockets/01n0397/01N-0397_tr00001_111401.htm.

PART III

Commercial Drivers' Health

CHAPTER 12

Commercial Drivers' Health

NATALIE P. HARTENBAUM, MD, MPH, FACOEM

> As significant changes occur, they will be noted at the end of each chapter in the online version of this book at least twice a year.

Similar to many occupations, operating a commercial motor vehicle (CMV) has a unique set of occupational hazards. In addition to the obvious risk from motor vehicle crashes, drivers' exposures and hazards include ergonomic hazards, exposure to diesel exhaust, noise, long hours, and a challenging lifestyle to maintain good health. Their lifestyle, unique set of stressors, and exposures can lead to an increased incidence of many chronic diseases. There is an increasing focus on driver's health and well-being, especially on fatigue and medical conditions that can lead to fatigue or impairment. This chapter is not meant to serve as an exhaustive review of driver health, but rather to provide background information and resources for those that are seeking additional information. As new reports become available, they will be noted in the online version of this book.

It is important to remember that the professional driver has many tasks beyond entering the vehicle and steering. The Federal Motor Carrier Safety Administration (FMCSA) had provided a very detailed description of the many factors that may affect a driver's health on the prior medical examination form.

> *Responsibilities, work schedules, physical and emotional demands, and lifestyles among commercial drivers vary by the type of driving that they do. Some of the main types of drivers include the following: turn around or short relay (drivers return to their home base each evening); long relay (drivers drive 9–11 hours and then have at least a 10-hour off-duty period); straight through haul (cross country drivers); and team drivers*

(drivers share the driving by alternating their 5-hour driving periods and 5-hour rest periods).

The following factors may be involved in a driver's performance of duties: abrupt schedule changes and rotating work schedules, which may result in irregular sleep patterns and a driver beginning a trip in a fatigued condition; long hours; extended time away from family and friends, which may result in lack of social support; tight pickup and delivery schedules, with irregularity in work, rest, and eating patterns; adverse road, weather, and traffic conditions, which may cause delays and lead to hurriedly loading or unloading cargo in order to compensate for the lost time; and environmental conditions such as excessive vibration, noise, and extremes in temperature. Transporting passengers or hazardous materials may add to the demands on the commercial driver.

There may be duties in addition to the driving task for which a driver is responsible and needs to be fit. Some of these responsibilities are: coupling and uncoupling trailer(s) from the tractor, loading and unloading trailer(s) (sometimes a driver may lift a heavy load or unload as much as 50,000 lbs. of freight after sitting for a long period of time without any stretching period); inspecting the operating condition of tractor and/or trailer(s) before, during and after delivery of cargo; lifting, installing, and removing heavy tire chains; and lifting heavy tarpaulins to cover open top trailers. The above tasks demand agility, the ability to bend and stoop, the ability to maintain a crouching position to inspect the underside of the vehicle, frequent entering and exiting of the cab, and the ability to climb ladders on the tractor and/or trailer(s).

In addition, a driver must have the perceptual skills to monitor a sometimes complex driving situation, the judgment skills to make quick decisions, when necessary, and the manipulative skills to control an oversize steering wheel, shift gears using a manual transmission, and maneuver a vehicle in crowded areas.

Another description of the standard skills required of a tractor-trailer operator, which was developed by the Professional Truck Driver Institute, includes the basic skills needed for tractor-trailer drivers[1] (Table 12-1).

It is estimated in 2014 that there were around 3,025.7 billion vehicle miles traveled (VMT) by all motor vehicles with large trucks traveling 279.1 billion of those miles (9.2 percent of the total), and buses traveling 16.0 billion of those miles (0.5 percent). There are several estimates of the number of licensed commercial motor vehicle operators but in 2014 this was estimated to be around 6 million.[2]

TABLE 12-1 Primary Function/Duties: Commercial Motor Vehicle Operator

1. Read and Interpret Control Systems
2. Perform Vehicle Inspections
3. Exercise Basic Control
4. Execute Shifting
5. Back and Dock CMV
6. Couple Trailer
7. Uncouple Trailer
8. Perform Visual Search
9. Manage and Adjust Vehicle Speed
10. Manage and Adjust Vehicle Space Relations
11. Check and Maintain Vehicle Systems and Components
12. Diagnose and Report Malfunctions
13. Identify Potential Driving Hazards and Perform Emergency Maneuvers
14. Identify and Adjust to Difficult and Extreme Driving Conditions
15. Handle and Document Cargo
16. Address Accident Scenes and Reporting Procedures
17. Address Environmental Issues
18. Plan Trips/Make Appropriate Decisions
19. Use Effective Communications
20. Manage Personal Resources While on the Road
21. Record and Maintain Hours of Service Requirements</TBL>

From Professional Truck Driver Institute[1]

In 2014, 3,978 large trucks and buses were involved in fatal crashes, a 5% decrease from 2013.[3] The Occupational Safety and Health Administration (OSHA) reports that there are roughly 475,000 large trucks with a gross vehicle weight rating of more than 10,000 pounds involved in crashes that result in approximately 5,360 fatalities and 142,000 injuries each year. Of the fatalities, about 74% were occupants of other vehicles (usually passenger cars), 3% were pedestrians, and 23% were occupants of large trucks.[4]

FMCSA and the National Highway Traffic Safety Administration (NHTSA) conduct an ongoing Large Truck Crash Causation Study (LTCCS) evaluating factors that contributed to crashes. Many of the factors had little to do with driver health. They found that between 2012 and 2014, only 3.9% of drivers of large trucks had at least one driver impairment–related factor (distraction was included in a different analysis).[3] Of the 3,697 drivers of large trucks involved in fatalities in this dataset, the most common factor was asleep or fatigued (Table 12-2).[5]

TABLE 12-2 Driver Impairment-Related Factors 2014

Factor	Percent
Asleep or Fatigued	1.8%
Under the Influence of Alcohol, Drugs, or Medication	1.0%
Ill, Blackout	0.5%
Other Physical Impairment	0.2%
Physical Impairment, No Details	0.2%
Emotional (Depressed, Angry, Disturbed, etc.)	0.1%
Deaf	0.0%
Blind	0.0%
At Least One Driver Impairment–Related Factor Recorded	3.9%
No Driver Impairment–Related Factors Recorded	96.1%
Total	**100.**

From Large Truck and Bus Crash Facts 2014[3]

Many of the injuries that drivers sustained are similar to those suffered by the general working population, with about 50% of injuries being sprains and strains; bruises, fractures, cuts and lacerations, soreness and pain, and multiple traumatic injuries are the other common injuries. Causes include overexertion, contact with object, being struck by an object, falling (on the same level), and transportation accidents.[4]

Structure of the Trucking System

The North American Industry Classification System (NCAIS) at the Bureau of Labor Statistics (BLS) places this industry in the transportation and warehousing sector and subdivides it further into general freight trucking and specialized freight trucking based on differences in equipment used, type of load carried, scheduling, terminal, and other networking services. General freight transportation establishments handle a wide variety of general commodities, generally palletized, and are transported in a container or van trailer. Specialized freight transportation is the transportation of cargo that—because of size, weight, shape, or other inherent characteristics—requires specialized equipment for transportation. Specialized freight includes military materials, construction machinery, steel, oversize or overweight goods, and hazardous materials (hazmat). The most common specialized vehicle is the tank truck, which may haul liquid or dry products such as petroleum products; food products; chemicals; and intermediate products such as paints, solvents, and cement.

The BLS reports only consider the "for-hire" trucking operations, not the "in-house" operations, trucks used by companies whose primary business is in other industries, but which run "in-house" trucking operations. These "private carriers" move freight owned by that company. These trucks are registered with FMCSA and would be included in their reports.[6]

The industry can also be divided by geographic scope, either long-distance or local (see discussion on intrastate versus interstate in Chapter 3). Another consideration is by size of each shipment. The smallest are the parcel carriers (United States Postal Service [USPS], United Parcel Service [UPS], FedEx). They would carry loads with weights from letter size up to 150 pounds, but with an average typically less than 50 pounds. The next group would be the less-than-truckload (LTL) with an average weight typically around 1,000 pounds. Both parcel and LTL operations would generally involve local terminals. Truckload (TL) carriers move freight with an average weight of 20,000 to 35,000 pounds.[6] Additional information on the trucking industry can be found in the Transportation Research Circular — Trucking 101.[6]

A majority of drivers are employees, including a small number of owner-drivers who consider themselves as "employed" by motor carriers. They may operate under permanent contracts with motor carriers to which they lease their trucks. Some are true owner-operators or subcontractors but many are dependent contractors.[6] True owner-operators own their vehicle and operate under their own authority, locating their own freight and managing their own financial and operational affairs. A dependent contractor operates under another motor carrier's authority. This distinction has led to a number of legal actions.

An estimate of average earnings of those in the trucking industry (as defined by NCAIS) can be found in Table 12-3.

TABLE 12-3 Earnings by Occupation in Transportation

Data series	Wages, 2015			
	Hourly		Annual	
	Median	Mean	Median	Mean
Bus and truck mechanics and diesel engine specialists	19.54	20.12	40,650	41,850
First-line supervisors/managers of transportation and material-moving machine and vehicle operators	26.87	28.02	55,880	58,280
Laborers and freight, stock, and material movers, hand	13.49	14.52	28,060	30,200
Truck drivers, heavy and tractor-trailer	20.14	20.87	41,900	43,410
Truck drivers, light or delivery services	15.67	17.46	32,590	36,320

From Bureau of Labor Statistics (BLS) Truck Transportation[7]

Equipment

There are many types of trucks a driver may operate. They can be straight or articulated. A straight truck is one that has the engine, cab, and cargo space built on a single chassis, or frame, regardless of the number of wheels. An articulated vehicle consists of a power unit, the tractor, and one to three attached trailers. Vehicles can be designed for specific tasks, such as to carry liquids or gases, cargo, bottles, livestock, refrigerated cargo, or other specific material. The U.S. Department of Transportation (DOT) classified trucks by gross vehicle weight rating (GVWR; Table 12-4).

TABLE 12-4 Classification of Truck by Size

- Class 1: GVWR ranges from 0 to 6,000 pounds (0 to 2,722 kg)
- Class 2: GVWR ranges from 6,001 to 10,000 pounds (2,722–4,536 kg)
- Class 3: GVWR ranges from 10,001 to 14,000 pounds (4,536–6,350 kg)
- Class 4: GVWR ranges from 14,001 to 16,000 pounds (6,351–7,257 kg)
- Class 5: GVWR ranges from 16,001 to 19,500 pounds (7,258–8,845 kg)
- Class 6: GVWR ranges from 19,501 to 26,000 pounds (8,846–11,793 kg)
- Class 7: GVWR ranges from 26,001 to 33,000 pounds (11,794–14,969 kg)
- Class 8: GVWR is anything above 33,000 pounds (14,969 kg)

GVWR = gross vehicle weight rating.

Schedules

Typical work schedules vary. Hours can be long and are often unpredictable. On turnaround or short relay trips, drivers may drive 4 to 5 hours, leave the truck they have driven, and return in another vehicle. On long relays, a driver will drive up to 11 hours, take a 10-hour break, and then return. Straight-through hauling is often cross-country, with 11 hours of driving and 10-hour rest stops. Drivers may drive as part of a team and utilize a sleeper berth for part or all of their sleep. Straight-haul and sleeper-haul drivers often are on the road for days to weeks.

A significant factor affecting a driver's schedule is the Hours of Service (HOS)[8,9] regulations which have gone through several revisions and challenges. The current HOS[10] standard was published in 2011, with a compliance date of July 1, 2013. One issue, the 34-hour restart, was placed on hold until the Secretary submits the CMV Driver Restart Study final report to Congress[11] which was done late 2016. Based on that report, neither the requirement of two off-duty periods between 1:00 a.m. to 5:00 a.m. nor the once-per-week limit on use of the restart will be enforced. The current HOS requirements can be found in Table 12-5 (see following page).

Health Issues

Several Medical Review Board (MRB) or Motor Carrier Safety Advisory Committee (MCSAC) meetings since September 2015[12] have included Driver Health and Wellness as a key topic. Reports on driver health, examples of successful programs, and useful resources can be found in the meeting materials.

In 2014, the National Institute for Occupational Safety and Health (NIOSH) conducted a national survey of long-haul truck driver health and injury.[13] Among the key findings were that, compared to the national working population, truck drivers had the following:

- Prevalence of obesity twice as high
- Prevalence of morbid obesity twice as high
- Prevalence of current cigarette smoking more than double
- Prevalence of self-reported diabetes elevated

They also found that just over 25% reported having hypertension, with 86% reporting a body mass index (BMI) above 30 and 17% reporting a BMI above 40. Over half were smokers and 73% reported getting at least 6 hours of sleep per 24 hours, 22% indicating they obtained at least 8 hours of sleep per 24 hours. When looking at risk factors of hypertension, obesity, and smoking, 88% had at least one risk factor

TABLE 12-5 Hours-of-Service Rules

PROPERTY-CARRYING DRIVERS	PASSENGER-CARRYING DRIVERS
11-Hour Driving Limit May drive a maximum of 11 hours after 10 consecutive hours off duty.	**10-Hour Driving Limit** May drive a maximum of 10 hours after 8 consecutive hours off duty.
14-Hour Limit May not drive beyond the 14th consecutive hour after coming on duty, following 10 consecutive hours off duty. Off-duty time does not extend the 14-hour period.	**15-Hour Limit** May not drive after having been on duty for 15 hours, following 8 consecutive hours off duty. Off-duty time is not included in the 15-hour period.
Rest Breaks May drive only if 8 hours or less have passed since end of driver's last off-duty or sleeper berth period of at least 30 minutes. Does not apply to drivers using either of the short-haul exceptions in 395.1(e) [49 CFR 397.5 mandatory "in attendance" time may be included in break if no other duties performed].	**60/70-Hour Limit** May not drive after 60/70 hours on duty in 7/8 consecutive days.
60/70-Hour Limit May not drive after 60/70 hours on duty in 7/8 consecutive days. A driver may restart a 7/8 consecutive day period after taking 34 or more consecutive hours off duty.	
Sleeper Berth Provision Drivers using the sleeper berth provision must take at least 8 consecutive hours in the sleeper berth, plus a separate 2 consecutive hours either in the sleeper berth, off duty, or any combination of the two.	**Sleeper Berth Provision** Drivers using a sleeper berth must take at least 8 hours in the sleeper berth, and may split the sleeper berth time into two periods provided neither is less than 2 hours.

but only 9% had all three. With the health issues identified, over twice as many truck drivers than the working population reported not being covered by health insurance or a health care plan.

Other risks identified in an older review included the following observations.[14]

1. Lung cancer can likely be caused by exposure to diesel exhaust, and the longer that exposure lasts, the more likely it is that a cancer will develop. It is likely that there is also a relationship between diesel exhaust and bladder cancer, but this finding is less robust.

2. There is some evidence that cardiovascular disease is caused in part by truck driving. Risk increases with the duration of driving and disruption of sleep cycle.
3. Noise-induced hearing loss may be the result of a lifetime working as a commercial driver.
4. There is likely a causative relationship between professional driving and vertebral disorders. This may be due to whole body vibration, but this relationship could not be established based on published literature.
5. It is suggested that there is a causal relationship between commercial driving and other musculoskeletal disorders, but this too was not proven in the literature.
6. An increase in gastrointestinal (GI) symptoms has been documented in drivers; however, there was insufficient evidence to implicate circadian disruption and varying shift assignments.
7. The literature suggests, but does not establish, that disruption of circadian rhythm may have negative impacts on the general health of workers. Drivers may experience an improvement in subjective health complaints if stabilized to a day schedule, but this does not occur if stabilized to night or evening schedules.
8. There was no definitive information concerning (a) the relationship between reproductive health and duration of driving, (b) the effects of prolonged work hours, or (c) increasing driving from 10 to 11 hours while decreasing overall work time from 15 to 14 hours on the general health of workers.

Fatigue

Fatigue is one area that has had a lot of attention in the trucking industry over the past decade and is not covered in other chapters of this book. Multiple attempts to "fix" the HOS regulations have met with challenges. The one thing that appears obvious is that there is not a one-size-fits-all solution to the fatigue problem. Fatigue is a significant issue in the life of the trucker. The Truck Driver Fatigue Management Survey,[15] conducted by FMCSA, found that 51% to 65% of drivers reported having experienced yawning, feeling drowsy, eyelids heavy, feeling sleepy, and struggling to be alert while driving. Many less-reported serious driving consequences from drowsiness include nodding off or falling asleep (13%), having a near miss (9%), running off the road (6%), or colliding with something (3%). There also appears to be a relationship between obesity, fatigue, and fatigue-related crashes.[16,17] One of the interesting findings is that there is a large inter individual difference in susceptibility to fatigue.[18]

Drivers will use many different techniques to manage their fatigue both on and off the job. Off the job, they will try to "get a good night's sleep," although for many this is not possible or effective. On the job, some of the activities they would engage in while driving included stretching/changing positions, adjusting ventilation, having a caffeinated drink, listening to music or the radio, talking on the cell phone or CB radio, or eating while driving.[15]

One of most comprehensive reviews of driver fatigue was recently published by the National Academy of Science (NAS).[19]

Key conclusions from the summary of that report are:

Conclusion 1: Insufficient sleep can increase the risk of developing various health problems, including obesity, diabetes, hypertension, and cardiovascular disease, all of which can impact an operator's level of alertness while driving and potentially impact crash risk.

Conclusion 2: Based on the evidence on drivers who are not commercial motor vehicle drivers, obstructive sleep apnea is known to increase crash risk, and there is no evidence base or compelling reason for thinking that the same would not also be true among commercial motor vehicle drivers.

Conclusion 3: Better understanding is needed of the effects of treating obstructive sleep apnea in commercial motor vehicle drivers with positive airway pressure (PAP) therapy with respect to the amount and quality of sleep they obtain and their cognition and driver performance following PAP treatment sessions.

Conclusion 5: Substantial data gaps limit understanding of factors that impact the health and wellness of commercial motor vehicle drivers. Closing these gaps would aid greatly in developing a better understanding of drivers' current status and long-term prospects with respect to health and wellness.

Conclusion 8: Insufficient information exists on (1) how the variety of fatigue management and health and wellness management programs available have been designed, (2) whether drivers/employers actually adhere to these programs, and (3) whether these programs are effective in achieving their goals.

Conclusion 10: There is no biological substitute for sufficient sleep.

Conclusion 12: Despite almost three decades of research on the topic, technological innovations for detecting driver fatigue in near real time and operational strategies for their use are still in the early phases of understanding and application.

Conclusion 13: Biomathematical models can be useful for the development of general work–rest schedules. However, existing models do not account for individual variation, so care must be taken in applying them to address likely impacts of irregular work schedules.

Although participants in the NAS panels were able to reach some conclusions, they still believed that the following research needs should be evaluated prior to modifying existing requirements on fatigue and driver health.

- How much sleep do typical CMV drivers need to maintain suitable sustained levels of alertness and to avoid being drowsy to the point of driving while impaired?
- To what extent would any proposed change in HOS regulations affect the amount of sleep obtained by CMV drivers in different industry sectors?
- What degree of hypopnea (severity level of obstructive sleep apnea [OSA]) results in enough sleep loss to increase the risk of crashes for CMV drivers?
- To what extent does regular use of positive airway pressure (PAP) and related OSA treatment technologies and measures mitigate that increased risk?
- To what extent are various collision avoidance and driver fatigue alert technologies (both in-vehicle technologies and infrastructure measures such as roadway rumble strips) useful for reducing the risk of crashes?
- What substances, if any, reduce impairment due to sleep insufficiency?
- To what extent is chronic sleep deprivation related to an increased risk of developing health threats or various medical conditions?
- To what extent do CMV drivers, their employers, corporate officials, fleet supervisors, safety and risk managers, and drivers' families make use of the North American Fatigue Management Program (NAFMP) materials on the Internet?
- To what extent do fatigue awareness training and fatigue management initiatives result in behavioral improvements in CMV drivers?

An underutilized tool that could assist trucking companies in addressing fatigue is the North American Fatigue Management Program.[20] A joint project of FMCSA and Transport Canada, the NAFMP is an interactive web-based educational and training program developed to provide commercial truck and bus drivers and carriers with an awareness of the factors contributing to fatigue and its impact on performance and safety.

The NAFMP provides:

- Information on how to develop a corporate culture that facilitates reduced driver fatigue;
- Fatigue management education for drivers, drivers' families, carrier executives and managers, shippers/receivers and dispatchers;
- Information on sleep disorders, screening and treatment;
- Driver and trip scheduling information; and,
- Information on Fatigue Management Technologies.

There are also ten educational modules with a different target audience ranging in duration from 30 minutes to 3.5 hours (Table 12-6).

TABLE 12-6 Complete Module Overview—North American Fatigue Management Program

Module	Title	Target Audience
1	FMP Introduction and Overview	Motor Carrier Executives and Managers
2	Safety Culture and Management Practices	Motor Carrier Executives and Managers
3	Driver Education	Commercial Drivers
4	Driver Family Education	Driver Spouses and Family
5	Train-the-Trainer for Driver Education and Family Forum	Carrier Safety Managers and Other Trainers
6	Shippers and Receivers	Freight Shippers and Receivers
7	Motor Carrier Sleep Disorders Management	Carrier Executives and Managers
8	Driver Sleep Disorders Management	Commercial Drivers
9	Driver Scheduling and Tools	Dispatchers and Driver Managers*
10	Fatigue Monitoring and Management Technologies	Motor Carrier Executives and Managers

FMP = Fatigue Management Program.

*Can also be considered an advanced module for drivers

Stakeholders, including those in Table 12-7, can go directly to those components of the tool that relate to them.

TABLE 12-7 Stakeholders

- Motor Carrier Executives and Managers
- Safety Managers and Other Trainers
- Dispatchers and Driver Managers
- Commercial Drivers
- Driver Spouses and Family
- Freight Shippers and Receivers

Another fatigue management tool was produced through sponsorship of the Federal Transit Administration, Toolbox for Transit Operator Fatigue.[21] This includes an overview of sleep, fatigue, and alertness, and discusses the physiologic principles of sleep and fatigue, concerns such as drugs and nutrition that affect alertness, and the performance consequences of fatigue in the workplace. The main portion of this document describes how to implement a fatigue management program and has tools that can be used for education, process tools that can be used to identify and correct conditions that can lead to operator fatigue, and countermeasures that can be used to offset the consequences of fatigue during work time.

One additional resource that can provide information on Fatigue Management Programs is the Fatigue Management in the Workplace report from the American College of Occupational and Environmental Medicine (ACOEM).[22]

Improving Driver Health

There are many reasons why a carrier may undertake a health or wellness program for its drivers. Many may look at this as a way to improve the likelihood that the driver will pass the medical examination. Others may be looking to improve performance, decrease the risk of crash or workers compensation costs, decrease overall health care costs, or ideally just to have healthier employees. These programs can work but only if many key issues are considered. A one-size-fits-all program will not work for all, as it is important to consider the size of the company, whether the drivers are centralized or dispersed, as well as the rate of turnover and trust for the employer and the commitment of the management. The trucker lifestyle can make these programs challenging.

They may have irregular schedules and opportunity for sleep. They may have limited access to healthy food or limited ability to engage in a regular exercise program. A 2007 report provided a review of literature available at that time on truck and motorcoach driver health issues; it described elements of employee health and wellness programs that could be used for commercial drivers and presented case studies of a few companies that had already implemented employee health and wellness programs.[23]

The FMCSA's MRB and MCSAC were tasked with identifying methods for the agency and its stakeholders to improve the health of CMV operators.[24] They were asked to focus on five areas: work conditions, diet and exercise, sleep and fatigue, personal injury, and lifestyle choices. Recommendations were sought on behaviors or activities that could be done before, during, or after work to make lasting improvements (Task 15-3). A subcommittee prepared recommendations and ideas for the development of a driver wellness website, which can be found in their discussion notes.[24]

The Owner Operator Independent Driver Association (OOIDA) Foundation[25] recently identified 12 challenges that face drivers and can lead to difficulties in implementing a wellness program:

- Hours-of-service regulations
- Pay by the mile
- Lack of parking facilities
- Poor food choices available at truck stops
- Scheduling problems
- Long hours
- Delays at loading docks
- Proper sleep
- Available health care
- Prolonged sitting
- Intermittent intense exercise during loading, tarping, tying down, and so on
- Vibration

They also identified keys to a successful program:

- The program must be customized to meet the individual's needs.
- Steps within the program must be incremental.
- There needs to be a feeling of anonymity, in which the driver feels free to discuss and openly express concerns.

- There needs to be accessible avenue to obtain information from just about anywhere the driver might be.
- Accessible professional information and advice.
- Ongoing monitoring of program and participation.
- Minimal cost.

There are several programs available. They may include health screening, seminars, coaching, or onsite fitness centers. Some are broad and others focus on specific health concerns, such as smoking, obesity, hypertension, or sleep apnea.

Given the diverse and mobile nature of the industry, many of the programs are online.[26-29] One focuses on medications and allows truckers to enter the names of medications they are taking—including prescription, over-the-counter, or supplements—and provides the driver with information on medication or food interactions and other driver warnings.[30]

Conclusion

Although many advances have been made in recognizing issues in driver health and safety, there are still many questions that remain. It is important that, as new or modified requirements in driver fitness and fatigue are formulated, they be based on a research-oriented understanding of the costs and benefits, recognizing that obtaining zero risk may not be attainable at an acceptable cost (whether financial or ensuring sufficient personnel to support the industry that is already facing a shortage of drivers). With any medical treatment or test, there is always a risk; the goal is to find that acceptable risk based on evidence, not gut feelings.

References

1. Professional Truck Driver Institute. Skill standards for entry-level tractor-trailer drivers. http://www.ptdi.org/errata/SKILL%20STANDARDS%20ENTRY%20LEVEL%20021517.pdf.
2. Federal Motor Carrier Safety Administration, U.S. Department of Transportation. 2016 Pocket Guide to Large Truck and Bus Statistics. https://ntl.bts.gov/lib/59000/59100/59189/2016_Pocket_Guide_to_Large_Truck_and_Bus_Statistics.pdf.
3. Federal Motor Carrier Safety Administration, U.S. Department of Transportation. Large Truck and Bus Crash Facts 2014. https://www.fmcsa.dot.gov/safety/data-and-statistics/large-truck-and-bus-crash-facts-2014.

4. Occupational Safety and Health Administration, U.S. Department of Labor. Safety and Health Topics—Trucking Industry. https://www.osha.gov/SLTC /trucking_industry/safetyinfo.html.

5. Federal Motor Carrier Safety Administration, U.S. Department of Transportation. Motor Carrier Safety Progress Report (as of September-30-2016). https://www.fmcsa.dot.gov/content/motor-carrier-safety-progress-report -september-30-2016.

6. Transportation Research Board of the National Academies. Transportation Research Circular Number E-C146 December 2010. Trucking 101: An Industry Primer. http://onlinepubs.trb.org/onlinepubs/circulars/ec146.pdf.

7. Bureau of Labor Statistics, U.S. Department of Labor. Truck Transportation: NAICS 484. https://www.bls.gov/iag/tgs/iag484.htm

8. Federal Motor Carrier Safety Administration, U.S. Department of Transportation. Hours of Service of Drivers. https://www.fmcsa.dot.gov/regulations/hours -service/hours-service-drivers.

9. Federal Motor Carrier Safety Administration, U.S. Department of Transportation. Hours of Service: Who Must Comply? https://www.fmcsa.dot.gov /regulations/hours-of-service

10. Federal Motor Carrier Safety Administration, U.S. Department of Transportation. Hours or Service of Drivers; Final Rule. *Fed Reg.* 76(248); 81134 – 81188. December 27, 2011. https://www.fmcsa.dot.gov/regulations/rulemaking/2011 -32696.

11. Federal Motor Carrier Safety Administration, U.S. Department of Transportation. Hours of Service. *Fed Reg.* 79(245);76241–76242. December 22, 2014. https://www.fmcsa.dot.gov/regulations/hours-service/hours-service-drivers.

12. Federal Motor Carrier Safety Administration, U.S. Department of Transportation. Medical Review Board (MRB) Meeting Topics. Updated 2017. https://www .fmcsa.dot.gov/medical-review-board-mrb-meeting-topics.

13. Sieber WK, Robinson CF, Birdsey J, Chen GX, Hitchcock EM, et al. Obesity and other risk factors: The National Survey of U.S. Long-Haul Truck Driver Health and Injury. *Am J Ind Med.* 2014 Jun; 57(6):615–626. Summary of findings at https://www.fmcsa.dot.gov/sites/fmcsa.dot.gov/files/docs/National%20Survey %20of%20Long-Haul%20Truck%20Driver%20Health%20and%20Injury.pdf.

14. Orris P, Buchannon S, Dinges D, Bergoffen G. Literature Review on Health and Fatigue Issues Associated with Commercial Motor Vehicle Driver Hours of Work. Synthesis 9. Transportation Research Board. 2005. http://trb.org /publications/ctbssp/ctbssp_syn_9.pdf.

15. Dinges D, Maislin G. 2006 Truck Driver Fatigue Management Survey. FMCSA. FMCSA-RRR-06-0. May 2006. https://www.fmcsa.dot.gov/advisory-committees /mrb/2006-truck-driver-fatigue-management-survey.

16. Wiegand DM, Hanowski RJ, McDonald SE. Commercial drivers' health: A naturalistic study of body mass index, fatigue, and involvement in safety-critical events. *Traffic Inj Prev.* 2009;10(6):573–579.

17. Thiese MS, Ott U, Robbins R, et al. Factors associated with truck crashes in a large cross section of commercial motor vehicle drivers. *J Occup Environ Med.* 2015 Oct;57(10):1098-106.

18. Van Dongen HPA, Baynard MD, Maislin G, Dinges TF. Systematic interindividual differences in neurobehavioral impairment from sleep loss: Evidence of trait-like differential vulnerability. *Sleep.* 2004;27(3):423–433.
19. Commercial Motor Vehicle Driver Fatigue, Long-Term Health, and Highway Safety: Research Needs. Panel on Research Methodologies and Statistical Approaches to Understanding Driver Fatigue Factors in Motor Carrier Safety and Driver Health. Committee on National Statistics, Board on Human-Systems Integration, Division of Behavioral and Social Sciences and Education, Transportation Research Board, National Academies of Sciences, Engineering, and Medicine. Washington (DC): National Academies Press (US); 2016 Aug 12. https://www.nap.edu/catalog/21921/commercial-motor-vehicle-driver-fatigue-long-term-health-and-highway-safety.
20. North American Fatigue Management Program. http://www.nafmp.org/en/
21. Gertler, J, Popkin, S, Nelson D, O'Neil K. Toolbox for Transit Operator Fatigue. TCRP Report 81. Transportation Research Board for the Federal Transit Administration, 2002. http://onlinepubs.trb.org/onlinepubs/tcrp/tcrp_rpt_81.pdf.
22. Lerman SE, Eskin E, Flower DJ, George EC, Gerson B, Hartenbaum N, Hursh SR, Moore-Ede M. Fatigue Risk Management in the Workplace, ACOEM Presidential Task Force on Fatigue Risk Management. *J Occup Environ Med.* 2012;54(2):231–258. http://www.acoem.org/uploadedFiles/Public_Affairs/Policies_And_Position_Statements/Fatigue%20Risk%20Management%20in%20the%20Workplace.pdf
23. Kruger GP, Brewster RM, Dick VR, Inderbitzen RE, Staplin L. Synthesis 15: Health and Wellness Programs for Commercial Drivers. Transportation Research Board. Washington, DC, 2007. http://onlinepubs.trb.org/onlinepubs/ctbssp/ctbssp_syn_15.pdf.
24. Federal Motor Carrier Safety Administration, U.S. Department of Transportation. MCSAC Task 15-3 Subcommittee Discussion Notes. 2016. https://www.fmcsa.dot.gov/advisory-committees/mcsac/mcsac-task-15-3-subcommittee-discussion-notes.
25. Federal Motor Carrier Safety Administration, U.S. Department of Transportation. Owner Operator Independent Driver Association (OOIDA). Meeting the Challenges of Reaching Long Haul Truck Drivers. 2015. https://www.fmcsa.dot.gov/advisory-committees/mcsac/meeting-challenges-reaching-long-haul-truck-drivers
26. Driving Healthy. - http://www.drivinghealthy.org.
27. Occupational Health Sciences at Oregon Health and Science University. SHIFT: Safety and Health Involvement for Truckers. https://www.ohsushift.com/welcome-shift.
28. Virginia Tech. Commercial Motor Vehicle Driving Safety Website. https://vtechworks.lib.vt.edu/handle/10919/71897
29. Virginia Tech. CMV Driver Health Outreach. https://vtechworks.lib.vt.edu/handle/10919/24206
30. AAA Foundation. Roadwise Rx. 2016. http://www.roadwiserx.com.

Index